"An enlightening look into Andrew Lloyd Webber's early life and
professional career."
—*Broadway World*

"Is there is nothing Andrew Lloyd Webber can't do . . . This memoir
proves that he can write stylish and witty prose too."

UNMASKED

ANDREW LLOYD WEBBER

UNMASKED

A MEMOIR

HarperCollins*Publishers*

HarperCollins*Publishers*
1 London Bridge Street
London SE1 9GF

www.harpercollins.co.uk

First published by HarperCollins*Publishers* 2018
This paperback edition published 2019

1 3 5 7 9 10 8 6 4 2

Text © Andrew Lloyd Webber 2018

Andrew Lloyd Webber asserts the moral right to
be identified as the author of this work.

A catalogue record of this book is
available from the British Library

ISBN 978-0-00-823761-5

Printed and bound in Great Britain by CPI Group (UK) Ltd, Croydon

Excerpts from 'That's My Story' – Lyrics by Tim Rice, published by EMI Music Publishing Mills
Music Limited and reproduced with the kind permission of Sir Tim Rice. Excerpts from Joseph and
the Amazing Technicolor Dreamcoat – Lyrics by Tim Rice © The Really Useful Group Limited.
Excerpts from 'Come Back Richard Your Country Needs You' – Lyrics by Tim Rice, published by
Novello and Company Ltd and reproduced with the kind permission of Sir Tim Rice. Excerpts from
Jesus Christ Superstar – Lyrics by Tim Rice © The Really Useful Group Limited. Excerpts from
Evita – Lyrics by Tim Rice © Evita Music Limited/Universal. Extracts taken from 'Rhapsody on a
Windy Night', The Poems of T.S. Eliot Volume I: Collected and Uncollected Poems and 'The
Naming of Cats', Old Possum's Book of Practical Cats by T.S. Eliot © Set Copyrights Ltd and
reprinted by permission of Faber & Faber. Excerpts from Aspects of Love – Lyrics by Don Black &
Charles Hart © The Really Useful Group Limited. Excerpts from The Phantom of the Opera –
Lyrics by Charles Hart, Additional Lyrics by Richard Stilgoe © The Really Useful Group Limited.

Title page art courtesy of Bob King Creative Ltd.

While every effort has been made to obtain permission from the photographers
and copyright holders of the pictures used in this book, the author and publishers
apologise to anyone who has not been contacted in advance or credited.

For my fabulously un-PC Auntie Vi, most of whose sayings I could not possibly share in 2018.

CONTENTS

PROLOGUE

I have long resisted writing an autobiography. Autobiographies are by definition self-serving and mine is no exception. It is the result of my nearest and dearest, aided and abetted by the late great literary agent Ed Victor, moaning at me "to tell your story your way." I meekly agreed, primarily to shut them up. Consequently this tome is not my fault.

I intended to write my memoirs in one volume and I have failed spectacularly. Even as things are you'll find very little about my love of art which, along with architecture and musical theatre, is one of my great passions. I decided the saga of how I built my rather unfashionable Pre-Raphaelite and Victorian art collection belongs elsewhere. The dodgy art dealers who tried to screw me can sleep peacefully – at least for the moment.

This medium sized doorstop judders to a halt at the first night of *The Phantom of the Opera*. Quite how I have been able to be so verbose about the most boring person I have ever written about eludes me. At one point I had a stab at shoehorning my career highlights into a taut tight chapter, rather like Wagner brilliantly packs his top tunes into his operas' overtures. This was a dismal failure. The only thing I have in common with Wagner is length.

So here is part one of my saga. If you are a glutton for this sort of thing, dive in, at least for a bit. If you aren't, I leave you with this thought. You are lucky if you know what you want to do in life. You are incredibly lucky if you are able to have a career in it. You have the luck of Croesus on stilts (as my Auntie Vi would have said) if you've had the sort of career, ups and downs, warts and all that I have in that wondrous little corner of show business called musical theatre.

Andrew Lloyd Webber

UNMASKED

OVERTURE AND BEGINNERS

Before me there was Mimi.

Mimi was a monkey. She was given to my mother Jean by a Gibraltan tenor with a limp that Mum had taken a shine to in the summer of 1946. Mimi and Mother must have seemed a really odd couple as they meandered through the grey bomb damaged streets of ration-gripped London's South Kensington. "South Ken" was where my Granny Molly rented a flat that Hitler's Luftwaffe had somehow missed which she shared with Mimi, Mum and Dad.

My dear Granny Molly came from the Hemans family, one of whom, Felicia, wrote the poem "The Boy Stood on the Burning Deck," a dirge which every British schoolchild was force-fed a century ago. Granny was an interesting lady, not least for her strange political views. She was a founder member of the Christian Communist Party, a short lived organization that arguably was rather a contradiction in terms. She had a sister, Great-Aunt Ella, who married a minor Bloomsbury Set artist and ran, I kid you not, a transport cafe for truck drivers on the A4 outside Reading in which she kept hens.

Granny had got married to some army tosser and divorced him asap, which was not what a girl did every day in the 1920s. She told me that she threw her wedding ring down the lavatory on her honeymoon night. But the military deserter must have lurked around enough to sire Molly's three kids Alastair, Viola and finally my mother Jean. Eventually he remarried some émigré Russian wannabe Princess Anastasia and that's all I know about him.

Unquestionably Granny had a raw deal. Her only son Alastair drowned in a boating accident near Swanage in Dorset after he had just left school at eighteen. I have a photo of the man who would have been my uncle on my desk as I write. It affected Granny hugely but it particularly traumatized my mother. Mum had a complete fixation on Alastair and was forever proclaiming psychic contact with him. Curiously I think she did have contact with him, although her promise to "get hold of me when she discovered how" made in a letter just before she died has so far failed to deliver.

In 1938 Granny found herself bereft of her beloved son and a single mum supporting two daughters. The army tosser had never properly supported her, so she was forced to sell a big house on Harrow Hill and move to the South Kensington rented flat on Harrington Road, SW7. When Mum met a plumber's son named William Lloyd Webber, a young scholarship boy white hope of the pre-war Royal College of Music, love blossomed. Soon, despite the Second World War, nuptials could not be put on hold. Dad had close to zero income. That's why he, Mum, Granny and Mimi shacked up under one roof.

A mere two years after VE Day, this postwar ménage à quatre came to an abrupt end. Mum got pregnant. Mimi became horrendously distressed and violently attacked my mother's stomach with bloodcurdling cries. In short, Mimi was the first person to take a dislike to Andrew Lloyd Webber.

A decision was taken that Mimi had to ankle out of the South Kensington ménage on the urgent side of asap. On March 22, 1948, I brought the number of residents up to four again.

CUT FORWARD TO THE 1960s and 10 Harrington Court, Harrington Road redefined the "B" in bohemian. At its 1967 occupational peak it housed Granny Molly, Mum, Dad, plus his huge electronic church organ, Tchaikovsky Prize–winning pianist John Lill, Tim Rice, my cellist brother Julian and me. No. 10 was on the top floor of one of those Victorian mansion blocks where the lift occasionally worked but most of the time you used the stairs. The traffic noise was deafening, but I doubt if the neighbours heard it, such were the sounds of music emanating from our household.

One afternoon, Tim Rice and I were descending the stairs out of the menagerie. Julian was practising the cello. A bloke from the flat below leapt out and accosted us.

"I don't mind about the pianist," he rankled. "It's that oboe player I can't stand."

However, as bizarrely bohemian as 10 Harrington Court may have been, I couldn't wait to get out of it, particularly as Mum from time to time threatened my brother and me with jumping out of the fourth-floor window. This got boring after a bit, so enter into this narrative my aunt – my impossibly, adorably, unrepeatably politically incorrect Auntie Vi, Granny's eldest daughter. She was married to a slightly pompous doctor called George Crosby for whom Granny had worked as a secretary when she was really down on her uppers. Vi had a brief career as an actress. She was hilariously funny and a great cook with several serious recipe books to her name. She knew a few glamorous names in theatre. She was everything my family wasn't and I adored her. She was my escape valve. Fifty years later I still daren't print her sayings. In the 1960s she was the author of the first gay cookbook. A chapter monikered "Coq & Game Meat" is headlined:

Too Many Cocks Spoil the Breath.

FRANKLY I WAS FALSELY CITED as the cause of Mimi the monkey's behavioural setbacks. Surely 10 Harrington Court was no place for a simian bent on swinging around the community? However, my mother stood by her initial stance. Ten years later she took brother

Julian and me to Chessington Zoo. On entering the monkey house she let out a great cry of "Mimi!," more than worthy of her limping tenor. The simian turned its head, puzzled.

"Look, she recognizes me. It's Mimi," said Mum triumphantly as the monkey leapt across its cage and climbed the wire in aggressive fashion uttering the most fearsome sounds.

"I told you it was Mimi." Mum looked at me pointedly. "She always hated the thought of you, now she's seeing you for real."

The story of my life? Maybe this is as good a place to start as any.

1

Perseus & Co.

I was born on March 22, 1948 in Westminster Hospital with a huge birthmark on my forehead that Mum said was cured courtesy of a faith healer. Others said it faded of its own accord, but Mum's graphic details had me convinced that it might recur at any time if I was a bad child. My first memory is of being in hospital aged three with acute appendicitis. This Mother told me was undiagnosed until it was just about to burst. My case was presided over by Uncle George, now Auntie Vi's "partner" (they hadn't married yet) who had undiagnosed the appendicitis in the first place. As my relationship with dearest Auntie Vi bloomed whilst I staggered into my teens, the saga of the undiagnosed appendicitis would be often recounted to me in increasingly distended detail. Mother also had a serious footnote about my being chucked out of hospital way too early due to my screaming which Uncle George found embarrassing to his standing in the medical profession. Mother was seriously pregnant with Julian at the time, so the saga must have been a pain to her to put it mildly.

Being told that I had a brother is memory number two. It was a bright spring day and I was playing in Thurloe Square gardens, to which my family had a key. I remember not quite understanding what having a brother meant, but here my memory goes blank. I can't remember anything about Julian as a baby at all, perhaps because Julian's popping onto the planet also saw the arrival of Perseus the cat. Perseus was a wonderful square faced, seal-pointed Siamese boy, not one of those angular faced jobs so beloved of today's breeders. I fell in love with Perseus instantly. Dad was also completely devoted to him. But I realize now that the family really shouldn't have had an animal like that cooped up in a flat. His incessant cries to get out still give me nightmares.

Such was Perseus's deafening low Siamese miaowing that when I was around seven I asked if I could take him on a lead to Thurloe Square when I wasn't at school. Both Mum and Granny said yes. How trusting parents were in those days. You wouldn't let a kid loose with a cat on a lead around South Kensington today – unless you were after a million hits on YouTube. So I became a regular spectacle walking Perseus like a dog across the old zebra crossing that led to the train station and the only bit of greenery Julian and I knew, at least in school termtime. One day Perseus escaped. Five hours later he was found among the pedestrians on the zebra crossing returning from the only piece of greenery that he, too, knew. Percy's kerb drill was impeccable.

Years later I had the job of looking after Percy when he was dying. The old cat raised himself tortuously from his basket and started miaowing in a manner all too reminiscent of his incarcerated cries. The poor old boy scrabbled at the front door as if there were a rabbit to catch outside. So I put his lead on. He didn't want to walk so he sat on my shoulder, a mode of transport which he always liked.

A year or two earlier the traffic at South Kensington had been reorganized into a fearsome one-way system. At the time it was claimed to feature the most complicated set of traffic lights in Europe. Perseus never mastered the new system, but it was clear that the old cat wanted to pad back to the gardens that he used to freely wander to before its advent.

We got to the site of the old zebra crossing. Percy tried to get off my shoulder and I put him down. He sat for a few seconds, looked out at the new traffic lights and hissed. Then on his own he turned, lead trailing behind him, back to our flat. Next day he died. I owe

Cats not only to Mummy's bedtime reading of T.S. Eliot's *Old Possum's Book of Practical Cats*, but also to Perseus.

My third memory of 1951 is so shocking that it might also account for my not remembering anything of baby Julian. It concerns my appearance on the cover of a magazine called *Nursery World*. Mum hired a photographer, thrust a violin and a bow upon my person and thus created a nauseous picture on the front of the grisly publication that haunts me still. It speaks volumes about Mother. For Mum was so ambitious for her offspring that she would have given Gypsy Rose Lee's famous showbiz mum a fair old run in the Great Child Prodigy Handicap Stakes. Sadly I was no such thing. Pushy mothers of the world beware. Offsprings rebel. Just as Gypsy Rose Lee took a career path her mother hadn't intended for her, so did I. Not as a stripper, though, at least not in public.

Mum was an ace children's piano teacher. Although she died in 1994 she is still a bit of legend among the great and the not so good who inhabit the leafier parts of southwest London. In 1950 Mother co-founded a pre-prep school called the Wetherby with a couple called Mr and Mrs Russell, the former being interested in bare bottom spanking. I was one of the first tots through the door. The place was a roaring success. Over the years luminaries from Princes William and Harry to Hugh Grant have joined the ranks of short-trousered ones who crossed Wetherby's threshold.

My mother had a big hand in the school's birth pangs. In those days parents from most walks of life wanted their kids to learn the piano. My mother's brilliance and patience in that department assured the Wetherby's swift ascendancy. Anyone who has ever sat beside a child while it plonks away at ghastly ditties with titles like "El Wiggly" or "Honk That Horn" will bear out that to do so you either need to be a saint or tone deaf or most probably both. Mum's patience might well redefine canonization. I reckon she must have given at least 100,000 piano lessons to beginners in her lifetime. Further, she really cared about her charges. There was a time when this confirmed, yet confused, socialist claimed to have taught a fair wedge of the Tory party.

I confess that her piano lessons gave me a head start in the basics of music. The trouble was that there were so many of them. And there was that wretched violin. Mum's general idea was that I would emerge on the international concert stage as some Yehudi Menuhin-style violin toting child prodigy. Her hopes didn't last long.

The next instrument out of the closet was the french horn. I was rather better at blowing than scratching. Indeed I rather enjoyed playing this overdeveloped hunting instrument until I was twelve. It was then that a crisis occurred. Mum's quest to have me garner serious music grades brought me full frontal with Hindemith's horn sonata. I have read somewhere that Hindemith developed a load of theories about the importance of amateurs to music. My theory is that some of his compositions were designed to make average instrumentalists like me abandon music for once and for all. He achieved a resounding success in my case. After attempting to play his epic I chucked my french horn in its case where it remains to this day.

Clearly Mum was transferring her ambitions from my father to me, but to grasp why you have to know something about him. Billy Lloyd Webber was a mild man who feared authority in any form. He once hid in a cupboard because he had mistakenly called out the fire brigade. It transpired that Granny had left a chicken in the oven and smoked the flat out. He was convinced he was going to get a stretch in the slammer for abusing the emergency services.

Billy's family was solid working class. His father was a plumber by trade but also a keen amateur musician. Like so many of my grandfather's contemporaries, Billy's father had sung in various church choirs. So Dad was steeped in the late High Church nineteenth-century choral tradition beloved by the Anglo-Catholic "smells and bells" establishments where Grandpa exercised the larynx. As a child Dad got music scholarships all over the shop. At an unprecedentedly youthful age he won a gong to the Royal College of Music. He also became the youngest person ever to become organist and choirmaster at St Cyprian's Clarence Gate, a splendid "Arts and Crafts" church by Sir Ninian Comper. But for all his talent Dad wouldn't say boo to a goose. All he wanted was a nice quiet routine.

By the time I was ten, Dad was increasingly content in his academic roles such as Professor of Composition at the Royal College of Music. In 1959 he became boss of the London College of Music which seemingly sealed the end of his composing aspirations. He felt his writing was out of step with its time and increasingly wrote "light music" under pen names or music for amateur church choirs. Mum found his lack of ambition infuriating. Still, she was very particular about taking me to listen to his cantatas and anthems, especially first performances. Even Julian, who was barely old enough, was dragged along to hear them but soon new compositions seemed to dry up – or so we all thought. After my father's death, Julian discovered a cache of compositions that had never been performed. Some of them were as good as anything he ever wrote.

2

Some Enchanted Ruin

The three great passions that were to shape my life – art, musical theatre and architecture – surfaced early. My love of architecture kicked off with a weird romantic obsession with ruined castles and abbeys which began as early as I can remember. By my teens this led to a full-blown love of architecture of all sorts. Quite where this came from is a mystery; the visual arts don't feature in the Lloyd Webber family DNA.

In the case of theatre and pop music, it is easy to explain why. My family had an annual Christmas outing to the London Palladium pantomime.* Everything captivated me. In those days the Palladium was synonymous with popular variety theatre. All the big names played there. The pantomime was a combination of big names, big sets and contemporary pop songs that must have been a heady mix to this five-year-old. One such pantomime, *Aladdin*, contained a line that I still cherish:

Aladdin rubs lamp. Up pops genie.
"What is your wish, sir?"
"To hear Alma Cogan singing 'Sugar in the Morning.'"
Curtain parts to reveal Alma Cogan singing "Sugar in the Morning."

* A uniquely British theatre entertainment for families that goes back to the nineteenth century, its appeal is wholly inexplicable to non-Brits.

Very soon I had built my first toy theatre. This was first an adapted version of a Pollock's toy theatre but eventually became a vast construction made out of play bricks baptized the Harrington Pavilion. Over the years its technical ambitions grew to such an extent that its stage acquired a revolve made from an old gramophone turntable. That revolve was a direct result of my aping the famous closing scene of TV's *Sunday Night at the London Palladium*. All the stars used to line up on the legendary Palladium revolve waving good night to millions in Britain for whom that show was *the* television show of the late 1950s and early '60s. To Britain it was as big as *The Ed Sullivan Show* in the USA. I pinch myself every morning knowing that today I own the theatre that turned me on to theatre.

London Palladium inspired pantomime and variety seasons at the Harrington Pavilion were short lived. Christmas holidays 1958 brought me full frontal with musicals for the first time. It was a baptism and a half. I saw *My Fair Lady* and *West Side Story* plus the movies of *Gigi* and *South Pacific* all in the space of four game-changing weeks. 1958 also coincided with the arrival of Harrington Court's first long-playing gramophone. With it came an LP of Tchaikovsky's *Nutcracker* Suite. Unfortunately for Dad the other side was Prokofiev's *The Love for Three Oranges* Suite whose gloriously dissonant chaotic start much appealed to Julian and me. The famous march had us dancing on our bed with joy. Thus began my lifelong love of Prokofiev, in my opinion one of the greatest melodists of the twentieth century.

My Fair Lady was the talk of London throughout 1958. The legendary musical based on Bernard Shaw's *Pygmalion* had opened on Broadway two years earlier to ecstatic reviews, apart from one Alan Jay Lerner told me about in *Variety* that said there were no memorable songs. The producers did a brilliant hyping job in Britain by banning the music from being heard or performed until just before the London production opened, with the result that the Broadway cast album was the ultimate in chic contraband. Naturally Auntie Vi had one, so by the time I saw the show I knew the score backwards and had long pondered whether Rex Harrison's semi-spoken song delivery had a place at the Harrington Pavilion. London's lather frothed even further as the three Broadway leads, Rex Harrison, Julie Andrews and Stanley Holloway, repeated their starring roles at the Theatre Royal Drury Lane and I was lucky enough to have a ticket to see all three – actually two because Stanley Holloway was off. It's funny how a disappointment like that stays with you forever. In my case that and the rustling front cloth depicting the exterior of Wimpole Street as Freddy Eynsford-Hill warbled "On the Street Where You Live" are what I remember most about that December Saturday matinee – apart from my showing off by singing along with the songs to show I knew them.

My love of the score took me to the movie of *Gigi*, the now impossibly un-PC story about a girl being groomed as a courtesan. Can you imagine what would happen if you pitched a Hollywood studio today a song sung by an old man entitled "Thank Heaven for Little Girls"? Thank heaven I was young enough only to agree and even today the overture from *Gigi* is something I relish hearing.

Curiously it was Granny Molly who banged on about *West Side Story* and it was she who took me to it. The American cast's dancing was like nothing I'd seen before. That two stage musicals could be so different, yet equally spellbinding, had me in a tailspin. Granny bought me the Broadway cast album for Christmas and pretty soon it was my favourite of the two. I related to Bernstein's score much as I did to Prokofiev's *Love for Three Oranges*.

However what completely pulverized me was the film of *South Pacific*. I went with Mum and Dad and I remember the afternoon I saw it as vividly as the legendary colour filters that would have clobbered a lesser score. I had to wait until my birthday the following March for the soundtrack album. I still treasure my battered worn copy –

incidentally it is the only album to have been No. 1 in the UK charts for a whole calendar year. By Christmas 1961 I knew the scores of *Carousel*, *The King and I* and *Oklahoma!* and had seen the *South Pacific* movie four times. But there was one other movie. It only had a few songs but it grabbed me nonetheless. Elvis in *Jailhouse Rock*. The "Jailhouse Rock" sequence had me standing on my seat. I still have the worn-out 45 rpm single that drove my parents to distraction.

Musicals were soon the staple diet of the Harrington Pavilion. I wrote tons of dreadful ones. An audience of bored parents, friends, relatives and anyone I could find would gather for the latest offering with Julian and me on vocals, and me alternating as pianist and scene-shifter. At its zenith the theatre's stage, were it to have been built lifesize, would have dwarfed that of the new Paris opera house at the Bastille. Subjects included everything from *The Importance of Being Earnest* to *The Queen of Sheba*. A whole fantasy town developed around the theatre. Everyone in this town was somehow dependent upon the theatre's well-being. The Harrington Pavilion had a box office through which the townspeople booked tickets. Hits or turkeys were assessed by the reaction of the audience of bored parents and friends.

I developed with Julian a complete world in which I could hide and where I was truly happy, a make-believe world with one common denominator, musical theatre. There were stars who came and went, made comebacks or passed into oblivion with billing to match. There were pretend directors, designers and programmes, even souvenir brochures, for I was very impressed by the stiff-covered job that went with *My Fair Lady*. There were special train services that ferried audiences from the fantasy town to the theatre on show nights and, when I was given my first tape recorder, original cast albums were quick to follow.

Praise be to the good Lord that the tape recorder in question was incompatible with any other. For some reason it had its own peculiar tape speed. Thus my prepubescent warblings, along with the gismo that recorded them, are mercifully lost to posterity. However I own up that two of the tunes survive in other guises. From *Ernest!* billed modestly as "A Musical of Gigantic Importance," one became "Chained and Bound" in *Joseph*. The main melody of "Chanson d'Enfance," appropriately titled under the circumstances, in *Aspects of Love* also came from this show. Quite how the latter could possibly have made sense dramatically in a musical based on Wilde's timeless comedy eludes me.

However my burgeoning love of medieval cathedrals, ruins and churches affected me equally as deeply. I built a vast play-brick Gothic cathedral (dedicated to St Elvis) at the other end of the nursery to cope with the Harrington Pavilion theatregoers' spiritual needs. St Elvis's Cathedral fell victim to the wrecker's ball and chain, i.e. Julian in a fit of rage knocked it down. But for many years the Harrington Pavilion, being glued together, survived unscathed. In the Sixties when I left home, my toy theatre was carefully dismantled and stored. But sadly it went missing when I moved house in 1974. All I have now are a very few photographs.

WITH THE TOY THEATRE shows came an increasing interest in me from Auntie Vi. Mum, frankly, whilst not disapproving of my puerile jingles, didn't exactly approve either. She had transferred her ambition for a classical musician of a son onto three-year-old Julian, for whom she had bought a baby-sized cello. Dad, however, was starting to show an interest in what I was up to. When I was ten he took some of my tunes, arranged them very simply for the piano, and had them published under my name in a magazine called *The Music Teacher* with the title "The Toy Theatre." Every now and again when I was experimenting away at the piano he'd come in and ask me how I had discovered some chord or another. I suppose that wasn't surprising: my father, for all his grand title of Professor of Composition at the Royal College of Music, truly loved melody. In fact he was the most open bloke about melody there could be.

Thus in addition to hearing all the current musicals, specially when I went to visit Auntie Vi, my father would play me music of all sorts, albeit with a heavy leaning towards Rachmaninov. Dad's taste in "serious" music did not embrace the modernists. He did, however, admire Benjamin Britten's orchestrations, though he would wave his cocktail-shaker in anger that Britten left for America in the Second World War as a conscientious objector. Dad repeatedly moaned that Britten thus gained a massive unfair advantage over composers like himself who stayed in bomb blitzed London and did their bit for the war effort.

In 1958 Dad decided to hit the organ keyboards again. He had given up his post at All Saints Margaret Street after the war to teach composition at the Royal College of Music. Now, a decade later, he was appointed musical director of the Methodist Central Hall in Westminster. The Central Hall services were polar opposite to the High Church trappings of All Saints. I gather his move caused quite a stir in circles where incense is a key conduit to God. But Mum was delighted. She distrusted Catholics. Catholics believe animals have no souls. The truth was that the Central Hall had one of the finest organs in Britain and Dad was itching to play publicly again. My cellist brother Julian tells me that performing was where Dad showed a steely side. Early in his career Julian asked Dad how he could overcome his pre-performance nerves. Dad rounded on him, saying if he had prepared himself properly he wouldn't be nervous.

Apart from the occasional blood and thunder sermon or rousing free-church hymn, the ray of sunshine in the colourless services that Julian and I were now dragged to every Sunday was the moment Dad goosed up proceedings with one of his organ improvisations. Of course Methodists are teetotallers so I hope nobody examined the mineral water bottle Dad had beside him in his organ console and which, after a swig, miraculously transported him to ever greater inspirational freedom.

2014 saw the centenary of my father's birth and there has been a welcome flurry of interest in him as a composer. This has been much encouraged by Julian's discovery of many pieces he wrote but kept under wraps because he openly felt his music was out of step with the contemporary serious music world. It was. But, rather as late Victorian painters continued in sub Pre-Raphaelite style long after the advent of Impressionism, Cubism and the like, today we see these artists still had something to offer even if it was out of its time. I feel the same way about Dad's music. He could have been a fantastic film composer. His work is crammed with wonderful big melodies, quite alien of course to anything in contemporary classical music, but of a scale and dramatic breadth equal to many of the famous twentieth-century film composers. I believe he knew it but couldn't bring himself to consider going down that road.

First, in the 1930s it would have seemed like a heinous case of letting the side down for a working-class boy who had won every sort of academic gong to demean himself in the world of "commercial" music.

Secondly, he loved a fixed routine. He could never have coped with overnight rewrites demanded by a temperamental director who wanted a musical rethink like yesterday. But listen to Dad's orchestral tone poem *Aurora*. I played it once for the movie director Ken Russell, who pronounced it an erotic, supercharged mini-masterpiece. The director of *Women in Love* should know.

I have one very vivid memory of Dad. Before we went to the movie of *South Pacific* he played me the Mario Lanza recording of "Some Enchanted Evening." Three times he played it, tears streaming down his face. The third time around he muttered something about how Richard Rodgers' publisher told him that this song would kick off the postwar baby boom.* When the record finally stopped he looked me straight in the face.

"Andrew," he said, "if you ever write a tune half as good as this I shall be very, very proud of you."

On that evening my love affair with Richard Rodgers's music began. I went to bed heady with melody. Sadly, however, Dad never raised the issue of whether in my later career I'd come even halfway to equalling "Some Enchanted Evening."

MUM, MEANWHILE, WAS DETERMINED that I should be a prodigy in something or other. So when I went to the junior department of Westminster School, known as the Under School, my mother's eagle-eye supervision of my homework meant that I rose through the school far too fast. By the time I was eleven I was in a grade where some of the class were nearly two years older than me.

Considering I was smaller than the other boys, useless at sport, still played classical music and was the school swot, it's not surprising that I was bullied. I needed a big idea. It came about in an unlikely way. Westminster Under School was in those days in a square that was walkable from Victoria station, two stops down the underground from "South Ken" station. Heaven knows what today's parents would think of a journey to school involving packed trains, a walk past a shop selling "Iron Jelloids" and the Biograph, London's first gay movie house, but that's the journey I took twice daily. On the morning in question a saddo tried to fondle me undercover of the tight standing crush on the underground train. I was too shocked to make a fuss. But I was furious, so furious that it gave me an idea that maybe was big enough to call an epiphany. Whatever, it changed my schoolboy life.

---

* Rodgers and Hammerstein's Williamson Music was represented by Teddy Holmes at Chappell's. As well as being Rodgers and Hammerstein's publisher, he was also my father's.

That afternoon was the end of term concert. I was slated to play some boring piano piece by Haydn. It was time to ring the changes. I ascended the stage to a deafening yawn and announced a change of programme. There was a small flicker of interest.

"Today," I intoned, "I am going to play some tunes I have written that describe every master in the school."

The flicker of interest was now a flame – on the small side, but a flame nonetheless. So I dedicated to each master one of the tunes I had written for the Harrington Pavilion. After the first there was baffled applause. After the second it was heading towards strongish. During the fourth song the school was clapping along and when, before the sixth, I turned to the headmaster and said, "This one is for you," even the other masters applauded.

At the end there was uproar. Boys were shouting "Lloydy, Lloydy!"

I was no longer the little school swot. I was Andrew. And I had become Andrew through music.

IT WOULD GREATLY SIMPLIFY writing this tome were I to claim that this was the moment I knew my destiny was to write music. But the truth is, it wasn't. Music was an increasingly important part of my life, my safety valve in fact, but it wasn't my overriding passion. Equal first was still architecture with art a close third.

My love of ruined castles and abbeys must have started very young because I have a scrapbook put together when I can't have been more than six. It is stuffed with guidebooks and postcards and very childish writing about the abbeys and castles around Southampton and Portsmouth. This figures, because my father's sister Marley lived around these parts in one of those twentieth-century houses which, like most of the sprawl on the English south coast, should be demolished forthwith.

I am pretty sure that my passion for architecture kicked off at Westminster Abbey. A few years ago I was invited to a meeting about some very exciting plans for the Abbey's future. The Dean of Westminster produced a letter that the Abbey archivist had found which he proceeded to read. It was from me aged seven offering my pocket money to the Abbey fabric fund. "Precocious brat" was written all over the faces around the table. I have had many discussions about getting involved with the Abbey subsequently, but they always stall over my insistence that the utterly inappropriate chandeliers that were hung in the church in the 1960s are sold to a hotel in Vegas.

I shall forever have a debt to my parents for indulging my childhood obsession. Every family holiday was somewhere in Britain where there were buildings I wanted to see. One summer the family found itself in a rented house near the massive steelworks of Port Talbot in Wales because I wanted to be near a place called Margam Abbey – which, by the way, has a great orangery. The best holiday was in Yorkshire. You have to be made of Yorkshire granite not to be moved by the stunning evocative ruins of Fountains Abbey. My favourite was Rievaulx. What did the abbey look like before Henry VIII's minions did an ISIS job on this medieval masterpiece? The imagination runs riot. The vistas to the abbey from the glorious mid-eighteenth-century park on the hill above Rievaulx are England at its Arcadian best.

What emphatically was not Arcadian was an incident still embedded irrevocably in my skull. My parents took me and Perseus the cat to Richmond Castle. The place was pretty empty, so Mum let Perseus off his dog lead. Out of the blue a bunch of cadets from the local army camp tramped into the castle courtyard as noisily as their boots would allow, caught sight of our terrified cat and chased him up the spiral staircase of one of the towers. Dad, of course, ran for cover. Even today I have a real paranoia of the army. Certainly it fuelled my childhood fear of conscription, which was still in action in Britain at that time, and ten years later heightened my sympathy with the pressganged US conscripts of the Vietnam War. That incident and the constant fearmongering headlines in the press about war over the Suez Canal throughout that hot 1955 summer led me to the dark thought that forces I could never control would some day destroy me and my little world of theatre and medieval buildings. It was during that otherwise idyllic holiday that I first prayed at bedtime.

VERY SOON THEATRES JOINED the list of abbeys, cathedrals, country houses and the like that so dominated my childhood. The 1950s saw the arrival of television. Soon the variety theatres that were so much a part of pre-war British life became sad, redundant, twitching corpses. Theatre after theatre succumbed to the wrecker's ball. I found their plight irresistible. Some theatres literally had become ruins. I remember prising my way into the derelict Bedford Theatre in London's Camden Town, a theatre made famous by the early twentieth-century artist Walter Sickert who painted it brimming full of vibrant life. Rain was pouring through a gaping hole in the roof. Two years later it was a memory.

Some of the lucky ones had a stay of execution by being turned into TV studios. The Chelsea Palace was one such. I was taken to a transmission of a then massive TV comedy series, *The Army Game*. The stalls had been raised to the level of the stage to create a huge flat floor on which the dinosaur TV cameras ducked and dived around teeny little sets. In the late 1950s that sort of show was broadcast live. For a brief period, the Harrington Pavilion was turned into a TV studio with a similar flat floor, but mercifully common sense prevailed and live theatrical performances resumed PDQ with a massive hit musical called *The Weird Sisters* based on *Macbeth*. Now the Chelsea Palace is yet another Kings Road shopping centre. What would a theatre producer give for such a wonderful building in that location now?

HOWEVER THE TV PROGRAMME that really game-changingly gripped me was a Saturday night rock'n'roll show called *Oh Boy!* It thrillingly made a virtue of being filmed in a theatre, a wonderful old variety house called the Hackney Empire, which intriguingly was designed by the same architect as the London Palladium, Frank Matcham. It was directed by Jack Good who went on to helm *Catch My Soul*, the rock *Othello*. He used the auditorium as if it were part of the set. Cameras swooped onto the stage over hysterical girls screaming at Brit male stars who all had surnames like Wilde, Eager or Fury. Equally great was the backing band Lord Rockingham's XI with their intriguing choreographed instrument moves. I moaned to my mother that Brahms would be much enhanced if classical orchestras would only do this sort of thing. Years later Cliff Richard confirmed to me just how staged each show was and how he had been directed down to the last camera eyeball.

Oh Boy! made a most profound impression on me. From then on the words rock'n'roll were synonymous with musical theatre and the Harrington Pavilion was soon ablaze with rock shows.

BY THE TIME I hit double figures my brother Julian was becoming a star on his half-size cello. The word "prodigy" was bellowed above the traffic din at 10 Harrington Court and unsurprisingly Mum's main interest switched to my younger sibling. Notwithstanding this, we both entered the Saturday morning junior school at the Royal College of Music, me toting my shiny french horn.

But as far as Mum was concerned I was at best a conundrum and so she gave up on my academic career and, buoyed by events at the school concert, I gave up on it too. Thoughts of my being the youngest ever Queen's Scholar at Westminster Great (i.e. senior) School evaporated. I wasn't even entered for the scholarship exam called "the Challenge." Mum's sole consolation prize was that I entered Westminster aged twelve, a full year earlier than usual. Meantime I was getting closer and closer to my deliciously naughty Aunt Vi.

3

Auntie Vi

A quick reminder. Auntie Vi was mother Jean's elder sister. She married Dr George Crosby, the dumpy somewhat pompous doctor for whom Granny Molly had once worked as a secretary. Vi called him "Potto" which was really rather appropriate. That glorious word "panjandrum" could have been invented for him. Vi and George plus a marmalade cat named Cooper lived in a top-floor flat in Weymouth Street above his medical practice, close enough to the centre of London's medical hub Harley Street, but the location was cheaper and actually rather nicer. I used to escape there as often as possible. The flat – or maisonette, as George puffed it up – seemed impossibly glamorous (my aunt would have said "chi-chi") after the seldom cleaned haven for traffic noise addicts that was Harrington Court.

There was an upstairs drawing room which had been knocked into the room next door by means of an ever so "chi-chi" arch. Therein lurked a stereo record player on which Auntie played those Fifties Latin American records which showed off the marvels of stereo with question-and-answer bongo solos panned left and right only. There was a dining room with a bar underneath and a wine rack containing George's collection of Barolo. Up to that time the only wine bottles I had seen had candles in them. There was Vi's kitchen where there were herbs, onions, garlic and wine and where she cooked her recipes for the modern woman. In 1956 she had written and had published a hit recipe book *The Hostess Cooks* under her maiden name Viola Johnstone. Its premise was that in the Fifties no one could afford home help any more. The recipes were designed so that our hostess could emerge from the stoves, mascara intact, to entertain out front as if an army of sous chefs had been slaving since dawn and she had had a decent post-lunch siesta. It was a far cry from the over-boiled brussels sprouts of Harrington Court.

Then there were Vi's friends. There was Tony Hancock of TV's iconic *Hancock's Half Hour* sitcom. Vi introduced me to him in his flat where he was teaching a parrot to say "Fuck Mrs Warren." Mrs Warren was his cleaner – whom he loathed – so he had embarked on a strategy to get her to quit. She didn't. Auntie told me that one day the parrot mysteriously cried, "Hancock has no bollocks."

There was film director Ronald Neame who had been David Lean's legendary cameraman on classic British movies like *Great Expectations*. One day I was to work with him on *The Odessa File*. There was Val Guest and his glamorous actress wife Yolande Donlan. I was in total awe of her as she was the lead in the movie *Expresso Bongo* with Cliff Richard. Ballet nuts might be intrigued to know that the rock'n'roll sequences in this epic were choreographed by Sir Kenneth MacMillan, another name who would cross my professional path. A few years later, Val discovered Raquel Welch in the movie *One Million Years B.C.* It was Val who created the iconic image of Miss Welch in a doe-skin bikini which he used as his Christmas card. I've still got mine.

Finally there was Vida Hope, the theatre director who had a huge hit with *The Boy Friend*, one of the few Fifties British musicals to hoof it to Broadway. Julie Andrews was the young lead and it was in *The Boy Friend* that she was headhunted for *My Fair Lady*. I remember Vida railing passionately against a Broadway musical she had just seen. "A nauseating show with a fifty-five-year-old woman pretending to be an eighteen-year-old nun, plus a load of saccharin cute children." She was referring, of course, to Mary Martin in *The Sound of Music*.

It's hard today to understand just how low the reputation of Rodgers and Hammerstein had sunk in the eyes of the British intelligentsia. I still remember the father of a school friend thinking I was a congenital idiot for loving the "sentimental twaddle" called *Carousel*. He collected cuttings of ghastly reviews and with great pleasure showed me one by John Barber describing the show as "treacle." Of course I was taken to *The Boy Friend* and frankly I'm still agnostic about it. It was yet another nostalgic British musical burying itself in the sand against the tide of rock'n'roll. However it was a lot better than *Salad Days*. I was dragged to this concoction by my godmother Mabel, who disowned me after Perseus the cat destroyed a fox fur stole she left in my care when she was dining with Granny. I remember thinking that if ever I worked in the theatre *Salad Days* was the sort of show I had to eliminate.

THE ATMOSPHERE AT 28 Weymouth Street was everything home wasn't. Aunt Vi had a real eye for interior design, two words my parents hadn't heard of. And it was Vi who taught me to cook. In the process I learned a few choice bon mots that hardly any boys of my age knew, let alone understood. However what really forced me into Auntie Vi's not inconsiderable bosom was Mum's latest obsession which affected the family deeply. Certainly the family was never the same again. Its name was John Lill.

John Lill was sixteen years old and Julian only nine when they met at the Saturday junior school of the Royal College of Music. John Lill was the school's star concert pianist and destined to be the second Brit to win the Tchaikovsky Prize in Moscow. Although Julian was seven years John's junior, somehow they had become friendly enough for Julian to ask him back to Harrington Court where John met Mum. It was a meeting that was to change all our lives. It's easy to understand why John, plus his back story, so grabbed Mum. John Lill was born into a working-class family who lived in the then run-down deprived northeast London suburb of Leyton in one of those slum houses that today sell for hundreds of thousands of pounds, such is London's housing crisis. John was selected for the local grammar school but it was at the piano that he excelled. He won a scholarship to the junior Royal College and scraped together his train fares there by playing pub piano in one of the East End's tougher bars. The owner would introduce John with gems like:

"Do you know your balls are hanging out?"

To which John would reply, "No, but sing the tune and I'll vamp."

At last here was the young musical genius Mum had been looking for. Better still, from a background that salved Mum's conscience big time about hours spent teaching privileged brats at the Wetherby School. Soon Mum was driving John back to Leyton from college and had befriended his parents. Before long Julian and I found ourselves in Leyton to see for ourselves John's family terraced house "in the slums" as Mum unmincingly chose her words.

There was another life-changing consequence to all this. Whilst Mum was up to good deeds, Julian and I were let loose on the streets of Leyton and we soon discovered the local football team, London's "Cinderella" soccer club Leyton Orient. Although for one brief season the O's did reach English soccer's top flight, we Orient supporters are a small bunch unsullied by success, principally because there's never been any. However once you have pledged allegiance to a soccer club, that's that. Julian and I support the O's to this day, although tragically as I write this, the club has gone out of the Football League.

Years later, it was at the O's that I was given some truly sage advice. Around the time the "Jesus Christ Superstar" single came out in Britain, I was invited to lunch in the O's boardroom by the club's then chairman Bernard Delfont. Bernie, later Lord, Delfont was half-brother to Lew and Leslie Grade. Between the three of them they controlled British show business. Bernie owned the theatres, Lew owned the top film and TV outlets and Leslie was agent to the stars. It was what is today called a 360 degree arrangement. So I was pretty overawed to be asked to watch a home game by the most powerful man in British theatre. Leyton Orient lost of course. But it's the conversation after the debacle that I recall most.

"My boy, can I give you some advice?" said Bernie, drawing me to one side.

"Of course, Mr Delfont."

"Just call me Bernie."

"Yes, Bernie."

"I've heard that song of yours, I've got this feeling you could go far. I've got some advice for you, my boy. You're not Jewish are you?"

"No I'm afraid not, I'm . . ."

"You're not one of the tribe?"

"No, I er . . ."

"Never mind, I'll give it to you anyway." He paused. "Never, my boy, never buy a football club."

From that day onwards Bernie became a friend I could always count on. It was Bernie who years later came to the rescue of Cameron Mackintosh and me when we couldn't get the theatre we needed for *Cats*.

NOT VERY GRADUALLY MUM imported John into the family. There were plusses here too. As John increasingly practised chez Harrington Court, I sometimes turned the pages of his piano scores and discovered a huge amount of music I would never have known otherwise and John's technical ability was inspiring to witness. But there were three boys going on the summer family holiday now. I am sure it must have been very awkward for John too but he seemed to accept everything Mum threw at him. Whatever Julian and I felt, we had acquired an elder brother. We had no choice in the matter. Nor did Dad. He admired John and recognized his exceptional gifts, particularly as an interpreter of Beethoven. But it must have been hard for this quiet, reserved man to stomach that his wife's attentions and ambitions were focused on someone else.

THE JOHN LILL SAGA was still in its embryo when, in the autumn of 1960, aged twelve and a half – a year younger than my contemporaries and frightened out of my skull – I started my first term at Westminster School. The school, circa 1960–65, was a bit like me, a curious mixture of rebellion, tradition, bloody-mindedness and neurosis, glued together by academic excellence, although the latter was arguably not strictly applicable in my case. It is supposed to have been founded by Queen Elizabeth I in 1560. In fact the school long predated the throne's most famous redhead. It was Henry VIII who did one of his rare decent deeds, apart from allegedly writing *Greensleeves*, by sorting out a chaotic Abbey school. After he annexed and plundered the monasteries in 1536 he found himself in a quandary about Westminster Abbey because this was where the monarch was crowned. Its destruction would have made the operation awkward. So the school became part of his Westminster scheme of things.

The school's location greatly defines its character. Westminster is at the epicentre of British tradition. It's where the monarch is crowned. The Queen's Scholars are by statute the first voices to shout "God Save Whoever" the moment after he or she is crowned. Westminster scholars are to this day allowed to attend debates in the mother of Parliaments. If you were a Scholar in my time you could have skipped the queues at Winston Churchill's lying in state, witnessed the vote that legalized gay sex and watched the Profumo Affair bring down the Macmillan government.

On arrival, new boys had to choose two special subjects to top up the usual diet of Maths, French etc. Annoyingly history was not an option. Westminster kids did not take the lower history grades as the senior history master rightly considered them useless. So I wound up doing Ancient Greek which I hated and biology (you had to choose a science-based subject) which was Greek to me.

For your first two weeks at the new emporium you were allocated a boy a year older than you, who was tasked with sympathetically demonstrating the niceties of the institution in which you were to spend the next few years. In fact you were regaled with tales of the headmaster's legendary beatings and the sadistic antics of the gym master, Stuart Murray. I was familiar with this bastard. He had practised minor versions of his craft at the Under School and drilled into me a loathing of exercise and sport that was only partially sorted out by a Californian swimming instructress called Mimosa in the 1970s. I don't think I'm vindictive by nature but when I read in the school magazine one morning years later that Mr Murray had died, I wrote two tunes and had a bottle of wine for lunch.

I LAY LOW FOR my first term but a plan hatched when I saw the house Christmas pantomime. This struck me as awesomely sophisticated stuff. But none of the music was original. I let the following Easter term pass by but come the summer it was time to strike. I played the card that I had played before. A highlight of the summer term was the annual house concert. I put myself down to play the piano, programme to be announced.

As the end of pre-Beatle days drew nigh, the British charts were home to a few local curiosities, none more so than Russ Conway. Mr Conway was a rather good-looking gay guy. He played pub piano on TV with a fixed grin, despite having lost two digits in an incident in the Royal Navy which need not detain us. He also wrote several chart-topping instrumentals, most famously "Side Saddle." John Lill featured a few of these in his pub gigs.

My offering at the annual house concert was a tune I had knocked up in his style. It had the desired effect. After two encores the housemaster declared that it would make everyone's fortunes. Next morning I was summoned to see the Head of House. He told me that another senior boy was writing next term's annual pantomime. He needed some songs. Would I like to meet him? That's how I met my first lyricist and came to compose my first-ever performed musical.

Its name was *Cinderella up the Beanstalk* and his name was Robin Barrow.

Any cockiness I acquired was short lived. Buoyed by my belief that I was God's gift to melody, I wrote a fan letter to none other than Richard Rodgers, courtesy of my father's publisher Teddy Holmes at Chappell Music. Rodgers actually received it and, to my amazement, invited me to the London opening of *The Sound of Music* at the Palace Theatre. So on May 19, 1961 I found myself at my first premiere. On my own in a back row of the upper circle, I was overwhelmed by the melodies. However, arrogant little sod that I was, I wrote on my programme, "Not as good as 'You'll Never Walk Alone'" beside "Climb Ev'ry Mountain" in the songlist. Even so, I knew I was hearing melodies that would become evergreen from a genius at the top of his game.

Unfortunately my marvel at this first night tunefest was not shared by the London critics. This was rammed home to me by my so-called school friends when I pitched up the following morning. They had considerately laid out all the reviews for me on the common-room table. "Look what they've done to your idol, Lloydy," they crowed. That's when I first experienced a feeling that's taken the shine off many an opening night. But at least I learned my first lesson in creative advertising. One of the reviews read, "If you are a diabetic craving extra sickly sweet things inject an extra large dose of insulin and you will not fail to thrill to 'The Sound of Music.'"

"You Will Not Fail To Thrill To The Sound Of Music" adorned the front of the Palace Theatre for eight poetic justice infused years.

NEXT TERM REHEARSALS FOR *Cinderella* began. I found myself a junior boy rehearsing the seniors in a show with words written by a school prefect. Unsurprisingly, the first two rehearsals were daunting. In those days the seniority code at any school was quite something. But it was amazing how once we got into the swing of things all this was forgotten. Melodies were offered up, criticized, rewritten, discussed. Songs were tried out, cut, reinstated and cut again. It turned out that the Head of House had a rather good voice, so creepily I gave him a couple of wannabe showstoppers. For the first time I was where I was to discover I am happiest – working on a musical. We did three shows. I played the piano backstage and every night I took a proud little bow.

Two incidents dominated Christmas. The first was news from Italy that Auntie Vi had been slung out of Pisa Cathedral for showing her tits to a sacristan who had said her dress showed too much of her shoulders. The second happened on Christmas day. Mum had propelled Julian and me towards the morning Christmas service at the Central Hall, Westminster, unwisely leaving Granny Molly in charge of the Christmas turkey. I suggested that I manned the stoves and that Molly went to hear Dad and his choir strut their stuff, but this suggestion fell on deaf ears. Throughout the service I was gravely concerned about the fate of the turkey and keen to get back to Harrington Court as soon as decently possible. So Mum volunteered to drive me home, leaving Dad and Julian to cadge a lift with a neighbour after the post-service teabag and packet mince-pie party.

Mum turned on the car radio and out of the tinny mono speaker came music that catapulted thought of the turkey into the middle distance. Mum had tuned in five minutes after the start of Puccini's *Tosca*. I was completely and utterly captivated. I couldn't understand a word of it (probably a good thing as the more you understand the plot of *Tosca* the more unpleasant it is) but I had never heard such theatrical, gloriously melodic music in my life. Mum did explain what was going on when we got to the Act 1 closer, the "Te Deum," as she parked in the mews by the French Lycée. I realize now why that "Te Deum" hit every nerve in my body. My love of Victorian church architecture equalled an affinity with High Church decadence and if ever a piece of theatre is that, surely it's the *Tosca* "Te Deum." To this day it remains the only piece of theatre I secretly would love to direct. Just that bit though. Sadly, you probably wouldn't see much of my directorial debut due to excess incense clouds.

Unfortunately Mum clocked Dad and Julian being dropped off home across the road and opined that, *Tosca* or not, it was time for Christmas presents. I begged her to let me stay in the car. She said something like, "I suppose music is more important than Christmas" and told me to lock the car door after I had finished with the keys which she left in the ignition. With that she ankled towards the family festivities. I listened spellbound to the second act, as the car got colder and colder, and I went as cold as the outside air when I heard what I later discovered to be "Vissi d'arte." By the time the third-act bells of Rome were chiming I was totally wiped out. This was truly theatre music that I never dreamed possible. And there were no words! It was then that my reverie was interrupted by ferocious banging on the car windscreen.

You have to think of things from the police officer's point of view. Here was a thirteen-year-old boy in floods of tears at 2 pm on a freezing cold Christmas Day seemingly in charge of a car and listening to opera on the radio at full volume, not everyday stuff for a police officer, let alone on Christmas Day. Furthermore the thirteen-year-old boy seemed extremely indignant, even aggressive at being asked to turn the music off and explain himself. Eventually the policeman sort of accepted my story with an "I suppose I'll believe you this time because it's Christmas," and let me go on condition that he walked me to the flat front door.

A week later Dad gave me a highlights album of *Tosca*. I resolved to save every penny of my pocket money so that one day I could buy a boxed set of the whole score.

I SAID WORKING ON a musical is when I am happiest, but that Christmas a present proved once again that this isn't quite true. I was given a book about ruined abbeys and once more I was off into my world of history and architecture. From then onwards every school half term was taken up with a train ride to somewhere I wanted to see. Without this stabilizing passion my life could have been very different.

Easter 1962 found me on my one and only school holiday trip. A bunch of us, including my new-found lyricist Robin Barrow, were taken to Athens and Rome, where we duly marvelled at the antiquities. I added a diet of churches. It was in Rome that the misreading of a street map led me to a building that truly changed me. With hindsight I suspect the essay I wrote when I got home, which cogently argued that the American Church in Rome with its mosaics by the great Victorian artist Sir Edward Burne-Jones was Rome's finest building, may have been my first written attempt at being provocative. If so, it had its desired effect.

My art master was furious. "How can you write such garbage?" he screamed. "Don't you realize that church is full of Victorian tat?"

It must have been galling for a 1960s art teacher to think he'd hauled a troop of teenagers around the marvels of ancient Greece and Rome only to find one of them had fallen in love with Victorian art.

THE FOLLOWING SUMMER TERM was the occasion for the annual Westminster scholarship exam called the Challenge. Eight boys are chosen to enter College, the house reserved only for scholars. This was the exam that was deemed pointless for me to try when I was at the Under School. However I was still young enough to have a crack at it. So I did. The first few papers, Greek, Maths etc., suggested that my decision to have a go was extremely unwise. History was the last paper and, secure in the knowledge that everything I had done so far reinvented the pig's ear, there was nothing for it but to let rip. My paper was a eulogy to medieval Britain, with the added thrust that the Gothic Revival improved it. I argued that, superb as the medieval glass in the clerestory of Westminster Abbey is, the glass by a Victorian named Kempe in the south transept eclipses the lot.

I sauntered out of the exam room that bright summer's day certain that I wouldn't be hearing more from the powers behind the Challenge. Next day I was summoned to an interview. Behind a desk was the bursar, the headmaster and the senior history teacher, a wonderful man called Charles Keeley. For some reason it was the bursar who asked the questions. Curiously we got onto the subject of the castles of the Welsh borders. Quite why I talked about Clun Castle escapes me but, if ever you find yourself stuck on this subject, the thing to remember is that Oliver Cromwell blew up its "keep" or main tower which duly slipped intact down the hill it stood on. I mentioned this. It transpired the bursar's family came from Clun.

That night I was told I had won a Queen's Scholarship to Westminster.

4

A Whiter Shade of Something
That Didn't Taste Very Nice
in the First Place

If, like me, you think that a story of adolescent angst, depression, unrequited you-name-it and general hormone imbalance is best consigned to a lovelorn teenager's chat site or a current hit musical, skip the next bit. Frankly I nearly did. In a nutshell I was pretty confused and unhappy for the next two years, partly because I was now away from home at boarding school, even if it was only three stops on the underground from Harrington Court. And yes, as was the case for so many public schools at that time, there was a master whose activities today would result in a medium-scale sojourn in one of Her Majesty's less salubrious addresses.

But the bottom line, appropriate words in the circumstances, was that I emerged from Westminster wiser in the ways of the world and having encountered some of the finest and kindest teachers any boy could have wished for. Top of the list were my housemaster in College Jim Woodhouse and the history chief Charles Keeley. It was Charles who went out on a limb to get me my scholarship and up until the last minute I singularly failed to repay the faith he showed in me.

The skippable bit starts in the summer of 1962, a summer I shall ever associate with Brian Hyland's bittersweet "Sealed with a Kiss." Auntie Vi and George the Panjandrum sold up their Weymouth Street flat and moved to a house they had built on the Italian Riviera, just over the French border in a village called La Mortola, famed for the Hanbury Gardens. Even now they remain my favourite spot on the Mediterranean. George had reached retirement age and the promise of sun and cheap booze had proved irresistible. At a stroke I had lost my London escape hole, although I soon found I had gained an outside plus. At La Mortola I got to touch the last golden autumn days of the bohemian Côte d'Azur that has vanished now into a sea of oligarchs and eurotrash.

The family holiday that year was in the north Norfolk village of Burnham Market. I chose it because Norfolk oozes churches. The problem was that John Lill came too and an upright piano was added to our cottage's rental bill. It was obvious that things were also beginning to weigh on Julian. One afternoon we were on an open-top bus. It was brilliantly sunny and I had forced my brother to join me on a church crawl. I vividly remember him asking me how we were ever going to get Mum to see what she was doing to the family.

Actually we both liked John. That holiday he was learning the fiendishly difficult last movement of Prokofiev's seventh piano sonata, a bravura tour de force in 7/8 time. I turned the pages for him. I became obsessed with the mesmeric possibilities of that oddball time signature . . . try counting in seven, here's a tip: count one two three, one two, one two in a row without a break. Next try counting one two, one two three, one two and vary it from there. You'll be popular in the subway. Every musical I have written has a section in 7/8 time. There's even a joke about it in *Phantom* which, so far as I know, has only been laughed at once – by the conductor Lorin Maazel who found it hilarious.

I suspect John would laugh at it too. He and I share a similar sense of musical humour. A few years later we went to a concert of unusual instruments in St Pancras Town Hall. The big draw was Vaughan Williams's Tuba Concerto. Unfortunately it was preceded by Vivaldi's Concerto for Sopranino and Orchestra. A huge man with the biggest hands I have ever seen ascended the stage with no visible instrument in sight. The conductor raised his baton. The goliath raised his chubby palms mouthwards from which emanated a sound so piercing and high that every dog and bat in the vicinity must have been begging scalpers for front row seats. To make things worse Vivaldi was, put it this way, not on peak form when he knocked up this particular epic. John and I got the giggles, which ended in my getting hiccups when a serious woman with glasses in front of us who was deeply studying a music score turned round and said "It may be funny but it's not that funny." When next up a diminutive chap staggered onto the stage dwarfed by an enormous tuba, an usher less than politely suggested that we left. Was this the first and only time a Tchaikovsky Prize winner has been ejected from a classical concert? On another occasion John told me that he once by mistake turned over a page twice when he was premiering a Philip Glass piano epic. After his performance, Glass congratulated him on his fabulous interpretation. In short I grew to like John very much. With hindsight, my problem was never with John. It was with my mother's obsession with him.

I can't speak for Dad but I suspect that he felt the same way too. Back in that summer of 1962 things must have become way too much for him. To everyone's amazement he announced that he was going to stay with Vi and George in Italy. Dad had never been "abroad" in his life. Mum had no intention of tagging on and a plan was hatched that he would spend a week with my aunt and uncle while I was to fly out a few days later.

My first memory of Nice Côte d'Azur Airport is of my father being freighted through the departure lounge, his speech slurred, his pale skin frazzled and peeling, giggling hysterically about girls' bottoms. Clearly the sun and the local brews had made an impression on him. My first memory of La Promenade des Anglais is that Dad's argument had a lot going for it. In those days bikinis hadn't had much of an outing in the dank mists of Britain. Soon we were motoring past the grand villas on the Bas Corniche and past Cap Ferrat through a then low-rise Monaco to the French border and a world of scents and colours, actors and wine, parmigiano and olive oil, famous film directors, David Niven and his pool built in metres when he had specified feet, artists and their partners who were always the same people but in different combinations every holiday, Aunt Vi's *azur*-painted piano and her plumbago-covered terrace with the purple bougainvillea etched against the deep blue of the Mediterranean Sea, La Punta, the dreamy little fish restaurant on the shore which you could only reach on foot, the Hanbury Gardens and La Mortola restaurant where Winston Churchill had a celebration lunch after Germany surrendered . . . I could go on forever about a now vanished world that totally infused my life.

FROM THEN ONWARDS VI'S house became my second home. It's not surprising therefore that pitching up to board at Westminster on a grey autumn afternoon was a shock to the system. Worse, because of the way boys in my new house were grouped by age, I lost a whole year of privileges. Because I was so young when I had arrived at the school I had been at the school for two years, the same length of time as the boys grouped above me. I protested to deaf ears. It seemed terribly unfair. All this paled into total insignificance a few weeks later. October 1962 was the month of the Cuban Missile Crisis. For several nights we would look out of our dormitory window onto the Houses of Parliament and wonder whether that would be the last time we'd see them. There wasn't one of us who truthfully didn't want a hug from our parents at thirteen successive bedtimes. The one thing that consoled us was that our Westminster address meant our end would be swift.

My demotion caused a big problem with rehearsals. The first consequent crisis erupted over rehearsals for my old house's Christmas pantomime. This had already become a musical called *Socrates Swings* and the partnership of Robin Barrow and Lloyd Webber had much to live up to. Just because I'd changed houses, I couldn't let the old side down. The issue was that rehearsals mainly took place after junior boys' bedtime and I was now a junior again. Robin, being a prefect himself, sorted matters out with his opposite number in my new house who reluctantly went along with my extended bedtime but subsequently got the opportunity to make me pay for it by beating me horrendously hard for something I didn't do. Thus I accompanied our *Socrates Swings* atop a three-inch cushion. Mum and Dad came to a performance and I think it was then the penny dropped that I was not going to be a model history scholar.

A couple of weeks before the world premiere of *Socrates Swings*, the London premiere of Benjamin Britten's *War Requiem* was given at Westminster Abbey. A few Queen's Scholars were chosen to be ushers and I was one of them. It was a thick "peasouper" foggy night and it was impossible to see more than a few feet, even inside the Abbey, so how the performers followed the conductor was a miracle. How anyone got to the Abbey was even more so, proving how in those pre-air-pollution-control days Londoners were inured to massive fogs.

The performance made a profound impression on me. The *War Requiem* is a piece of breathtaking theatricality with its juxtaposition of Wilfred Owen war poems and the Latin Requiem Mass. As ever with Britten his orchestrations are a master class, perhaps never more so than here since he uses three elements – a full orchestra, a chamber orchestra and a "positive" organ (an organ used by early Baroque composers like Purcell with a very particular sound) to accompany his detached, ethereal boys' choir. It was that performance that led me to Britten's operas, *Peter Grimes* and *The Turn of the Screw*. Britten's use of a single brushstroke on a snare drum to describe the sound of a tug in *Death in Venice* is genius personified.

AT THE END OF the same week as the *War Requiem*'s London premiere, another debut occurred. That Christmas a song called "Love

Me Do" by a relatively unknown Liverpool band named The Beatles entered the pop charts. It only got to No. 17 but it was the harbinger of 1963, the year when The Beatles had the first of their seemingly infinite run of No. 1 hits and pop music was changed forever. Liverpool's Mersey Sound erupted and Swinging London was born. Westminster was right in London's epicentre, only a walk away from the music publishers of Tin Pan Alley* and the clubs and concert venues where everything was happening. All I wanted was to be a part of this new music scene and there it was, a mere hop and a skip from my enforced cloistered doorstep via a short cut through the Abbey. I was desperate to prove that I too, not just John Lill, could be a success.

Maybe because my father had seen my Christmas 1962 two-performance smash *Socrates Swings* and thought I needed help, or perhaps because we had found something in common re La Promenade des Anglais in Nice, in the spring of 1963 he decided to send me part-time to a specialist music college in the school holidays. The "college" actually was a place that taught musically illiterate songwriters how to put their efforts on paper. It was run by a guy who, it transpired, Dad had known in student days called Eric Gilder and Dad thought I'd pick up a few practical tips. Indeed Mr Gilder did show me a rather nifty key change trick which I occasionally still use. It makes a change from the usual half-step upwards. The most valuable thing Gilder taught me was how to prepare the piano score of a musical. The guinea pig was a show I had started based upon one of the worst ideas ever conceived for the stage short of a musical about the humanitarian work of Genghis Khan. It was called *Westonia!* and was a sort of send-up of the Ruritanian concoctions much beloved by Ivor Novello. Nearly 60 years later my embarrassment is such that nobody – not even my dearest or closest – knows where I have hidden the score.

* The nickname for Denmark Street in Soho.

Westonia! came about because I was desperate. Robin Barrow was now university bound and there were no other budding lyricists lurking in the Westminster cloisters. The meteoric rise of the Fab Four had sent my contemporaries' interest in musicals plummeting from zero to minus ratings. The only person I could find to write lyrics to my juvenilia was a brassy Australian ex-actress friend of my aunt's called Joan Colmore. Thus *Westonia!* was born.

Thanks to Mr Gilder, the score of this horror was presented in a rather professional way. So when I sent it to the top West End producer Harold Fielding, accompanied by a letter stressing I was fourteen, it got noticed. The producer of *Half a Sixpence* and *Ziegfeld* let it be known that he thought the music was promising. Somehow word spread enough for a couple of agents to enquire of Dad whether I needed representing. Naturally I thought a West End opening was imminent and my skiving off school to meet publishers and the like reached fever pitch.

Eventually I got a sweet letter from Harold Fielding saying that I should press on with the music, but in no way was *Westonia!* headed for the West End any time soon. Along the way I had a short stint represented by a top agency, the Noel Gay Organisation, who promptly dropped me once Fielding put me back in my box. I came down to earth with a mega bump. Musicals, I decided, were dead ducks – especially if top producers couldn't see the obvious quality of cutting-edge works like *Westonia!* It was time to be a pop songwriter. But firmly in the way was the inescapable fact that I was stuck in a boarding school that I was less than partial to and the Lill saga dominated home life.

Towards the close of the Easter holidays I was deeply depressed. Mum's John Lill obsession was making her increasingly moody and erratic. Home was a cauldron of overwrought emotion and jealousy, fuelled increasingly in Dad's case by alcohol. Another term at boarding school loomed like a grey sledgehammer. My adolescent hormones told me I'd had enough.

One morning I stole some Veganin tablets out of the bathroom cupboard, went to the post office and withdrew my savings – all £7 of them. Then I bought aspirin from two different South Ken chemists and headed for the underground station. In those days the "underground" penetrated as far as Ongar in the then deep Essex countryside. I bought a one-way ticket. When I hit the end of the line I wandered into the town, bought some more aspirin and a bottle of Lucozade and headed for the bus station. I planned to take the first bus, get off somewhere remote and swallow my arsenal of pills behind a convenient hedgerow.

I saw a bus with "Lavenham" on its front. Something told me to take it – the name rang an architectural bell. The ancient bus trundled through the Essex countryside and as we hit Suffolk the sun came out. By the time we arrived at Lavenham an overcast morning had turned into a glorious spring day.

Lavenham! I'd never seen such an unspoilt English village before. But it was the church that did it. All I remember now is sitting inside for what must have been two hours and saying "thank God for Lavenham." I headed back to the bus stop and London thinking things weren't so bad after all. But I kept the pills.

It would be elasticating the truth if I claimed that my Westminster days didn't have plusses. First, Westminster kicked off my burgeoning love of Victorian architecture. One of the College prefects was a guy called John House, who sadly died in 2014, having had a distinguished career as an art curator and becoming Slade Professor of Fine Art at Oxford University. John was the first person to introduce me to the great Victorian architects and, together with my increasingly inseparable friend Gray Watson, I began combing Britain for Victorian churches.

By my second year in College there were few parts of London I didn't know. My architectural crawls took me to parts of Britain's cities that I suspect very few of my Westminster contemporaries saw. Most of the finest Victorian churches were built as mission bases from which to scupper Satan's enticements to the defenceless poor. So I got into some near misses with local youths who did not take kindly to an effeminate boy in a smart school suit clutching poncy architectural guidebooks. As a result I discovered I wasn't totally un-athletic. I could run.

By the time I left school I had a pretty fair knowledge of at least a dozen British cities. This was the era of mass demolition of housing deemed uninhabitable, for which read housing of a human scale. It was the 1960s that saw the brutal creation of urban roads that swathed through Britain's town centres thanks to the new planning mantra that separated pedestrians from God the car. Everywhere there was an orgy of government-inspired destruction that ripped the heart out of Britain's cities far more effectively than Hitler's Luftwaffe ever did. Of course Victorian buildings, being considered the runt of all architecture, were top of the list for the wrecker's ball, theatres being particular targets. I remember lying down in Pall Mall with a group of my aunt's friends in vain protest at the demolition of London's gorgeous St James Theatre. The preservation of Britain's most vulnerable architecture became a lifelong passion.

The other plus was the arguments with Granny. Gray Watson and a group of us College boys salivated over hopping on the underground to Harrington Court where we berated the co-founder of the Christian Communist Party with our ever more right-wing, ludicrously politically incorrect views. She secretly loved it, of course. I began to discover increasing depths to this remarkable woman. She confided about her bohemian open house in Harrow and that her sister Ella's greasy spoon for truck drivers was called Jock's Box. Was she beginning to see in me a glimmer of her own son so tragically taken from her when he had barely left school?

However there was one thing she didn't notice. Harrington Court was becoming so dirty and scruffy that it was becoming embarrassing to ask friends home.

IN THE WINTER OF 1963 my new-found role as ace pop songwriter paid off big time. Or so I thought. A publisher at United Artists Music had sent a fistful of my efforts to an A&R chief at Decca Records called Charles Blackwell. Blackwell was a big cheese who steered top artists like P.J. Proby, the singer who provocatively split his trousers whilst performing in a cinema in Walthamstow to much tabloid shock horror. I witnessed this minor piece of rock history, having sneaked out of school one Saturday night. Unfortunately a photo of Proby, split trousers and audience with me in it (now lost), got into one of the rags but thankfully nobody at school saw it.

Blackwell decided to record one of my songs with a singer called Wes Sands. Wesley (real name Clive Sarstedt) was the brother of pre-Beatles-era singer Eden Kane (Richard Sarstedt) and of Peter Sarstedt who one day was to have a huge hit with "Where Do You Go To (My Lovely)?," a song Tim Rice at the time rechristened "Where Do You Go to My Ugly," but now says he rather likes. Sarstedt, rather than Kane/Sands, was the real family name. The song Blackwell chose was called "Make Believe Love." To top it all, I had written the lyrics. Modesty and common sense prohibit my reproducing the lyrics here. Suffice it to say I was certain that my career was off and running. I acquired a new agent, a thirtyish very camp publisher called Desmond Elliott. I was invited to the recording session. I could oversee the creation of my first runaway hit!

Unfortunately the new commander of the Westminster School Combined Cadet Force had other ideas. In those days kids at schools like Westminster were forced to become cadets in the army, navy or airforce. My military career started inauspiciously when I failed the army basic test. I was hauled up in front of the commander for sowing the seeds of mutiny. The basis for this false accusation was my answer to a question about what you did when under enemy fire and confronted by a closed gate. I opined that I would open it and proceed through it asap. This was apparently not what a cadet was supposed to do. It seemed you either burrowed underneath or vaulted over said gate. I pointed out that neither option would work in my case. In reply to the suggestion that I was unpatriotic and disloyal to Her Majesty the Queen, School and Country, I countered by suggesting that I composed a school cadet corps march that would kick "Land of Hope and Glory" into the long grass.

The commander either believed me or feared that my presence on the parade ground was fatally disruptive, even if hard to prove. For a year I got permission to swan around listening to military bands and inadvertently learned a lot about writing for brass instruments in the process. However the new school year yielded a new CCF commander and he was having none of this. Having heard, I think, on the school grapevine that I was having a song recorded, he ordered me away on an army field trip. I pleaded with him that this recording session was my big chance and he replied that school was not about being a pop songwriter. A taste of the army assault course at Aldershot was what I needed.

I was totally distraught. I was – I still am – paranoiac about the army and I was terrified out of my skull. I found my stock of aspirin and took an overdose. I woke to find a doctor's face pressed close to mine demanding what the hell was I doing frightening my parents like this. I can't tell you if it was a cry for help or whether I meant it. I don't know.

A psychiatrist concluded that my paranoia about the army was genuine and, if not exactly an illness, mirrored a problem that also bedevilled my father. Apparently he had frozen during a military assessment when he was conscripted in the war. I will never know what else the report about me said but I do know it found that I had vertigo. I could have told them that. I once seized up completely when I was very small and made to stand on a box as a punishment. These days I get vertigo if I just stand up.

So my army days came to an inglorious halt. I got a dire warning from the Commanding Officer that the incident would go on my permanent record at MI5, thus scuppering any chance of a career in public life. But my wonderful housemaster Jim Woodhouse was sympathetic. So the end of 1963 saw me still hanging on to Westminster life, not kicked out as a misfit as a lot of schools would have done. The year end was a yawn. Robin Barrow had left so there was no Christmas show to compose. I got a few offers to be a pretty boy pianist at Desmond Elliott's publisher friends' Christmas parties and earned a few quid and the sort of tweak of the bottom that might aggravate Taylor Swift. 1963 may well have been the year The Beatles saw and conquered, but for me it was like the French wine vintage. A whiter shade of something that didn't taste very nice in the first place.

IT WAS WINE THAT ushered in my 1964 with a cock-up that could have put paid to my Westminster career big time. Auntie Vi knew a wine merchant and I was allowed to coat-tail onto a tasting of 1961 clarets. 1963 may have been for both French wine growers and myself an "*année de pissoir*" but 1961 was hailed as the reason people bother to grow grapes. The wine tasted and looked like ink to me, but I was firmly told that in 50 years' time things would be different and that the ink would probably outlive me. So with my Christmas party earnings I forked out on a couple of cases of Château Palmer. This apparently was the bargain of the vintage, a wine from a lesser-known château that had punched beyond its weight. Wine bores will confirm that Vi's wine merchant knew what he was salivating about.

The snag was that instead of delivering the stuff to my parents' flat it somehow got delivered to Westminster School. Since alcohol and smoking were offences punishable by expulsion, I assumed that my teatime summons to the study of John Carleton the headmaster meant the end was nigh. I explained what had happened: that no sane person would drink this wine for decades and it had simply gone to the wrong place. The headmaster asked me rather too pointedly if I liked wine. I couldn't lie. I simply said that my uncle collected Italian wine and, yes, I had tasted the odd glass of his best and, yes, I did like it. The headmaster thought for a moment and then ordered me to come back and see him in a couple of hours. These I spent agonizing about the even more agonizing two minutes that almost certainly awaited me if he had decided that those two hours were not my Westminster swansong. But instead of a scowling HM clasping his infamous six foot cane he stood there beaming. A small table had been laid with a decanter and two glasses.

"I have a small dinner party tonight and I am serving a 1945 Château Léoville Barton," declared the man the school nicknamed Coote. "I thought you might like to taste it with me."

Thus began my friendship with the headmaster. I valued my time with him, even if it did sometimes mean sitting very close to him on his sofa.

5

"Mr Lloyd Webber,
Do You Like Cats?"

Come 1964 Swinging London was really taking off. I had a bit more freedom at school now. Carnaby Street spewed out "mod" clothes. Beatlemania and Beatle boots lurked everywhere. Even big American pop stars were making desperate attempts to sound hip in Britain. *Two Yanks in England* was the latest Everly Brothers album offering. Even Bobby Vee experimented with *The New Sounds from England*, albeit with an occasional Buddy Holly hiccup.

In January I somehow got a ticket in the cheap seats for the theatrical event of the year – for me perhaps of all time – the opening performance of Franco Zeffirelli's production of *Tosca* with Maria Callas and Tito Gobbi. So much has been written about the few legendary performances they gave that all I will say is that it was life-changing for me. I saw just how much two world-class opera performers at the top of their game can bring to an all too familiar work.

It certainly opened the eyes of many opera critics. Because Puccini was the commercial backstop of every opera company he had become devalued as a composer. To serious opera buffs his stock was similar to the Sixties intelligentsia's view of Rodgers and Hammerstein. Every time an opera house needed bums on seats they wheeled out a tired old production of *La Bohème, Tosca* or *Madame Butterfly* played by a disinterested orchestra and regarded by the management as a necessary ill to pay for the real stuff of opera which unfortunately the ignorant public had no desire to see.

Everyone has a *Tosca* story, e.g. the fat soprano who threw herself off the rooftop of the Castel Sant'Angelo only to bounce up over the ramparts from the trampoline stationed beneath. *Tosca* had been called a "shabby little shocker." *The Oxford Companion to Music* (Seventh Edition by Percy Scholes) had this condescending entry – about a third the length of Bartók's – about Puccini. It speaks volumes.

> The music is essentially Italian in its easyflowing melody . . . his harmonies just original enough to rouse the attention of the conventional opera goer . . . he employs not so much his own system harmony as that of his immediate predecessors served up with new condiments.

Here at last was a production that took the music seriously, gave it first-class production values and proved what a master theatre composer he was. Parenthetically, much as I love *Tosca* the only other Puccini opera I know well is *La Bohème*. For some reason, I have never got to grips with *Madame Butterfly* or *Manon Lescaut*. In fact my knowledge of opera is not as deep as all that. One of my problems is that I can't hear the words. It's worse when they're unintelligible and supposed to be being sung in English.

IN FEBRUARY 1964 TWO ex-Westminster boys joined the Swinging London party. Peter Asher and Gordon Waller were both prefects during my early days at school. Gordon had fronted various Elvis-type school acts and had definitely been the school's hot dude. Little then did I think that only a few years later he would play Pharaoh in the first stage production of *Joseph and the Amazing Technicolor Dreamcoat*.

Peter's claim to fame was that his sister Jane was Paul McCartney's girlfriend. This was helpful as far as Peter and Gordon's debut single was concerned since Paul wrote it. "A World Without Love" went to No. 1 on both sides of the Atlantic. It was the first time anyone from a British public school had done such a thing. I thought Westminster needed to commemorate this momentous feat. I booked up to see Headmaster John Carleton who heartily agreed that once again Westminster was ahead of the curve.

Not only did he give me complete use of the school theatre, but he allowed the whole school a special holiday to see my celebration. My enterprise was much abetted by Desmond Elliott. Whether he or I came up with the abominable title *Play the Fool*, I can't remember so I'll blame him. What I do remember is that the invites were sent out to random key people whose addresses I stole in envelopes that looked like writs. The response was astonishing. Soon people who hadn't been invited were clamouring for tickets to this happening under the nose of Westminster Abbey.

There wasn't much musical content from me, apart from a show-stopping bid with my Wes Sands song "Make Believe Love" which completely failed. It was much upstaged by an outfit called Twinkle and the Trekkers, Twinkle being a rather posh girl in a wafty dress who had been drafted in by one of the boys to front his house band. She had written a death motorcycle epic called "Terry" with incisive lyrics like: "He rode into the night / Accelerated his motorbike / I cried to him in fright / Don't do it, / Don't do it." A motorbike was an essential part of the staging but we couldn't find one. Nonetheless "Terry" went fine. Shortly afterwards Twinkle had a big UK hit with it on Decca Records. I think somewhere along the line Tim Rice had a short association with Twinkle, but I may be misinformed.

A huge array of lower echelon radio and TV producers turned out to see the first show I had masterminded. So it was as a producer rather than composer that these guys first heard of me. Nothing like this had happened at Westminster before and I was very proud of it.

Even masters mouthed "Well done." I had promoted the show, cast it, found the technicians, found someone to light it, sorted the sound system, chosen the music and created a decent running order out of a ragtag potpourri of bands who ranged from hormonal teenage girl sulkbags to a rough North London mob oddly named Peter and the Wolves who wanted to smash the Merseyside boys. Their songs were pretty dire, but their cover versions had the whole school rocking and Compline (evening prayers) was abandoned in St Faith's that night. All those episodes of Jack Good's *Oh Boy!* had rubbed off on me. Soon, I presumed, someone would take me on as an apprentice at a TV company and I could leave Westminster just like that! It's nice to dream.

THE SUMMER TERM WAS when we took A levels. The results of these determined whether you tried for a university. At Westminster there were a series of "closed" places to Oxford and Cambridge, i.e. scholarships and the like which are charitably funded and only open to Westminster boys. I don't know if this monstrously unfair system applies today, but in my day these "closed" places siphoned off the best Westminster talent. Rarely did a Westminster boy enter the "open" exams that pitted you against all comers.

My A-level results were appalling. I had only two passes, a D grade in History and E in English; the worst ever result by any Westminster Scholar. My songwriting and producing activities had finally caught up with me. I sat the Christ Church exam along with everyone else, but knew I had no hope of getting a place. I went to the interview like a zombie. Needless to say, I was told to try again next year. Suddenly it hit me. All my friends would be leaving for Oxford and I would be left skulking behind, trapped in a school I was bursting to get out of. Now all my friends seemed to be talking in groups about what would happen when they left. Should they travel round Europe together? What about a trip to New York before Oxford term starts? They were talking about New York, the home of musicals! And they were talking without me. I had blown it big time and it was all my fault.

There was only one tenuous hope. Talk about Last Gasp Saloon time but I realized that the "open" exam for entrance to all the Oxford colleges took place a fortnight later and there was still time for me to enter. Dear Jim Woodhouse took pity on me and the entry forms were signed and dispatched, but not without a resigned look from both Jim and my history master Charles Keeley. I resolved to take myself on a kamikaze crash course of the medieval history I loved and to pray that I got an exam paper with the right questions for me to heroically bluff my way through.

It was coming up to the end of term and the other boys were already university bound so lessons were token. I asked permission to skip them. I threw myself into book after book for twelve hours a day and spent the remaining hours dreaming up historical theories that were so ludicrously at odds to accepted academic thinking that at least I might interest an examiner. Perhaps, if I backed my outrageous ideas up with enough facts, I might stand a chance of blagging my way into one of the smaller colleges. But it all depended on the questions in the exam paper and whether I could twist them my way.

The college you chose as a preference was another major consideration. I chose Magdalen College as my number one. I knew a lot about its architecture, it had a Pre-Raphaelite connection through Holman Hunt and its Senior History professor was the medievalist K.B. McFarlane whose books I had read. My number two choice was Brasenose College because I liked its name.

IT WAS MID-NOVEMBER WHEN I sat the exam, all alone as I was the only Westminster boy to enter the "open" exam. The paper was a dream. I waffled on about how Edward II was a far better king than Edward I, how the Victorian additions improve the medieval original at Cardiff Castle (I can personally vouch that this view is not shared

by HM The Queen), that Keble College, for years wrongly considered a red brick Victorian eyesore, is in the top three of Oxford's
best buildings; that the classicist Christopher Wren had advised that
Westminster Abbey's tower be finished in the Gothic style (it is still
an unfinished ugly stump by the way), etc. I doubt if such an outpouring of muddled factual diarrhoea has ever hit an examiner. At least I
had given it my best shot.

Three days later I got a letter from Magdalen inviting me for an
interview. It said that I might need to have a second one and to come
prepared to stay overnight at the college. I pitched up late morning at
the porter's lodge and was shown to a rather nice Victorian bedroom
and told my interview would be at 3 pm. I didn't know Oxford that
well, but I had time to check out that I was right about Keble College
and, importantly, that Gene Pitney was top of the bill at the Oxford
New Theatre that night. That was my evening sorted out.

After lunch with a lot of nervous young men who for some reason
didn't want to make conversation about Gene Pitney's "Town Without Pity," I joined a small group of the about to be interviewed outside
a sort of common room and took a seat. It was then I noticed the
Siamese cat. Or to be accurate, the Siamese cat noticed me. Now it
takes two to know one and the cat was in no doubt. It jumped on my
knee, purring loudly, and butted against my fist whilst engaging in
the sort of intelligent conversation and occasional rub against the face
that only proper Siamese cats do. After a while it settled down and
kneaded my leg for Thailand.

When the door opened and someone said, "Mr Lloyd Webber,
will you come in please?" I obviously couldn't put the cat down. So I
carried it in. I was invited to sit down and my new best friend settled
contentedly on my knee. Facing me across the centre of a medium
sized dining table was Professor McFarlane, flanked by various dons
one of whom asked an easily answered trick question about the date
of the nave of Westminster Abbey. I am to this day a genuine fan of

McFarlane's books and it was actually a joy to be interviewed by this great medievalist. It took a while but eventually he got around to serious questioning.

"Mr Lloyd Webber, do you like cats?"

I didn't reply "how long have you got?" but the nub of my answer caused him to end the interview by saying that that would be all and that I didn't need to stay overnight for another interview.

I was a bit alarmed, but on balance I thought things had gone pretty well. I bade farewell to the cat who followed me back to the little room I had been given. The big issue now was that I was told I wasn't needed the next day and I wanted to see Gene Pitney. What if they wanted the room for some poor blighter who had to go through the hoop a second time? I decided to wing it. That night I heard "I'm Gonna Be Strong" for the first time.

I took the train next morning and went straight to my parents' flat. Granny really wanted to know how I had got on. I explained about the cat. She looked exasperated and muttered something about how one day cats would be my undoing. I naturally took a different view. But I was masking huge jitters about the outcome of my interview. It wasn't exactly textbook. So I phoned Magdalen College and asked if there was by any chance a list yet of new undergraduates for next year. Eventually I got through to a very important-sounding woman who said she was the bursar's secretary. I asked her if the list of next year's undergraduates was ready yet.

"I am afraid we only have the list of scholarship winners but the list of the names of the new undergraduates will be published in two days' time."

Two days was a long time to wait. "By the way to whom am I talking?"

I mumbled my name.

"Oh wait a second," she said, "you are Mr Lloyd Webber, just let me see. Ah yes. Mr Lloyd Webber, congratulations. You have won a

History exhibition.* We so look forward to seeing you at Magdalen next year."

I was speechless. Granny blinked back a tear. Here was I, a boy who had wasted a complete year at Westminster and I had won the only open award Westminster had to Oxford that year. I said good-bye to Granny, ran to South Kensington station where the train to Westminster took an eternity to arrive. I ran down Tothill Street into Dean's Yard and to my long-suffering history master's classroom. He had just finished a lesson. I told him the news and he went ashen. All he said was "Bless you, my boy."

It was then that I realized just how far he had stuck his neck out to get me a scholarship to Westminster and how terribly I had betrayed his trust. I spent the rest of the day contemplating the ineffable powers of the cat.

---

*   Magdalen College's terminology for a junior scholarship.

6

Enter Timothy Miles
Bindon Rice

It was just before Christmas when my agent Desmond Elliott un-
leashed a project that was to dominate the next two years. Desmond
ran a small publishing company called Arlington Books which spe-
cialized in niche areas such as cookbooks. He also represented Leslie
Thomas, an author who a year later had a huge success with his novel
The Virgin Soldiers. Leslie was a "Barnardo Boy," in other words an
orphan raised in a Barnardo home. These "homes" were founded by
a Victorian philanthropist Dr Thomas Barnardo. He had witnessed
the plight of orphaned children in London's Dickensian East End
and, future wife on arm, started a rescue home that mushroomed
into one of the world's leading charities for homeless kids.

Desmond immediately divined in the Barnardo story a massive
post-*Oliver!* musical. Kids, jolly cockneys, Dickensian locations, a
hero who nearly lost the love of his life in his crusade against the Victorian establishment – this, Desmond decided, was stuff that would
make *Oliver!* look like *Salad Days*. Leslie was supposed to come up
with a storyline and I was to knock up a few tunes so Desmond could
stitch up a producer. It was to be called *The Likes of Us*. Connoisseurs
of musical theatre disasters will already have twitching noses. Years

later a musical about Dr Barnardo (not mine) did reach the West End. Tom Lehrer was in the audience and was heard to mutter "a terminal case for abortion."

There was a minor snag to creativity. I was still at school. Nowadays nobody would dream of having pupils who had outlived a school's usefulness hanging disruptively around the cloisters. But January 1965 saw me back in College one more time. I simply had to get out. So I invented a story that I had been offered a part-time job by an antiquarian bookseller. It was an elegant solution for all. In February I was free and I wanted to start work on the musical. The trouble was there was not a lot of input from Leslie Thomas. With hindsight I wonder how much he knew about it. Leslie is a novelist not a scriptwriter.

IT WAS A WEIRD feeling suddenly having time on my hands, waking up not knowing how to fill the day. When you are old you fill blank days by doing pointless things like writing autobiographies, but that wasn't on my radar at the time and Oxford was months away. So I spent the early part of the year looking at buildings. It was then that I cemented my knowledge of Britain's inner cities.

Today there's much talk about the new generation looking forward to a worse future than their parents. Based on some of the things I saw in 1965, it would have been hard for the new generation not to have had a better future than their forebears. It was common for four families to be stuffed into a clapped-out small terraced house sharing one toilet at the back of a stinking misnomer of a garden. If the era of Rachman, whose name was so toxic that "Rachmanism" entered the Oxford English Dictionary, was supposed to have been over I didn't notice it. He was the notorious British slum landlord who bought run-down properties in rough neighbourhoods and packed them with immigrants before in 1962 he did something unusual, i.e. not for profit – he dropped dead.

Coming from a protected, albeit bohemian environment, I admit to being shocked and not a little frightened by how quickly large city areas were changing character out of recognition. Once I was backed onto the rickety railings of one of the terraced houses that surrounded St Mary Magdalene in Paddington by a not particularly threatening, if extremely large, Jamaican guy pushing me "de weed." A gang of three passing white yobs surrounded us, opining articulate bon mots such as "He may be a fucking poncy posh nancy-boy but he's white and you take your fucking black hands off him." Something told me this was not the moment to engage in conversation about High Victorian Gothic. Today the houses around St Mary's are long gone. It's odd to reflect that those that survive in Notting Hill and Paddington now sell for millions of pounds.

I SPENT EASTER WITH Auntie Vi at La Mortola which was in full Mediterranean flower mode. She was spending a lot of time in the kitchen from which emanated cries like "God bugger the Pope," followed by a lot of meticulous writing up of recipes in a notebook. I tinkled away dreaming up tunes for the Barnardo show on her blue piano while I gazed at the virulent purple bougainvillea that had flowered early on her terrace that spring. But still there was no story outline from Leslie Thomas and I began to concoct one myself. Back in London, out of the blue I received the following letter.

11 GUNTER GROVE LONDON SW10

April 21, 1965

Dear Andrew

I have been given your address by Desmond Elliott of Arlington Books, who I believe has also told you of my existence.

Mr Elliott told me you "were looking for a 'with it' writer" of lyrics for your songs, and as I have been writing pop songs for a short while now and particularly enjoy writing the lyrics I wondered if you consider it worth your while meeting me. I may fall far short of your requirements, but anyway it would be interesting to meet up – I hope!

Would you be able to get in touch with me shortly, either at FLA 1822 in the evenings, or at WEL 2261 in the day time (Pettit and Westlake, solicitors are the owner of the latter number).

> Hoping to hear from you,
> Yours,
> *Tim Rice*

Naturally I was intrigued. I thought it might be unwise to call his work number so I dialled the FLAxman. In those days all phone numbers were prefixed by abbreviations in letters of names or towns. The numerical equivalents still survive, for example in London 235 is short for the "BEL" of BELgravia. A school friend's uncle had a 235 phone line which until his death in the noughties he answered with "BELgravia whatever the-number-was." He also referred to Heathrow Airport by its 1938 title the London Aviation Station and pronounced the Alps "the Oorlps." Once he moaned to me that a sojourn in his country house had been upset by his company holding a board meeting on a Wednesday. "It will ruin two weekends!" he fumed. But I digress.

A very well-spoken young man answered and explained that he did write pop lyrics – in fact he had also written some "three-chord tunes," as he put it, to go with them. He had done a course at La Sorbonne in Paris and was now 22, working as an articled clerk in a firm of solicitors and was bored out of his skull. The Desmond Elliott connection was that he had an idea for a compilation book based on the pop charts. He thought Desmond might publish it. Apparently Desmond had declined this opus (Tim was later to resurrect it as *The*

Guinness Book of British Hit Singles). Clearly Desmond had thrown me into his rejection letter as a sop. We arranged to meet one evening after Tim got off work.

I spent some of the in-between time pondering what a "with it" aspiring pop lyricist with a public school accent who had been to La Sorbonne looked like. Somehow I imagined a stocky bloke with long sideburns and a Beatle jacket, possibly sporting granny glasses. Consequently I was unprepared for what hit me when I answered the Harrington Court doorbell three days later. Silhouetted against the decaying lift was a six foot something, thin as a rake, blond bombshell of an adonis. Granny, who had shuffled down the corridor after me, seemed to go unusually weak in the knees. I felt, how shall I put this, decidedly small. Awestruck might be a better way of describing my first encounter with Timothy Miles Bindon Rice.

VERY SOON IT DAWNED on me that Tim's real ambition was to be a heartthrob rock star. I learned that he had been to Lancing College in Sussex, that he was born in 1944 and was therefore nearly four years older than me, that his father worked for Hawker Siddeley Aviation and his mother wrote children's stories. He brought a disc with him of a song he had written and sung himself. Apparently there was tons of interest in it and also in Tim as a solo pop god answer to Peter and Gordon. I was wondering where on earth I could fit into this saga of impending stardom.

So the first song and lyric I heard by Tim Rice was "That's My Story." It was a catchy, very appealing demo with Tim singing his three-chord tune in a laid-back, folksy way, accompanying himself on acoustic guitar. But it instantly struck me that the simple, happy, hooky melody seemed at odds with the rather bittersweet lyric about a guy dumping his girlfriend except the story was a charade. The guy had been dumped by his girlfriend. The punchline was "That's my story but, oh Lord, it isn't true."

Anyway, I thought it would make Tim a huge star by the end of the year. I reckoned that it would be nice to say I had met him before he was world famous and that was about it. I somewhat diffidently broached that, although I loved pop and rock, my real love was musicals. To my surprise Tim said he'd been brought up on his parents' cast albums and he actually liked theatre songs. I didn't sense that he had an overpowering passion for musicals, but he certainly didn't rubbish them like most of my friends. I don't think I mentioned the Dr Barnardo project and *The Likes of Us*, but after he had met my parents, who were both charmed by him, we arranged to meet each other again.

I really liked Tim. He had a laconic turn of phrase and a quick wit I had never found in anyone before. He met my school friends who liked him too, particularly the gay ones. Eventually I tentatively broached Desmond Elliott's Dr Barnardo musical and played him two tunes. Tim seemed quite taken. All I had was the rough synopsis I concocted in the absence of anything from Leslie Thomas, but at least it was a start. One melody was meant for two teenage cockney lovebirds who were the basis of a subplot. The other was for an auction told in song. In it Dr Barnardo, after a few fun lots to set things up, saw off all bidders and bought the Edinburgh Castle Gin Palace in London's cockney epicentre, the Mile End Road. This he would turn into a temperance centre for general do-gooding. It was that sort of show.

A few days later Tim showed up with two lyrics. The first was the auction song which he had called "Going, Going, Gone!" The first lot to go under the gavel was a parrot. The first couplet I read by my future collaborator went thus:

> *Here I have a lovely parrot, sound in wind and limb*
> *I can guarantee that there is nothing wrong with him.*

How could I not smile? To this day only Rice would come up with a parrot sound in wind and limb. The quirkiness and simplicity of

Tim's turn of phrase grabbed me immediately. By some strange osmosis with "Going, Going, Gone!" we had written a plot driven song that was a harbinger of the dialogue-free style of our three best-known shows. Tim titled the other song for the lovestruck subplotters "Love Is Here." The first verse went:

> *I ain't got no gifts to bring*
> *It ain't Paris, it ain't Spring*
> *No pearls for you to wear*
> *Painters they have missed it too*
> *Writers haven't got a clue*
> *They can't see love is here.*

Desmond Elliott however was not best pleased when I broke the news that I had decided that Tim should be my writing partner for *The Likes of Us.* A with it pop lyricist should stick to with it pop lyrics, was his opinion. That was, until I played Desmond the songs. Very shortly Tim too was managed by Desmond Elliott of Arlington Books.

DESPITE THERE BEING STILL no plot outline from Leslie Thomas, Tim made some song suggestions and we started writing. Desmond co-opted a "producer" who was in fact another book publisher, Ernest Hecht of Souvenir Press. Ernest Hecht was a Kindertransport émigré from Nazi Germany who once told me that a publisher's first duty to an author is to remain solvent. He had dabbled in theatre and in 1967 presented the farceur Brian Rix in *Uproar in the House.* What qualified him in 1965 to present a musical is anyone's guess. But it was Desmond's gig and I presumed he knew best.

Meantime I acquired a music publisher. During my skiving off school days I had got to meet some of the guys at Southern Music, an American-owned publisher with a big country and western catalogue and a very active London office in Tin Pan Alley. Soon I was taken under the wing of the CEO, a guy called Bob Kingston. Bob was later to give me one of the greatest pieces of advice of my career, thanks to which quite a few people have made a considerable fortune. He spotted that I was an oddball seventeen-year-old with a curious appetite for musical theatre – the pariah of my generation – and that my passion just might rub off on other people. So he did a deal with Desmond to publish *The Likes of Us*.

Bob was very enthusiastic about our embryonic score but felt we lacked a killer ballad. He kept banging on about another "As Long as He Needs Me." The consequence was a string of tunes, all with three long notes, as per the "he needs me" bit of Lionel Bart's mega hit. Proof, if needed, that it is unwise to create songs by formula can be found in "How Am I to Know" which made it through to the recording of *The Likes of Us* at the Sydmonton Festival many years later. I suppose it got included because Tim and I thought it the best of many attempts to emulate Bart's classic. It would have exited were the show to have made it to rehearsal because it had been usurped as pole position banker by another putative winner "A Man on His Own." Guess what? The tune was "Make Believe Love" (the song that failed to launch my career as a lyricist). Bob pronounced we had a smash hit on our hands and the score was complete.

A demo recording with bass, drums and a very ancient pianist was made featuring a couple of session singers and Tim and I filling in gaps. The ancient pianist had only one style, stride piano. Even the big ballads acquired a honky-tonk sheen. The sound engineer had an addiction to his new echo machine. So bits of the demo were helpful, others emphatically less so. All of them sounded as if they had been recorded in Penn Station at three in the morning. No matter. Back home I was able to render friends soporific with my first show LP. Surely the West End was a matter of months away.

The summer of 1965 wasn't exclusively taken up with *The Likes of Us.* I toured Italy with a group of school friends and spent loads of time with Vi and George at La Mortola. It was that summer that I properly met Vi's friend, the film director Ronnie Neame. Ronnie had recently directed Judy Garland in a movie called *I Could Go on Singing.* This was also the title song. It had an unfortunate lyric since it continued "till the cows come home" which prompted a version on *That Was The Week That Was* in which the singer was stampeded by a herd of rampant bovines. I had the cheek to play Ronnie a tune I thought better that I had wanted to send him when he was making the movie, but Vi had stopped me. He said it sounded a bit "classical." It later surfaced as "I Don't Know How to Love Him."

Ronnie had been David Lean's cameraman and producing partner on classic movies like *Great Expectations.* I was enthralled when he told me how, in an emotional scene with co-star Dirk Bogarde, Judy Garland had without warning veered totally off script into a super-charged autobiographical monologue. Ronnie feared the cameraman might stop shooting this unrehearsed pure gold so he eased the guy off his camera and took over himself. Ronnie tightened the shot and, by inching the camera slowly back on its track, lured Garland to keep monologuing her way forward into his retreating lens. Thus he created a seminal Garland moment in a not particularly special movie.

Also that summer I met Tim's parents for the first time. I had just failed my driving test, so Tim drove me in a pre-World War Two Austin car that his parents lent him to their converted farmhouse near Hatfield, about 20 miles north of London. Joan and Hugh were very kind and asked me a lot of questions about my family and what my ambitions were. They asked me quite a bit about Oxford and I, maybe wrongly, thought there was a question too many in front of Tim on the subject of university. I didn't tell them of the role of Professor McFarlane's cat in my academic achievements.

There are songs you vividly remember when and where you first heard them. I first heard Richard Rodgers' "Something Good" at the home of John Goodbody, an aptly named Westminster boy as he was Britain's junior weightlifting champion, not necessarily the first achievement you would think of in a Westminster boy. John was a trainee journalist and during his long career in newspapers he became the highly respected Sports Editor of the London *Times*. He shared my huge love of the Everly Brothers and it was at his parents' house in North London that I turned up one Saturday night clutching my unplayed newly purchased soundtrack LP of *The Sound of Music* film. John's friends were slightly older and more cynical than I, so they doubtless shared the view of the *New York Times* that *The Sound of Music* was "romantic nonsense and sentiment."

I wonder if they noticed me turn colder than your average Austrian ski slope during my first encounter with the stupendous overture. Out of the glorious modulation at the end of "My Favorite Things" burst one of Richard Rodgers's most brilliant and characteristic melodies. And it was new! Rodgers hadn't written anything to touch it for at least five years. "Something Good" is right up there with his very best, complete with his "Bali Hai" tritone,* the halfway note in the scale that hits the word "Hai" and is there in some of his most typical greats. Hearing this melody for the first time is as vivid a memory as my debut encounter with *Sgt. Pepper*.

THE CLOCK TICKED TOWARDS October and my first Oxford term. However any qualms that I had over the daunting prospect were somewhat hijacked by another of Mum's domestic dramas. This time she burst into my bedroom at four in the morning proclaiming that something terrible had happened to John Lill and that she could feel his pain. Later in the morning it transpired he had fallen off his

---

* The technical definition of a tritone is a musical interval composed of three adjacent whole tones. However, I am referring to what is called an augmented fourth or diminished fifth.

motor scooter. Maybe there was something in Mum's psychic claims or, perish the thought, John had phoned her after the accident and I hadn't heard the phone because I was asleep – although I am inclined to believe the former, since Mum was long on psychic contacts. There were two consequences of this bizarre affair: (1) I decided I would find a way to move out of Harrington Court asap and that Oxford was not a bad stepping stone. (2) Mum decided John Lill needed to move into Harrington Court as living in Leyton subjected him to too many hazardous road journeys.

Despite all this it was John who drove me to Oxford on a chilly October night to begin the Michaelmas term at Magdalen, one of those journeys where you wish the distances between villages were just that little bit longer. I had been tipped off that it was wise to get in first and ask in advance if there was a room in the "New Building." I got one. But I was unprepared for what hit me. After Harrington Court my room wasn't a room. Today it would be called the Presidential Suite in a country house hotel – a bit of a run-down one maybe, but I never say no to faded grandeur. The New Building was constructed in 1733 and, despite being a mental Victorian Gothic man, I had no objection to a massive panelled drawing room plus bedroom, kitchen and bathroom overlooking Magdalen's famous meadow, home of a load of deer and Snake's-head Fritillary, the latter being an extremely rare flower, not a heavy metal band. One gripe. It was a bit on the cold side. And there was no piano.

In the weeks before I went "up" to Magdalen, I mooted to Desmond the idea of getting our show staged by one of the Oxford University dramatic societies, OUDS being the mainstream one, the other the Experimental Theatre Company or the ETC. This was an extremely arrogant thought for a seventeen-year-old freshman. Both societies were widely recognized in the theatre and appeared outside Oxford frequently, sometimes internationally. Desmond was rather sniffy, but he didn't entirely perish the thought. So I rented a tinny upright piano from Blackwell's in Oxford High Street. Nobody in the college minded. Next I wrote a letter of introduction to the presidents of the two drama societies, fairly crawling stuff, I recall, but tinged with a faint hint that I was God's next gift to the West End and they would be wise to meet me whilst they still could.

Lady Luck dealt me a great card at my first lunch in Magdalen's pleasingly Gothic hall. I found myself sitting next to a fellow fresh-man law student called David Marks. His ambition was to be an actor. He turned out to be no ordinary hopeful. After winning every acting prize Oxford offered he went on to become President of OUDS. Less than a year after we met he premiered the role of Rosencrantz in the first production of Tom Stoppard's *Rosencrantz and Guildenstern Are Dead* at the Edinburgh Fringe Festival. David never pursued a career as an actor and became a successful barrister, saying he found acting too repetitive. He also agreed to be the first person to play the role of Dr Thomas John Barnardo.

Very soon I had met all the student top brass. OUDS was headed by Bob, now Sir Bob Scott who was to become the arts and sports czar of Manchester. David Wood honchoed the ETC. David has had a successful career as actor, writer and lyricist and it was the ETC that became the most likely home for *The Likes of Us*. We had several meetings and it was even mooted that as he could sing he might usurp David Marks and play Dr Barnardo. A plan developed that it could be staged after summer term 1966 in the Oxford Playhouse. There was, however, one outsized snag. There was still no script. As it was Desmond's project, I obviously couldn't suggest he ditched his best-selling novelist Leslie Thomas for some unknown budding dramatist Oxford student.

Thus *The Likes of Us* was in remarkably different shape to a play that was the big talk of Oxford. Written by a second year undergrad-uate, *When Did You Last See My Mother?* was staged by OUDS and a production in London quickly followed. It rendered its author the youngest to have a play produced in the West End. The author's name was Christopher Hampton, he had been to the same school as Tim Rice and the play is said to have been influenced by homosexual activities at Lancing College. This is a subject I have not raised with Sir Tim, as I sense that he might be exceptionally unqualified to contribute to this topic. Chris is a couple of years older than me, but clearly *The Likes of Us* couldn't hang about if I was to grab the "Youngest Author in West End" title myself. I didn't of course, but 25 years later Chris and I would get Tony Awards for *Sunset Boulevard*.

Meantime word was dribbling through Oxford's dramatic community that there was a socially awkward seventeen-year-old with an outsize room overlooking Magdalen meadow and a piano in it to boot. So, aside from *The Likes of Us*, I met with several budding writers and lyricists, some of whom have subsequently had respectable theatre careers. But I quickly became rather too aware that absolutely none of them had Tim's rhyming dexterity and, more importantly, his highly individual turn of phrase. Years later I sometimes notice a similar turn of phrase in Chris Hampton's work. I wish I had met their Lancing College English master.

1965 was decades before mobile phones and the only contact with the outside world was a coin phone box outside the porter's lodge which invariably had a big queue. I started to make too many day trips to London. I was already a little fearful that Tim would forget about his junior Oxford collaborator. I simply wasn't allocating my time properly and I was trying too hard to do too many things. My History tutor asked to see me. He said I had been admitted to Oxford a year too early at seventeen. I should take the rest of the academic year off. He really couldn't have been kinder and even offered to look after some of my things if I couldn't take them home. I immediately thought how was I to get *The Likes of Us* on in Oxford if I wasn't there, but my attempts to say I really could cope were greeted with the reply "See you next October."

7

Teenage Operas, Pop Cantatas

My unanticipated time off from Oxford equalled a newly blank diary until October when I was supposed to restart at university afresh. Clearly with me based in London again, *The Likes of Us* was unlikely to happen that summer in the Oxford Playhouse. The songs had been demoed. There was still no script. My father arranged for me to have a few lessons at the Royal College of Music. I made several trips to Vi and George in Italy and got taken to the Sanremo Song Festival by Southern Music's American owner where I met Gene Pitney. I hung out with old school friends, revisited David Marks in Oxford, saw Tim a bit who was still working at Pettit and West-lake, got my driving test at the third attempt, dropped my brother to school, that's about it, i.e. not the sort of stuff to grip reader or publisher apart from possibly one anecdote which I have many times told elsewhere. The problem is that all these years I've been dissem-inating fake news.

The story as previously told goes as follows. Back in 1966 I used to frequent a shop in the nether regions of the Fulham Road which sold cheap copies of current LPs that somehow had fallen off the back of a lorry. Nearby was a bric-a-brac shop. One day I saw a filthy dirty canvas in its window which looked remarkably like Lord Leighton's *Flaming June*, probably one of the most famous of all Victorian paint-ings. Even though Victorian pictures were still considered nearly worthless, the £50 that the shop owner was asking for it seemed cheap to me. (Today £890.) So I begged Granny to let me borrow the money. When she asked what it was for she opined that she wasn't going to have Victorian rubbish in her flat.

The way I have been telling the story is that it was bought by the pioneering Victorian picture dealer Jeremy Maas. He then sold it to a Puerto Rican cement baron called Luis A. Ferré who was starting a museum in Ponce, his home town on the south of the island. Apparently Ferré had a policy of never paying more than $5000 for anything. In those days you could buy several acres of Victorian canvases for $5000 and consequently Mr Ferré hoovered up some great paintings such as Burne-Jones's masterpiece *Arthur in Avalon*. It is ironic that such important "aesthetic movement" paintings created in the pursuit of beauty should have found their home in an island so cruelly treated by nature. Today *Flaming June* is billed as "The Mona Lisa of the Southern Hemisphere," has been in the Tate Gallery, the Frick, you name it, and is worth millions. Thus Granny denied me a Victorian masterpiece. I've been writing and dining out on this for decades.

Unfortunately I was wrong. I recently learned that Jeremy Maas bought the real thing from his barber a few years earlier. So I take this opportunity to grovel with apology for a falsehood that I even perpetuated in a Royal Academy exhibition catalogue and revel in the fact that I didn't lose out on a great deal after all.

IT WAS AROUND EASTER when Bob Kingston, boss of the London office of Southern Music, called me into his office. I am not the only one who should be eternally grateful for what he told me. Everyone from Tim Rice to all those who made tons of money out of our early shows should erect a monument to him. Without it the rest of this book would be completely different, not to mention the rest of my life – and probably that of countless others. Bob Kingston was the first person to tell me about Grand Rights. The meeting came about because either Desmond Elliott or Ernest Hecht had had a faintly encouraging response from Harry Secombe's management to *The*

Likes of Us demo disc. Harry Secombe was a very successful British comic who was unusual in that he had a more than OK, if slightly strangulated, tenor voice. This propelled him into occasional flights of light opera and the title role in an *Oliver!* influenced musical called *Pickwick* which had opened in London in mid-1963, directed by Peter Coe and designed by Sean Kenny, repeating a partnership they had begun with Lionel Bart's classic. Both these had, of course, also been approached about our epic.

Based on an over optimistic chat with the excitable Desmond, Bob felt it was time to sit me down and explain the music business facts of life. In those days income from songwriting came from three sources. First was record sales. Second were fees from performances on radio, TV and public places. Third was "sheet music" sales, i.e. printed song copies. The publisher split the income from the first two categories 50/50 with the writers and doled out 10% of the proceeds from the third. Income from international sources was split 50/50 based on what the local publisher remitted to the UK publisher. Naturally all the major publishers set up their own local firms who skimmed off a big cut of a song's income with the result that the publisher in practice could end up with a far bigger share of the income than the authors. For example, a song earns $100 in the US. The US publisher (owned by the UK publisher) takes a 50% cut, remits 50% to the British publisher who splits that 50/50 with the writers. Thus many writers at that time only received 25% of the gross international income. This practice has long since been challenged, but it was the norm in 1966. Bob explained that these three income streams are called Small Rights.

What Bob then spelt out was that there is another rights category, Grand Rights. He told me that Tin Pan Alley publishers rarely understood what they were. Grand Rights are the royalties that arise whenever an entire dramatic work is performed on the stage or on film. Bob felt it was not morally right for a pop music publisher to participate in this income. The agreement Tim and I had been given for *The Likes of Us* was a standard contract whose wording implied that we had signed away absolutely everything to Southern Music. Bob proposed giving us back our Grand Rights. *The Likes of Us* was never to earn a penny, but the advice Bob gave me that morning was unquestionably the most precious of my entire career.

THAT MAY TIM'S BOSSES at the law firm Pettit and Westlake told him to destroy some highly sensitive legal documents. Unfortunately he shredded the wrong ones. This caused Tim's law career to come into question and so his father Hugh lent on some contacts he had at electronic giant EMI with the result that in June Tim joined EMI Records as a management trainee. Almost immediately Tim was assigned to the A&R department, A&R standing for artists and repertoire, the department responsible for finding artists, choosing their songs and overseeing their recording careers.

Today the initials EMI mean little even in the music business. But in 1966 EMI was the undisputed giant of the record industry. It owned a vast litany of artists headed by The Beatles, an unequalled roster of classical musicians, a huge manufacturing base not only of the software but the hardware of the music business, plus the world's most famous recording studio complex at Abbey Road. It is hard to believe that today this once proud company's initials survive only in the names Sony/ATV/EMI Publishing and Virgin/EMI Records. In 2012 the then owners, venture capitalists Terra Firma, became infamously infirm as the giant turned into a munchkin. After complex shenanigans, Japanese giant Sony acquired the music publishing and the record division was swallowed up by Universal Music, who merged it with the Virgin label.

At almost exactly the same time as Tim started at EMI I got a letter from Magdalen. It got straight to the point. The college bigwigs had heard that I was working on a musical. They wished me luck but hoped I realized that when I returned I was expected to concentrate on my studies. If I wanted I could discuss changing the course I was reading, but if I returned they expected me to live up to my exhibitioner status.

Reality had caught up with me big time. I thought about switching from History to Music. My father knew Dr Bernard Rose, the highly regarded director of Magdalen College's fabled choir. But Dad was hugely against my studying music. He felt that the Oxford course would be far too academic for me. So my only future at Oxford was to return and read history seriously. Even give or take a little bit, realistically I would have to take a three-year break from musical theatre or at least from attempting any professional involvement.

Meantime Tim, nearly four years older than me and understandably ambitious for his own future, was starting a job in the creative department of the world's top record company. Even if Tim was at the bottom of the ladder, he had his foot in the door. Tim could easily have a hit on his own or with another writer. He might easily lose interest in a younger hopeful whose real interest was theatre, a world far away from chart-obsessed EMI and the white-hot heat of Swinging London. Furthermore I knew full well that Oxford offered nobody who could hold a candle to his lyrics.

Should I go back to Oxford or leave? It was the biggest decision of my life and there was nobody I felt I could turn to for advice. My family would point to two dismal A-level results as my only academic qualifications. I had the odd music grade, but no way was I a performer so there was no hope down that alley. The most anyone could say about me was that I wrote tunes, had an oddball love of musicals and a bizarre love of architecture and medieval history. I knew that my family would be appalled if I chucked in the lifeline that Magdalen had offered me.

I took myself away to agonize. What if musicals were on the way out? What if I was no good at them anyway? I knew I was no lyricist. So was it not lunacy to try a career where my music was greatly dependent on the words that went with it and stories that might be lousy? What if the writer of those words, in this case Tim, no longer wanted to work with me? What if that writer didn't come up with the goods? Most musicals are flops. Why should mine be any different? That is, if I ever got one on.

I went over and over in my head what an Oxford degree would mean for me. I couldn't imagine a career I'd enjoy where it would do me any good. But my family had no money; they didn't even own the Harrington Court flat. I would have to make a living somehow, someday. But with or without a degree at what? At least staying at Oxford would stave off a career decision for three years. True I would have to knuckle down and work to get a decent class of degree. But on the flip side of the coin I fretted that I was an exhibitioner who was taking up a college subsidized place that would probably have gone to someone far worthier than I had it not been for Professor McFarlane's cat. Should I not let that worthier someone have my place?

However, there was the certainty of what a decision to leave would do to the family. Granny Molly would be consumed with anxiety. Aunt Vi and Uncle George would be livid. Mum might just take it on the chin, but I couldn't tell what Dad would make of it. Of all the family I was closest to Molly. I strongly sensed that my increasingly frail Granny would regard my leaving Oxford as an insane, suicidal move. Could it somehow rekindle in her a myriad of associations with the loss of her son Alastair? She cared that much about me. But then what if I lost Tim? The thought went round and round in my head and drilled into it like an unmelodic earworm. Finally I made my decision. On July 17, 1966 I wrote to Thomas Boase, Magdalen College's admission tutor, informing him that I did not want to continue as a History exhibitioner.

I thought my bombshell was received pretty well; a few long faces, a bit of muttering, as far as I was concerned that was about it. I took three school friends to stay at Vi and George's. They seemed on the sombre side of OK, but pretty soon Vi and I were experimenting with olive-oil recipes in her glorious seaview kitchen. It's only recently that I learned things were not quite as I thought. First my brother Julian remembered that he had never witnessed such a family row as happened after I told Mum and Dad of my decision. Then I discovered among some of Mum's papers the outline of her autobiography. It seems I was dead right about Granny equating what I was doing with the loss of Alastair. In her view I was throwing my life away and she felt appalled that Dad was doing nothing to stop it. Vi and George were safely out of the way in Italy. It was difficult and costly in 1966 to make international phone calls, you had to book them via the operator, but they made their views patently clear in letters that were kept from me.

Years later, according to Mum, I was staggered to learn that it was Dad who not only defended me but supported my decision. Apparently he strongly argued that in all his experience with students at the Royal and London Colleges of Music he had not come across anyone with such determination to succeed and that it would be completely counter-productive to put roadblocks in my way. With hindsight this is borne out by a conversation that Dad and I had before I took off with my school friends to Italy. First he reiterated that he would not support my trying for the Royal College of Music. I remember his reason, "it would educate the music out of you," quite a statement from the senior Professor of Composition at the Royal College and the head of the London College of Music to boot.

Secondly he strongly felt that I should take a course in orchestration. The orchestra, he opined, provided the richest palette of colours in music if you knew how to use it. I was thrilled when Dad said he would fix for me to take a part-time course at the Guildhall School of Music and Drama. I was fascinated by the tone colours of composers like Britten and how a high romantic like Richard Strauss could take the orchestra to ever more overripe extremes. I remember thinking that learning orchestration is like learning the basics of cooking: just as I knew from Vi how to make a soufflé or a mayonnaise, now I would learn how to make my orchestral ideas a reality. That Guildhall course has stood me in good stead. It is the only academic course I have taken seriously.

MEANTIME TIM WAS SETTLING in at EMI. I suspect he was too busy finding his feet to worry about my decision and I often wonder if he realized just how big a factor he was in my making it. But the fact that he had a toe in the door of the world's number one record company could open doors for both of us and I was keen to coat-tail. Tim was assigned to the department of one of EMI's most successful old-time arranger/producers, Norrie Paramor.

Norrie was a supremo of the pre-Beatles old guard. He was the guiding light behind the legendary British pop star Cliff Richard, who has the distinction of having a number one hit in five different decades. Norrie was still a very major force in the British record industry, even if younger musical Turks had overtaken him. But come mid-1966 Norrie's star at EMI was again in the ascendancy. This was because the cream of EMI's top producers had left to form an independent company, disgusted by the low pay and derisory royalties (if any) they got in return for making EMI untold millions. Stars like Beatles guru George Martin had had enough.

This left good old reliable Norrie in pole position. And with artists like Sinatra again pulverizing the action with songs such as "My Way," the top brass at EMI might have been forgiven for thinking they made the right call in letting go the George Martins of this world. So Tim was in the right place at the right time. I suspect that old-school Norrie Paramor saw in the contemporary pop ears of the very personable Tim Rice a presentable way into a young world that was no more his natural habitat. Furthermore Tim wrote lyrics. It wasn't long before Tim was being allowed to produce acts that EMI wanted to drop, but was obliged to record in order to see out their contracts.

Pop was changing fast in the last half of the 1960s. 1965 had ushered in "fusion," the idea that any instrument could go with anything. As early as 1964, Sonny and Cher had featured an oboe on "I Got You Babe." Paul McCartney sang "Yesterday" accompanied by a string quartet. In 1967 *Sgt. Pepper* took things still further, including adding the merest hint of a narrative structure. By the end of 1968 even the Rolling Stones were recording with the London Bach Choir. I was learning the rudiments of classical orchestration at exactly the time as its marriage with rock was romping all over the zeitgeist.

In that summer of 1966 the Beach Boys' "Good Vibrations" kicked off a genre that was to spawn perhaps the ultimate Sixties "fusion" single, Jimmy Webb's six-minute "MacArthur Park" with Richard Harris. Then there was the concept single. The most successful was "Excerpt from 'A Teenage Opera,'" a sort of mini-opera in itself with a kids' choir. The "Teenage Opera" never was completed but the idea hugely caught the spirit of the moment. None of this passed me by.

THE UNWANTED ACTS TIM was assigned to humanely lay to rest were pretty dire – with one notable exception. This was a handsome 23-year-old singer called Murray Head. EMI had unsuccessfully tried to launch Murray and had put a fair bit of clout behind him. But now he was "de trop" and Tim was ordered by Norrie to cut his last contractual single. Murray had, however, been cast as one of the leads in a Roy Boulting movie titled *The Family Way* opposite John and Hayley Mills. Paul McCartney composed the soundtrack and Murray had written a song called "Someday Soon" that was supposed to feature in the film. This was the song Tim recorded.

Murray had a light tenor rock voice, really rather lyrical yet passionate and earthy when he wanted it to be. Tim was very good about letting me meet Murray who must have thought me highly curious. I was hopelessly out of place and felt very shy in his dope-filled flat. But he would often accompany himself on guitar. What struck me was his incredibly musical riffing. It was always melodic and always highly individual. I shared Tim's belief that given the exposure Murray and the song would get from the movie, Tim might have produced his first hit. Unfortunately this was not to be. Most of "Someday Soon" ended up on the cutting-room floor. But I agreed with Tim. Murray was very special.

1967 dawned with still no *Likes of Us* script from Leslie Thomas, though I vaguely remember a synopsis appearing that had no relation whatsoever to what Tim and I had written. Hopes of a theatre production pretty much evaporated. I continued to take my orchestration lessons. Mum negotiated that we rented an additional flat at Harrington Court, primarily so she could move John Lill in. To be fair it also had a decent room for my increasingly arthritic granny. There was one spare room which Mum wanted to rent. I suggested offering it to Tim, who accepted, and at a stroke a ménage à trois was created to rival South Kensington's weirdest. Add me and my turntable next door, Julian on cello and Dad on electronic organ and new meaning was given to the words "bohemian rhapsody."

AT THE END OF February I got a letter from the music master of Colet Court School, the junior part of St Paul's School in Hammersmith. His name was Alan Doggett. Alan had taught Julian at Westminster Under School and had become friendly with our parents. Alan was openly gay, but not, he pointedly professed, a predator of little boys. Indeed Julian, who was not bad looking himself, knew of no such baggage at the Under School. But nonetheless Alan made no secret of having adult gay relationships. He also loved early classical music.

This caused Julian and me to have a private joke at his expense.

There was a flat near ours in Onslow Gardens whose occupant left the window open in summer from which emanated hugely precious harpsichord music. You could see enough of the decor to know that it was not the home of a rugger ace. Julian and I used to call places like this doggett houses. Alan proposed that I compose a "pop cantata" for his charges. His choir had premiered and recorded two such epics already, *The Daniel Jazz* by Herbert Chappell and *Jonah-Man Jazz* by Michael Hurd. Their main attraction was telling a Bible story in light pop music, nothing too dangerous, just enough novelty to make parents smile and keep a class of unmusical kids out of detention. Lyrics were not their strong point. Apparently the educational publishers Novello and Co. had done very well with them. Novello published Dad's church music and he confirmed that this was true. *The Daniel Jazz* was their top seller.

So on March 5, if an old diary doesn't lie, I met with Alan for a drink. He explained that he wanted something for the whole school to sing but there must be a special role for the choir and school orchestra. There could be soloists too, but he reiterated that it was vital that there was something for everyone to perform, even the tone deaf. Skirting around why he thought I was the right bloke to compose for the latter, he suggested a collection of poems by American poet Vachel Lindsay called "The Congo" as ideal fodder for me to musicalize. One of them read like lyrics for the Eurovision Song Contest – I quote: "Rattle-rattle, rattle-rattle, / Bing. / Boomlay, boomlay, boomlay, BOOM." "The Congo" is full of similar nonsense words based on Congolese chants. Somehow I wondered if the poem would ring true in the hands of the very white pupils of a posh, fee-paying West London preparatory school, although I could see that kids could have a lot of fun making silly percussive noises with it. However I broached Alan's offer with Tim.

Tim wasn't instantly ecstatic at the thought of writing something for a bunch of 8–13-year-old school kids. It was a bit of a comedown from hopes of a West End premiere and the white-hot heat of EMI in the year that company launched *Sgt. Pepper*. But Tim had schoolday memories of Gilbert and Sullivan operettas and Gilbert's witty lyrics in particular. Also the notion of a "pop cantata" did chime with what was happening at the time. We liked the idea that there would be no script – not that we ever had experience of one, since Leslie Thomas had still failed to deliver anything for the increasingly dust-gathering *The Likes of Us*. So we tossed a few ideas around. At first we felt another Bible story wasn't cool. Maybe something from English history? I don't remember if the subject we subsequently toyed with, King Richard I and his minstrel Blondel, surfaced at the time. We certainly combed our history books, but nothing grabbed us. A James Bond themed idea was temporarily our frontrunner, but it was soon shown the egress as we thought it would date and anyway it needed a plot.

Salvation came in the form of *The Wonder Book of Bible Stories*. Books like these are excellent source material for musicals. They save a lot of reading time and effort. The plots are nicely condensed, the print is big and there are lots of pictures to bring important moments to life. Tim fell on the story of Joseph and his coat of many colours. I liked the idea. It had the primal ingredients of revenge and forgiveness. There could be humour, particularly if Joseph himself was made out to be a bit of an irritating prick who in the end turns out to be OK. And then there was Pharaoh. I wondered what would happen if we built and built Pharaoh's entrance and he turned out to be Elvis. Plus there is a nice happy ending when Joseph is reunited with his dad and family. It seemed a natural.

At first Alan Doggett wasn't convinced. This would be the third biblical cantata the school would have done. Couldn't we think of something more original? But he melted when one evening I played him the opening two songs. He beamed at Tim's turn of phrase

And when Joseph tried it on
He knew his sheepskin days were gone
His astounding clothing took the biscuit
Quite the smoothest person in the district

It's the use of everyday colloquialisms that makes *Joseph*'s lyrics so great. It was 1967, we were writing a "pop cantata" and who cared whether rhymes were perfect. Confirmed bachelor Alan melted still further when I introduced him to Tim. Soon *Joseph* was slated for the Colet Court End of Easter Term Concert, 1968. The work that launched our careers was under starter's orders.

8

Elvis with Mellotron and Tambourines

From Easter 1967 our pop cantata simmered leisurely on the back burner, but with *The Likes of Us* in the deep freeze Tim and I started writing pop songs. The first Rice/Lloyd Webber song to be commercially released was "Down Thru' Summer." The artist was Ross Hannaman and the arranger/producer Mike Leander who had arranged "She's Leaving Home" for The Beatles. Ross was a contestant in the London *Evening Standard* Girl of the Year, 1967 competition. Those were the days when such contests were only just beginning to be deemed un-PC. We had noticed in Ross's blurb that she sang. Tim asked his bosses if he could sign her if she won the competition. Surprisingly the answer was yes. So we piled off to hear her sing in some club where we encountered a very pretty teenager with an OK folksy voice, very much in the Marianne Faithfull mould. Tim immediately fancied her, but she had two blokes who managed her, one of whom was her boyfriend, so Tim was temporarily stymied.

You could vote as many times as you liked for your favourite Girl of the Year provided you voted on a coupon in your *Evening Standard*, presumably a marketing wheeze to sell more newspapers to the competitors' nearest and dearest. Tim and Ross's manager found a heap of unsold *Standards* that were about to be pulped and duly voted with the whole lot of them. Her resulting victory was so obviously false that Angus McGill, the witty veteran doyen of Fleet Street diarists who organized the competition, had to declare Ross a joint winner. He couldn't disqualify her because the rules said you could vote as many times as you liked. But he hadn't reckoned on someone hijacking the odd thousand unsold copies in a recycling plant. Actually Angus was amused. The contest was hardly serious and he liked the idea that one of the winners might become a pop star. I was introduced to Angus and soon we became real friends. I would often meet him in his Regent's Park flat from where we would drive to his shop Knobs and Knockers which sold exactly what was on the ticket.

The tune I wrote for Ross was tailor-made for her wispy soprano, a wistful folk ballad that I heard in my head simply arranged for acoustic guitar and a small, sparely scored string section. Tim provided a suitably obtuse flower-powery lyric. "Down thru' summer you would stay here and be mine." It *was* the Summer of Love, after all. The recording session was not at Abbey Road, but Olympic Studios, studio of choice for the Rolling Stones and in those days boasting one of the best sounding rooms for an orchestra in London. Little did I guess when I pitched up that morning what a huge part Olympic was to play in my life. Unfortunately Mike Leander's perception of my little tune could not have been more different from mine. Instead of an acoustic guitar and chamber strings, Mike had arranged the song for a full out galumphing electric rhythm section plus a thrashing drummer whose unsubtle playing was so loud that it spilled over the microphones of the entire orchestra. Nothing could have been more at odds with how I heard my tune and I sat in the corner of the studio, disconsolate.

I thought the B-side, a sort of "Semi-Detached Suburban Mr James" re-run called "I'll Give All My Love to Southend" (we were in the "Winchester Cathedral" era), fared rather better, even though Tim and I had a "beat group" in mind rather than a pretty folksy girl soprano. I always liked the tune of "Down Thru' Summer" and reused it as the middle section of "Buenos Aires" in *Evita*. When the melody accompanies Eva's premonition of her fatal illness in Act 2, the arrangement isn't far from how I had heard Ross's single.

Angus arranged various promotional stunts for Tim and me and the *Evening Standard* joint winners ranging from a day at Royal Ascot to a night in Mark Birley's newly opened Annabel's. This may have made good copy for the *Standard*, but was hardly likely to ingratiate our hopeless single on the record-buying public. Amazingly Tim swung it that we got a second chance with Ross. The song was titled "1969" and the lyric was about someone having a trippy premonition, "a Chinese band marched by in fours," that sort of thing. The chorus went "Hey, I hate the picture, 1969." Tim the soothsayer didn't predict 1969 to be a bundle of laughs. This time the tune was only partially by me because we decided to make something out of Beethoven's "Für Elise." I added what I thought was a rather hooky chorus and a spooky descending tritone linking section. This time the arrangement by ex-Shadows drummer Tony Meehan was far closer to my intentions and I don't find it totally unlistenable to today. The B-side, "Probably on Thursday," had a really lovely wistful lyric even if, like so many of Tim's songs, it told a pessimistic story: "You're going to leave me, possibly on Wednesday, / Probably on Thursday." Twenty years later I rewrote the melody of the verse and recorded the song with Sarah Brightman.

That summer we wrote a song for *Joseph* that we thought might just be a pop hit. Most pop lyrics emanating from the Summer of Love displayed a somewhat opaque side – witness that legendary pop-synth fusion album *Days of Future Passed* by the Moody Blues or any of Donovan's hits. The song was "Any Dream Will Do" and the lyrics were no exception. But more of this anon.

A STOCK CHARACTER IN pop showbiz films is the record company postboy. Invariably this character delivers mail to the top executive brass and refuses to leave their offices until they listen to some act he's discovered. Just to get him out of the door, the top brass reluctantly go to one of the act's gigs. The act, after various cliffhanging story twists, turns out to be pop's answer to the Second Coming. EMI had such a postboy. His name was Martin Wilcox. I don't know if he ever blagged his way into the top honcho's offices. But he did get as far as Tim Rice. The act he was peddling had a suitably Sixties name, the Tales of Justine. Its guiding force was a teenager called David Daltrey, naturally presumed to be a distant relative of Roger Daltrey of The Who, but I've never seen any proof. He lived in Potters Bar in Hertfordshire, not that far from Tim's home in an area that by 1967 was a sprawling monotone London suburb. Maybe as an escape David had written songs with titles like "Albert (A Pet Sunflower)." He also had a pleasant singing voice and was friendly with an outfit called the Mixed Bag, who did competent cover performances of current hits.

Tim managed to get EMI to sign the Tales of Justine, "Albert (A Pet Sunflower)" was the first single and Tim winged it with his bosses that I arranged it. Albert owed a debt to British music hall, so I stuck a *Sgt. Peppery* brass band on top of the group which made the record rather fun. We all thought it was catchy enough to be big. Tim and I also signed the band up to ourselves as managers – we called ourselves Antim Management – and we added them to our roster of one, Ross Hannaman, who had ditched her previous team, possibly because she'd had a brief fling with Tim. Unfortunately Ross's stay with Antim didn't last long. She shacked up with the begetter of "Excerpt from 'A Teenage Opera'" Mark Wirtz who immediately issued a press release informing the world that we would hear a new Ross Hannaman. In fact we heard nothing at all, the pair got married and were divorced two years later.

Antim Management was undeterred by Ross giving us the heave-ho. Being cutting-edge representatives of our clients, we now designed and printed up some psychedelic sleeves for the Tales of Justine's "Albert." One night after hours we inserted all the promotion copies into these sleeves. Our theory was that since no EMI single ever had special promotion covers, radio producers and reviewers would think EMI's entire might was behind this release.

Unfortunately the head of EMI's promotion department, a thirty-ish guy called Roy Featherstone, was extremely unimpressed as was the British public. Sales were zilch. Roy gave Tim a hell of a roasting. I was therefore pretty scared when I got a message from Granny at Harrington Court saying that a Mr Featherstone had called and wanted to see me in his office. I was unprepared for a smiling Roy Featherstone and the offer of a cup of coffee when I quivered into his office two weeks later. Tim had recorded quite a few songs with David Daltrey and I had done all the arrangements. Mr Featherstone said he thought the songs were OK, but the arrangements were terrific, particularly one called "Pathway" where I had experimented with all sorts of effects. He would like to help me get a few more arranging gigs with other artists. This was the first time anyone in a record company had noticed my music, even if it was only my orchestrations. The timing couldn't have been better because Tim had just hit me with news that had left me axed as if by a pole.

Norrie Paramor announced that, like George Martin and the other top EMI producers before, he was leaving EMI and setting up on his own. He wanted Tim to go with him as his key man. It was an offer Tim could not refuse. Nor should he have done but it was clear that Norrie, despite hints from Tim, did not envisage a role for me in his new venture. Furthermore he employed instead ex-Westminster boy Nick Ingman as arranger and composer with whom Tim was to write B-sides and the like. Ironically Nick had been the lead singer of the group that performed "Make Believe Love" at my Westminster concert for Peter and Gordon.

I was very alarmed. Tim was turning 23, had a job with real prospects and entrees into songwriting. I was 19, had chucked up Oxford for Tim and a musical that was never going to be produced. At least

Roy Featherstone had thrown me a sort of lifeline and in fact I was to have a great relationship with Roy. But it was not until ten years later. My only real lifeline was a Friday afternoon school concert.

FRIDAY, MARCH 1, 1968 was a grey, drab, drizzly day but not over-cold for the time of year. Around 2 pm a gaggle of two hundred or so parents, mostly mothers as it was a weekday afternoon, gathered with no particular sense of anticipation in the rather cramped entrance hall of Colet Court School. Conversation centred on their fervent hope that this special end-of-term concert of *Joseph and His Amazing (Technicolour) Dreamcoat* was short enough for them to drive their children home before the weekend rush hour. One young mum commented that Johnny Cash was marrying June Carter that afternoon, US time. They were probably surprised, after they were ushered onto those hard low chairs you only find in school halls, by what was on the stage.

Lloyd Webber and Rice had fielded the entire Antim Management artists' roster. Stage centre was a pop group rig, drums and amplifiers manned by Potters Bar's very own cover band, the Mixed Bag. Seated next to a mike stand was no less than Potters Bar's star vocalist and songwriter, David Daltrey. There was an elephantine keyboard contraption looking like an electronic organ which I had badgered the school to hire called a Mellotron. These now long-extinct dinosaurs were a forerunner of the synthesizer and much loved by the Moody Blues. They didn't generate their own sounds but used a cumbersome battery of pre-recorded tapes. Seated in serried ranks was the school orchestra, augmented by a few student mates of mine from various colleges of music. Behind all this were two groups of boys. The first batch were the 30-strong school choir and the second the three hundred or so kids who couldn't sing or were tone deaf or both. Some of these had tambourines. Lurking backstage was Tim, gearing up for an Elvis impression as Pharaoh. So there was a mildly curious buzz from the parents in between anxious glances at watches, hoping the whole thing would crack on and finish PDQ.

The headmaster, a suave traditional cove called Henry Collis, ascended the stage and made a brief speech which decidedly hedged its bets on the forthcoming entertainment. He then introduced Alan Doggett in a fashion that suggested that if things went tits up it was all Doggett's fault and he needn't turn up on Monday. Alan bounced on stage, sporting a natty bow tie, raised his conductor's baton and off we went, straight into the story at bar one because the now signature trumpet fanfare introduction didn't exist in those days.

Joseph and the Amazing (Technicolour) Dreamcoat (the word "Technicolour" included a "u" and was for some reason billed in brackets) was away to the races.

THE CONCERT WAS A total blast. The mummies, particularly the yummy ones, forgot about the weekend rush hour and virtually the whole 22-minute cantata was encored. Everyone loved Tim's Elvis impression as Pharaoh, but it was the piece as a whole that was the star. Some mothers clamoured for a repeat performance on another day so that their other halves could hear it. For the record, here is the hugely condensed plot of what we performed that afternoon.

Jacob had two wives and twelve sons. Joseph, his favourite and a dreamer, irritatingly predicts to his brothers that one day he will rise above the lot of them. When Jacob gives Joseph a coat of many colours it is the final straw. They decide to kill him. Luring Joseph into the desert, they encounter some roving Ishmaelites. A sudden twinge of remorse and a chance to make a shekel or two prompts them to sell Joseph as a slave to be taken to Egypt. They dip Joseph's coat in goat's blood, telling his grieving dad he was killed bravely fighting. Joseph gets chucked into gaol, presumably as an illegal alien, where he sings his big ballad "Close Every Door." His interpretation of his cellmates' dreams catches the attention of Pharaoh who is having nightmares.

Joseph interprets these as signifying seven years of impending food glut, followed by seven of famine. Pharaoh makes Joseph boss of a rationing scheme to provide for the bad years. Joseph's famine-stricken brothers pitch up in Egypt, begging for food. They don't recognize their brother but he recognizes them and puts them to a test: he plants a cup in Benjamin, the youngest brother's, food sack, accusing him of stealing. The brothers rally to his defence, offering themselves up for punishment instead. Realizing they are now responsible citizens, Joseph reveals to his astonished siblings who he is. Jacob is brought to Egypt to be reunited with the son he thought was dead. A happy ending is enjoyed by all.

This simple primal tale had everything. Tim had made a brilliant choice. I didn't realize it at the time, but in my attempt to write music that would never allow its kid performers to get bored, I was unwittingly creating what was to become my trademark, a "through-sung" musical, i.e. a score with little or no spoken dialogue where the musical structure, the musical key relationships, rhythms and use of time signatures, not just the melodies, are vital to its success. Nothing in *Joseph* was random. I wrote it by instinct as I had no experience. But the fact that there was no spoken dialogue meant that I was in the driving seat. Once Tim and I had agreed the essential elements of the plot and we had decided where the key songs would go, it was down to me to control the rhythm of the piece. Of course spoken dialogue can be invaluable – on many occasions it is by far the best way to express dramatic situations – but for me my through-composed shows are the most satisfying.

It is the strength of the heart of *Joseph* that allowed it to expand like Topsy into a stage musical with its various pastiche set pieces. This central core has its own, if naive, musical style and above all a real emotional centre. The only pastiche in the Colet Court version was "Song of the King" which turned Pharaoh into Elvis. I have to claim that as my idea. I thought we needed something to lighten the mood after Joseph's "Close Every Door" in which Joseph sings that Children of Israel are never alone, one of the simple central messages of the piece. Unusually the title was also my idea, although hardly original. It was inspired by the Alan Price single "Simon Smith and His Amazing Dancing Bear." "Technicolour" got added as it seemed a cool way of saying "many colours." Moreover Technicolor dreams, with all their 1960s connotations were definitely the stuff of the moment.

Thrillingly, after the concert there was an on-the-spot offer of publication. Unbeknown to Tim and me, Alan Doggett had invited the team from Novello and Co., the top classical music publisher who had strayed highly successfully into the educational market with *The Daniel Jazz*. They also published much of my father's church music and I wonder if he too had a hand in their giving up a Friday afternoon to hear our effort. Anyhow they wanted to sign *Joseph* there and then. We referred them to Desmond Elliott.

DESMOND HAD SHOWN SCANT interest in our pop cantata. In fact he had shown scant interest in anything I was doing. For a long while his attention had been more or less exclusively devoted to a school friend of Tim's called Adam Diment. Adam was a novelist who had written a couple of alternative James Bond type books with titles like *The Dolly Dolly Spy* and *The Bang Bang Birds* featuring a character not unlike Austin Powers. Desmond persuaded Adam to grow his hair, got publishers Michael Joseph in such a tizzy about him that they paid him a massive advance and then fielded him on TV chat shows around the English-speaking world dressed in "mod" outfits. London bus sides proclaimed "If you can't read Adam Diment love him." For a brief while Adam made a heap of money and was quite a celebrity.

It was not surprising then that having a young, good looking male pop star author of his own creation under his belt so to speak, Desmond was no longer as enthused about me as he once was. So when he negotiated a £100 advance for both Tim and me out of Novello's, peanuts to what Adam Diment was making, he assumed my father (the legal age you could sign a contract in 1968 was 21) would ink the agreement immediately. (Today £1670.) Fortunately Bob Kingston's homily echoed round my skull and I added the words "excluding Grand Rights" to the document, which I got Dad to initial as well as adding his moniker.

The resulting explosion in Desmond's St James's Street office could be heard above the teatime quartet in the palm court of the neighbouring Ritz Hotel. How could I be so stupid as to jeopardize this deal? I was wasting his time. Anyway there never would be Grand Rights involved with a 20-minute pop cantata. Nobody would perform it in a theatre. He ended a diatribe of a letter to my father with "enough is enough." Tim stood back aloof from the fray, possibly savouring the saga. I stood my ground. I argued that Novello's would hardly be bothered about Grand Rights income if there was never going to be any, so let's leave the wording in, just in case. I was right: Novello's didn't even murmur. The contracts were signed excluding Grand Rights. My relationship with Desmond was never the same again.

The clamour for a repeat performance of *Joseph* simmered just enough for Tim, Alan and me to take it seriously. The problem was a venue. Here my father stepped in. He suggested a performance at the Central Hall, Westminster after the 6:30 pm Sunday service. There were two snags. The Central Hall, Westminster is big – three thousand or so seats. Could we fill it? Secondly *Joseph* was only 22 minutes long. There would have to be something else to go with it. Now my mother surfaced. The first half of the concert could be classical. Julian could do a bit, Dad could play the organ and John Lill would be the Act 1 closer. May 12 was fixed as the big night. There's a strange coincidence in this. May 12 was also the date of the first public performance of *Jesus Christ Superstar* in Pittsburgh three years later.

Rehearsals went just about OK. The vastness of the Central Hall swallowed up the Mixed Bag and without a proper PA system I got very worried David Daltrey's vocals would be lost. Alan Doggett had never conducted in a hall of this size and didn't have the control that an experienced musical director would have had. I got so nervous that I wanted to cancel the performance and Tim's laid-back approach to the issues wound me up still further, something not lost on him. I found the playing untogether and feared it was all going to be too amateurish for a performance open to the public.

I need not have been so stressed. Despite the classical first half being way, way overlong, the joy of *Joseph* and the infectious enthusiasm of its young performers carried all before it. Although it was past most of the kids' bedtimes, there were once again several ecstatically received encores, a harbinger of what was to happen to *Joseph* in the future. Desmond Elliott at last showed some interest, although I don't think he saw a future in *Joseph* beyond schools. We had made one alteration. In a quest to make what possibly could be a single on the lines of the hugely successful "Excerpt from 'A Teenage Opera'" the previous summer, we lengthened the sequence in which Pharaoh makes Joseph his second in command. We also added a "teenage opera"-style hooky kids chorus. "Joseph how can we ever say all that we want to about you." This has become one of the central themes of today's *Joseph*, although we were soon to rework this whole section.

But thoughts like that were a million miles away after the huge reaction to the performance. I wanted that night to go on forever. Would there ever be another performance of *Joseph* like this?

9

Any Dream Won't Do

I woke on the morning of May 13 to the radio blasting that there were massive student riots in Paris and they were spreading all over France and already threatening Nice. This bothered me. I had anticipated post-*Joseph* cold turkey by booking a cheap night flight to Vi and George's place, and the local airport to La Mortola is Nice Côte D'Azur. That lunchtime I got a telegram from Aunt Vi saying the airport was blockaded so I had to say *arrivederci Nizza*. I fixed up dinner with my school friend David Harington. David was and still is always good for a cheer up. He is also the father of *Game of Thrones* actor Kit Harington. David is, like me, a serious foodie.

One of the greater current myths purveyed by today's food writers is that London was a gastronomic desert before they came on the scene. This is, as my Aunt Vi would have eloquently stated, clotted bollocks on stilts. Britain may not have heaved with top-notch cooking, but it had many fine restaurants. One such was the restaurant David and I graced that night. It was called Carlo's Place and was way down the Fulham Road next to a newsagent that sold reviewers' copies of new LPs at half-price. The decor, all exposed pipes and brickwork, would look cutting edge today in New York's Meatpacking District and the marinated pigeon breasts were to die for. Carlo's Place was special to me. It was there that a year later I wrote what became the signature theme of *Jesus Christ Superstar* on a hastily summoned paper napkin.

It was just as well I had planned to meet David. That morning a review of *Joseph* appeared in the *Times Educational Supplement*. After a few gratuitous knocks at my father's organ playing in the Wagnerian length Part 1, it opined that *Joseph* was pleasant enough but none of the tunes was outstanding, "being of the Christian pop crusading type," and it was rhythmically based too much in "chugging 4/4 time." This much upset me as I was very proud that the moment where Joseph accuses his brother of theft is in 7/8 time. I consoled myself that the combination of the Mixed Bag and the Central Hall's acoustic could indeed have rendered this less than obvious to Meirion Bowen, the reviewer. However what really got to me was that he finally damned with faint praise saying that *Joseph* provided "abundant" evidence that I could one day "become a successful composer/arranger."

Damn it, man, I wanted to be one now. If I'd stayed at Oxford I would have been a hugely employable graduate by the summer! Anyway the dinner with David perked me up, David having questioned the latter statement, and I took off to Brighton to mooch around Victorian churches and generally forget about things. Perhaps, I thought in the phenomenal brick nave (far taller even than Westminster Abbey) of the internationally important Victorian masterpiece St Bartholomew's, I should contact Roy Featherstone at EMI and, armed with Mr Bowen's prediction, remind him of what he had said about my arrangements of David Daltrey's songs.

EVENTS TOOK A DECIDEDLY unexpected turn on Sunday. For in the *Sunday Times* under the rather insipid headline "Pop Goes Joseph" was the rave review every first-timer prays for. The only stricture that pop/rock critic Derek Jewell had was that "the snap, crackle and pop" of *Joseph* zipped along too fast. Where was Tim? Had he seen it? He had said he was going away on a "private" weekend which I assumed was with some girl or other. I couldn't wait to get back to London, find Alan Doggett and buy him a drink. Tim eventually found me at Harrington Court and I detected a crack in his normal easy-going nothing-really-matters veneer. Tim was ecstatic. We had been hailed as having made a breakthrough for pop! Not lost on both of us, buried at the bottom of the review was a less than flattering appraisal of the new offerings from Norrie Paramor's star artist Cliff Richard.

Next day the action started. Possibly riled by the Cliff Richard dig and possibly feeling that it would be no bad thing to be associated with "a breakthrough for pop," especially since this alleged breakthrough was under his nose, the great legend Norrie Paramor decided to get behind *Joseph*. Very shortly he obtained an offer from Decca Records to make a *Joseph* album and not only that, Decca were happy that it should be with our original performers. This was great news, although it did cross our minds that it might just be that named artists would cost Decca and Norrie a lot more money.

There were two snags. *Joseph* was only the length of one side of an LP. The second was that Norrie wanted to publish it, i.e. cream off some of our potential income for himself. *Joseph* was already contracted to Novello's, a genuine traditional publishing house, rather than Norrie who had had a rough time a few years previous when the TV show *That Was The Week That Was* uncharitably suggested that artistic reasons might not be the reason Norrie Paramor compositions just happened to crop up on the B-sides of the top artists he produced at EMI.

Norrie's brother Alan was wheeled out as head of the so-called Paramor publishing division. Unbeknown at least to me, he had already contacted Novello's about muscling in on their publishing deal. Novello's, being a classical outfit, had signed *Joseph* on classical music terms not on the extortionate "50% of what the publisher chooses to account for" terms that were standard then in the pop world. And of course, thanks to Bob Kingston and no thanks to Desmond Elliott, they had zilch of the Grand Rights. What Alan Paramor proposed was that to accommodate Norrie the contract was redrawn on pop terms with the Grand Rights included. No agreement, no Decca record. Of course this was blackmail. Furthermore Tim was dependent on Norrie for his job and was in no position to battle. What happened next was the first of many times I got cast as the bad guy in negotiations. Yet all I was doing was trying to protect us both from being bullied into something manifestly unfair. I have no doubt that any wavering thoughts Norrie might have had of bringing me under his wing ended after a one-on-one tussle I had with his so-called publisher brother.

I pointed out that Tim was an employee of Norrie with a guaranteed income and I had no such support. Therefore why should I, frankly also Tim, give up potential earnings on a project Norrie had absolutely no involvement in developing? Alan was furious. He thought I would be a pushover. Eventually the Paramors, who obviously had also threatened out-of-their-depth classical publisher Novello's with the same no deal, no record scenario, proposed upping the publisher share to 40% not the 50% of the standard rip-off pop publishing contract. But the Grand Rights had to be thrown in. I resisted. At another one-on-one with Alan, where he told me I was an ungrateful troublemaking upstart, he offered to leave control of the Grand Rights with us but he wanted 20% of them, or bye bye record. I was in no position to argue any more. It still seemed far fetched to think a 22-minute school cantata would have life in theatre and film. But even so, that meeting rankles with me to this day. At least I kept us 80% not 50% of our theatre and film income, despite having no idea of whether there would ever be any.*

WITH THE PUBLISHING ISSUE decided, Tim and my next task was to expand *Joseph* to LP length, i.e. about 40 minutes. This was easy. Most of the songs had been deliberately kept very short lest the kids got bored and they needed expanding anyway. But we added two

---

* Tim and I now own 100% of *Joseph* as a result of my company being offered the chance to buy the publishing rights years later.

new songs. In the Colet Court version we had skipped the story of Egyptian mogul Potiphar and his wife who fancied Joseph. The new song "Potiphar" contained a typical Rice lyric:

> Potiphar had very few cares
> He was one of Egypt's millionaires
> Having made a fortune buying shares
> In pyramids.

The second, "Go Go Go Joseph," is an archetypical Sixties song that tells the story of Joseph's dream-solving activities in gaol and is now the Act 1 closer in the theatre. Little did we premeditate that when we wrote it.

Norrie Paramor wanted to keep a watchful eye on what I was up to with the orchestrations, so I did a lot of writing in his office. My stock with the great man got even worse when he opined that he had been to the opening night of *Cabaret* and that it had no hit songs and was an average musical at best. I had seen it in preview and, aside from the subplot with a boring song about pineapples, I thought it was great, flamboyantly directed by a name I banked, Hal Prince, and with sensational performances by Judi Dench as Sally Bowles and Barry Dennen as the MC. I told Norrie that I thought it was the best thing I'd seen on the London stage since Callas in *Tosca*. Even if that was absurdly comparing apples and oranges, *Cabaret* opened my eyes to a new seamless way of staging that chimed with my growing certainty that musicals could be through-composed.

Cabaret arguments notwithstanding, Norrie seemed pleased enough with my arrangements and the Decca recording was green lit. There was a minor hiccup, however. We got a letter from Technicolor demanding that we drop the word from our title as we were infringing a trademark. I replied saying that was fine by us, as we were doing a deal with Eastmancolor who were keen to be associated with vibrant new cutting-edge stuff. Practically by return we got a letter saying we could use Technicolor provided we spelt it correctly. Naturally we had been spelling it the British way with a "u" in the colour bit.

When you write an orchestration it's a bit like an artist with paint. You have musical colours in your head and the palette is infinite. The big difference is that an artist executes a picture himself. A composer relies on others to execute what he has written. I, like all composers who orchestrate, hear the complete work in my head as I want it to sound. Unfortunately the reality doesn't always turn out that way. Come the *Joseph* recording, the delightful but very amateur playing of our Potters Bar stars was shown up hugely when combined with the hardened orchestral session musicians that Norrie hired for our day in Decca Records' long-vanished North London recording studios. Alan Doggett, an amateur conductor himself, was way out of his comfort zone. I found the solo vocal performances under par. In short I was not the happiest bunny in the control room.

I worked myself up into such a lather that I didn't stay till the bitter end. My lather foamed further when I heard the finished mixes. Some of the playing was so ragged that I wondered if the recording would even be released. The production values I had hoped for were zero. Lather turned to meltdown. Tim was scheduled to play the finished tapes to Norrie the next day. I told him we couldn't play him such amateur night out stuff.

How wrong I was. Norrie loved it and so did Decca. The homespun quality of the "pop group next door" combined with the kids for whom *Joseph* was written exactly conveyed the irresistible joy that happens when people make music just for the fun of it. But as a recording to rival *Sgt. Pepper* or "MacArthur Park," as I had hoped, *Joseph* didn't stand a chance. The vocal performances were merely pleasant and not remotely charismatic enough for there to be a serious shot at a hit single. "Any Dream Will Do" had to wait over 20 years to chart when Jason Donovan's recording went to No. 1 in Britain.

Parenthetically in 2002 "Any Dream Will Do" was sniped at from an unexpected quarter. The Archbishop of Canterbury, Dr Rowan Williams, chose the annual Dimbleby Lecture to challenge the lyric for suggesting "The personal goals recommended were simply activating your potential in any direction you happen to set your heart on." He caused quite a stir and Tim was not best pleased. My quibble with the lyric is its pessimism, "May I return to the beginning / The light is dimming / And the dream is too. / The world and I / We are still waiting / Still hesitating / Any dream will do." It is interesting that in the original Colet Court version the lyric read "My dream is dimming" rather than "the light." I wonder how many of the school kids who have sung my jaunty tune over the years were aware that what Tim is saying is world weary – the lyrics aren't jaunty at all.

Looking back, I realize that my angst in the studio was the first of many meltdowns I have had when faced with less than bullseye performances. Bad sound is one of my pet hates and even today I go to too many musicals where it seems the creative teams have cloth ears. My problem always has been, and still is, that I am a perfectionist. Any substandard performance drives me bonkers. I think I have got slightly better at controlling myself in my old age but only slightly. Anyway, shortly after Decca announced they were happy we were offered a performance of *Joseph* in St Paul's Cathedral. But it was not until November. Furthermore Decca decided they would release *Joseph* in January 1969. The record company honchos figured it might get more noticed than if it was smothered by the Autumn/Christmas schedule. So I had an outsize hole in the summer. It was filled by the not inconsiderable bulk of darling Auntie Vi.

YOU MAY RECALL THAT I alluded earlier to the matter of Auntie Vi and too many cocks spoil the breath. This issue was about to percolate into my life in a major way. It began with a telegram that read thus:

GOD BUGGER THE POPE STOP ARRIVING IN UCL HOSPITAL
TOMORROW STOP SORRY HOLS OFF CALL STOP VI STOP

Just as well the postmistress in La Mortola has scant English, I
thought, as I booked a call to find out what on earth had happened
on the Costa Fiore.

The matter had two nubs. Nub one, my uncle George explained,
was that poor Vi had very badly broken her leg in three places. She
was being freighted back to England by air ambulance and would be
ensconced in UCL Hospital in London. Since I was her favourite relative, I was expected to rise to the occasion. So far so good. Hospital
visits to see Vi would doubtless be colourful and George, being a doctor, would see she got great treatment.

It was nub two that proved more troublesome. She had started
writing a cookbook and wanted me to help her continue with it in her
hour of need. The manuscript to date was in the post via registered
mail. Had I received it? I hadn't. No matter, first off after arrival her
leg would have to be reset, but George was sure Vi would be compos
mentis fairly soon after the surgeons had strutted their stuff. Then
she would need cheering up and help with the book was the prescribed tonic. None of this sounded unreasonable. I loved nattering
food with Vi. Then the manuscript turned up. The title page of the
draft in the registered brown envelope said it all.

THE QUEENS OWN COOKBOOK
Camp Cooking for Town Dwellers
by Rodney Spoke

Auntie, no doubt inspired by her many theatrical friends, and
maybe Kenneth Williams on the BBC World Service, was writing a
gay cookbook.

Before you say "what's wrong with that?," you have to remember this was more than 50 years ago. London may have been swinging and recipes like Coq Up and her version of Spotted Dick might have hit my funny bone, but away from the Kings Road things hadn't swung far enough for mainstream publishers to embrace this volume wholeheartedly. I quote the introduction.

> Running mascara, eye-lashes slipping, nose unpowdered, nails unvarnished and even a hint of stubble. There is no excuse for it. You can stop messing about in the kitchen and come out in the sitting room. Here at last is a cook book for the Bona Viveur.

It struck me there was only one publisher for Auntie. Desmond Elliott. I was right. Soon after Vi's leg was reset, she had a deal set with Desmond's Arlington Books. Vi had broken her leg very badly and her stay in hospital through that hot summer was a long one. I enlisted my friend David Harington to help Vi concoct chapters like "Game Meat" and we did keep Vi merry as she created the character of Rodney Spoke, whose "graceful hand has been behind so many of London's leading restaurateurs." The book eventually was published in 1970 and I spent most of that year and a few years after praying that nobody discovered that Rodney was my aunt or that I had anything to do with it.

THE REVEREND MARTIN SULLIVAN, the New Zealand-born dean of Sir Christopher Wren's masterpiece St Paul's Cathedral, was not averse to publicity in the name of Jesus. He inaugurated a summer youth festival called Pop-In at St Paul's by abseiling down the cathedral's West Front. Traditionalists were not keen. There are historical connections between St Paul's School in West London and the cathedral and Rev. Sullivan thought *Joseph* would be a perfect follow-up to his summer high jinks. Not a few eyebrows shot up at the announcement that a pop cantata was to be performed on November

9 in the cathedral hailed as one of the better consequences of the Great Fire of London.

Unfortunately when Sir Christopher designed his iconic dome he did not have a rock drummer in mind. The St Paul's Cathedral echo is a good twenty seconds long. And there's more than one of them, as anyone who has climbed the steps to the Whispering Gallery at the rim of the dome will testify. In short, St Paul's Cathedral isn't top of the venue list for a highly public performance of a piece which much depends on hearing the words. So there were a lot of heads buried in the words in the programme when the Joseph Consortium, as our massed forces were now named, gave the first performance of *Joseph* Mark 2.

The dome did a great job of masking the Joseph Consortium's rhythmical deficiencies and once again the overwhelming feeling was joyous. There was a good review from Ray Connolly, the *Evening Standard* music critic whom we had come across when we were unsuccessfully trying to propel their Girl of the Year Ross Hannaman into the stratosphere. The sadly now defunct satirical Peter Simple column in the *Daily Telegraph* ran a story about a new pop cantata "Mr Moses and the Amazing 200ft Cybernetic Funcalf," music by old Etonian Adrian Glass-Darkley, which neatly pulled the rug from under any serious thoughts of a sequel in this direction, at least for a bit. When we did fleetingly flirt with the Moses story, we thought of starting it with the tune that I had scrawled on a table napkin in Carlo's Place. What was to become the big *Jesus Christ Superstar* theme had first-draft words that went "Samuel, Samuel, this is the first book of Samuel." We became friends of Martin Sullivan, who hugely encouraged us to choose another biblical story as our follow-up. In fact he was the first of many who suggested the story of Jesus, but for the moment the launch of the *Joseph* album blanked out thoughts of a successor.

DECCA'S DECISION TO RELEASE *Joseph* in the New Year meant that the run-up to Christmas churned through agonizingly slowly. I increasingly panicked that if *Joseph* didn't strut the stuff I would have to get a job. It was time to make plans. My mother had got to know a feisty fun ex-model called Pam Richards who had a flat in the block next door. She lived on her own, but seemed to have a bevy of friends of whom one of the younger was an aspiring heartthrob pop star called David Ballantyne. David's singles were all over the pirate radio stations and I was intrigued to discover who was paying for them. He told me he was being supported by a property developer with a taste for dabbling in show business called Sefton Myers. My family became friendly with David and soon Julian and I met his very pretty sister Celia. Julian was very smitten, so much so that a few years later they got married. I banked Sefton Myers's name.

The *Joseph* album finally lurched out in January 1969 to a few really exceptionally good reviews, several hailing it as genuinely ground-breaking. But that was about it. I pushed for one more performance to launch the album at the Central Hall and raised a bit of money to advertise it. It was a mistake. Now that *Joseph* was a major Decca Records release, the stakes were far higher. A third public performance proved to be one too many for the parents of Colet Court. Although we did get quite an audience, the atmosphere was totally different. "Forensic" might be the word. Instead of anticipatory celebration the audience wanted to know what all the fuss was about.

The first problem was the playing. Our Decca album performers, bless them, were just what they were, a perfectly nice bunch of amateurs from Potters Bar. Since we could not afford professionals, we got students from the Royal College for our orchestra. They were simply not up to it and Alan Doggett was neither tough nor experienced enough to whip the disparate forces together. The teetotal Methodist Central Hall was not the ideal venue to launch an album that would supposedly transform pop. We were putting a square peg into a round hole big time. I knew it and wanted to cancel the whole

thing which was utterly unprofessional as I had pushed for it in the
first place.

The fallout didn't take long. Tony Palmer, pop critic for the *Observer*, the rival newspaper to the *Sunday Times*, seized his moment.
After castigating the out of tune playing, he concluded that "if Joseph
is a new beginning for pop, it is the beginning of the end." Frankly,
based on that performance he had a point. Still 1969 saw *Joseph* bed
down very nicely from Novello's point of view, a gratifying number of
schools performed it and a new piano score was commissioned to include the new songs on the LP. But it was hardly going to support me
and both my family and I knew it. It was time to find out a bit more
about Sefton Myers. A property man who dabbled in showbiz might
just conceivably be a man with a lifeline.

David Ballantyne didn't seem to know much about Myers other
than that he was often seen around Variety Club events. That figured. The Variety Club of Great Britain was then, as it is now, an
excellent charity that provides for disadvantaged and sick children
through glamorous events where donors rub shoulders with British
stars. In the 1960s its patrons were a Who's Who of the showbiz
establishment with a big Jewish contingent. I found out via a contact
at the charity that Sefton was seriously stagestruck. So I knocked up
a letter.

Throughout life I have found that the best way to get something
you want from people is not to dangle your real carrot in front of their
nose. Lob it into the mix in passing whilst pushing something else.
That way, if you get a nibble, you can act all coy and say it's not really
up for discussion. It also saves you embarrassment on the 99% of occasions when your semi-hidden bait gets zero response. So I wrote
to Sefton asking if he would back a museum of pop memorabilia and
help find a property for it. Actually time has proved it was a good
idea, except I would have been useless at running it. But I also en-

closed the *Joseph* album and a few choice reviews. Two days later I got a letter telling me to call him and arrange a meeting.

We met at his offices in Charles Street, Mayfair, bang opposite the now sadly shadow of its former self Mark's Club. There was another man at the meeting who remained silent throughout and was introduced as Myers's show business advisor. His name was David Land. With hindsight this must be the only meeting ever when David Land remained silent. It went as I had hoped. There was no interest in my pop museum. But what was the story behind this *Joseph* album? Sefton's show business pal David had been given it to check out and he had loved it. And who was this Tim Rice who had written the words? I made out that he was a cutting-edge record executive with Norrie Paramor and that I was busy on multiple musicals all destined for the West End. Sefton asked if I could come back for a second meeting in a few days' time.

If you'll excuse the mixed metaphor, next week the bacon came home to roost. Sefton offered me a management contract with a guaranteed three year income and an option to continue the arrangement for ten years, £2000 a year rising by £500 annually as an advance against a commission of 25% of our earnings. It was a whopping commission but £2000 per year was a lot of money in those days (today approximately £32,000). Furthermore there were no strings attached to what I could write. David Land was rather more vocal at this meeting pronouncing, "My boy, these are serious ackers you can't refuse."

There was just one condition. Tim had to agree to sign up too. I needed no persuading. This offer would provide me with three years of secure income and prove to my family that I hadn't left Oxford in vain. But how best to persuade Tim to chuck up a seemingly safe career path with Norrie Paramor? It would be a tough ask. Tim didn't seem a natural risk taker. This wouldn't be easy and, boy, didn't I know it.

10

"Did Judas Iscariot Have God on His Side?"

Of course Tim took loads of convincing. After all he was more than three years older than me and, non-existent as that age gap feels now, then it seemed massive and thoughts of a secure future pressed even heavier on him than me. Tim admits to never having been as passionate about musicals as I am and the thought of giving up a seemingly much safer career path in the then all-powerful record industry must have been agonizing. I believe Tim even tried to persuade Norrie Paramor to take me in-house, but Norrie was having no truck with the long-haired troublemaker who had committed the mortal sin of loving *Cabaret* and burbled on about Hal Prince. We acquired a lawyer called Ian Rossdale, who negotiated that we each got a £500 advance and that our guaranteed weekly money was definitely non-returnable. (Today £7,950.) I think this was a real carrot for Tim. But most importantly I believe his parents advised him to take the plunge and if that's true I owe a big posthumous hug to Hugh and Joan Rice. Tim signed the deal and handed in his notice to a less than ecstatic Norrie Paramor.

OMG! Three secure years ahead. I could write anything I liked. But with the contract under my belt, writing took equal billing with another top priority, moving out of Harrington Court. Granny had set up a trust fund with about £4000 in it that was mine when I was 25. (Today £63,600.) I persuaded her to advance it to let me buy a flat. I found a basement in a house in Gledhow Gardens near Earl's Court. It had one big room and backed onto a large garden so it was blissfully quiet. But it was £6500 and to buy this I had to get a mortgage. (Today £103,350.)

When *Joseph* was rehearsing in St Paul's Cathedral, Tim and I had just for a laugh popped into the local branch of the highly exclusive bank Coutts and Company, top client HM The Queen. In those days it redefined pomposity. Every member of staff from bank manager to humblest clerk wore Fred Astaire-like white tie and tails – and, no, you didn't expect them to launch into a tap dance routine on the marble staircase. A visit to Coutts was designed to inspire awe and trepidation in the chosen few of the great and good allowed into its echelons.

Fully expecting to be shown the tradesman's entrance quicker than promptly, Tim and I marched in and demanded to open an account. We were ushered into the deathly silent office of the assistant manager, a frock-coated character called Tom Slater. He seemed to know about *Joseph* in St Paul's which we took as a definitive negative, especially in this hush-toned realm that only needed incense to make it religious. To our astonishment, he proffered the forms to open an account and a week later we joined the Queen in entrusting our worldly wealth to Britain's most exclusive bank. Although I got to know Tom well over the next few years, he never told me why on earth he admitted us. Had he got a score to settle with his bosses that day? Anyway it was to Tom I turned for my first mortgage and buoyed by my new contract I got a loan for £2500. At last I could move away from the dreaded Harrington Court.

My new flat meant that belatedly I began to be confident enough to build a social life. For the very first time I felt secure about inviting home girls. I needed someone to help me pay the mortgage and so I persuaded my school friend David Harington to rent the bedroom and I installed a cunningly concealed Murphy bed in the big room

for myself. We turned a sort of garden shed into a tiny psychedeli-
cally decorated dining room, uprated the kitchen with a dishwasher
of which I was hugely proud and lit the blue touchpaper for a series of
Auntie Vi recipe inspired dinner soirées. I became very friendly with
two girls, Sally Morgan and Lottie Gray via some Oxford friends,
thereby unwittingly brushing with the uppermost echelons of British
spy families. It was not long before Sally and Lottie introduced me
to a girl who changed my life. I also now had a room where I could
install a decent sound system. Along with the dishwasher I bought a
15 ips reel-to-reel tape recorder. I figured that a guy with a three year
writing contract absolutely needed one of those.

Sefton Myers laid out the red carpet. Tim and I were installed
on the second floor of his Mayfair office. Not only were we given a
line manager/minder called Don Norman who also managed jazz
singer Annie Ross, but we also acquired a girl called Jane who wore
the shortest miniskirts ever and a gopher/publicist called Mike Read
who went on to become a top Radio 1 DJ. Mike is a charming bloke
who became a firm friend of Tim's as well as writing and starring in
two legendary West End disasters about Oscar Wilde and Norrie's
protégé Cliff Richard.

Then there was David Land. The only way I can describe David
is, were you to phone Central Casting seeking a caricature warm-
hearted, gag a minute, East End Jewish show business manager, they
could turn up no one better than David Land. One day a plaque
boasting Hope and Glory Ltd appeared outside David's door. I asked
him what on earth this company did. David said it was so he could
answer phone calls with "Land of Hope and Glory." When I asked
how he came by his surname he explained that when his father fled
Eastern Europe the immigration office thought "Poland" stood for
"P.O. Land." I grew to truly love this man.

A minor problem was that nobody in the business seemed to know
much about David other than that he managed the Dagenham Girl

Pipers. The Pipers are a sort of community outfit hailing from the sprawling east of London town which gave the Girls their name. It is the British home of Ford Motors and not a thing of beauty, but neither are bagpipes unless you are one of those who find the sound of the Scottish glens deeply moving. There are surprisingly many of these including, apparently, Hitler who is alleged to have remarked, on hearing the Girls when they were touring Germany in the early 1930s, that he "wished he had a band like that." Which proves he was tone deaf.

One of the most debated memories of my Sydmonton Festival is the sight and sound of the Girls dressed in fake Scottish kilts piping full tilt on my staircase when rain forced them indoors. David revelled in their press cuttings, particularly those that read "all this evening needed to make it truly horrendous was the Dagenham Girl Pipers." Nonetheless under David's stewardship the Girls piped their questionably tuned way from Las Vegas to the Royal Variety Show. Undeniably the Dagenham Girl Pipers fulfil an admirable social purpose and still give lots of people a great deal of pleasure. He secretly was very proud of them and was chuffed to bits when their redoubtable leader Peggy Iris got an OBE from the Queen.

"Dagenham Girl Pipers" is cockney rhyming slang for "windscreen wipers."

THE FIRST FRUIT OF our new contract was *Come Back Richard Your Country Needs You*. It was terrible. *Come Back* – and I hope it doesn't – was conceived as a follow-up to *Joseph* and was performed by the City of London School where Alan Doggett had become the new director of music. I discovered some of the justly forgotten score when I researched this book and I cannot believe how we ever allowed such slapdash sorry stuff to appear in front of an audience. Having abandoned the Bible as source material, Tim thought the story of England's Richard the Lionheart was a suitable case for treatment. In truth there is hardly any story. Richard spent most of his reign away from home warmongering on crusades, hence our title. He got captured in Austria on the way back from one of his military forays and his faithful minstrel Blondel is supposed to have gone round Europe warbling Richard's favourite songs until one day from a castle window his master emitted a cry of recognition. This gave rise to a typical Tim lyric I think worth quoting:

> *"Sir 'tis I," cried Blondel.*
> *"For you I've travelled far."*
> *"Rescue me if you can," said the King,*
> *"But lay off that guitar."*

I don't know why Tim was so obsessed with this story, but undaunted by the tepid reaction *Come Back* got, years later he wrote a full-blown musical on this slender theme called *Blondel*. I was not invited to be the composer.

From what I remember of our opus horribilis, three tunes surfaced elsewhere. One became the Act 2 opener of the full-length *Joseph* and the tune of the lyric I quoted got altered a bit and became the chorus of "Skimbleshanks the Railway Cat." The third, "Saladin Days," became "King Herod's Song" in *Jesus Christ Superstar* and contained a line about scimitars and Christians which I feel is inadvisable to quote. This melody had been rejected by the Eurovision Song Contest under the title "Try It and See" in Norrie Paramor days and was therefore published by Norrie. This led to a confusing credit in the booklet of the US album version of *Superstar* which in turn led a few people to mistakenly think Tim and I had not written one of its biggest moments. A single of "Come Back Richard," sung by Tim, was issued under the name Tim Rice and the Webber Group. It got nowhere.

AFTER THIS DEBACLE, WE needed to write something decent and do it pretty quick. *Come Back* was not the sort of stuff Sefton Myers had put his money on the line for. On paper our next project must have looked even worse. Obviously post-*Joseph* we had been urged to choose another biblical subject and many progressive churchmen had urged us to consider the story of Jesus Christ which we resisted. Tim, however, had mentioned several times Bob Dylan's question, "Did Judas Iscariot have God on his side?" He became fascinated about Judas in the historical context of Roman-occupied Israel. Was Judas the rational disciple trying to prevent the popular reaction to Jesus's teaching from getting so out of hand that the Romans would crush it? Was Jesus beginning to believe what the people were saying, that he truly was the Messiah? What if we dramatized the last days of Jesus's life from Judas's perspective? I could see massive possibilities in this, particularly theatrically. Unsurprisingly, nobody else thought this was remotely a subject for a stage musical, but we did write one song whose lyric encapsulated these questions. It was called "Superstar" and its chorus was destined to become the best-known three-chord tune I have written, the same chorus I had jotted on a table napkin in Carlo's Place and which had briefly been about Samuel.

It was all very well writing the song, but the question was what to do with it. David Land was nonplussed. "How do I explain this at the Marble Arch Synagogue?" he opined, but no way did he block our creative juices. Tim had an idea. Jesus and religion were having a bit of a vogue in pop culture with singles like Norman Greenbaum's "Spirit in the Sky." Dennis Potter's play on the life of Christ had the nattering classes chattering. It emerged that Tim had at some point discussed the possibility of some kind of musical piece about Jesus with Mike Leander, the composer/arranger who had produced our first single with Ross Hannaman at EMI. Mike was now the A&R chief at MCA Records, then a division of Universal Studios, and he was apparently rather enthusiastic. The boss of the British office was a pensive Irishman called Brian Brolly. It was to this odd couple that I first played our song on their office piano with Tim doing his best on vocals.

They bit big time. Brian asked me how I heard the arrangement. I replied that I wanted it to be a fusion of symphony orchestra, soul brass section, gospel choir and rock group with a bluesy lead vocal to go with our three-chord verse; in other words nothing fancy. Astonishingly Brian did not say baulk at my extravagant suggestions, in fact very soon afterwards he called me in to discuss them. Happily I brought with me the unreleased David Daltrey song "Pathway" that I had orchestrated. Brian asked a lot of questions about whether I could handle such disparate forces. He had obviously heard the *Joseph* album and I told him I wanted to make a single that took the fusion of an orchestra and rock group further than ever before. The "Pathway" demo convinced him. Brian swallowed the bait.

We were given the budget for a full symphony orchestra plus all the other trappings and, joy of joys, allowed to produce it ourselves. I could hardly believe it. There was one issue: MCA wanted to own everything. I was to discover later, to my great benefit, that Brian understood the importance of buttoning up all areas of copyright. In return for financing the single, MCA was to have the worldwide rights to any future recording of the as yet unwritten "opera" plus Leeds Music, Universal's publishing arm, acquiring similar publishing rights on standard pop terms.

However there was no mention of Grand Rights. Sensing Brolly was a sharp operator, I let sleeping cats lie. David Land was a close friend and, I soon discovered, sparring partner of the boss of Leeds Music Cyril Simons. I thought we could tackle this in the unlikely event we ever wrote the complete piece. A deal was signed for the single (and any eventual album) which provided a 5% royalty in Britain and 2½% in the rest of the world, out of which we had to pay back not only the recording costs but any royalties to singers. It was a terrible deal. But MCA were risking a lot of money and we were in no position to turn it down. The big question now was who could perform it?

Tim's first thought was Murray Head. I agreed. His acting skills meant Tim's words would be secure. Best of all he had a real bluesy soul voice which he could turn to silk in a heartbeat. Tim's lyrics were a series of pertinent questions. From the opening couplet "Every time I look at you I don't understand / Why you let the things you did get so out of hand?" to the chorus "Jesus Christ, Jesus Christ / Who are you? What have you sacrificed?" Tim touched on issues just as relevant 50 years later. This was not lost on Murray when we approached him but he was bemused by the song and sceptical about its chances. However he had been dropped by EMI and eventually concluded there was no harm in fronting the single, although understandably he wanted to see what the rest was like before committing to the whole project.

It was Murray who suggested the musicians and thanks to him I acquired a superb rhythm section, bass and drums from Joe Cocker's backing group the Grease Band plus Juicy Lucy's Chris Mercer on tenor saxophone and Wynder K. Frog, alias Mick Weaver, on keyboards. The bedrock of a great rhythm section is the bass and drums. Alan Spenner (bass) and Bruce Rowland (drums) played as if they were joined at the hip. Somehow they knew instinctively what the other would do. At last I was working with top musicians and from day one of rehearsals my mind raced with ways to push the band further.

OLYMPIC STUDIOS IN THE southwest London suburb of Barnes was Britain's hottest rock studio, but its big room could accommodate a full-sized symphony orchestra. It was the natural choice for our single. The in-house engineers straddled both rock and orchestral music since major films were regularly scored there. When Keith Grant, Olympic's legendary recording engineer, saw the scale of my arrangements he suggested that the rock band recorded to a metronome in their headphones. Nowadays this is called a "click track." With a "click" as a guide, an orchestra only has to follow it to be totally in time with the original track. But a "click" dictates that the musicians will play mechanically and not with each other.

No great rock band plays like a machine and there are bound to be minor variations in speed in any performance, hence Keith Grant's worries about overdubbing a juggernaut of a symphony orchestra without a "click" to guide it. I gambled that a great rhythm track totally outweighed the risk, but the issue never arose as Keith assigned our project to a young engineer my age called Alan O'Duffy. Alan is a tall, liltingly soft-spoken, big hearted Irishman who became the rock that pulled our disparate forces together. His experience in a studio that recorded everything from happening bands to symphony orchestras had prepared him for everything I threw at him. A metronome was never on his radar either, so we recorded the band and the soul singers ahead of the orchestra in the big studio where the Rolling Stones made many of their greatest hits.

Murray provided indefatigable guide vocals. A gospel choir, the Trinidad Singers, was hired for the chorus and the "soul trio" were a pair of seasoned white session girls, Sue and Sunny, augmented by Lesley Duncan, the singer-songwriter who later famously duetted with Elton John. Ironically the white soul singers at first sounded blacker than the gospel choir who seemed rather overawed and kicked off more Ascot Gavotte than Caribbean. But when it all eventually started to cook, everyone was astonishing. I tried several variations of the final choruses with the band, but on the master take Alan and Bruce took things into their own hands and played syncopations that defied gravity. Afterwards I wrote them all out, but although I've got rock sections to replicate what they did, it never sounds quite the same.

The timekeeping problem did prove a nightmare for the orchestra. I had scored the big "Superstar" chords in full Guildhall School of Music textbook "Also Sprach Zarathustra" overdrive. Recording that was easy. But recording the linking bridge section, where the full orchestra plays syncopated phrases precisely in time with the rock section, might have had my father's Methodist minister craving a sip of Dad's so-called water bottle. With the session clock ticking, we finally got a great take, only for Alan O'Duffy to announce to the whole studio that he had failed to put the tape machine into record. I went nuts. Calmly he got the orchestra to do another take and miraculously it too was perfect.

When the 70-odd players had gone Alan asked if I would like to hear back my orchestra. The sod had recorded them twice. My 70-piece orchestra now numbered 140. Maybe it was this naughty rock'n'roll Heath Robinson vibe in the studio, maybe the sheer adrenaline that comes when you create something spontaneously that you can't really write down or maybe the vocal creativity that Murray brought to take after take, but whatever the reason that original recording of "Superstar" has never been bettered.

The B-side was orchestral and in two sections. The first was a very Richard Straussian arrangement for heavily divided strings of the melody that eventually became "Gethsemane." I already knew what I would compose for the crucifixion and my instinct was that this music would become its coda. I wanted the antithesis to the stark horror of Jesus's death, something overripe and more stained-glass window than wood and nails, that hinted at how Jesus became sentimentalized in paintings like Holman Hunt's *Light of the World* or the Baroque excesses of southern Italy. Tim dubbed the music "John 19:41" after the verse in St John's Gospel describing Jesus's body resting in his tomb. The second part never made it to the final "opera." It was a fun tune in 7/8 time which I thought might come in handy if we wanted something celebratory, possibly after Jesus's triumphant return to Jerusalem. We didn't.

When Tim, David Land and I played the single to Mike Leander and Brian Brolly, Brian was euphoric. He truly thought it was a major – he even used the word "cathartic" – breakthrough for pop. He pronounced that his American masters would unquestionably finance the rest of the unwritten "rock opera," as it was decided the non-existent opus would be billed. David Land kept mumbling about what he would say at some friend's son's imminent barmitzvah, but the discussion quickly centred on what the single should be called. We settled on "'Superstar' from the Rock Opera 'Jesus Christ.'"

Everyone agreed that we needed a leading clergyman to endorse the single. An obvious target was Martin Sullivan at St Paul's Cathedral. Martin was delighted to help and wrote, "There are some people who may be shocked by this record. I ask them to listen to it and think again. It is a desperate cry. Who are you, Jesus Christ? is the urgent enquiry and a very proper one at that." Martin immediately offered St Paul's Cathedral for the premiere if and when we finished "Jesus Christ." We never took up the offer. Events overtook us. But he did give us this advice. Strict, or as he put it, fringe Christians would be bound to denounce our work, but that didn't bother him. He was certain that most Christians would actively embrace it. His concern was that we could inadvertently offend Jews.

We were taken aback. We were supported by two Jewish businessmen and this possibility had never been touched on. It was not on our radar to write anything that could be remotely interpreted that way. Tim told Martin that his take would spring from whether history had treated the motives of Judas Iscariot and Pontius Pilate unfairly and that he couldn't see how that could be offensive to anyone. I added that Sefton and David, plus their many connections in London's Jewish community, would surely flag any problem. For years

Martin's warning seemed unfounded. It wasn't until the film of *Jesus Christ Superstar* was released in the US that it proved real.

BRIAN BROLLY WENT INTO overdrive. "Superstar" would lurch out in the UK on November 21. He secured releases in every major territory and a few I'd never heard of. Of course the most important was the USA where Brian's ultimate boss Mike Maitland quickly became the project's unstinting champion. The American release was set for December 1. Back in the UK there was high excitement because we were offered a live performance on David Frost's Saturday night ITV show. This had two consequences: outraged viewers jamming the ITV switchboard and the beginning of my deep friendship with David that continued up to his far too early death in the summer of 2013.

A rather irritating storm was fabricated by the *Daily Express*. A creative journalist managed to get quotes that implied we had asked John Lennon to play Jesus. This was ludicrous. For openers there was no score or script to show him. Even today this fabricated rubbish persists as fact. But despite the huge TV plug and this mini furore, the UK reaction was disappointingly ho-hum. Britain wasn't ready for the single that Brian Brolly hailed as "cathartic" and, it turned out, nor was the USA. True there was a ripple of interest, but the big Christmas releases and the subject matter meant airplay was minimal. Thankfully the single did take off in a strange assortment of territories like Holland and Brazil and Brian Brolly confirmed a then massive budget of £20,000 for us to record our "rock opera." (Today £318,000.)

Having got this nod from MCA we realized we'd better write it. My relative new wealth meant that I had tried most of London's gastronomic hotspots, so I thought it time to get our creative juices flowing in the countryside. I alighted on a then ace watering hole, Stoke Edith House Hotel in deepest rural Herefordshire, having checked out there was an annex with a grand piano and that it served duck "en croute," a dish whose pastry, Auntie Vi opined, would taste like "clotted greasy bollocks." Tim remembers that we didn't do too much writing. I certainly remember scouring every record shop in a damp Christmassy Hereford for our single without much success. I also remember writing a rude note in the Hereford Cathedral visitors' book cursing the Dean and Chapter for heinously chucking out the superb nineteenth-century chancel screen by Gilbert Scott. Their crass, insensitive stupidity can be gauged in the Victoria & Albert Museum where the screen now lives. Hopefully one day it will be returned.

What we did do was map out the storyline of what was now confirmed as a double album. Overriding everything was that we were telling our story in sound and sound alone. We had none of the visual elements of theatre and film to fall back on. A cast-iron musical and dramatic structure was the key. In my department, rhythm, orchestral textures, time signatures and melody had to be deployed to keep our listeners' styluses in the grooves. Crucially important was how to reprise and pace material for dramatic effect. Dialogue had no place on a record, so the music and lyrics had to carry everything.

We did take one major decision in Herefordshire which was an important first step in creating the musical structure. It was where to put the pre-existing single "Superstar." One thought which we rejected was to use it as a prologue to the album. I suggested that, if ever our work was staged, it could accompany Jesus's journey from the place of his trial before Pilate to Golgotha where he was crucified. Thus Judas would become a narrator commenting on a version of the Stations of the Cross. In any event it felt completely right for Tim's questions to come towards the end of the piece and before Jesus's ultimate sacrifice.

This decision meant that the big "Superstar" chords had to be the climax of the trial. I had an instinct that whatever I composed for the trial should be condensed and become the overture. Also I figured that the overture had to show off my hugely varied musical forces of synthesizers, orchestra, rock group and choir in two minutes. The overture does this in precisely that order. It is indeed an edited version of the trial with the questioning motif that ends the opera sung by the choir as a prelude to Judas setting out his stall with "Heaven on Their Minds." Tim comes straight to the point. "My mind is clearer now / [. . .] if you strip away the myth from the man / You can see where we all soon will be / Jesus you've started to believe / The things they say of you / You really do believe / This talk of God is true" before begging the man who he admires and even loves not to let his followers get so far out of hand that the occupying Romans crush them once and for all.

In truth we were writing a musical radio play. Ultimately this gave us one enormous advantage. Audiences came to know our recording so well that no future director or producer could add musical passages for scene changes or tamper with the construction. The score had become set in stone. There is a famous story regarding my *Cats* collaborator Trevor Nunn directing Mozart's *Idomeneo* at Glyndebourne Opera. During a rehearsal he asked conductor Simon Rattle if he could repeat a section to cover a complicated stage move. Rattle shot back, "This is Mozart not Andrew Lloyd Webber." Thanks to the record not even Trevor could ask this of *Superstar*. Actually on second thoughts I am not so sure.

The New Year dawned with young American conscripts still being killed in Vietnam. Back home the troubles in Northern Ireland were festering, although on the mainland we were then still pretty much unaware of them, and there was a divisive General Election looming. But there was little inkling of this that winter. Brian Brolly wanted the double album for release in the fall of 1970. We set ourselves a target to complete the writing by Easter with my target to have the orchestration finished by May. In fact we finished way earlier which was just as well. For there was, as P.G. Wodehouse put it, a fly in an otherwise unsullied ointment. I fell deeply, passionately, head over heels in love.

11

Love Changes Everything, But . . .

I first met Sarah Hugill at a birthday party thrown by my friend Sally in Christ Church, Oxford, organized for Lottie Gray. I can still remember the date. January 21, 1970. Sarah was just a slip of a 16-year-old schoolgirl, but it isn't hard to explain why her parents had allowed her out for this bash. They had a little something in common with Sally and Lottie's families.

Sarah's father Tony had individually won the Croix de Guerre for bluffing a German commander into surrendering an entire French village. He had served in the 30 Assault Unit set up by James Bond author Ian Fleming. Tony wasn't over-keen on Fleming. He told me that he spent too much time in Whitehall and not with his men on the front line. Worse, when Fleming did get there, he had a habit of polishing off all their best brandy and cigarettes. Nonetheless Tony gets a big name check in *Casino Royale* and is supposed to be one of the role models for James Bond himself. Tony's day job was research chemist to the sugar company Tate & Lyle with special responsibilities for the plantations in Jamaica. But when he was appointed head of the FAO (the United Nations Food and Agricultural Organisation), one of his best friends told me never to take things at face value, although neither Sarah nor I know to this day exactly what this meant. Hence the connection with the parents of the party hostess.

I of course knew none of this when his deliciously open-faced daughter offered to be my secretary. Falling in love with Sarah didn't take long. I asked her to dinner at the bistro opposite the Michelin building in what London real estate agents poncily now call Brompton Cross. I thought she was ordering ludicrously small, simple things. She didn't know whether she was supposed to pay her share of the bill. That did it. I had to see her again.

By the end of January I had all the main melodies for our "opera" and Tim's lyrics were flowing as fast and furious as I was falling for Sarah. My new flat came in very handy. It was only a few hundred yards from Sarah's school. Since she was supposed to be revising for her summer exams she had loads of free time. So most days she would clock into school and promptly ankle round to me. Fairly soon I gave her a spare key. There are worse things when you're 21 than a pretty schoolgirl waking you up in the morning. Come March it was time to meet her parents. Thanks to the manners Auntie Vi drilled into me, I got on well with my elders and Tony and Fanny Hugill were no exception.

I had dinner at their flat near Kensington High Street. My love of architecture soon had small talk regarding their country home veering towards local churches, thus deflecting possible discussion about the length of my hair. I was invited for a weekend and made a note to wise up on north Wiltshire where their out-of-town pad was located. Over the years I have found that when meeting prospective in-laws it goes down well if you know more about where they live than they do.

LOVE MAY WELL CHANGE everything but in my case it had me writing fast and even more furiously. By mid-February *Superstar*'s structure was advanced enough for me to break the score down into record sides. My sketches for Side 1 are dated February 21 and the final fourth side dated March 4. Unusual, irregular time signatures are a vital part of *Superstar*'s construction. They give a propulsive energy to the music and thus to the lyric and the storytelling. There is a December '69 note that Mary Magdalene's first song must be in 5/4 time and two months later a big exclamation mark above the 5/4 time signature when it had become "Everything's Alright." There's a double exclamation mark above the 7/4 time signature of the Temple Scene in my notes for Side 2. The biggest note is a reminder to myself about writing a musical radio play with "clarity" scrawled across it and endless reminders about light and shade.

The writing may have sprinted apace but finding our singers was less plain sailing. With a guaranteed record release in the bag, Murray came on board quickly so the key role of Judas was cast. We were anxious to snare a known name as Jesus and Tim pursued Colin Blunstone, the lead singer of the Zombies, whose big hit was "She's Not There," written by fellow Zombie, Rod Argent, a fine musician with whom I was to work many times almost a decade later. I had a niggling feeling that Colin's voice was not rocky enough but the Zombies' record label CBS shot my worries in the foot by refusing permission for him to record for us point blank.

Help arrived unexpectedly. I had been invited a few months before to the Royal Albert Hall premiere of Jon Lord's *Concerto for Group and Orchestra* which featured Lord's band Deep Purple and the London Symphony Orchestra conducted by a friend of my father's, fellow composer and lover of cocktails, Malcolm Arnold. There I met Deep Purple's manager Tony Edwards, a smart businessman who like Sefton also dabbled in show business. I found the music bland, so I droned on about how daring it was to fuse a rock group with an orchestra. I discovered that Deep Purple were contemplating a wise career move and about to go heavy metal. I mentioned something about *Superstar* and Tony Edwards was intrigued.

Now, several months later, we got a call saying Deep Purple had a new lead singer and would Tim and I like to come round to Tony's very smart Thames-side house in Barnes and hear some of his rough tapes? His name was Ian Gillan. The moment I first heard the famous Ian Gillan primal scream was the moment I found my Jesus. He would be red blooded and full of spunk, not some bloke in a white robe clasping a baby lamb. That night I went back to my flat and rewrote the moment Jesus slings the moneylenders out of the temple.

Work on *Superstar* took a temporary back seat and not only because of Sarah. Out of the blue I got an offer to write a film score. The film was called *Gumshoe* and was directed by a first-timer, the future twice Oscar contender Stephen Frears and starred Albert Finney. Albie, as everyone called him, had set up a small independent film company with the actor Michael Medwin called Memorial Enterprises. Michael, an urbane pin-striped suited chap who frequently played the role of upper-class spiv in British B-movies, had been impressed by the mini buzz around the "Superstar" single and apparently had heard me jaw on about film musicals on some radio programme. The plot of *Gumshoe* involved Albie as a small time Liverpool bingo caller who fantasizes about being a glamorous Bogey-style private dick. Stephen, who unlike the suave Michael Medwin seemed a man ill at ease with the new Conservative government, wanted a score in Max Steiner style which would be a sort of homage to Bogart and Bacall and, coupled with very British working-class locations, would raise a wry smile. He also wanted a touch of rock'n'roll. I agreed I was their man. At worst this would be a laugh.

A large contraption called a Moviola was manhandled down my basement stairs. This dinosaur was the then standard editing kit for movies and became extinct almost exactly the time *Gumshoe* was made. You literally marked up the film where you wanted to cut it. Rather like analogue tape, it has recently made a slight comeback. Stephen would get the operator to run a sequence whilst I improvised on the piano until he got out of me what he felt fitted the pictures. Then I orchestrated it. I had a ball writing pastiche but I composed one deliberately filmic tune I was very pleased with. Two decades later I completely reworked the melody as the title song of *Sunset Boulevard* which I reconceived in 5/8 time. I'm pretty sure this makes it the only title song of a musical in this time signature. The recording sessions were hassle free and I got back to "Superstar" with the delightful team at *Gumshoe* seemingly contented. I didn't hear anything more about the movie for months.

WITH MURRAY AND IAN in the bag as Judas and Jesus, I began firming up our band. Joe Cocker was taking a rest from gigging so Grease Banders Alan Spenner and Bruce Rowland on bass and drums were nabbable. Tim and I approached Eric Clapton's manager Robert Stigwood in a pie-in-the-sky attempt to procure his client as lead guitarist, but an audience in Stigwood's grand Mayfair offices ended up with us graciously being shown the door. So we went with another Grease Band member Henry McCullough, who subsequently was lead guitarist in Paul McCartney's Wings. Chris Mercer, the Juicy Lucy sax player on our single, signed on and brought with him guitarist Neil Hubbard.

Finding a keyboard player, however, was hairier. I needed someone who spanned rock and classical, someone who could play rock by feel but could also stick to the musical script when required, in other words actually read music. There was a progressive trio creating quite a ripple in the sweet smoky haze of the live rock circuit called Quatermass. I can't remember who first played me their virtuoso Hammond organ dominated tracks, but big thanks to them for introducing me to Peter Robinson. Pete ticked every box. Not only was he a great rock player, but his musical knowledge spanned everything from Led Zeppelin to Schoenberg, and he introduced me to Miles Davis. Next Quatermass's singer John Gustafson became our Simon Zealotes. We were almost ready for the studio.

At the beginning of June we were invited by a Father Christopher Huntingdon to be his all-expenses-paid guests at the US premiere of *Joseph*. The first-ever public performance of a Rice/Lloyd Webber epic in America was taking place at the Cathedral College of the Immaculate Conception, Douglaston, Queens, New York. Father Huntingdon was in charge of the place. We jumped at it. Neither of us had been to America before. Had I known we would be staying at the Harvard Club in central Manhattan I just might have given my shoulder-length hair a tweak and been spared the censorious looks hurled my way in this epicentre of Ivy Leaguedom.

In truth I remember my first Broadway show better than I remember the *Joseph* performance which was fine, but the Elvis wasn't up to Tim's. It was Stephen Sondheim's *Company*. I had suggested to Tim that we saw it because I had clocked Hal Prince's name on the poster. It was a matinee and both afternoon and theatre were stiflingly hot. Somehow I had got into my head that my first Broadway show would be big and brash, at the very least with staging like *Cabaret*. But of course I saw something groundbreaking and utterly the reverse. I was completely unprepared for it and musically it was a million miles away from what was going on in my head at the time. Tim was taken with the lyrics, but I was a 22-year-old in love with a 16-year-old girl and not yet ready for middle-age angst. My rose-petal-strewn state of mind was considerably more the last scene of the same writer's *Merrily We Roll Along* than the first.

Back in London Sarah quizzed me about how we got on and I told her about Father Huntingdon and the Harvard Club. She replied that she wished I had told her who'd invited us. Father Huntingdon was her mother's Ivy League American cousin.

THE FIRST DAY WITH the band loomed and it dawned on me that only I knew how the music would fit together. Aside from the set-piece songs, much of what we recorded would feel alien to the rock musicians because they would appear like unconnected isolated fragments. I needed the feel and pacing that comes from having rehearsed a complete work many times, so most days I'd get them to jam the music I scheduled for the day for half an hour. Then I'd give Alan O'Duffy the nod and we'd record the short segment while the band was still hot. That's how "What's the Buzz" happened along with the moneylenders sequence in the Temple. It took a while for the band to free up in the 7/4 time signature, but just by playing the section round and round the rhythm became second nature to them. That day we recorded Ian's incredible screamed "My temple should be a house of prayer."

I was happy with how most of the main songs turned out first time around with one big exception: "I Don't Know How to Love Him." This was a real case of third time lucky. We originally reckoned on Annabel Leventon to play Mary. Annabel had been a big name as a serious actress on the Oxford University scene during my brief stay there. She also had quite a reputation as a singer and was in the London version of *Hair*. There had been real pressure on Tim and me to create a standalone single and Mary Magdalene's song was supposed to be it. Of course I tried too hard and so my arrangement had none of the spontaneity of everything else. There was nothing wrong with Annabel's vocal, nor with the playing. It just sounded conventional. A second attempt was no better.

The Mary issue was temporarily shelved whilst we searched for Pontius Pilate. I badly wanted to record the trial. It was our most ambitious shot at something operatic and I thought it top priority to check out if it worked. Don Norman, the guy whom Sefton had employed as our day-to-day manager, also represented a jazz singer – I can't remember his name – who was performing at the Pheasantry in Chelsea. Don pitched him for our Pilate. Tim wasn't so sure. At any rate I alone went to check the guy out. He did a really good set but diction wasn't top of his agenda. We needed an actor who could sing, not a singer who might be coaxed into vaguely acting. I was just about to mutter a few platitudes and leave when an incredibly young looking long-haired Hawaiian beauty took to the stage plus a battered acoustic guitar. From the moment she sang I got the shivers. Yvonne Elliman's voice was quirky, youthful, sexy and highly individual. I never found a phone box faster. I called Rice and said he had to get to the Pheasantry fast. We had found our Mary.

One down, Pontius Pilate to go. I kept thinking "musical radio play." Whoever sang Pilate must sound very different to the rest. Would Barry Dennen, the actor who had made such an impression on me as the MC in *Cabaret*, conceivably consider us? Contact was made via his agent and I was overjoyed when Barry said he'd meet me. Over several cups of coffee I gleaned that Barry was American, a musical theatre animal through and through and had been in an on and off relationship with Barbra Streisand for whom he had put together her early stage acts. We hit it off instantly and immediately tried out the Pilate material. I knew at once his highly distinctive voice was what we needed. Not only that: Barry was prepared to take real vocal chances: witness how he delivered Pilate's final hysterical cry to Jesus "Die if you want to, you misguided martyr!" Barry and Yvonne wound up as the only artists on the record to star both on Broadway and in the 1972 movie.

Tim suggested his friend Mike d'Abo, who had recently taken over from Paul Jones as lead singer of Manfred Mann, to sing the cameo role of King Herod. With an assortment of friends and scantily employed MCA wannabees filling the smaller parts, our casting was complete.

THE TRIAL WAS THE first scene to be completed. As usual we had recorded the band ahead in sections and these were edited together so Barry could give a proper performance. Hearing a real actor in a real scene inspired the team hugely and for the first time people thought I might just have a clue about how the musical bits fitted together.

"I Don't Know How to Love Him" was another matter. I was desperately thinking of ways to make the arrangement interesting. The conundrum was becoming as intractable as giving King Kong a bikini wax. One evening I was round at Alan Doggett's place. Playing in the background was a particularly boring early church music LP featuring an early "positive" organ which has a very distinctive snuffly fluety sound. I had an idea. Why not get Peter Robinson into Bach mode and make this the featured instrument? Alan, of course, knew where such a contraption could be hired.

Yvonne had sounded great simply accompanying herself on acoustic guitar. Was that, coupled with the snuffly organ, a way to go? And had the conventional drum part fatally holed the two previous versions? Bruce Rowland thought percussion was the answer. An afternoon session was booked which gave Bruce lunchtime to lay out the biggest selection of tom toms ever seen on the floor of Olympic Studio 2. Four men staggered into the studio baying for the blood of whoever hired the ancient organ as no one had told them it had to be humped up a staircase. I ducked all responsibility and blamed Alan Doggett. Yvonne sang beautifully, unfazed by the sight of Bruce crawling around his tom toms like a stoned Pocahontas. At last "I Don't Know How to Love Him" was in the bag.

SO WHAT WITH ONE thing and another I was in exceptionally high spirits when I boarded the train to Brighton on a sunny morning two days later. I had received an invitation from the headmistress of no less than Roedean School to judge their summer end-of-term music competition. Roedean is one of Britain's top posh boarding girls' schools. The school motto is "Honour the Worthy" and it sits atop a cliff on Britain's south coast from where it glares defiantly at the English Channel. In those days there were rumours that its teenage charges, arguably due to enforced separation from the opposite sex, were unusually receptive to any young man who shimmied through the hallowed school portals. Clearly I was in for a blissful afternoon.

What made it particularly satisfying was Rice was furious. At the very least, he muttered, the school should have asked both begetters of *Joseph*. I opined that it was a music competition and words were not on the agenda. In those days there was a fabulous first-class-only Pullman Car train from London to the south coast. Unlimited food and drink was plied at every seat. Since Roedean was paying I naturally made a special point of taking it. A mimosa arrived shortly after we pulled out of Victoria station and by the time we hit the glorious sun-drenched Sussex downs heaven was well and truly on my mind. In fact it was hard to believe the real address had anything better to offer.

Maybe the delectable head girl who met me at Brighton station did look at me a little curiously. But I let that pass. The poor thing had been long incarcerated in deepest Sussex and the sight of a male 22-year-old cutting-edge educational music composer must have been unsettling, especially one with hair my length. Nor was I fazed by the school's facade, one of those neo-Jacobean jobs designed to make you think twice about entering. A hardened Victorian fan like me is not unnerved by a *Harry Potter* type structure perched atop a cliff facing the English Channel, even if it was designed to instil British fortitude into its inmates on windy January nights. Nor, frankly, did the sideways glances during common-room drinks at my Deborah and Clare floral shirt suggest anything seriously was amiss. It was over lunch that the penny dropped. And oh boy did it drop big time. *Joseph* was published by Novello's who also published my dad. The headmistress had presumed *Joseph* was written by my father.

I don't know if you are familiar with *Right Ho, Jeeves* where the luckless Gussie Fink-Nottle is forced to dole out the gongs at Market Snodsbury girls' school prizegiving. If you aren't, you'll just have to take on trust why I anticipated truth and fiction were about to intertwine in a particularly cruel fashion. Other than the excruciating moment when I brought out an exceptional bottle of wine to chat up my prospective in-laws and my only corkscrew broke, I had never before experienced such blind panic. I asked if I could phone my father. Luckily Dad was cocktailing at the London College and when I read him the categories of the forthcoming contest he immediately grasped that my plight was exceptionally serious. I was particularly worried about my total lack of knowledge of woodwind instruments.

"Remind the clarinetists about their embouchure and the position of their lips, tongues and teeth," he advised, "and talk about flutter tongue technique to the flautists. If in doubt give the top prize to the youngest class."

I have fond memories of my father and I hope nothing in this book suggests otherwise. But if ever you find yourself judging a music competition involving several hundred teenage girls, take my advice and don't talk about embouchures or about the position of lips, tongues or teeth and never allude to flutter tongue technique. Put it this way, I still occasionally meet women I don't know who give me a wry smile and talk about the happy time they spent at Roedean in the late 1960s.

ONE OF THE LAST bits of *Superstar* to be recorded was "King Herod's Song." The simple answer to the question "why a vaudeville song?" is that it felt right. Every instinct told me that after the full-on intensity of "Gethsemane," our five-minute set piece for Jesus, and before the final scenes of Judas's death, Jesus's trial and the harrowing crucifixion, we badly needed something to puncture and lighten the musical mood. A song that stood out stylistically seemed exactly what the constraints of a record demanded. Listeners could imagine their own picture of King Herod and his court of many colours. Ian Gillan's extraordinary performance of "Gethsemane" was among the last we consigned to tape, along with Murray's deeply felt interpretation of Judas's death. I vividly remember the night we recorded it and how completely wiped out he was when the session was over. These were for me the highlights of the vocal sessions that were now taking place at Island Studios. We had to move to Island as we had used up our booked time in Olympic 2 and Island was the only studio with the same recording desk.

Last to hit the oxide was the orchestra and the choirs which were overdubbed in Olympic Studios. Mixing was a slow process. Computer memory was far in the future, so Alan O'Duffy had to remember a huge number of complex balancing moves. The overture, for instance, with its synthesizers, heavy rock band, chamber orchestra section, full orchestra and classical choir all featured in two minutes, was a case in point. Sometimes we would settle on a less than perfect mix just because it felt right. If you listen very carefully to the two bars before the big orchestral "Superstar" chords in the overture you will hear Alan Doggett counting the orchestra in with a "one, two, three, four." We'd forgotten to switch his track off.

One sequence was cut. St Matthew in his Gospel summarizes its plot rather succinctly. "And seeing a fig tree by the wayside he went to it and found nothing on it but only leaves. And he said to it, 'May no fruit ever come from you again!' And the fig tree withered." Tim wrote his own version of Jesus's curse including the couplet "I hope your leaves go brown / May a vandal chop you down." Like the fig tree this sequence shrivelled out of our album.

Brian Brolly arranged a listening session for the British MCA/ Universal bigwigs at Advision Studios in central London. About ten mostly besuited execs turned up, some of them ruefully asking how long the album was and would there be a pee break in the playback? (It was after lunch.) David Land hustled in his mate Cyril Simons, our publisher and boss of MCA Leeds Music, all the while elaborating on his now familiar monologue about how this would go down at the Marble Arch Synagogue. When playback finished there was a lengthy silence. It was punctured by Cyril. Turning first to David Land and then to the assembled honchos he gloomily intoned, "There's not a lot here for Ruby Murray."*

---

* Ruby Murray was an Irish balladeer, popular in Britain in the Fifties, whose last hit in the UK charts had been in 1959 – a world away.

This was the first verdict passed on *Jesus Christ Superstar*.

Brian himself, however, was truly ecstatic. Almost as enthusiastic was Mike Leander. It was Mike who suggested that we added "Superstar" to the working title "Jesus Christ." Everyone agreed, it seemed so blindingly obvious. Very soon we learned that the American record company was if not on cloud nine at least pushing cloud eight and a half. Our double album was scheduled for British release on October 16 with America following a week later.

BY NOW IT WAS early July and time to head to Auntie Vi, but this time with a twist: her nephew was not just passionate about musicals but insanely consumed by affairs of the heart. During the last weeks of recording my beloved Sarah had been dispatched on a working holiday to a family in France and had fetched up in the deep southwest town of Albi. I was hugely missing her and slightly envious of her too as I have always wanted to check out Albi's pink-bricked cathedral and still haven't. Although her parents were a bit twitchy, the plan was that she would then join me at La Mortola. I guess they must have weighed up that she would only mope at home and make Ophelia seem like a rib-cracking stand-up act. This posed a delicate issue for broadminded Auntie. Sarah was now only just seventeen and there was only one spare bedroom.

A simple solution was found: I was kicked out. The Neames were away and I was banished to the maid's room in their villa next door. The maid, if indeed there was one, must have had something highly distasteful in her blood because no other way could she have survived the army of mosquitoes that caused Dr George to worry if I had smallpox. Soon I was back in my old bedroom and passion resumed as usual, constrained only by serious itching. Sarah and I were well and truly in deepest young love territory with moonlit dinners by the sea at La Punta and love songs composed on Vi's piano. The only blot was that the test records I had brought with me so Vi could hear *JCS* had been largely destroyed by a bottle of aftershave that broke open in my suitcase on the flight to Nice. The only bit that was playable was "King Herod's Song," so Auntie for months tried to enthuse over an opera about Jesus written entirely in the style of English music hall.

The idyll nosedived when a telegram arrived from Sarah's mother ordering her home at once. Her elder sister Olivia had been very seriously mugged in New York and had been flown back to Britain. Sarah's mum wanted her by her side. Quite what good Sarah could do back home eluded her. It was the busiest weekend of the summer and not only were the flights overbooked but the traffic queues at the old border between Italy and France were a nightmare. The only way to get to Nice Airport was by car and elderly George was the only chauffeur. Sarah got a stay of execution for two days but of course when she got home she was bollocked for failing to conjure up a non-existent plane seat. Olivia was all right but had received a very serious blow to her head. She needed total rest without younger sisters fussing about. I stayed on a week feeling generally deprived and morose and composing lovelorn dirges.

I HAD ONLY JUST hit the homeland when there was an urgent message to call David Land. Cyril Simons had belatedly discovered I had written "excluding Grand Rights" on the *Superstar* song publishing contract. David wanted to know what I meant. I reiterated what Bob Kingston had told me, that they were the theatre and film rights and it was vital we kept them for ourselves. I got the feeling David doubted an album with nothing on it for Ruby Murray would make even tiny waves on the stage let alone the screen. However he said he would come with me and together we would battle it out with Cyril. A meeting was arranged at Leeds Music's presidential offices at the bottom of Park Lane. My night before didn't brim with sleep. Any future for *Jesus Christ Superstar* beyond a double album depended entirely on the outcome of this meeting. Did David remotely understand what was at stake?

The Grand Rights meeting went approximately thus. I'm sorry about the jokes, they were stale even in 1970.

Land: Morning Cyril.

Simons: Morning Land. Make this quick. I need songs for Ruby's album by lunchtime.

Land: The boy wants the Grand Rights. How do we know Jesus was Jewish?

Simons: How do we know Jesus was Jewish, Land?

Land: He lived in his parents' house till he was 30, worked for his dad and his mama thought he was God. This is an opera, Cyril, so I want the scores bound.

Simons: I want you bound, Land. What are these Grand Rights?

Land: Don't know, Cyril, you're the publisher you should know.

Simons: I've got to find ten songs for Ruby and let me tell you the boy's songs aren't one of them.

Land: Just give the boy the Grand Rights, Cyril.

Simons: How can I give away what I don't know I've got?

Land: Ask the boy what they are.

Simons: You ask the boy what they are. You're his agent.

Land: You ask him.

Simons: What are Grand Rights? Make this quick.

Me: Er . . . they mean if you go to the theatre . . .

Simons: Heard the one about the Jewish mother and the school play?

Land: Yes, Cyril, but you're going to tell me anyway.

Simons: Boy tells mama he's been cast as the Jewish husband, mama says bubbeleh go back to the teacher and tell him you want a speaking part, listen Land for once and for all, what are these rights?

Land: I've told you I don't know, they're to do with shows, the boy
   wants them that's all . . .

Simons: *(interrupting)* Look, Land, who wants to hear loud show
   music and pay for it unless they take their clothes off like that loud
   American hippy show . . .

Land: *(interrupting)* This isn't a loud American hippy show, it's a loud
   show about Jesus and the boy wants . . .

Simons: *(interrupting)* I know what the boy wants but you don't know
   what the boy wants so how do I know what it is the boy wants if
   you can't tell me what he wants so . . .

Land: *(interrupting)* Why not just give him what he wants if he wants
   it so badly and then we can . . .

Simons: *(tetchily)* OK the boy can have them but tell him he needs to
   write something a bit mellower if he wants Ruby to . . . [etc. etc.]

That's how I got back the entire theatre and film rights to *Jesus
Christ Superstar*. To this day I wonder whether David Land was utterly clueless or played a total blinder. Something tells me it was the
latter.

12

JCS Meets RSO

I first heard that Sefton Myers was seriously ill three days before the album release date. It came as a complete shock but with hindsight it was obvious something was wrong. He kept cancelling a meeting I asked for to download what Bob Kingston had told me about theatre and music publishing. One afternoon I was waiting in vain in his office when I couldn't help noticing an unsigned letter lying on his desk. It was headed "Andrew Lloyd Webber/Tim Rice/New Ventures Theatrical Management Ltd" (the name of his holding company). It was a reply to a missive from his bank manager and it said he would cancel our contract and pay Tim and me off if *Superstar* flopped. I wondered whether to tell Tim but decided not to. So everything was riding on the album and the first signs weren't encouraging.

Brian Brolly had gone into complete overdrive with the album sleeve. He commissioned a package that opened up into a star and revealed a load of hideous children's drawings of Jesus. Unfortunately the star's edges were made of the sort of wafer-thin cardboard that slices your fingers open. Maybe someone thought that blood-inducing copies of an album called *Jesus Christ Superstar* was a marketing move too far. Hastily it was withdrawn and replaced with a conventional sleeve. We had personally sent an advance copy to Derek Jewell, the *Sunday Times* critic whose *Joseph* review kick-started our careers. I don't know what it did to his fingers, but next Sunday he pronounced that *Superstar* would find life tough as it would be "caught in the crossfire" of people offended by a rock treatment of Jesus and rock fans who thought the subject was uncool.

In reality it was met with a massive dose of British indifference, even condescension. There were a few nice comments, but as there were no big names involved I doubt if any of the major rock critics heard the whole thing out. Before I had too much time to fret we were told to get ready to fly to America for two weeks. MCA USA had decided there would be launches in New York, Los Angeles and Toronto. They were to be in "low-key" churches which I pessimistically presumed meant the USA reaction would also be tepid to cool. David Land said at least the American company was going through the motions, so we should smile and give it our best shot. Two first-class TWA air tickets arrived at the office which we changed to Air India because I thought the in-flight food would be more interesting. Over an onion bhaji I pondered the odds of New Ventures Theatrical Management Ltd giving us the heave-ho by Christmas.

THE SIZE OF THE stretch limo was the first inkling that MCA Records might be sniffing something. We were greeted by two record execs and a bouncy publicist called Barry Kittleson. It was in the back of the stretch monster that we first saw the American album packaging. We were confronted with a plain brown opera box adorned with a simple inlaid logo of a pair of facing golden angels that looked a bit like a bangle. Inside was an elegant oblong booklet containing the cast list and the lyrics. I was taken aback. It couldn't have been further from the lethal finger scyther back home. I totally failed to spot that those angels would become the first mega logo in musical theatre history. Next we were ushered into suites in the now demolished Drake Hotel. It may have been a fading Manhattan grand dame but I had never stayed in a place like it.

The record execs turned out to be Dick Broderick, the boss of the New York MCA office, and a guy who was to be our minder called

Ellis Nassour who had written real estate columns for the *New York Times* and vaguely knew its feared theatre critic, a Brit called Clive Barnes. Mr Broderick cashed in on the *Superstar* saga with a book that claimed I was an alcoholic. I can't blame him. Pretty much on arrival we were told we could order anything we liked from room service. My eye alighted on the Drake Hotel wine list. Tell me, what is a boy supposed to do if room service has the best list of 1945 red burgundy he has seen and someone else is paying? Most of it was undrinkable as the Drake had failed to cellar it properly and its destination was the sink. But that wouldn't have been obvious to Mr Broderick when his office processed the bill.

The publicist Barry Kittleson said he'd brief us in the morning, but for now we should read a folder full of the early press comments and reviews. They were staggering. What totally poleaxed me was *Time* magazine which was eulogistic about the music. I phoned Sarah whose mother was none too pleased because I had forgotten that back home it was one in the morning.

The next few days are a blur. The New York playthrough may have been in a low-key church, but the Q&A afterwards revealed a phalanx of critics and feature writers who were anything but B-list. I was terrified and Tim did most of the talking. When Tim's latest girlfriend pitched up in town, an urbane lady called Sara Bennett-Levy, things got too much for me and I hibernated in my hotel room penning lovelorn letters to Sarah. Next we made an LP of answers to scripted questions so DJs around the US could pretend they were interviewing us by popping their own versions of questions like "Do *you* think Jesus Christ was what they said he was?" and "If Jesus came back now, would he have flowers in his hair?" in the gaps.

That evening I got a message to call "Tony." It transpired to be Sarah's dad who was in New York doing whatever he really did. It was a blessed relief from being second fiddle to the super-couple. We had a seriously old-fashioned dinner in the hotel restaurant, debated where

New York restaurants got their rubbery shrimps from and a novel Tony was thinking of writing about his wartime spying experiences in Portugal. It didn't hurt my chances of acquiring a father-in-law when I ostentatiously signed the bill, knowing MCA would pick it up.

Next up was a repeat operation in Los Angeles. I fell in love with tinsel town from get go. The bustling pavement cafes and the bougainvillea caressed trees reminded me of Auntie Vi and my beloved La Mortola. We did a repeat playthrough in a functional modern church hall off Vine and gave an exclusive one-on-one interview with a caricature John Lennon granny-glassed critic from *Rolling Stone* straight out of central casting. A gorgeous looking swimming instructress named Mimosa fastened on me saying she could teach me how to sing "Elusive Butterfly" underwater. I asked her to prove it. She certainly gave new meaning to the line "something there that glided past you followed close by heavy breathing." Much to Tim's delight, who was on his own now, we met a micro-skirted cross-legged Linda Ronstadt in a house on the ocean in a vain quest to have her record "I Don't Know How to Love Him." Next we were freighted to Toronto where we were album of the hour. MCA abandoned the handsome opera box and replaced it with a bog-standard gatefold sleeve because they couldn't manufacture the boxes quick enough.

The backlash started when we got back to New York. *New York* magazine pronounced the album a cynical piece of marketing exploitation cashing in on the zeitgeist of "Spirit in the Sky" and the "Jesus Movement." Since back home neither had resonated in the way the review described, it seemed grossly unfair. It was then pretty much a lone voice, but it was a harbinger of things to come.

BACK IN BLIGHTY WE megabumped back to reality. Outside our inner circle the word was that *Jesus Christ Superstar* was headed for the curiosity shop. But I had something more important on my mind. Sarah. We both had missed each other terribly. Although after my dinner with her dad in New York her parents had clocked that her curious boyfriend might have a vague future, they were anxious to remind me she was still a schoolgirl. So they imposed a strict curfew that she must be home by 11:30 pm which was made up for by her clandestine visits to my flat in the morning after she clocked in at school. I was thrilled in late November when they made a great point of asking me to stay at their country home for Christmas.

Back at Harrington Court the news wasn't brilliant. Granny Molly's health was declining fast. Her arthritis had become unbearable and for huge chunks of the day there was nobody to look after her when Mum and Dad were at work. I booked a call to Vi and George. My *Superstar* news delighted them, but when I suggested we got Molly into a nursing home they became surprisingly distant. I asked our family doctor to help. Before he could even see her, MCA Records urgently needed us back in New York. Granny would have none of me staying to sort things out and Mum insisted she would cope. So after a tearful two hours with Sarah it was back to Heathrow Airport.

It was around then that David Land told us that Sefton Myers had terminal cancer. He explained that the runaway success of *Superstar* meant that New Ventures Theatrical Management now had a real value and the family would have to sell the company for death duties. It threw me completely off balance. I had always hoped that if we were successful we would tear up our management contracts and partner up in business with Sefton. He and I spoke the same language. Much as I had grown hugely fond of David Land, I saw the future with Sefton. Tim and I were about to lose the mind that could steer us through the minefield of overnight success precisely when we needed it.

The minefield manifested itself in the form of a hotel suite that resembled the Chelsea Flower Show on the eve of a visit by the Queen. Congratulatory notes from theatre producers who "would be honored to meet" peeped from mighty gladioli and an invitation to the opening of *Hay Fever* at the Helen Hayes Theatre was aptly accompanied by monster scented lilies with huge stamens which stained two of my fingers yellow for weeks. However the most eye-watering attraction was the limo sent by Robert Stigwood. The poor thing looked like it had been stretched on the automobile version of the rack. David Land had instructed us firmly that should the Australian pop magnate summon us we were to sit up and take notice. Thus it was that on an early November weekday night we met the man who had refused us Eric Clapton. Little did we know that night that he was about to play a key role in our lives for the next few years.

Stigwood had rented a vast townhouse on East 78th Street. Not that you would think it was rented. Robert had imported a butler from England (who I learned years later ran off with the silver) and was holding court as if the fabric of Manhattan society would rend asunder without him. Dom Pérignon flowed like a river in spate, although he himself drank rum and coke in large quantities with no evident effect. My request for white wine elicited Le Montrachet, Le Domaine de la Romanée-Conti of course. But what impressed Tim most was that Robert's house guest was none other than Peter Brown, the legendary fifth Beatle as Tim informed me in the limo afterwards since I hadn't a clue who he was. Peter was a close friend of The Beatles and had been an even more intimate friend of their manager Brian Epstein dating right back to their early Liverpool days.

I learned years later how he fitted into the Stigwood firmament. Robert was an Australian who burst onto the British show business scene in 1960 as the manager of actor/singer John Leyton. He was a pioneer in more ways than one. Through London's gay scene he met Sir Joseph Lockwood, the chairman of EMI, whom he charmed into releasing John Leyton's singles by making the first-ever lease tape deal, i.e. Robert made the master recordings and leased them to EMI for a period of time, after which they reverted to him. Nothing like this had ever been done in the record business before. Record companies made and owned everything. Sadly Robert went bankrupt shortly afterwards producing package pop concerts. He subsequently went under twice more. Most recently Robert had gone belly up promoting a young milkman from Coventry called Simon Scott. He had blitzed every major British DJ with lifesize busts of his baby-faced protégé to propel his single "Move It Baby" chartwards. Inconveniently it didn't move. So Robert wound up a lodger in a flat owned by Terence Stamp's famous looker of a brother Chris who managed The Who and Jimi Hendrix.

One evening Chris was paid a visit by Peter Brown. Brian Epstein came along for the ride and took an instant shine to Robert. Not long afterwards Epstein asked the blond Australian to join the management arm of NEMS Enterprises, the company through which he managed The Beatles and his other big Liverpool acts. Stigwood soon was key to the success of new NEMS signings like Eric Clapton and Cream. Robert was close to a young city whizz-kid called David Shaw, a pioneer of a notorious tax planning scheme called "bond washing," whose bad books I got into three years later when I created a fictitious band called The Bond Washers.

One weekend the trinity of Brian, Robert and David disappeared to Paris. To The Beatles' and everyone at NEMS's horror, Brian returned to say he was merging his business with Robert and that David Shaw would steer the new company to the Stock Exchange. The fallout was so frightful that this never happened. But from then on any previous resentment The Beatles and the original Epstein artists had for Robert quadrupled. So when Brian died in August 1967 and Robert was the obvious successor to the empire, The Beatles and Cilla Black would have none of it. Robert left NEMS, taking with him his main acts like Clapton and Cream plus a new signing, three brothers: Barry, Maurice and Robin Gibb, who called themselves the Bee Gees. Robert blamed Peter Brown for The Beatles rebuffing him, but in reality there was nothing Peter could have done.

The distrust the Fab Four harboured for Stigwood wasn't allayed by his championing of the Gibb brothers who just happened to be writing rather good songs at a time when things were becoming highly sensitive in The Beatles camp. Someone even spread a rumour that the brothers had drawn lots to decide who should take one for the team with Robert or Brian as the way to get a contract with NEMS. The muck-spreaders soon looked stupid. In a short time Robert steered the Bee Gees to huge international success. Furthermore Robert now independently had his own fistful of highly valuable acts. So he took a huge gamble. Ever the chancer, he came up with the wheeze of doing with David Shaw what he had been stymied from doing with Brian Epstein. He would float the Robert Stigwood Organisation on the London Stock Exchange. Shaw was smart and bundled a few other media companies under the Stigwood Organisation umbrella so it looked to the City like it was a multi-faceted kosher outfit. The Robert Stigwood Organisation (RSO) made its debut on the London Stock Exchange in 1969 in one of the most disastrous flotations ever. But Robert now had paper shares with a quoted price.

It was those shares that were so attractive to the team surrounding the terminally ill Sefton Myers. Robert merely had to issue Sefton Myers and David Land RSO shares with a paper value to acquire the company that owned 25% of Tim and my earnings. Furthermore, by acquiring our management contract Stigwood could automatically steer our work to his own production company. From Sefton's advisors' perspective they now had shares whose value could be crystallized for death duties whilst maintaining via Stigwood stock an interest in Tim's and my fate. It was no wonder that before we knew it we had a new manager and a producer to boot. New Ventures Theatrical Management was sold to the Robert Stigwood Organisation.

Robert was, as ever, smart. Before we had time to get independent advice he gave us an instant cash advance of £15,000 each. (Today

£238,500.) It was more money than we had ever seen and of course by banking it we tacitly agreed to the takeover. David Land was retained as our day-to-day point person through a new company called Superstar Ventures which operated out of his Wardour Street offices, thus providing a semblance of independence from the main Stigwood HQ in Mayfair. But the truth was a mere few weeks after our record was released we had been gobbled up by a publicly quoted company fronted by the biggest gambler in show business.

When I returned to London the doubts set in. Waiting at my flat was a telegram. It had been sent to my parents' address and they hadn't realized it was important. It read:

I AM THE PRODUCER OF WEST SIDE STORY, FIDDLER ON THE ROOF AND CABARET AND WISH TO ACQUIRE THE RIGHTS TO PRODUCE AND DIRECT JESUS CHRIST SUPERSTAR. PLEASE CONTACT SOONEST. HAROLD PRINCE.

I literally buried my head in my hands. The Stigwood deal was done. Besides, when I asked David Land if it was too late to add Broadway's leading producer and director to the mix he had absolutely no clue who he was. I can't help wondering how different my career would have been if that telegram had found me sooner and Hal Prince had directed that first *Jesus Christ Superstar* Broadway production.

ISN'T IT STRANGE HOW some dates, phone numbers and the like etch themselves on the brain while others don't? No matter how long the gap between working together, I can remember lyricist Don Black's home phone number in a heartbeat. Quiz me on my private office line and I glaze over. It's the same with show openings. I can remember *Cats* London but not *Phantom*. I can do *Phantom* NY but *Cats* is early Alzheimer's. I only remember two dates in 1970. January 21, when I met Sarah, and November 22. That's when I met Peter Brown properly for the first time. He was no longer the fifth Beatle. Now he was President of the Robert Stigwood Organisation USA.

Tim and I had flown back together from Los Angeles, this time plus David Land. The three of us had been meeting with Stigwood in La La Land about a possible *Superstar* movie. Norman Jewison, director of *In the Heat of the Night* and *The Thomas Crown Affair*, had contacted MCA/Universal about helming a film, so we all met with Ned Tanen, head of Universal Studios, who had just been informed by legal that he didn't have automatic rights to any film thanks to the meeting with Cyril Simons and David a few weeks back. Not that this inhibited him from presuming that Universal was the movie's only natural home.

I liked Ned. He and Norman agreed that any film would be based on the record and not screwed up by added dialogue. Furthermore Norman Jewison was directing the movie of *Fiddler on the Roof*. So he had street cred not only with steering a musical from stage to screen but also with a Jewish story. He sounded the perfect fit and the meeting was as positive as meetings always are in Hollywood. Ninety-nine percent of the time you leave buzzing with the fantastic power pow-wows you've had and then never hear from anyone again, but this meeting proved the exception.

David, Tim and I took the Sunday morning flight from LAX and arrived at Kennedy in the early evening where we were met by Stigwood's new US chief. Peter has impeccable manners so deeply impregnated in his DNA that it was unthinkable that he wouldn't greet RSO's new wunderkinds at the airport himself, even if it did mean fouling up his Sunday night. Peter was charm and courtesy personified and naturally offered us dinner but couldn't hide his relief when Tim and David said they were knackered and wanted to head hotelwards. I, however, was firmly on Pacific time. I had denied myself the ghastly American Airlines catering and was highly hot to trot to a decent watering hole. Peter's face dropped a visible inch when I perkily said that dinner was just my ticket.

What had fazed him, Peter explained to me over a third bottle four hours later, was that no decent restaurants were open in New York on a Sunday night, incredible to believe half a century later. I don't remember where we went and neither does Peter. But that was the night I met my oldest, loyalest and dearest friend. Peter and I bonded so firmly that we were still nattering at 2 am on Monday morning. I learned that his parents hailed from the Wirral, the smart opposite bank of the Mersey to Liverpool. He had worked in Brian Epstein's family record store and therefore knew The Beatles and Cilla Black from the start. Despite this he had no hint of a Liverpudlian accent, but then Epstein sounded almost as plummy as the Queen.

Peter was Epstein's closest confidant and his premature death obviously affected him deeply, even though he must have seen it coming. We didn't have friends in common, our worlds were very different then, but we found in each other that something you can't put into words or, for that matter, music. In the ensuing years we have both been through pretty seismic ups and downs, but our friendship has never once wavered. Years later Cilla Black and I played a beastly trick on Peter. He had become the doyen of high-powered New York publicists, with clients ranging from Nancy Reagan via the BBC to the state of Qatar and his accent had matured to match. Cilla and I invented a BBC radio show called "How They Sounded" and told Peter that the producers had got hold of some tapes of him from the late Fifties and he was the second subject after Margaret Thatcher. This sent him into such a tailspin that he phoned the BBC Director General begging him to kill the programme. Cilla also confided that in his record-stacking days Peter was nicknamed Peggy Banger due to his addiction to sausages.

· · ·

BACK IN BRITAIN I proposed to Sarah which was a stupid formality. We had long presumed we would get hitched as soon as she legally could. I had the cash to buy a smart BMW 2002 so as an unofficial engagement present to Sarah I gave her my old Mini which she promptly drove into the back of a lorry on the Earl's Court Road. More serious was the Granny situation. It was blindingly obvious that it was way too much of a problem to look after her at Harrington Court but my parents still wanted to keep her at home. They claimed they kept a watchful eye on her but the poor woman could hardly get out of bed. The trickiest thing was that although nothing was said I sensed my parents resented my worrying.

I decided to tackle Vi and George in person. The vagaries of the Italian parcel post system gave me an excuse to fly down to La Mortola clutching a box of *Superstar* sets which they wanted for Christmas presents. If anything they were even more distant about Granny. Auntie Vi was as outrageous as ever, she was very taken with a Russian recipe she'd concocted called Boyar's Sole, but it was like she was giving a performance to change the subject. They asked fondly after Sarah and eyebrows only shot up a centimetre or two when I told them I was going to get married as soon as we legally could.

In mid-December, David, Tim and I went to a big meeting at Robert's estate in Stanmore, a village which in the eighteenth century boasted the country seat of the Duke of Chandos. Now it's a northwest London suburb. Robert's mansion was a curiosity, a sixteenth-century half-timbered house that he said had literally been transported from Worcestershire. It lurked in a large, landscaped garden that had all the rock mogul trimmings – a swimming pool, tennis court and a gypsy caravan fabled for shenanigans etched in the rock'n'roll hall of infamy. I was totally overawed. In truth I found all the early Stigwood meetings really difficult. Tim was revelling in the new surroundings and David Land just acted the court jester as expensive bottle after expensive bottle was served up by beautiful house boys. It was like a scene out of *La Dolce Vita*. Reality seemed millions of miles away and I felt cripplingly shy. Robert announced that he was slating a Broadway production of *Superstar* for next fall.

It didn't take long for Tim and David to get revved up about billing. Tim was worried that as his name was shorter than mine he would get less space on the posters. David's solution was simple. Our names would be in separate, equal-sized boxes – "Like in *Variety* at the London Palladium, the Cyril Ornadel Orchestra gets all bunched up but Yana's name looks huge." I have long been baffled about Tim's preoccupation with billing. On all our shows he has insisted his name goes first. I couldn't care less. I just think Lloyd Webber and Rice sounds better than the other way round, as does Rodgers (music) and Hammerstein (lyrics) whilst Gilbert (lyrics) and Sullivan (music), Lerner (lyrics) and Loewe (music) have a far better lilt than the reverse. It's not just with me. With Elton it's Rice and John, though I can't make a huge case for John and Rice sounding better.

Much more important though was to discuss the show's creative team. A boozy pre-Christmas lunch was certainly not the moment to do so, let alone to drop in the name Hal Prince. During the chauffeured drive back to my flat in Robert's beautiful vintage white Rolls-Royce, I wondered whether there'd ever be a right time to drop in Hal's name, let alone have a serious creative discussion.

I ASKED MY PARENTS if they'd like something special for Christmas and drew a total blank so I bought them a fridge. The Harrington Court antique should have been condemned as a health hazard decades ago. Filial duties thus discharged, on Christmas Eve I drove Sarah in my boy-racer BMW to her parents' Gloucestershire home in Ashton Keynes near Cirencester. The Hugill clan was out in force. Gathered together were Tony's brother Michael, mathematician and headmaster of Whitgift School, her two elder sisters Olivia and Victoria, Olivia still rather weak after her New York ordeal, her younger brother Charles and her maternal Granny Imogen, widow of the High Sheriff of Rutland. Imogen Gore Browne was a character straight out of *Downton Abbey*. Sarah and I once took her to a restaurant in Chelsea where she eyed up the menu over a large glass of sherry before pronouncing censoriously, "You can always judge a restaurant by whether it has hot puddings." It hadn't.

Christmas Day passed in a haze of church, presents, more church, and a strange family version of mah-jong, the gambling game you see on the street corners of Hong Kong. I think the family was relieved when they prised out that I was politically a left of centre Conservative. The success of *Superstar* had not been lost on the American side of the family. Father Huntingdon, after all, had been behind the New York premiere of *Joseph* and as the first man to present a Lloyd Webber/Rice – sorry, Rice/Lloyd Webber – show in the USA was arguably way ahead of the entire Broadway pack. Come Boxing Day it was time to raise what the whole family knew was coming – a date for our wedding which Sarah and I wanted to be yesterday. Sarah's parents were adamant that she finished school so at least she had got grades in something. Then we could marry away to our hearts' content. We planned the wedding day for July 24, barely six weeks after Sarah turned eighteen.

Next day Tony not unreasonably wanted to have a frank conversation about my financial future. There was zero guarantee that *Superstar* and I weren't one-hit wonders. However, it was clear that our album was going global with only Britain the odd man out. Tony wanted me to meet an investment advisor called John Carington and, come the New Year, to get an independent review of where things stood.

Tim and I had never received any tax advice. Tim delightfully maintained that he would love a tax problem because it would mean he was rich. I can't say I find tax a scintillating subject but I soon learned that there's nothing like an 83% going on 98% income tax rate to concentrate the mind. It was through John Carington that I met John Avery Jones, perhaps the finest tax mind of his generation. John got our *Superstar* activities on a proper footing but not before I was put into a supposedly unbeatable tax efficient forestry scheme. I was steered into buying a mountainside in Wales, where I upset the system by insisting on planting hardwood rather than baby fir trees. No matter your tax problem, don't get into forestry. My forest developed a sinkhole of such national importance a large chunk of it had to be roped off. Soon, as those who read on will discover, it burnt down.

1970 WAS THE BEGINNING of a property bubble, so banks like Coutts were all too ready to fuel it with mortgage deals. I had been desperate to live in the country since I was little. Now Robert's advance meant that I had plenty to fund a deposit on something not too grand, so Sarah and I went on a househunting spree. Gothic fantasists will understand why we settled on a farmhouse on the Wiltshire/Dorset border. It was close by where William Beckford, that infamous nabob of worrying sexuality, built the ultimate romantic Gothic folly Fonthill Abbey in wild countryside that today is still remote and stunning. Unfortunately its legendary 200 foot octagon collapsed and the mansion that beat Disneyland to it is but a memory. By the following May our rather less showy farmhouse was up and running. With a combined age of 39, Sarah and I had set up our first home.

In mid-January Granny was taken into hospital a few days before *Superstar* went into the US Top 10. When I told her she replied "That's wonderful darling, but are you getting enough to eat?" The hospital was vague about what was wrong with her but her arthritis was beyond debilitating and a nursing home now seemed inevitable. My parents were insistent that they and Vi and George sorted everything out, my mother adding that I really must concentrate on my career as I might never get this opportunity again. To be fair, to the day she died Mum maintained that people have an almost religious responsibility to exploit any talent they have above everything else.

In February my eye was taken off the ball Granny-wise by a phone call from Columbia Pictures. They were in trouble with *Gumshoe*, but they loved the music. Would I compose some more? I talked it over with David Land. We had forgotten about *Gumshoe* and it was curious that the film hadn't been released. We discovered that Columbia had funded the movie on the back of Albert Finney. But they thought it was muddled and were re-editing it, hence they needed more work from me. Obviously with *Superstar* strutting its stuff in the US, David could have asked for an arm and a leg, but he advised that we shouldn't. I would get the chance to work alongside a top film editor. I knew nothing about movies and here was a chance to get a well-paid apprenticeship. It would help David's negotiations that I had a Columbia Pictures credit on my CV should Universal make the *Superstar* movie.

I agreed, but I was worried about working without Michael Medwin and Stephen Frears's blessing. They had taken a punt on me before *Superstar* and it was their movie, not mine. But they were fine about it. Stephen and I even discussed Gene Vincent voicing the rock song, a pipe dream that remained exactly that. So I found myself on the best crash master class of my career – and better still I was being paid! The editor Charles Rees was an old-timer who had seen it all. He literally de- and re-constructed the movie in front of me, even altering lengths if I needed a few extra seconds here and there for the music. Intriguingly the *Sunday Times* reviewer Dilys Powell had seen the original cut and reviewed the film as an object lesson in what a skilled editor can do.

Gumshoe still has a cult status of sorts. The music got better reviews back home than *Superstar*.

13

Jesus Goes to Broadway

1971 was rather eventful. I got married; *Superstar* opened on Broadway; I met my hero Richard Rodgers; my father made uncannily accurate prophesies about Tim Rice; Stigwood launched three huge *Superstar* arena tours and Tim and I got a mega putdown from John Fogerty of Creedence Clearwater Revival. This occurred on a flight during the publicity tour when *Superstar* went to No. 1 in the US. We were in a row of three seats – me, Tim and at the end of the row the legendary Mr Fogerty who had boarded in true rock-star fashion at the very last minute. Naturally it was Tim who opened conversation.

"We're huge fans," crawled Rice.

I nodded in obsequious agreement.

"What we love about Creedence is you're a true three-chord band."

Fogerty looked pained.

"Man," he drawled, "we're a two-chord band."

I WAS STILL NURSING the two-chord putdown when I met Richard Rodgers. I was invited to his Manhattan apartment in the Pierre Hotel which I remember being rather dark and rammed with Impressionist paintings. I was greeted very courteously by his wife Dorothy and shown into a sitting room overlooking Central Park. The great man was perched on a ridiculously uncomfortable-looking French armchair. In hindsight I wish he hadn't sent me tickets for his latest Broadway musical *Two by Two* which I had seen the night before. This was the show about Noah's Ark starring Danny Kaye, who infamously created mayhem after breaking his leg and returning to the production in a wheelchair. Mercifully I saw the show pre this event. But it was a creaky, old-fashioned affair with only a hint that the melodic genius behind some of the greatest shows in musical theatre history had composed the score.

I had a day's worth of questions. In his first collaboration with Lorenz Hart did he truly write all the melodies first with the lyrics written to the music? Was it really the other way round with Oscar Hammerstein, or was it a bit of both? Why was his melodic style so different in the two collaborations? "Some Enchanted Evening" doesn't sound like it was by the same composer as "The Lady Is a Tramp." However, Rodgers had his own agenda.

He wanted to know whether I thought the future of the musical was through-sung. Was the day of the "book" musical over – i.e. a show with songs and spoken dialogue? I said that a through-sung musical put the composer in the driving seat but surely it was horses for courses. Today it would be like saying that post *Hamilton* every musical must be written in hip hop.

Next Dick Rodgers – he insisted I call him Dick – gave me three precious insights. The first resonated like an oversized dinner gong. The human ear cannot take in more than two or three melodies at one listening. So was this why we released *Superstar* on record before a stage show? I explained that nobody was interested in producing it and the only way we could get our work heard was through a recording. He said we had hit on something very smart. He repeated that no one, not even he, could take in a crock of melodies in one listening, so critics often said a great score was tuneless or not up to previous best. He cited *The King and I* as a case in point. He said it wasn't until the movie that the score was recognized. I found this astonishing, the score is a classic tunefest, made even more extraordinary as all the main melodies are written within just one octave because its star, Gertrude Lawrence, had a tiny singing range.

Secondly, not all his melodies ended up in the shows where they started. "Getting to Know You," the song Anna sings to the children in *The King and I*, was originally written for *South Pacific* and titled "Suddenly Lucky." He cited it as the perfect example of the wrong tune in the wrong place. In *South Pacific* it was intended for the second lead Lieutenant Cable to sing about his new-found love, the Tonkinese girl Liat. But the melody with its lyric "Suddenly lucky / Suddenly my arms are lucky" was far too flippant and it was replaced with the classic "Younger than Springtime." However, it was perfect for the much flightier moment in *The King and I*.

Thirdly, he complained that critics were afraid of sentiment and are not trained to read musical scores. Who am I to disagree with arguably the greatest melodist of the twentieth century?

BACK IN BRITAIN I found out that Granny had been ensconced in a nursing home in Surrey. The news worried me deeply. Why wasn't she in a home in London? Mum said Vi and George had recommended the place. Had anyone seen her? I asked. The answer was it only happened a few days ago and that the nursing home was a top-drawer establishment trusted by all. Sarah and I drove there immediately and my worst fears were confirmed. We found Granny in a cold, first-floor bedroom of a converted Victorian house straight out of *Bleak House*. She was lying in bed, emaciated, shivering and crying. The shocking pain of her arthritis had crippled her, but the most distressing thing was that she was begging for something to eat. I couldn't find any nursing staff who might have had a vague clue about what was going on so I drove to the village store and bought some basics like bread, ham and cheese which she wolfed down whilst Sarah and I gazed out of the window onto an ugly main road and fought back the tears.

How, why had this happened? I couldn't be bothered to make a scene with whoever ran the place. I just had to get her out of it fast. I found a phone box and called our family doctor, Brian Pigott – the one I had called about Granny before Christmas. Brian had been my uncle's junior partner and had taken over his practice when he retired to Italy. He didn't sound surprised. I told him that we had to find a London nursing home for her immediately and that I would pay. He said that he knew of just the place – in fact he had recommended it to begin with. I told Granny I was moving her to London as soon as possible. She clasped my hand as best she could. I will never forget the sight of those pathetically swollen arthritic fingers or the tears of thanks when I promised her she would be out of this cursed place as soon as I could get everything together.

Brian Pigott moved fast. By the time I had got home, he had arranged for her to be picked up by ambulance and driven to a private nursing home in Pimlico, near Westminster. He warned me he had spoken to Vi and George and that they were furious with me. That evening I talked it all through with Sarah. Neither of us could work out why moving her to London was such a big deal. Next day Granny was moved to a beautifully run nursing home in St George's Square, two doors along from the home of a master who had taught me at Westminster.

She wasn't there long. My beloved Granny died a few days later.

I couldn't go to her cremation. *Superstar* beckoned again, this time somewhere in Europe. I could have cancelled but Granny would have emphatically not wanted me to. Vi and George didn't fly home. They sent flowers. What was the reason everyone was so weird about the woman who had provided the home for my family and done so much for all of us? I didn't put two and two together at the time, but when I took my first faltering steps towards writing this book the penny dropped. Granny had worked for George as a secretary. After a year or so he met her 20-year-old actress daughter Viola. Granny Molly was a very attractive divorcee and George divorced his first wife fairly soon after she worked for him.

George had had an affair with my grandmother and then married her daughter.

EARLY IN THE YEAR we were summoned for lunch at Robert's Stanmore pad to talk about Broadway directors. Things started promisingly. Robert had bought some go-carts he was hugely pleased with, so Tim and I obliged by racing each other round his not inconsiderable grounds. Unfortunately during a promising overtaking move I took a corner too fast and ended up in a rhododendron bush. There followed a touching moment when Rice, perhaps fearing that *Superstar* would be our last work together, abandoned his go-cart and sauntered over to check that his collaborator was all right. Unwittingly he left his go-cart running. From my bushtop vantage point I could see a crisis developing. The go-cart was slowly making its way towards Robert's new swimming pool. Abandoning all thoughts of his injured colleague Tim sprinted manfully after the accelerating vehicle. Every time he tried to grab it, it seemed to edge forward just that little bit faster.

I don't know if the go-cart's performance in the swimming pool was typical of the genre but frankly it got to the middle rather elegantly, merely skimming the surface and giving rise to huge hope that it would make it incident-free to the other side. Then it sank.

Back in the 1950s Noël Coward was asked for an opening night verdict on the actor Edward Woodward in *High Spirits*.

"Edward Woodward," he replied, "sounds like a fart in the bath."

Until its immersion the go-cart's amphibious debut had been gloriously silent. But then it rent the air with a high-pitched shrieking sound like a demented kettle and plummeted to the pool floor in a stream of Edward Woodwards that lasted fully twenty seconds. From nowhere three young men in tight white trousers sprinted, screaming "Oh my God!" to the poolside where a foul looking, dark brown slick was now challenging the water's immaculately balanced pH factor.

Robert was very gracious and feigned far more concern about my split lip, but when lunch was announced something told me once again this was not the moment to raise the Hal Prince issue. During the first course I got hiccups. From my dining-room seat I could see vain attempts to bring Tim's go-cart to the pool surface which was now black. This sideshow rather clobbered conversation. Thankfully the tight-trousered saviours decided their quest was futile just as the main course was dished up. Robert pronounced this was the moment to get real about theatre directors and that we must think "outside the box." With these words I realized that any hope I might have had of Hal Prince getting into the mix was doomed.

Two theatre directors were mooted. I simply can't imagine who suggested the first, Frank Corsaro. Frank was a bona fide, cutting-edge opera director – not an obvious name to come out of the Stigwood firmament. He had recently directed a much talked about production of Janacek's *The Makropulos Affair* and was a regular player at New York City Opera. When we subsequently met I liked him immediately. His idea was that the stage should be filled with banks of TV screens as if the Jesus story was breaking news. It was truly ahead of its time. I had misgivings about how this would work: TV screens were small back then and projection in its infancy, but his knowledge of music and his feeling that the staging should embrace media technology was original and exciting.

The only other candidate, at least presented to us, was Tom O'Horgan, then the "it" man of the theatre because he had directed *Hair*. Stigwood had come across him when he produced the London version. Our meeting did not go well. I don't think I have ever heard such modish bullshit as he spouted and I got the strong feeling he was going through the motions and wasn't genuinely interested in our work. So I strongly urged for Corsaro and that seemed fine with everybody. I never thought to ask why these were the only two names on the table, possibly because a huge issue overtook us that came totally from left field. It led to Stigwood making legal history and establishing case law of massive importance not just for Tim and me but for everyone who today works in musical theatre. This is what happened.

Early 1971 was seeing a mushrooming of *Superstar* concerts in the US presented by opportunist producers who saw a fantastic opportunity to quickly cash in on our album's runaway success. There had never been a through-sung dramatic piece that could be produced in concert quite like this before. Consequently there was no legal precedent to stop anyone simply hiring any old musicians and singers, taking a huge hall and charging the public what they could get whilst paying us practically nothing for our work, let alone caring about performance standards. By simply arguing they were presenting the songs of an album in concert, these promoters paid only the basic standard performing license fee for the songs rather than a box office royalty, whilst passing off that theirs was a properly authorized concert.

Stigwood leapt into action. Peter Brown suggested he hired music business lawyer Lee Eastman to put an injunction on every producer he discovered presenting what he called "unauthorized" performances. I got to know Eastman's son John, whose sister Linda was to marry Paul McCartney. Together with a highly effective advocate Robert Osterberg, the Eastmans ensured that Stigwood was successful in injuncting most of these performances. The saga ended in what John Eastman describes as a "critically important judgement" in our favour in the US Court of Appeals Second Circuit. It defined grand rights performances for the first time and established that a complete dramatic work performed in concert, even if performed without staging, was a grand right. It is impossible to overestimate how much today's composers, authors and producers owe to what Stigwood with Eastman and Osterberg achieved with this judgement.

But getting an injunction was one thing. Enforcing it was another. I remember a judge telling us that *Superstar* had gone so huge it would never be possible to prevent every "unauthorized" performance. The only way to beat these pirate producers was to mount our own versions like yesterday.

Robert's experience as a pop promoter now stood us in huge stead. No 1970s theatre producer could remotely have achieved what he now did. First he realized he could not take on the US single-handed so he brought in Universal as a partner, a by-product of which was that our US album royalties were doubled to equal the British royalty rate. He hired the William Morris Agency and its top booker Steve Leber to set up the tour. Then he linked arms with me. No rock tour had featured a full symphony orchestra before and Robert realized I was key to getting the concerts right. I worried about them clashing with my upcoming wedding, but he turned on his considerable charm and assured me all would be well.

ROBERT SLATED THE TOUR to begin at the Pittsburgh Civic Arena on July 12, leaving plenty of time for me to be home for nuptials on the 24th. So I wound up as musical honcho of the biggest rock touring behemoth attempted to date. Casting was vital. We had to have names from the album to give us credibility and distinguish us from the pirates. Yvonne Elliman was a natural choice and Barry Dennen came on board on condition that he was confirmed for Broadway. But there was no way we could get our original Judas and Jesus. Murray Head was pursuing his film career and Ian Gillan was committed to Deep Purple. After hastily arranged auditions, two clear favourites emerged: African American Carl Anderson as Judas and a rock singer from Texas Jeff Fenholt as JC.

The big issue now was the sound. In those days live sound mixing engineers were virtually unheard of. Rock bands set themselves up on stage, did their own balance and that was about that. The concept of balancing individually close-miked voices was way off anyone's radar, let alone plus a 60-piece orchestra and full chorus. Ideally someone had to be found who could actually read music! In the end that proved too difficult and we ended up with a guy with a script and me shouting cues down his ear.

I shudder to think what an audience would make of the sound today. The orchestral amplification was a few boom mikes hoisted over the musicians and although we experimented with screens to isolate the rock players, the truth was that the orchestral mikes picked up everything. Still the rock band, 60-piece orchestra, soloists, choir and our three "soul" girls made an impressive sight.

The need to get the concerts up and running fast meant rehearsal time was short. I was so immersed that it wasn't until a nervous dinner before our Pittsburgh debut that I asked Robert when Tim would be turning up. Apparently he was now scared of flying and preferred travelling on ocean liners. So he was giving these early shows a miss. I remember how much I wished he could have seen the excitement outside the arena with the ticket touts plying their trade and over ten thousand people jostling to hear our rock opera live for the first time. How far away it seemed from the Stoke Edith House Hotel. I sat next to Robert by the primitive sound desk and watched the audience file almost reverently into the massive arena. Even the seats behind the stage had been sold. When we started there wasn't the usual massive cheer. The audience seemed strangely muted, even after Yvonne gave a blinding performance of "I Don't Know How to Love Him." I was slightly panicked. Robert told me not to worry and to wait till the end of "King Herod's Song." Jeff was a bit tentative at the start of "Gethsemane" but nailed the top notes brilliantly. Still the audience seemed down. Then it was "King Herod's Song." Robert was right. The audience went totally ballistic. It was like the lid being taken off a pressure cooker. The first-ever live performance ended in triumph.

But why did the audience behave like they were at a seance for so long? The answer wasn't complicated. Because *Jesus Christ Superstar* was constructed for records none of the songs had theatrical applause grabbing endings. Our aim had been to get the story from A to B as quickly as possible. The only song with any sort of big finish was "King Herod's Song." Some of the songs do have endings now. Theatregoers like to be reassured that their neighbours are enjoying themselves. But I believe *Jesus Christ Superstar* works best the closer it is to a well-staged concert. That Pittsburgh premiere remains one of the most precious moments of my career.

By next morning Robert had gone into overdrive. Despite the announcement that our "official" concert tour was up and running, rogue concerts were still sprouting everywhere. Now I saw his showman's grasp of an opportunity full frontal. We had the blueprint for the concert. There wouldn't be one, there would be two additional arena tours immediately. The Pittsburgh original would now hoover up the East Coast cities whilst the new identical production would play the West Coast. Eventually the two tours would cross over in middle America, giving repeat concerts on the coast they hadn't played. The second new tour would play a scaled-down version for towns with smaller venues.

He was as good as his chutzpah. By the fall, three arena tours were plying the USA. I was about to head home and prepare for the wedding when Robert nabbed me, saying he needed me at one more performance. Before the show we had a catch up about Broadway where we discussed trying out some possible additional material on the tour. I asked whether Frank Corsaro had yet finalized anything with the design team. Two young men, Peter Neufeld and Tyler Gatchell, had been engaged as the Broadway "line producers," i.e. the guys who oversaw the nuts and bolts of the show from contracting the actors to getting the sets built at the right price. They were surprisingly noncommittal. Tyler Gatchell became one of my closest friends in the Broadway community but back then he didn't know me well enough to confide in me what was going on and anyway my mind was on the wedding and getting home asap.

That evening Tyler and I were braving the crush outside the arena main entrance when I heard a familiar voice.

"Programmes, programmes! only a dollar!" the voice proclaimed. "Programmes, lovely souvenir programmes, cheap . . ." The voice stuttered to a halt when its owner caught sight of me.

There, dressed in a white coat sporting "official" on its back, was none other than David Land. Noticing Tyler, he conspiratorially drew me aside.

"Let's keep this our secret," he whispered. "We can share programme money, you and I, all cash, no questions asked."

"What about Tim?" I muttered.

"He's not here, only you and I need know. Look, Andrew, there's a few bob in this for both of us."

Again I asked if Tim knew about this.

David looked pained. "I was once beaten by my father for nicking threepenny bits," he said.

Probably a good thing too, I said.

"But you see my boy, my dad didn't cane me for stealing three-penny bits. He beat me for stealing *his* threepenny bits."

14

A Bad Case of the Edward Woodwards

Our wedding day dawned cool but mainly sunny. The news that *Jesus Christ Superstar* was America's best-selling album had not permeated the village of Ashton Keynes.

Outside the church a few curious village kids perched on a wall constituted the crowd. A photographer from the local newspaper summed up the press interest. On my side of the aisle were Mum and Dad, Julian, David Harington and a couple of other school friends plus Tim Rice, Robert Stigwood, Peter Brown and, possibly making his debut in an English country church, David Land and his wife Zara. Sally and Lottie arguably belonged in Sarah's family's pews but were seconded to mine to balance the numbers. Sarah's mob was considerably bigger as various cousins had been wheeled out, mostly Gore Browne relations of Sarah's mother. All in all there were roughly a hundred in tow. Alan Doggett had been commandeered as director of music and a professional choir assembled so the music was in good shape.

Apart, that is, from an anthem composed by me. For a while Tim and I had been wondering whether there should be a big solo number for Jesus in what would now be Act 1. So we wrote a new song to follow Jesus's triumphant entry into Jerusalem. Titled "Hey Father," the lyric was based on the Lord's Prayer, although in the order of service it was billed as "The Lord's Prayer, words by Tim Rice" which was news to some. The music much depended on a rock gospel treatment. Quite why I thought that our wedding was the right forum for this tryout eludes me. Also why I imagined a very staid church choir could have handled such a premiere was poor judgement rendered idiotic by under-rehearsal. The reaction or rather non-reaction of the wedding guests put paid to "Hey Father" ever hitting the boards.

The wedding belonged to Sarah. She glowed with incandescent triumph. The service was simple and beautiful. The reception was held in her parents' garden where Peter Brown complained that there were only sandwiches. I managed to spill champagne all over Sarah's wedding dress but otherwise it was a great day. Everyone seemed to realize how insanely in love we were and I drove Sarah, who had changed into hotpants, off to a great cheer. We planned to honeymoon at the Sacher Hotel, Vienna and then head for the Salzburg Festival but our first port of call was Bath and dinner at Britain's then top restaurant, the Hole in the Wall.

It was halfway down the old A4 road that I noticed Sarah was crying. I pulled the car over and took her in my arms. The reality of what I had done truly hit me. I had taken a girl barely eighteen straight out of school and propelled her away from her family into a new life that just happened to include being the wife of the composer of the first British musical to premiere on Broadway. It was only weeks away and Sarah had never even been to the USA. All I could think of to say was how much I loved her. For the first time in my life I felt responsible for something whose outcome I couldn't control.

VIENNA MAY BE AN architectural feast but that August it was hot, dusty and achingly pompous. There is something desperately conservative about Austria. The restaurant in the Sacher Hotel had no air-conditioning and was stiflingly hot, yet you had to wear a jacket and tie even though the temperature had hit the high nineties and the famous Sachertorte chocolate cakes were melting into a sludge the colour of Robert Stigwood's pool in the wake of the go-cart drama. Viennese food circa 1970 was schnitzel going on schnitzel and soon we had had enough.

We headed to the Salzburg Festival where we fell on an excellent performance of Janacek's *Glagolitic Mass*. I do like Janacek. Pretty soon we realized why we had got into the concert. Too few share this love. My mind wandered to Frank Corsaro and his production of Janacek's *The Makropulos Affair*. Why had I heard nothing about Broadway casting? But although I can't speak for Sarah, I was soon immersed in a sea of Slavicity (if there is such a word). As all the big-name concerts were sold out and over-manicured Salzburg was heaving with tourists, we headed for La Mortola.

Vi and George hadn't made the wedding. Vi's leg, "grotty," as she dubbed it, was still playing up so they were really pleased to see us and excited to show us off. Their Riviera friends were far more clued up about *Superstar* than everyone back in Britain. Ronnie and Beryl Neame held a small party where everyone was charmed by Sarah's open innocence and we wondered why on earth we hadn't gone straight to Italy in the first place. We invited Vi and George to Summerleaze, our Wiltshire farmhouse, for Christmas and left for home in high spirits.

Sarah was feeling much better about everything now, George having diagnosed that she was not helped by being put on the pill. I was getting more and more excited about the impending Broadway opening. I was going to be collaborating with an exciting director with opera in his lifeblood. I was 23 and my dream was about to come true.

ALL SEEMED CALM WHEN we got home. David Land was on holiday at his seaside home at Rottingdean near Brighton, a village famed as the home of the great Pre-Raphaelite Sir Edward Burne-Jones and a mite too close to Roedean School for my taste. Tim had just bought a townhouse with a pretty wrought-iron veranda in a seriously up-and-coming Notting Hill street called Northumberland Place and Tim had moved in there with his latest girlfriend Prudence de Casembroot. Sarah and I were highly curious to see what he'd done with it so we popped round one afternoon for a snoop. We got on really well with Pru who had gone out of her way to befriend my child bride. After Pru split up with Tim, she reappeared big time in our lives as David Hemmings's other half when he starred in the ill-fated *Jeeves* musical.

After a quick tour of the new Rice pad, the four of us headed to his funky new kitchen for a cup of tea. It was there that Tim dropped the mother of all bombs. He did it almost nonchalantly. Frank Corsaro had been replaced by Tom O'Horgan – presumably someone had told me? he added. I was speechless. I said surely he couldn't have gone along with this, but I sometimes wonder if he was enjoying my distress. He certainly wasn't over-worried.

I headed home and called Stigwood three times. Each time I was told he was busy and would ring back later. Eventually I called David Land on holiday. To say he was evasive was an understatement. Apparently Frank Corsaro had been in a car crash, was incapacitated and had been forced to pull out. I called Tyler Gatchell in New York and was told much the same thing. Tom O'Horgan was definitely now at the helm. Robin Wagner was to be the set designer with Jules Fisher lighting the whole caboodle. It was, Tyler pointed out, a crack A-list team.

Something didn't stack up. We were now in early September and our show started previewing in late October. There was no way totally new set designs could be built in that time. Previous conversations with Tom O'Horgan didn't suggest he'd had an epiphany and converted to minimalism. Furthermore our Broadway theatre was the Mark Hellinger, one of the biggest Broadway houses with one of the best stages in Manhattan, where *My Fair Lady* had played. This all must have been put in motion months before and I had been kept out of the loop.

I talked everything through with Sarah and we felt my only option was to make the best of it and get to New York as soon as possible to try at least to get the music into good shape. There was one very promising bit of news. Ben Vereen had been cast as Judas. I knew a little about Ben. I loved him in the movie of *Sweet Charity* and there had been very good word about him in London when he was Sammy Davis's understudy in *Golden Boy* at the London Palladium.

THE FIRST "CREATIVE" I met in New York was the newly hired musical director, a nice if soon to be frazzled guy called Marc Pressel. It was immediately screamingly obvious that no decent rock player would play for a Broadway show eight times a week. But this worry was as nothing to the nightmare I experienced when I checked out O'Horgan's latest Broadway oeuvre *Lenny*. This was a play, an extremely thin play, based on the life of comedian Lenny Bruce. If ever the words "shabby little shocker" had meaning, this was it. The sight of gratuitous naked prophets and clawing lepers was gruesome enough. But the ugly sets were by *Superstar*'s new designer and lit by our new lighting guy, who also racked up a credit as co-producer.

When I told Robert and his gang that *Lenny* was the most unpleasant evening I had ever spent in a theatre I was told firmly to zip it. I detected the merest head movement from Peter Brown that suggested tacit agreement, but he stopped short of saying anything, not that he could have done anything anyway. Where Peter was stellar was with Sarah. He realized she was plunged into a world far removed from her genteel West London girls' school. Peter rented a beautiful apartment on Central Park West where he still lives today. Back then the Stigwood offices occupied a corner but the apartment soon became a home from home for both of us, specially the increasingly homesick Sarah. It became her refuge from the small suite in the Waldorf Hotel where Robert had ensconced us whilst he lorded it up in the hotel's vast penthouse. Meanwhile there was still no confirmation of when Tim was arriving.

What with me seething about *Lenny* and wittering on generally, Peter thought it a good idea to get Sarah and me out of New York. We headed to Long Island where I saw something I thought I'd never see again, although I did years later in Japan. Behind the bar of a rather smart restaurant was an upside-down bottle of Château Lafite 1961 being served by the measure. The label had been steamed off and restuck on the inverted bottle. It was $40 a glass. What with this and *Lenny*, this was the only moment in my life when I seriously thought about seeing a shrink.

Rehearsals began the following Monday. From the outset it was clear that O'Horgan's vision of *Jesus Christ Superstar* had the vision and subtlety of Caesars Palace. The cast, however, was excellent. Jeff Fenholt was culled from the tour as Jesus. Barry and Yvonne repeated their roles as Pilate and Mary Magdalene, Barry bringing much needed theatrical sanity to the gold lamé ship. Ben Vereen proved to be one of the most outstanding performers I have worked with. If anything he was too polished and professional to play our Judas but that was hardly his fault. I regret I never had a chance to work with him again.

On the evening of the first day I was dealt a major curve ball. Peter Brown received a call from top agent Norman Weiss. Would we audition at the very last minute a new girl client he had signed? Apparently she had been singing in some gay public baths and he thought she would make a sensational Mary Magdalene. Yvonne Elliman was obviously already cast, but I agreed to go through the motions and hear her. If ever an audition could have undermined a casting decision this was it. Bette Midler's rendition of "I Don't Know How to Love Him" was mindblowing. Her interpretation of Tim's brilliant storytelling lyric was truly moving. I called Robert and told him I had heard a performance without equal. But, quite rightly, there was no way the commitment to Yvonne could be dishonoured. I console myself knowing that if Bette had made her Broadway debut in the upcoming glitzfest it would have been a chronic waste.

REHEARSALS CHURNED ON. THERE was one real plus: everyone agreed that we needed a new song for Mary Magdalene. She virtually disappears in the second half of the original album. So Tim and I wrote a duet for Mary and Peter after his denial that he has ever met Jesus called "Could We Start Again, Please?" It was great to hear it come alive.

But I don't remember O'Horgan once discussing text with the actors. Everything was about staging. Away from the rehearsal room the music department was in a mess. The Broadway "rock" musicians played all the right notes but there lay the problem: they didn't feel the music at all. Rock isn't about perfection.

Sound was a huge issue. Theatre sound as we know it today simply didn't exist. Up to the 1970s what passed as amplification was a row of "float mikes" pointing upstage, operated from the prompt corner by an assistant electrician. Robert decided to engage a sound designer, then a virtually unheard of thought in theatreland. Tom O'Horgan suggested Abe Jacob, who had worked on the West Coast version of *Hair*. Abe demanded that a proper mixing desk be installed in the auditorium which caused the theatre owners to have a seizure. Never mind if *Superstar* was blasphemous. The gravest cardinal sin in commercial theatre was about to be committed: losing seats. Eventually a mixing board was installed at the very back of the mezzanine. Union rules meant it was operated by one of the theatre's electricians. The gum-chewing, doughnut toting guy assigned to us didn't radiate music as his number one interest.

It didn't help that Abe had never done anything with an orchestra quite like this. The orchestra pit was covered over so it was like a recording studio isolated from the theatre. That way the sound could be completely controlled from the mixing desk, a risky thought considering its operator. The problem was that everything sounded swaddled in cotton wool. The brass resembled a bad case of the Edward Woodwards. Meanwhile as Abe grappled with the sound, the hugely elaborate set was being installed. The pièce de résistance was an enormous below-stage lift which hoisted Jesus aloft whilst a giant spangled golden cloak unravelled beneath him. It was a spectacular image, but it was so alien to my music that I still wince at the thought. Unfortunately an effect like this takes days to "tech" – i.e. get right. So a huge fight for theatre time began between the sound department and O'Horgan and his gargantuan effects team. Eventually it led to the kiss of death savoured by theatre ghouls the world over. Cancelled previews.

But there was still worse to come. Abe decided to experiment with radio mikes which in 1971 were barely out of the cradle. It isn't ideal if after Pilate screams at Jesus "die if you want to, you misguided martyr" the sound system crackles: "Homer, there's a pickup at the corner of 45th and 8th." So radio mikes were ditched in favour of old-fashioned handhelds whose cables turned the stage floor into a three-dimensional tangle of a tarantula's web. Someone had the idea to disguise them as ropes.

THEATRE WAGS DESCRIBED THE delayed first preview as "How To Succeed In Crucifying A Musical About Jesus Christ Without Even Blinking." One matinee I was with publicist Barry Kittleson. A girl bubbled up to him at the interval giggling, "Barry, Barry, isn't this just the worst show you've ever seen!" Barry had no option but to say, "Meet Andrew Lloyd Webber, the composer." The Archbishop of Canterbury came to a preview during an official visit to New York. Sarah and I were introduced to Michael Ramsey, the 100th Archbishop, sitting in the lobby of the theatre looking highly discombobulated. We were surrounded by press and he tried to be as nice as possible. I was caught between keeping the side up and a desperate yearning to apologize.

I'll grant that O'Horgan's beginning was stunning. On arrival the audience was faced with a giant wall. During the overture the actors clambered over its top whilst the wall folded backwards to form the stage floor. It was a brilliant effect – simple, highly theatrical and starkly effective. What followed is not worth recounting and there was no Tim in New York for moral support. Sarah recalls that I begged him to fly over. She concluded that he was too scared to come. Either that or he was unconcerned about what was happening. He had chosen the SS *France* with his girlfriend Pru as his preferred mode of transport to New York which docked a mere four days before opening night, rather too late for him to be of much help.

All I could do now was to try to galvanize the music but endless technical re-rehearsals made even this impossible. My pleading for theatre time earned me the reputation of being a petulant brat which was duly amplified to Rice. It is said that D'Oyly Carte controlled Gilbert and Sullivan through "divide and conquer." There was a lot of that going on now. At last Tim turned up with three previews to go. His contribution was to pronounce he wasn't sure if he liked what O'Horgan had done or not.

The first night dawned. David Land chartered a plane for 200-odd relatives and hangers on who had been promised the night of their lives. From Robert sideways and downwards it seemed the after-show party was all anyone cared about. The box office advance was huge. Hadn't it occurred to anyone that if the audience didn't like what was on stage *Superstar* would eat up its advance and that would be about it? My parents came to New York and I was glad they did. Dad sensed my forebodings, but said surely if the score was played well any decent critic would see through the production.

Actually the score wasn't badly served on opening night. The cast was on flying form. An old couple sitting in front of me turned to each other after "Everything's Alright" and stage-whispered that it was rather a good tune. The orchestra sounded much less swaddled than before as huge holes had been cut into the covered pit. There was the usual OSO (obligatory standing ovation) and Robert threw his vaunted party at the Tavern on the Green. The rent-a-mob made the right noises but the movers and shakers knew what they dared not say. Sarah and I left early.

When we got back to the hotel we both burst into tears. Sarah had been a bedrock for me way beyond her years in the last few weeks she had witnessed my desperate attempts to get Tim and David Land to support me. But she knew what I knew all too well. All my hopes, everything I had ever dreamed of, had collapsed in sickly tatters around us. Was it all over for me on Broadway at the age of 23? Next morning Dad said that when I got back home he would like a proper chat.

15

Suddenly There's a Valet

The morning press wasn't too bad. The *New York Daily News* review by Douglas Watt was a rave. It read like an old-timer desperately wanting to be trendy. "Stunning, vibrant, reverent," he screeched as if knowing this would appear with his by-line on a billboard close to Times Square. Clive Barnes in the *New York Times* damned with faint praise by calling *Superstar* the best British musical since *Oliver!*, an achievement akin to Brazil beating Lichtenstein at beach volleyball. He also opined that the production reminded him of the Empire State Building. But it was the subsequent press that was really damning. My father's hope that reviewers would close their eyes to the production and appreciate the score was wishful thinking. Late that morning, much against my wishes, I was interviewed by the *New York Times*. Any temptation to say what I really thought was clobbered by strict instructions that I shouldn't let the side down. I found myself defending the indefensible. I spouted incoherent drivel.

To be fair, Robert knew that he'd screwed up. But what he now did taught me a lesson that became my mantra. *Superstar* would be staged around the world as soon as possible. It has wrongly gone into theatre folklore that *Cats* was the first global musical. This, as Auntie Vi would say, is clotted bollocks on stilts. Robert Stigwood was first to grasp this nettle and he did so with both fists. He immediately spun a masterful PR campaign. Around the world the Broadway opening was reported as a triumph. In Britain some jingo-tinged stuff on the wire services meant the bad reviews got scarcely a murmur. Next he sought out the top theatre producer in every major territory. By Christmas Robert had co-productions on the go with Harry Miller in Australia, Keita Asari in Japan, European premieres in Sweden, Germany and France and a London production slated for 1972 summer. He also announced a West Coast production in the open-air Universal Amphitheatre in LA. The difference with today's world dominating blockbusters is that the Broadway production failed to provide a global blueprint. Every country's creative team would be different. But the premise of a quick rollout was the same.

Robert also hatched a cunning ruse. By announcing the LA production in an open-air venue it forced O'Horgan into a total rethink which resulted in the LA production being far better than Broadway's. The giant cherrypicker survived but this time Jesus's cloak was made of rags. Open-air productions sometimes get away with a lot – you can forgive much on a balmy night – but this image of Jesus silhouetted against the twinkling lights of the La La Land night sky was both effective and curiously moving. The show became a tinsel town must-see. Groucho Marx turned up late for one performance due to picking up a young waitress en route to the show. He loudly asked a lady in the row in front "Is this all right for Jews to watch?"

In the circumstances, Robert was very smart to allow each production to have its own creative team. If any of them hit bullseye, it could become the definitive model to roll out. In fact that never happened. The New York production played 711 performances, not a disaster but a very poor outcome for the premiere production in the nation that had embraced *Superstar* so unequivocally.

SARAH AND I WERE overjoyed to be back home, but goodness it felt curious. Robert's spinning had been so successful that you would have thought we'd opened *Oklahoma!* The album that had been a stiff for a year suddenly became the stuff of the British chattering classes and dinner invites mushroomed from people we barely knew. One such was from London Weekend Television. They were throwing a dinner in honour of Leonard Bernstein after the filming of his one-act opera *Trouble in Tahiti*. I found myself next to Bernstein and opposite Prime Minister Edward Heath. Conversation drifted to Prokofiev whom Bernstein dismissed as "merely chic," a remark I seethingly felt he should stick up his recently composed *Mass* which had received much the same critical response as the Broadway *Superstar*. I was so annoyed that for nearly three days I forgot that *West Side Story* was one of my favourite musicals.

Another memorable meal was with Dad. I had been postponing lunch with him as Sarah and I wanted to be in the country and he wanted to meet at the London College of Music. Dad was very proud of his achievements there. We had a tour of the building with his Registrar John Burn, who taught me at Westminster and whom I introduced to my parents. John had very similar musical tastes to my father and I had a hunch that he and Dad would get on. It was a joy that together they were turning the LCM into a real force in musical education and I was struck by how much knowledge and insight Dad seemed to have about his students.

Dad wanted John to join us for lunch which was sandwiches (and for John and Dad cocktails) in his office overlooking the stage door of the London Palladium. Dad gossiped about Harrington Court, told John Burn about how Tim shared the flat with Granny and John Lill and how he'd seen Tim and me working together on *Joseph*. He chortled that a master at Julian's school had become a musical director for me and a master at Westminster a right-hand man for him. Then he asked what really had gone on in New York. How was my relationship with Tim? I told him pretty much everything, how I wished Tim had supported me more in New York, but that he was a brilliant lyricist and my dream was we would have a long-term partnership like Rodgers and Hammerstein or Gilbert and Sullivan.

There was a pause. I saw Dad catch John Burn's eye. Then he said straight to my face, "You won't have a long-term partnership with Tim." I was very taken aback. I asked if he thought my perfectionist tantrums drove Tim crazy. Dad didn't really answer. He simply said, "Tim will be very successful but it will be with things that come easily to him."

AROUND THIS TIME DAVID Land got an enquiry from Frank Dunlop and the Young Vic to stage *Joseph* at the 1972 Edinburgh Festival. 1971 had seen quite a scrimmage to discover if Tim and I had written anything before *Superstar*. In the US our original *Joseph* album was released in packaging that implied it was a follow-up. David thought if someone felt they could find a way of staging *Joseph*, good luck to them. Dunlop proposed that *Joseph* would be the second half of an evening that began with Old Testament medieval mystery plays as a sort of prequel. "*Joseph* will be just like the bill-topper at the London Palladium," David crowed. Twenty years later the full-length version *was* the bill – and the most successful production in the Palladium's history.

Financially, things were becoming rosy that year end, mainly thanks to the three US concert tours. I flew Vi and George back from La Mortola for our first Christmas at Summerleaze. We decided to sell the Gledhow Gardens flat, copy Tim and buy a London townhouse. It was an extraordinary time for central London house prices which were doubling overnight for no obvious reason. I was sauntering past an estate agent near the Victoria & Albert Museum when I saw in the window details of a five-storey townhouse at the good end of Knightsbridge's Brompton Square. At £70,000 it seemed massively undervalued. (Today £910,000.) Fearing it would be £140,000 before I blinked, I called Sarah. We got shown round the place and agreed the asking price then and there. Coutts & Co were only too happy to provide the mortgage. It was the best property deal I ever did. Two years later I flogged it for way over double, which saved our bacon in the 1974 crash big time.

We took possession early in the year and held a furniture-free, food-throwing housewarming party, much enlivened by Norman Jewison who was now the director of the *Superstar* film. Tim was offered first crack at writing the screenplay. His concept unfortunately necessitated sets that made *Ben-Hur*'s budget look diminutive, so Tim was replaced by Melvyn Bragg which some thought odd as Melvyn was then best known for his novels about his native Northern England. I met Melvyn, liked him a lot and we have remained friends ever since. However my main preoccupation was to get on and write something else, preferably lighthearted.

I, like Tim, am a devoted fan of P.G. Wodehouse's Jeeves stories and I was overjoyed when we both enthusiastically decided to write a Jeeves musical. We chose *The Code of the Woosters* as our prime source material and Tim was very chuffed with the title "Suddenly There's a Valet." David Land was charged with clearing the rights. But Jeeves had to play second fiddle to a new-year start of setting up home and beginning to buy Pre-Raphaelite art. Sarah and I spent a lot of time improving Summerleaze whilst Tim globetrotted, checking out, among other things, Robert's *Superstar* rollout.

I had one other rather daft project up my sleeve. I proposed that I record veteran comedian Frankie Howerd as narrator of Prokofiev's *Peter and the Wolf*. Frankie's innuendo-filled humor was riding high in such romps as *Up Pompeii*. He was managed by Robert who fancied the scheme.

Robert was away at the time so Frankie and I commandeered his Brook Street office for an afternoon. As we sat talking, Frankie lunged at me and bit me viciously on the neck, saying, "Take this home to your child bride." I was totally shell-shocked and didn't know what to do. Frankie was a national treasure. If I said anything it would inevitably overshadow *Superstar*'s theatrical debut in Britain. Worse I didn't know what to say to Sarah so I said nothing and nor did she. We went ahead with the recording as if nothing happened.

The next big thing was the London opening. I was like a stuck vinyl record, repeating that what happened in New York couldn't happen again back home. Tim reported back very favourably on the Australian production. I never saw it but a recently discovered private recording owned by its late star Jon English makes me wish I had. It's extraordinary, in some ways rawer and rockier than our original. The production was a humongous hit and made *Superstar* very special to Australia. It confirmed its director Jim Sharman as the man to smash it to the British. The opening date was set for August at the Palace Theatre, formerly the London residence of *The Sound of Music*, which had subsequently garnered an unenviable record of flop musicals.*

I found a load in common with Jim Sharman. He had an in-depth knowledge of opera, having directed a risqué version of *Don Giovanni* when he was 21. His father ran a famous boxing sideshow that toured Australian showgrounds so Jim was good for ripe stories as an evening progressed. After *Superstar* he went on to direct *The Rocky Horror Show* having met its author Richard O'Brien when he briefly played King Herod in our London cast.

The musical director was the vastly entertaining Anthony Bowles. Anthony was a diminutive, extremely camp gay guy with an exceptionally high-pitched voice and a waspish tongue to boot. His put-downs were as legendary in West End circles as the waspish Sir Thomas Beecham's in the concert hall. At one audition a large baritone proffered himself as a potential Pilate.

"What are you going to sing?" shrieked Anthony.

"I would like to perform my own arrangement of 'The Impossible Dream,'" boomed the baritone.

"God spare us but start if you must," Anthony muttered.

The baritone intoned but not for long.

---

* *110 in the Shade, The Desert Song, Two Cities, Belle Starr, Phil The Fluter* and, astonishingly, *Cabaret.*

"Excuse me!" Anthony squawked.

"Yes, Mr Bowles."

"You are singing 'The Impossible Dream' in 4/4 time."

"Indeed, Mr Bowles," retorted the baritone. "It is part of my special reinterpretation."

Anthony rose to his full five foot two. "'The Impossible Dream' was written in 3/4 time," he howled. "You are singing 'The Impossible Dream' in 4/4 time. Thus you are making an insufferable experience one-third longer."

The casting was intriguing. Dana Gillespie as Mary Magdalene certainly ticked the boxes for the lover of the Rubens figure. Her previous movies such as *Secrets of a Windmill Girl* and *The Vengeance of She* suggested an empathy with the role, but what qualified her even more was her great bluesy voice which permeated several early David Bowie recordings. Tall and spindly Stephen Tate, whom Sharman cast as Judas, was the actor of the outfit with classical theatre training. Even so, little did I think when he rocked out with the *Superstar* soul girls – one of whom was called Elaine Paige – that one day he would premier frail old Gus the Theatre Cat.

Another future cat was Paul Nicholas. His casting as Jesus caused a clutch of raised eyebrows and more than a squeak in the UK's satirical magazine, *Private Eye*. Paul is the son of one of Britain's most prominent show business lawyers, the late Oscar Beuselinck. His career started young in the backup band for the aptly named Screaming Lord Sutch. By the mid-1960s he was in the Stigwood firmament and signed to Robert's label. Under the pseudonym Oscar he cut various chart-lite singles, the third of which "Over the Wall We Go," was produced by a young David Bowie, a fact unmentioned in the latter's obituaries. Paul went on to get his kit off as the lead in Robert's London production of *Hair*. Talk of his close friendship with Robert meant his casting as Jesus proved a touch too provocative for London's theatre mafia and his good looks only fanned jeal-

Mum and Dad on their wedding day in 1942. At least – unlike Granny Molly – Mum did not throw her wedding ring down the lavatory on her honeymoon night. *Photo: personal collection*

The first person to take a dislike to me: Mimi the monkey with my adorable Auntie Vi. *Photo: personal collection*

It don't mean a thing if it ain't got that swing. Dad and me (c.1950). *Photo: personal collection*

Mum's piano lessons gave me a head start in the basics of music – now the serious composing could begin. *Photo: personal collection*

And then there was that wretched violin (c.1952). A nauseating picture that haunts me still: Nursery World. *Photo: personal collection*

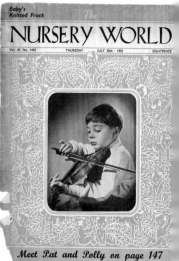

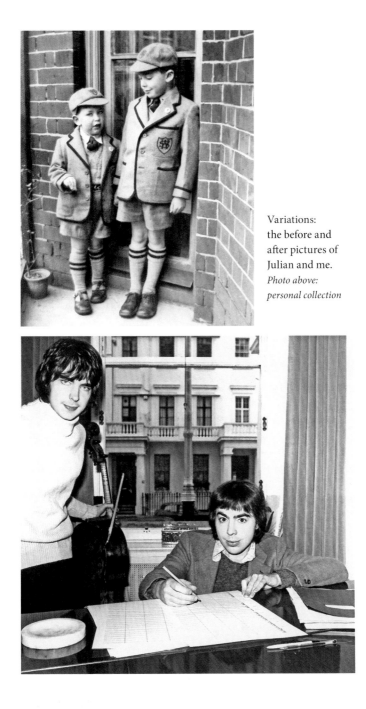

Variations:
the before and
after pictures of
Julian and me.
*Photo above:
personal collection*

My toy theatre, the Harrington Pavilion, survived unscathed for many years but sadly went missing when I moved house in 1974. All I have now are a few photographs which I took myself.

Photo: personal collection

Perseus just before I took him out for the last time. *Photo: personal collection*

Dad was as devoted to Perseus as I was. *Photo: personal collection*

I took these photographs when I was thirteen. The two above are the streets of Notting Hill and the one below is the interior of the ruined Bedford, Camden Town. I think it was in the street featuring the little boy that I discovered that I could run. *Photo: personal collection*

In the Norfolk
countryside
with John Lill.
*Photo: personal
collection*

With Timothy Miles
Bindon Rice. Granny
seemed to go unusually
weak in the knees.

Sarah and me on our wedding day, August 1971. *Photo: Tom Hustler*

My life's longest runner of forty-five years and counting: the architectural mongrel that is my home, Sydmonton Court. With Sarah in front of our "nineteenth-century, bog-standard, estate church." *Photo: Roy Jones/Arena Pal*

With Don Black and Marti Webb. Note my important Deborah and Clare floral shirt.

The cast of *Jesus Christ Superstar*. It took London by storm and became the longest running West End musical to date.

Paul Nicholas's casting as Jesus caused a clutch of raised eyebrows and more than a squeak in the UK's satirical magazine *Private Eye*. But Paul looked and sounded great. *Photo: John Haynes/Lebrecht Music & Arts*

With my musical hero, Richard Rodgers, at the Pierre Hotel, New York. I had a day's worth of questions. *Photo: personal collection*

With Tim, Jane and Sarah in Biarritz. This may have been the high point of the Rice–Lloyd Webber relationship. Here we were, two young, happy, married couples together, with a new project we were excited about and everything to play for. *Photo: personal collection*

"If it's alright with you, kid, it's fine by me," was Hal Prince's verdict on Elaine Paige. Rehearsing *Evita* with Hal and Elaine. *Photo: © Zoë Dominic*

"Setting sail on the Mayflower . . ." Breakfast on the terrace of the Mayflower Hotel, New York, 1982, with my theatrical soulmate, Cameron Mackintosh.

"There's a girl in *Hot Gossip* that's going to change your life," Arlene Phillips told me. "She has a voice from heaven. Her name is Sarah Brightman." *Photo: personal collection*

Sarah Brightman as Valencienne in *The Merry Widow.*

"Taut and tight" is how Gillian describes this
revealing shot of her in *Cats* rehearsals.

Mum showing where her true love lay, with our two Russian Blues, Dimitri and Sergei (Shostakovich and Prokofiev, of course). *Photo: personal collection*

The wooing of Valerie Eliot. From our first firm handshake it was clear that she was a fierce custodian of all things T.S. Eliot. *Photo: PA Images*

With Judi Dench in hospital after she broke her Achilles tendon. Had she sung "Memory" as Grizabella I know it would have been a very moving performance – but it was not to be. *Photo: PA Images*

Sarah Brightman   Kenn Wells   Finola Hughes

Three cool cats.

ous flames. Others said Paul was miscast. I can't agree. Paul looked and sounded great, even if he looked more rock matinee idol than carpenter king.

The London rehearsals were as happy as the Broadway ones were not but Tim was getting tetchy. I kept a note from him dated July 5, which reads as follows:

> Dear webber [sic – his typewriter seemed incapable of capital letters]
>
> just for the record here are all the extra film lyrics that i have just sent to n.jewison's office. i am fed up with writing extra bits for superstar and j.sharman wanting another verse for hosanna is the last straw. funny how people are never happy with the new bits even if better than old because they're used to the old. like the everlys re-doing all i have to do is dream if you think about it. save this card and print it in book of your life story in 1996. must do suddenly there's a valet v. soon as one more superstar lyric will drive me insane. aaaaaaaaaaaaaaagggghhhhhh
>   (signed t rice)
> c.c the pope, sir alf ramsey

IT IS IMPOSSIBLE TO exaggerate how much Stigwood hyped up the first night. Despite it being the August holiday season it was the hottest West End ticket in memory. No stone was left unturned. Robert clocked a group of nuns protesting outside the theatre during previews. He instructed our publicist Anthony Pye-Jeary to ensure they turned up for the opening by paying for their meals and accommodation.

As ever the first night was nerve-racking. *Superstar* was no shoo-in with London's old guard theatre critics who were pissed off about being in London during the Edinburgh Festival. I unwittingly made a fan of one of them just before the interval. I got up to help an old lady who turned out to be the legendary actress Dame Sybil Thorndike. What I didn't realize was that this was observed by the equally legendary *Sunday Times* critic Harold Hobson. Rave reviews appeared for my music for the rest of his tenure, even including my ill-fated *Jeeves*. The *Observer* film critic Penelope Gilliatt once famously opined, "One of the most characteristic sounds of the English Sunday is the sound of Harold Hobson barking up the wrong tree."

Tim and I were too nervous to sit through Act 2 so we stood together at the back. All went swimmingly until the crucifixion scene. Jesus plus the cross were supposed to rise through the floor, centre downstage. The problem on opening night was they didn't. The electric lift had broken. Anthony Bowles made frantic signals to the Moog synthesizer player who covered the gap with such agonizing atonal improvisations that Tim and I wondered whether we should run down the aisle and bring the nightmare to a halt. Eventually Paul and cross were winched up manually and things proceeded to the ritual OSO* and far better reviews than Broadway.

Jim Sharman had put the rock band on stage so the show felt closer to the arena tours than a conventional musical. *Superstar* works best the closer the director embraces its rock album roots. My favourite review was in one of the classical music magazines. The critic, having excoriated my score for having banal things like tunes, regretted that there were not more moments like the "tense searing musical invention scored for Moog synthesiser" that preceded Christ's "consequentially moving" death on the cross.

The party was at Robert's pad in Stanmore and huge fun. A joyous rumour spread that upstairs in Robert's bathroom there was a peep show worth viewing. Apparently a guest had ventured into it for a leak and discovered the not inconsiderable sight of the show's lyri-

---

* Yet again OSO = obligatory standing ovation.

cist and Mary Magdalene entwined on the floor. Robert's assistant Bill Oakes, who married Yvonne Elliman for a while, reminded an amused Sarah that he and Tim made a pact to score with every Mary Magdalene and Maid by the Fire by the end of 1972.

Superstar took London by storm. Throughout that autumn, backstage post-performance was *the* place to be. Night after night it was the hangout for the Bowie set and it was where Richard O'Brien incubated *The Rocky Horror Show*. Gore Vidal was a regular pursuing King Herod in the form of an American Robert had cast – Paul Jabara. Dana Gillespie was rumoured to have organized a cock measuring contest in her dressing room. I didn't enter. Auntie Vi told me it was bad form to enter a contest you know you're going to win.

The London production of *Superstar* ran for more than eight years and had 3358 performances, making it the longest-running West End musical to date. Among the proudest moments of my career was when one of my heroes, Dmitri Shostakovich, saw the production in 1975, said that he wished he'd composed it and really liked the way the rock section underpinned the woodwind and brass.

THE LONDON REVIEWS MAY have been fine but they were nothing compared to our next batch. The hoopla in London meant we had forgotten about David Land's "bill-topper" *Joseph* at the Edinburgh Festival. None of us were at its first night. Billed as part of an evening unpromisingly titled *Bible One*, there was a consensus that *Joseph* was way superior to *Superstar* and might just be the best British musical ever, a curious notion as *Joseph* was then only 35 minutes long.

Frank Dunlop had staged *Bible One* in the round. Almost four sides of scaffolded seating surrounded a floor which had been painted yellow, presumably to suggest the desert. The first half, or to be accurate two-thirds, consisted of the medieval mystery plays which were dirges based on the Old Testament with which strolling players apparently lit up the market squares of Ye Olde England. After an act of these fossils you might say that anything would be a blessed relief but *Joseph* really was a blast. Frank Dunlop had created a role of narrator, suavely played by Peter Reeves, whilst Gary Bond, an established West End juvenile heartthrob, was a handsome Joseph who sported a loincloth that looked like a nappy when he wasn't twirling his coat of many colours. Frank Dunlop had changed some of the lyrics from the third to the first person to give Joseph more to sing. Thus Frank unlocked the door to the full-length *Joseph* that is performed today. To top it all Pharaoh/Elvis was played by Gordon Waller, the Gordon half of Westminster School's very own Sixties chart toppers Peter and Gordon. *Joseph* was the unchallenged smash of the 1972 Edinburgh Festival.

Plans were immediately made to bring *Bible One* to London. The production had to be in the round, so no conventional theatre could house it. A home was found at London's Roundhouse in Chalk Farm, a former railway locomotive shed that had become a thrilling theatrical space. Once again *Joseph* was a runaway success. By now the medieval first two-thirds had become a half and Robert decided the sellout business meant a new production should be mounted next year in a West End theatre. The first half would be ditched in favour of a prequel to be written by Tim and me. That, at least, was the theory.

THE WEST END *JOSEPH* seemed miles away so Tim, David and I turned our attention to the *Superstar* movie which had been churning along apace and was now in principal photography in Israel. It was time to check it out. Sarah decided that she'd had enough of *Superstar* so it was only David, Tim and I who headed off on an El Al jumbo. *Superstar* veterans Barry Dennen and Yvonne Elliman were once again playing Pilate and Mary and Norman had cast the arena tour's Carl Anderson as Judas, Carl's chagrin at being passed over for Ben Vereen on Broadway having long ago turned to thanksgiving. Ted Neeley, Jeff Fenholt's Broadway understudy, was the movie's Jesus, Jeff having shacked up with Salvador Dalí's wife after Señor and Señora Dalí had met him backstage at the Mark Hellinger.

Since we had been virtually banned from the movie, the plan was to make a token appearance on the set, say hi to Norman and the cast, generally spread goodwill and then do a spot of sightseeing at Universal Pictures' expense. But things started badly. The airport security was interminable and we were very late for our rendezvous on the film set. So we ditched our bags in the hotel lobby and hastily headed into the desert in a Universal stretch limo driven by an Israeli who had a limp from a wound acquired in the Six-Day War. Consequently when David kept lecturing him, "I wouldn't have fought over that land if I was you," it failed to hit the spot.

Things got worse just as we neared the set. On the roadside was a bedouin with a dead camel waving frantically. David told the driver to stop, pressed down the electric window and shouted, "What's the matter buster, Wall Street gone through the floor?" Again our driver was unamused. So shortly was Norman Jewison. On arrival we were steered towards a low tent whose boiling hot interior sported a massive lighting rig. Inside Yvonne Elliman was sitting cross-legged and looking microwaved whilst Norman was crawling across the sand floor behind a massive camera.

Maybe it was bad timing just as another take was starting. Maybe David shouldn't have prodded Norman's shoulder causing him to jump. Whatever, David's opening gambit, "I have a message from Robert Stigwood, stop pissing about and get on with the movie," was received poorly. In fact Norman was fucking furious.

Over the next few days we had a hilarious time. David got very cross with me when we visited the Wailing Wall and I asked our poor driver to tell us something of its history. Hours later we finally sat down to lunch. David pointed a finger. "Never, Andrew, never ask a Jew about religion."

Looking back, I am sure this was his way of covering up that he was far more affected by his spiritual homeland than he would admit. One evening in Tel Aviv we found ourselves strolling on our own along the seafront. He was unusually quiet and we fell into a long discussion about the differences and similarities between the Jewish and Christian faiths. We agreed that two things were uniquely common to both. The quality of forgiveness and the power of redemption.

It was that special evening that I remembered at this deeply human man's funeral years later as the sleet fell over Willesden Cemetery.

16

Syd

Gentle reader, I crave your forgiveness for I am about to commit a cardinal chronological sin. I am going to stop yabbering on about musicals, veer widely – well, a few months – off piste and write about how Sarah and I happened on my life's longest runner of 45 years and counting, the architectural mongrel that is my home, Sydmonton Court.

Sarah says that once I got my first taste of country living at Summerleaze farmhouse, it was inevitable that my love of architecture would get the better of me and soon I'd want to make our main home in a slightly bigger house like Blenheim Palace. There were a good many fine country houses around our farmhouse and it wasn't long before my eye turned from appreciative to covetous. So in 1972 I began seriously searching for an architecturally important house for sale. I came perilously close to buying a wonderful pile called Hale Park, south of Salisbury, designed by one of the finest eighteenth-century architects, Thomas Archer. Sarah and I viewed it repeatedly and her mother Fanny was already eyeing up practical things like where you did the laundry. But I had a problem with a pylon line in its view.

I was about to shelve my quest for architectural squiredom when I saw a small advertisement in the London *Times*. It was for a big house and 20 acres 60 miles west of London in north Hampshire. Sarah and I vaguely knew the area. It was the first patch of unspoilt countryside we drove through on our way from London to Summerleaze. I was curious.

I vividly remember our first journey to Sydmonton. Sarah drove and I map-read. The route didn't immediately send our spirits strato-spheric. In those days the quickest way was via the vast nuclear works at Aldermaston. But past the village of Kingsclere the view became breathtaking. On our left was Watership Down, made famous by Richard Adams's novel about rabbits. Straight ahead was Beacon Hill and Highclere Castle, decades later to achieve worldwide fame as the TV set for Julian Fellowes's *Downton Abbey*.

The view was so great that my chequebook nearly climbed out of my pocket. There was loads wrong with the house, of course, but something felt very right. It took a German Jew, Dr Nikolaus Pevs-ner, to describe what makes the English visual arts tick in his seminal book, *The Englishness of English Art*. Sydmonton could be nowhere else but England. I got to know Pevsner well. He once described Syd-monton as the sort of English architectural mongrel you want to res-cue and love for the rest of your life.* We sold up in London and in

---

* "Sidmonton" or "side-mountain" began life after the Norman Conquest and was mentioned in Domesday Book as a grange, i.e. a rent-collecting base of Romsey Abbey. When Henry VIII crushed the monasteries in 1536, the grange and its land was given to one of the king's cronies, Sir William Kingsmill. He built a house of which a fair por-tion survives today. In the early nineteenth century it was massively altered by Thomas Hopper, an ubiquitous architect who churned out designs in whatever taste his clients wanted, in this case a bit of mock Tudor here, a bit of mock Georgian there. Sydmonton bumbled along in the Kingsmill family, never a top-tier grand house but not exactly a poor one either, until the Second World War. Then, as with all sizeable country houses, it was requisitioned and turned over to the military – in this case the US airforce whose main southern England base was at nearby Greenham Common. Several hundred US servicemen were housed in the house and grounds and in 1944 it became tarred with a major hushed-up scandal. A group of drunk, drugged or both airforce men descended on Kingsclere and shot up the locals in the pub. So great was the concern about an anti-US backlash that the "Kingsclere Massacre" was classified for forty years. I only heard about it when MI5 warned me that the embargo was about to be lifted and the press might make something of the link to my home, which they duly did. The Kingsmill family used their war-damage money to demolish large chunks of the house and modernize the rest, but in 1971 Colonel Bill Kingsmill died leaving no direct descendant. The house, the mainly let farms and a hefty death-duty bill passed to his nephew by marriage, who had to take the name Kingsmill to inherit. He decided to get rid of the big house and make a go of the remains of the estate.

November, with the aid of another big mortgage courtesy of Coutts & Co, bought "Syd," as everyone calls the house that is my home.

People thought I was suicidally bonkers to have bought a country mansion in November 1973. My closest friends openly said I was irresponsible to lumber Sarah with such a millstone. Black political storm clouds were gathering apace. Barely a month after I bought Syd, Britain was in the grip of an all-out miners' strike and was working an enforced three-day week. In March 1974 Prime Minister Heath called an election and his government fell. On the day the new socialist regime took hold of Westminster, 20-year-old Sarah and I took possession of a twelve-bedroom pariah of a country mansion and the new finance minister, Denis Healey, declared he would "squeeze the rich till the pips squeak."

I saw in Sydmonton a chance to make something very special. It would never be a fine house, but if somehow the estate could be put back together, the property would be unique. Its view of Watership Down was peerless. There was a classic eighteenth-century landscape view to a lake, overgrown and unloved but one day I might be able to own it and bring it back to life. There was a nineteenth-century, bog-standard, estate church smack in the main lawn. This clobbered the sale price. There were few takers for the prospect of country weddings every weekend outside their drawing-room window. I saw the chance that one day I could turn the church into a theatre. It happened quicker than I imagined.

Nonetheless I very nearly pulled out of the sale. What forced me to take a dip in the river of risk was the second great piece of advice of my life so far. It came from Bill Walworth, a Wiltshire estate agent who had befriended Sarah and me. He surveyed Sydmonton and pronounced it sound as a bell. He also chatted up its vendor. Bill concluded that he was probably alcoholic, had no strong ties to the estate and bit by bit would sell it off when he needed a few quid. If my career kept going I might have a unique chance to buy the pieces as and when I could afford them. Today the Sydmonton Court Estate farms 4500 acres. Bill Walworth failed to spot an additional bonus. The vendor had a beautiful daughter, Lucinda. I used to drop her to school and today she is one of my closest friends and lives next door.

NEW YEAR 1973 DAWNED with *Joseph* slated to hit the West End on February 17 and a cast rehearsing a first act that had no script. Memories of Leslie Thomas and *The Likes of Us* stalked proceedings like the ghosts of turkeys past. The problem with Robert's *Joseph* prequel idea was that if it was any good we'd have already written it. In truth Tim and I were keener on our *Jeeves* project than trying to come up with a *Joseph* curtain-raiser. Because the mystery plays were just that and had no music, Robert thought that even a vaguely amusing script that told the pre-Joseph Old Testament "story so far" would be more than an adequate set-up for our man in a dreamcoat, especially with a few new songs to spice things up. I kept flagging that people would bring totally different expectations to a West End theatre than they did to the funky old Roundhouse, particularly with our names plastered across the whole evening. The Albery, formerly the New Theatre, had been *Oliver!*'s home and is as West End mainstream as you can get. David still thought of *Joseph* as a variety act. "When people book to see Tom Jones at the Palladium they don't care about the jugglers," he burbled on unreassuringly.

Tim knocked up a script that featured God as an off-stage voice but no one liked it. So Robert drafted in Alan Simpson and Ray Galton, two top comedy writers he also managed. Alan and Ray were the writers of the legendary *Hancock's Half Hour*, whose star Tony Hancock I had met as a child, and the hugely successful TV series *Steptoe and Son* (*Sanford and Son* in the USA). They called their script *Jacob's Journey*. We added a few new songs, of which by far the best was "Seven Years" which worked because we compressed narrative in the way *Joseph* did. The melody subsequently appeared with a rather complex Rice lyric as "Disillusion Me" which Gary Bond recorded as a single.

The *Jacob's Journey/Joseph* double bill was doomed from the outset. West End audiences simply would not tolerate a first act that was a warm-up and Frank Dunlop's direction was far less effective behind a conventional theatre proscenium. I do, however, have one fond memory of the Galton/Simpson script . . .

> God: Jacob, I have decided thou shalt discard thy name and
>   henceforth be known as Israel.
> Jacob: Israel? But why?
> God: Just think of it as an old man's whim.
> Jacob: Yes, but Israel?
> God: Well, alright. How about Venezuela?
> Jacob: Doesn't sound very Jewish.
> God: Well, not at the moment no, but when people get used to it . . .

Come Easter we bowed to the inevitable. *Joseph* must be expanded to a full-length evening. One night in late June *Jacob's Journey* was ditched and the show that should have opened in the first place made its debut. Business increased, but not fast enough to save the day. Come the end of September *Joseph* closed.

That just might have been that. But immediately an offer came for a new production at the now defunct Haymarket Theatre in Leicester. Directed by Robin Midgley, it starred the son of a local celebrity Maynard Williams as Joseph and was an immediate local smash. Soon there was a highly successful UK tour, directed and produced by Bill Kenwright. In 1976 Frank Dunlop directed the lengthened *Joseph* at the Brooklyn Academy in New York. Finally, after various off-Broadway runs, it made the Great White Way, directed by Tony

Tanner in 1981 with the late great Laurie Beechman as the narrator. Laurie's performance was so definitive that from then onwards the narrator has usually been played by a woman.

In 1992 I produced a new version in the London Palladium, starring Jason Donovan which broke all Palladium box office records. That production subsequently played Broadway, Australia and toured the USA plus returning to the West End in 2007. The new elongated version has been made available to schools since the mid-1970s and has been performed throughout the English-speaking world ever since. Over 20,000 schools and colleges have performed *Joseph* to date.

JUNE 1974 FOUND US in Chicago promoting the *Superstar* film. I don't know why we were bamboozled into going. We had seen the movie. I thought it sounded awful. I was miffed because I had been fired from the orchestrations in favour of Norman Jewison's anointed musical director André Previn who, gallingly, got nominated for an Oscar for them. Considering the movie soundtrack used the original rock tracks from our album, I strongly felt that David and Robert should have fought to get me a co-credit. However I haven't seen the movie for 45 years, so I may well be better off without it. All I remember is liking the opening which I think featured a troupe of touring players arriving in the desert in a bus to enact the story of Jesus. Tim disliked the insertion of the words "Cool it man," moaning that if that's what got Melvyn Bragg a screenplay credit, what about him? I hated bits of interpolated music that I didn't compose and presume Previn wrote.

The reason the movie premiered in Chicago rather than New York or Los Angeles soon became clear. The Reverend Martin Sullivan's warning had come true. An outfit called the Jewish Defense League complained that the film's treatment of the High Priests and the mob was anti-Semitic because it implied the Jews killed Christ. There had been rumblings around the Broadway opening. Tim had successfully argued on TV with a rabbi called Marc H. Tanenbaum that it was a fact that both the victim and his oppressors were Jewish and that his lyrics deliberately took no sides. Furthermore the central point of the New Testament is that Jesus chose to die following God's will. This time the complaint caused serious damage. Ironically, not only was Norman Jewison's last movie *Fiddler on the Roof* but he had gone out of his way to mitigate criticism by having us write a new scene for the priests to deal with this issue. Looking back, I wonder if the scene exacerbated the problem.

I was upset about the anti-Semitic charge. Sefton Myers had discussed *Superstar*'s content many times. None of his Jewish friends had any issues and I believe Sefton raised *Superstar* with the then British Chief Rabbi Jonathan Sacks, who years later discussed with me the possibility of combining elements of the Christian and Jewish faiths into a text that I could set to music. I know Rabbi Sacks was very aware of the lyrics of "Close Every Door" from *Joseph*. Once again Tim won every public argument, but the pressure put on Ned Tanen and the Universal hierarchy was too great. The movie was effectively killed in the US. Maybe the Universal honchos were threatened by the JDL like the producer of the movie *Bridget Loves Bernie*. In 2001 the Jewish Defense League was classified by the FBI as a right-wing extremist movement.

TIM AND I SPENT a lot of time together that summer. We drove through France to La Mortola in his new BMW to do some more grindingly slow work on *Jeeves*. We had numerous contacts with P.G. Wodehouse's old book writer/collaborator Guy Bolton, whom the great man once described as "like mulligatawny soup . . . advisable not to stir." I was reminded that Wodehouse was the lyricist of the hugely successful trio Wodehouse, Bolton and Kern (Jerome Kern wrote the music) and he (PGW) famously wrote the lyrics of one of my favourite songs "Bill" in *Show Boat*. No one knew what hold Guy Bolton had over Wodehouse, but he (Guy) had heard about our *Jeeves* plans and even though he was nearly 90 years old tried to get in the mix. We had several meetings where he suggested we write songs for various enterprises that he had failed to get produced.

Robert Stigwood's in-house theatre man was an entertaining hard left-winger called Bob Swash. His politics, however, did not preclude him from seeing pound signs if he could steer the *Jeeves* project into the capitalist swamps of the West End via some of its best restaurants. Bob Swash knew progress with Tim was slow. Maybe a helping hand with the book might push things along. Enter playwright Alan Ayckbourn. His *Absurd Person Singular* had just opened to critical raves and Bob thought that a *Jeeves* project written by the trio of Rice, Webber and Ayckbourn would send luvvies into an orgy of frenzied anticipation. So he arranged for us to meet.

I immediately got on well with Alan, especially when the conversation got onto Burmese cats, and I thought we were seriously in business. But the fact that Tim allowed such a high-profile third person into our marriage should, in Wodehousian words, have put the Persian among the pigeons. For on September 20 Tim pulled out of *Jeeves*. It wasn't so much this that upset me. He had every right to withdraw from a project that he had qualms about. It was how he pulled out. I learned the news by way of a letter he wrote to Guy Bolton which he openly copied to me and David.

However my initial upset soon turned to delight. Tim having ankled from the three-way collaboration, Alan instead immediately offered to write the lyrics himself. I was triumphant. At last I had a real theatre collaborator and not only that but the British theatre man of the hour. This would show Tim a thing or three. Alan Ayckbourn was the artistic director of the Stephen Joseph Theatre in Scarborough where he always premiered his new work. He was already writ-

ing his play for 1974, *Absent Friends*, and was heavily involved with
the impending West End transfer of his most ambitious work to date,
a trilogy called *The Norman Conquests*. So *Jeeves* had to be put on ice.

There is a footnote. In November, P.G. Wodehouse himself wrote
to me, offering himself as my lyricist and suggesting an existing *Jeeves*
script by Guy as the basis for a Wodehouse, Bolton and Lloyd Webber partnership. Things had gone too far with Alan by then. But my
goodness, if only I had realized at the time just how amazing "Lloyd
Webber and Wodehouse" would have looked on my CV.

WHILST I WAITED FOR Alan I was kept busy thanks to Vi's old
friend, film director Ronnie Neame. I was seeing a lot more of Vi
now. Italy and her leg had proved too much for each other, so I helped
Vi and George buy a small house in the backstreets of Brighton. Although the Granny saga still rankled it was never mentioned and
they glowed when friends wanted help with house seats for *Superstar*
which was still London's hottest show.

In September Ronnie Neame asked Vi where he could contact
me. He was shooting the movie of Frederick Forsyth's novel *The
Odessa File*. Would I write the score? The plot was about the hunting
down of a notoriously sadistic Nazi war criminal. It was evocatively
set in a wintry Germany immediately after Kennedy's assassination
which appealed to me. Also *The Odessa File* was the follow-up to
Forsyth's massive hit *The Day of the Jackal* and with Jon Voight in
the lead it was guaranteed a high profile. The clincher was that the
film's veteran British producer John Woolf wanted a theme song
that could have been a German hit in Christmas 1963, sung by an
American artist who was big there at the time. Top of my list was
the Everly Brothers.

Unfortunately their fraternal relationship mirrored that of Joseph
and his brothers, so I was lumbered with a real old-timer, the mellow-

voiced Perry Como, hardly the rocker I had in mind. Perry Comatose would have been a better name for him. His performance rivals this book in guaranteeing even the most chronic insomniac hours of un-alloyed sleep. I asked Tim to write the lyrics although a large chunk ended up in German. Titled "Christmas Dream," it is my favourite "unknown" song we wrote together. US airplay was limited due to misinterpretation of Tim's couplet "Watch me now, here I go, all I need's a little snow." This was supposed to be a plea for a picture-postcard Christmas in a violent age but radio programmers divined an alternative meaning and banned it. There's a much better record-ing than Comatose's by the Leicester Haymarket Joseph Maynard Williams which, needless to say, didn't make the movie despite my hints.

The Odessa File was released in the fall of 1974 to OK reviews, the consensus being that the direction was pedestrian. The music came out of it rather well. But no one has asked me to score a movie since!

IN MARCH 1974 I had a meeting that turned out to have huge con-sequences, although the project that it was about didn't exactly ma-terialize as I thought it might. When I was very young I treasured two picture books. One was called *A Valley Grows Up* about how an imaginary town developed from prehistoric days to the twentieth century. My other favourite was *Thomas the Tank Engine*.

Thomas is the little steam railway tank engine star of a series of book stories set in vanishing rural England. It is the British equiva-lent of *The Little Engine That Could*. The moral of the books is that a properly brung up engine must be Really Useful all the time. I wanted to turn the stories into an animated musical TV series. So I met with their author, a retired clergyman, the Reverend W. Aw-dry. It was a pleasant meeting, although as I brewed instant coffee in the empty shell of my new vast country seat he must have wondered if he had come face to face with someone three stops down the line from Plaistow.* What would the Reverend Awdry have thought if he had known that his charming little books would indirectly inspire a gargantuan roller-skating musical and the name of a company on the Stock Exchange?

---

* I have been longing to get this expression into this doorstop. It is cockney for "mad." In Britain you talk of someone being "barking mad." Barking is a suburb of East London. It is three subway stops away from Plaistow.

17

Driverless Juggernauts
Hurtling Down a Hill

Whenever I am asked the old chestnut, "What's the secret of a hit musical?" I quote Oscar Hammerstein: "Fools give you reasons, wise men never try." Big hit musicals are very rare beasts. Every ingredient, story, music, lyrics, set design, choreography, direction and casting, to name but seven, have to come together and gel perfectly. It's far easier to explain why a musical doesn't work. Obviously most turkeys are just plain awful. Others – take *Chicago*, for instance – didn't have the right production first time around. It took fresh eyes and the O. J. Simpson zeitgeist for that great score to hit home.

In the case of *Jeeves* the team on paper looked really strong. At 25 I was the youngest but my form didn't look bad. Alan Ayckbourn had scored on both sides of the Atlantic with *How the Other Half Loves* and his latest trilogy *The Norman Conquests* confirmed him as catch of the day. Furthermore he brought with him another man of the hour, British director Eric Thompson, father of the actress Emma. Eric had not only directed Alan's recent successes but also plays like *My Fat Friend* and he was basking in his fame as the voice and script-writer of the BBC TV show *The Magic Roundabout*. The choreographer Christopher Bruce was feted as top dog at Ballet Rambert. The designer Voytek came with a pedigree featuring film work with Roman Polanski and a recent RSC production *The Marquis of Keith*, which had been raved about for a dazzling stage effect involving a vast disappearing dress. Shame he never met Tom O'Horgan. Stigwood decided to co-produce with Michael White.

Michael "Chalky" White was best known for producing *Sleuth* in the West End and had co-produced *Joseph* at the Albery, although I truthfully don't remember him being involved in any creative discussions whatsoever. He brought *The Rocky Horror Show* to the Theatre Upstairs at the Royal Court, was producing the movie *Monty Python and the Holy Grail* during *Jeeves*'s unimmaculate conception and had a knack of surrounding himself with the right beautiful people at the right moment. But he never saw *Jeeves* until it was well into its tryout. Here lay the problem. *Jeeves* had no producer. Robert had decided movies were his forte and would never see *Jeeves* until opening night. Michael was not the "lead" producer and was happy to let us theatre luminaries get on with it. Stigwood's man Bob Swash was great on nuts and bolts but no creative leader. The only person who had any creative experience in musical theatre was me. I had never worked on a new musical before and anyway who was I, a theatre newcomer ten years younger than Eric and Alan, to challenge a duo who had had so much success together?

It is impossible to overestimate the importance of a creative producer to a new musical. They are very rare beasts. In Britain at that time home-grown musicals could be counted on the fingers of an inexperienced sawmill operator. Hardly any exported. Tried and tested Broadway imports were the norm. There were several producers who had their names above local productions of Broadway shows, like Robert with *Hair*, but successfully importing an existing ready-made hit is really to be a glorified manager. Theatre bitches call them babysitters. It's not like being the guiding force behind creating a hit from scratch. If ever a disparate group, no matter how great their individual talent, needed the flair and firm leadership of a musical theatre producer, the *Jeeves* team was it.

. . .

THINGS STARTED REALLY WELL. Alan and I coincided in New York at the beginning of October. We had a look over some of the songs but our big excitement was our visit to Remsenburg, Long Island, so Alan could meet "Plum," as Wodehouse was known to his friends. I had visited the great man once before. The first time was when Tim, Sarah and I were in New York in 1972 following the London opening of *Superstar*. The really strange thing is neither Sarah nor I remember anything about it. I must have played some music, but Tim certainly didn't have any lyrics that he was happy to share with Wodehouse. Tim remembers opening his camera by mistake thereby destroying any evidence that the meeting ever took place. However, I remember our second visit extremely well. Alan, Sarah and I set off with Peter Brown plus a fey-looking photographer, whose task was to record the cathartic meeting and who Peter eulogized about. No mere snapper he. Here was the major artist the occasion demanded.

It was Sarah who heralded the first harbinger of Wodehouseland. Just as we came off the main highway towards Southampton she spotted a vast billboard proclaiming the Bide-a-wee Home for Lonely Dogs and Cats. We turned the corner into the Wodehouse drive where a pickup truck was revving furiously. Its cab was occupied by a tall, thin old lady and its flatbed sported three trays of freshly roasted chickens.

"Hello, I'm Ethel!" shouted the venerable woman above the din. "Just off to feed the cats, Plum's in the lounge, see you in a minute," with which the truck screeched into the middle distance. We headed for the house asap. It would have been unwise to be hanging around the drive when the pickup returned. In the porch stood the great man.

"Hello I am Plum," he said. "You must be Mr Ayckbourn, Mr Brown and Mr and Mrs Webber," the fey fellow having evaporated into the ether.

A huge dust cloud and an explosion of gravel announced Mrs Wodehouse's return and we all sat down for coffee – that is, all of us bar the fey photographer. After a rather stuttery chat it was time to play some music. There was a grand piano by the window and my nerves were not calmed when the great man said Jerome Kern had played *Show Boat* on it. Since singing was not top of either Alan or my credits, we had prearranged that Alan, script in hand, would mutter his lyrics in Wodehouse's ear whilst I banged the tunes out. When we got to "Half a Moment" he was visibly moved. After I had finished he fixed me in his eye. "Mr Webber, I don't think my characters can sustain an emotional song like this." It was a nice way of saying that what I'd written was a hopeless mismatch for his stories.

Things looked up when we played "When Love Arrives," a song which went down well even in the carnage of our first night. We had just finished when Wodehouse shouted, "Ethel, come here, there's a camera crawling around our shrubbery."

Alan and I swivelled round. There in the bushes outside the lounge window was Peter Brown's fey photographer, crouching and looking distinctly furtive.

"You there masquerading as an azalea, come out and show yourself!" commanded Plum.

By the time Peter had explained that this was his acclaimed photographic protégé bringing his unique artistic flair to the permanent record of our historic meeting, it was time to go. The Wodehouses had had enough. With an unforgettable parting shot to me, "I'd love to have had a go at writing that pretty ballad if ever you get stuck with the lyric," I was thanking Plum and Ethel from the car and we were on our way. What with Rice opening his camera and Peter's man in the shrubbery there is no decent photo to prove we ever met.

The melody of "Half a Moment" remains hugely personal to Sarah and me and sometimes I think that of all my ballads it might just be my favourite. I often wonder what it would sound like with a lyric by the man who wrote "Bill."

. . .

DESPITE EVERYTHING WE WERE in high spirits when we got back to England. The casting seemed excellent. David Hemmings was already confirmed as Bertie Wooster and on paper ticked every box. Ned Sherrin was spot on when he described him as a "debauched cherub." David was the quintessential film star of the Sixties, finding overnight fame in Antonioni's *Blow-Up* and marrying actress Gayle Hunnicutt. He famously described their marriage as "the poor man's Burton and Taylor." However by the time *Jeeves* was brewing he was living with Tim's now ex-girlfriend Prudence de Casembroot, Tim having ditched Pru for a cast member of the West End *Joseph*. Whether this was a factor in Tim's sudden *Jeeves* bailout I can't say. But I can say that Pru was a rock throughout *Jeeves* and everyone was delighted when later she and David got married.

David Hemmings was one of "Benjamin Britten's boys" and it is said Britten had a major crush on him. As a boy soprano he premiered the role of Miles in Britten's *The Turn of the Screw* and the marvellous aria "Malo" was inspired by his voice. I asked David if Britten's infatuation with him ever overstepped the mark but he was emphatic that Britten was scrupulously proper. Eric Thompson cast the splendid character actor Michael Aldridge as Jeeves to great approval from Alan Ayckbourn. Indeed all Eric's casting paid huge attention to character, even if it meant that the cast was made up of actors who could sing rather than vice versa. To top it all, the wonderful Anthony Bowles was there to keep our spirits up.

The first hint of impending doom was the script. This was no phantom Leslie Thomas job. It made *Gone with the Wind* look like a pamphlet and the songs made up barely 20% of the running time. When I squawked to Bob Swash, he said not to worry. Alan and Eric were a team of consummate pros. He was sure Alan had spewed all his thoughts out in a first draft which the pair would fillet away until the script was as razor-sharp as Brian Brolly's *Superstar* album sleeve. I was very alarmed. Of course I knew that there would be spoken dialogue, Wodehouse's humour massively stems from his turn of phrase, but everything I had done to date was music-driven. The songs seemed like appendages and rarely a part of the storytelling. Nevertheless I kept telling myself that Alan and Eric's recent successes couldn't have happened by chance.

MAYBE BECAUSE OF ALL this, my mind was already wandering. My first notes on *Evita* date from around the end of 1974. Despite Tim bailing from *Jeeves* the previous April, he and I agreed that if we found the right subject we'd have another crack at writing together. I had of course pointed out that this would have to wait until I came off the massive high of my imminent second West End smash. Our pact was struck after a preview of the musical *Billy* at the Theatre Royal Drury Lane starring Michael Crawford, with music by film composer John Barry and lyrics by our mutual friend Don Black. *Billy* was based on the film *Billy Liar* and the ingredients for a decent British musical looked unusually strong. I came away humming the title song and another called "Some of Us Belong to the Stars." The fact that I can remember the tunes over 40 years later speaks volumes. There was also a nice supporting performance by a soul girl from *Superstar* called Elaine Paige.

Tim and I decided that our meaningful discussion would happen over dinner at Covent Garden's then top restaurant Inigo Jones. Just as the menus materialized Tim leapt up and said he'd left his coat in the theatre. He promised he'd be back with it before you could say "*Poulet de Bresse à l'estragon farci à la mousse d'écrevisses et sa petite sauce de vin jaune doux de Jura aux échalotes.*" Ten minutes passed. Then another ten. Post-theatre diners looked at me sorrowfully and I would use the word "piqued" to describe my state of mind at this point, if it wasn't that I was embarrassed rigid. I had a dilemma. Should I stomp off furiously, muttering to a passing waiter that the partnership that was supposed to be the salvation of British musical theatre was damned for all time, or did I merely order off London's finest dinner menu and sit tight? I chose the latter option.

I was well into my first course when Rice returned. He needed a yarn worthy of Billy Liar himself to wriggle out of this one.

"Webster," his voice had a placatory tone, "I went to the front door to get my coat, the guy there had seen me wearing it when we went in, realized I'd left it behind and gave it to the stage door man."

"So?" I replied.

"Just as the stage door man was giving me my coat I bumped into Don Black."

I said I hoped Tim had been nice about the show.

"Oh I was," said Tim, "hence the cock-up, Don kept asking what I thought about various scenes and I found myself in a production meeting."

"Who was there?" I asked.

"Oh, just John Barry, Michael Crawford and the director [Patrick Garland]. Every time I said you were waiting in a restaurant they asked me about another scene, at one point they wanted me to come and get you. Look," said Tim after considerately ordering a steak tartare as it involved no cooking, "this could be a great idea for a musical. Bloke goes back to theatre to pick up forgotten coat. Backstage he meets the cast and creators. Ends up changing the plot, rewriting the songs, playing the lead and winning a Tony Award." I am still occasionally taken with a musical about a show whose plot morphs from Florence Nightingale as a girl into Donald Trump as Professor Bigley, the nutty rocket professor, in Kim Jong Un's *Kung Fu Capers*.

Tim too recalls that we discussed the idea of a musical based on Eva Perón before he exited *Jeeves*. I don't think we did that night at Inigo Jones, but I do remember Tim saying not long after that he had heard a James Dean profile in a BBC Radio 4 series about 1950s idols and there was a trailer for next week's subject, Eva Perón. Why on earth was an Argentine dictator's wife fodder for a series featuring

James Dean? My only vague recollection of Eva Perón was her face on a postage stamp. But by Christmas 1974 I realized that the Eva Perón saga had captivated Tim. He was very keen for me to see a documentary about her by an Argentine director Carlos Pasini Hansen called *Queen of Hearts*. Eva Perón acquired that epithet four decades before Princess Diana annexed the phrase.* I would have to get a handle on Eva Perón's story fast.

1975 DAWNED AND REHEARSALS began in a church hall in then terminally dreary Clerkenwell. I turned up for the meet and greet, eagerly anticipating a new lean and mean script, but instead what I and an instantly wary cast were handed was something the size of the European Convention of Human Rights. Equally unpromising was the litre of cheap supermarket wine that appeared at midday on Eric Thompson's work desk. From day one it was clear that Eric had a real drink problem. Assistant stage manager Hugh Wooldridge (Hugh went on to a successful career particularly as a director of theatre concerts) would plonk a litre of a brand wine called Hirondelle on his director's desk come 12 pm, followed by a second late afternoon which Eric glugged openly. Consequently the cast had little respect for him. Meanwhile choreographic rehearsals were taking place in another room with no guidance about how dance might fit into the story and in yet another Anthony Bowles and I were rehearsing close harmony numbers that eventually made no appearance other than in the entr'acte. There was absolutely no sight of a producer who could get a grip.

There is a weird sense of mañana that overtakes a disaster musical as it careers towards opening night. Disaster musicals are like driverless juggernauts hurtling down a hill. It's impossible to put the brakes on and turn the brutes around. Despite not even doing a rehearsal

---

* "I would like to be the queen of people's hearts," she said, in a BBC *Panorama* interview in November 1995.

room run, we left for our Bristol tryout with ridiculous optimism that somehow *Jeeves* would all come together once we had sets, costumes and an audience. It was the same during our dreadful time in the Bristol Hippodrome. There were endless excuses, like the theatre was too big (it was) and it will all come together in the half-sized Her Majesty's in London. The truth was the show was ridiculously long – the first preview was nearly four hours. Nothing coalesced, the design did not fit the script and my score didn't fit it either. A whole plot strand involving Bertie Wooster's food-obsessed favourite Aunt Dahlia was cut, thus unemploying the wonderful actress Betty Marsden and cutting two of the songs.

David Hemmings literally drowned his sorrows after shows in the hotel bar where he ordered whiskies and performed close magic tricks for any travelling businessman who would keep him company at two in the morning. When finally co-producer Michael White did turn up, it was blindingly obvious that the London opening should be aborted. He too clung on to the straw that some "deus ex machina," as Jeeves might have said, would come out of the closet and save him and his investors. He did, however, move Eric Thompson sideways and put Alan in the director's seat.

Jeeves opened in London on April 22 to excoriating reviews. Alan and I spent the second act round the corner in the bar of Le Petit Club Français, the greatly lamented, long-lost St James's Street club that General de Gaulle held court in during the Second World War. Despite our gloom we did make a pact that someday we would rewrite *Jeeves* from scratch.

Lucklessly for us the peerless Hal Prince production of Stephen Sondheim's *A Little Night Music* opened the week before and critics had a field day comparing the two. There were a few reviews that said the songs weren't too bad with Jack Tinker in the *Daily Mail* writing that my "catchy tunes were left high and dry" by the script. However, the venerable *Sunday Times* critic Harold Hobson, perhaps recalling my chivalrous behaviour to Dame Sybil Thorndike at the *Superstar* opening, pronounced *Jeeves* to be close to a masterpiece. He continued his encomia for three weeks, thus earning a special *Private Eye* section "Hobson on Jeeves" in its Pseuds' Corner. A year later he pronounced *A Chorus Line* as almost as good as *Jeeves*. He was retired shortly afterwards having barked up the wrong tree once too often. Sarah and I went to Venice where it hit me how huge the strain of Sydmonton and now *Jeeves* had been on her. She had lost a ton of weight and her hair was looking like she was having chemotherapy. I noticed through rehearsals that she seemed to be unusually thirsty, but in Venice she was drinking gallons. When we got home she went to see her doctor who said she had a classic case of stress and prescribed valium.

Just as I thought things couldn't get bleaker a letter appeared by hand. It was on Savoy Hotel headed paper and read: "I've just seen Jeeves. Bank the score. Remember you can't listen to a musical if you can't look at it. Are you writing anything else? Harold Prince." It's impossible to put into words how much that letter meant to me. I was struggling over a reply when instinct said call him. I met Hal in the American Bar that evening. He was unbelievably encouraging. I poured out how sorry I was about the *Superstar* saga. He reiterated that a stage design has to be right for the material. *Jeeves* needed something simple and elegant, what was on stage was elephantine and ugly. So chin up and get moving. What was I writing next? I said I was probably going to write a musical about Eva Perón with Tim Rice. Hal made me swear that if we finished it I would bring it to him first.

18

Eva and Juan

If you think the 2008 financial crisis was serious stuff, take a look at what happened a third of a century earlier. Things were desperate in the USA. The Dow lost 45% – nearly half its value – compared to 20% in 2008. But that was as nothing compared with what happened in Britain. By January 1975 UK stocks had lost three-quarters of their value in a single year. Imagine the impact of such a crash today. Jim Slater, the financial guru of the moment, summed up Britain in 1975. "People need just three things, baked beans, krugerrands (gold) and a gun to protect your family." The *Wall Street Journal* went further. An article that coined the phrase "Britain is the sick man of Europe" concluded "Goodbye Great Britain, it was nice knowing you."

It's no exaggeration to say that by 1974 Britain was on the verge of political meltdown, some even felt revolution was possible. The problems began in 1970 with the election of a Conservative government under Edward Heath. The hard left, wrong-footed by his victory, began a campaign to overthrow his administration. 1973 saw open war erupting between government and the trade unions, exacerbated in November 1973 when OPEC announced a 70% increase in oil prices.

In February 1974 the Miners Union called an all-out strike and Heath put Britain on a three-day working week. Power cuts were introduced on a rota which theatres, like much of industry, tried to get round by installing generators. In March Heath called an election; result, a hung parliament. Heath resigned and Harold Wilson came to power leading a Labour administration. Later in the year another election handed Wilson a tiny majority. Across the board wage increases in the public sector got the lights back on. But government expenditure rose by 35% while inflation galloped towards 20% and income tax was raised to as much as a staggering 98%. In June 1974 the fascist National Front clashed with the International Marxist Students Group, one of whom was killed. Army colonels were rumoured to be forming private armies to fight a Communist takeover.

Enter the Irish Republican Army, now under the control of dedicated Marxists as evinced by an extraordinary American TV interview given in 1974 by Seamus Twomey in which he admitted that it had been IRA strategy to get British troops into Northern Ireland to protect Catholics from Protestants so the IRA could point to British troops on the streets and label them occupying "oppressors," a strategy he claimed could eventually be employed to overthrow capitalism in the USA. A vicious bombing campaign began across the British mainland. In late November, 21 people were killed in the bombing of two Birmingham pubs. Every London restaurant window was protected by iron grilles, the IRA having chucked improvised bombs packed with rusty nails and ball-bearings through the windows of several of London's eateries. Even the exclusive basement club Annabel's in Berkeley Square was surrounded by sandbags.

Given all this it is not surprising that the story of Eva Perón resonated with me back in 1975. The pro-fascist Peróns came to power by harnessing the Argentine trade unions to overthrow what was the most liberal democratic country in Latin America. Despite Tim claiming his treatment was an apolitical Cinderella story when the record of *Evita* was launched in 1976, it is surely implausible that what was going on in his home country didn't rub off on him somehow.

THE DAY AFTER *JEEVES* opened I had an emotional phone conversation with Tim. I asked him point blank if after the reviews he still wanted to work with me on his Eva Perón project. He told me not to be so daft. Maybe because we'd taken ourselves away to a hotel when we started writing *Superstar*, but by the end of the call we had decided we'd try our luck again. We settled on Biarritz, a fading seaside resort on France's southwest Basque coast, close to the Spanish border. I had not been to Biarritz. It became famous when the Empress Eugenie, wife of Napoleon III,* built a summer palace there which is now a faded grand hotel. This seemed a great excuse to see it. We booked a suite, ordered a piano to be installed therein and set off for a few days on our own with our wives following on later. Yes, our wives. Tim was now a married man.

Maybe, as David Land suggested, it was because the *Superstar* tours were grinding to a close so the supply of Mary Magdalenes and Maids by the Fire was drying up. Whatever, Bill Oakes ended the Oakes/Rice trawl through that particular New Testament zone by marrying the doyenne of the Mary Magdalenes, Yvonne Elliman herself. For a short while Tim's attentions had hopped back a testament to one of Jacob's wives during the *Joseph* run, but by 1974 he had moved on. Sarah and I realized that Tim was unusually serious about Jane McIntosh when he took her on an *Evita* fact-finding trip to Argentina early in 1974. By the summer they were married with a child on the go.

Sarah and I were thrilled. Jane is an absolutely gorgeous, petite, Scottish lassie of the glens, sparky, intelligent and always fun to be with, brimming with life enhancing fun. When they met she was working at Capital Radio where Tim was doing a spot of disc jockeying. However she knew her way around theatre, having been a production assistant on various musicals including *Grease* starring Richard

---

* A good trivia question is where are Napoleon III and his wife buried: Notre Dame Cathedral in Paris, Elba, or next door to London's private jet centre Farnborough Airport? Answer: next door to Farnborough Airport. The exiled duo were rather matey with Queen Victoria and built an abbey at Farnborough to house their remains. The abbey looks as if it ought to be in the Loire Valley. Next door the Empress built a palace in exile, which resembles a vast, demented Swiss chalet.

Gere which flopped at the New London, a fact much rubbed into me when seven years later the theatre was announced as the home for *Cats*. When Tim met Jane, she and Richard Gere were an item and Tim made much of Jane changing Gere for his urbane charms. Jane seemed fiercely ambitious for Tim and hugely loyal. Sarah and I enthusiastically raised a glass to the newly weds at their reception in the Savoy with high hopes that the marriage would lead to a long, happy relationship between the Lloyd Webbers and Rices. I believed, in spite of my father's prediction, that the old firm was back in business.

BY THE END OF 1974 Tim had done a lot of work on the Perón plot. He was particularly pleased with his discovery that Che Guevara was Argentine and a contemporary of Eva. Guevara applied for a patent for an insecticide he invented which was turned down during the Perón regime. Was this the catalyst for him switching from being a nice middle-class capitalist to a card-carrying revolutionary? Tim found the thought as intriguing as it was amusingly provocative. Also by introducing Che into the story, Tim once again had a character who could step outside the action and act as narrator.

The story of Evita is simple. Eva Duarte was the illegitimate child of a small-town family in the Argentine pampas who cajoled and slept her way to Buenos Aires where she became a local pinup actress star. After an upwardly mobile set of rough and tumbles she became the bedfellow of a hungry-for-power colonel called Juan Perón. Soon she was his glamorous wife, playing a vital role in achieving his political ambitions. She tirelessly whipped up support for Perón among the *descamisados*, the shirtless ones, with "for the many not the few" platitudes. Together they ruthlessly eliminated anything or anyone that stood in the way of Perón's goal of becoming President of Argentina. "Evita," as she became known, acquired the aura of a saint among her beloved *descamisados*, whilst being perceived as a common slut by the Argentine establishment. She had not long turned 30 when she was diagnosed with terminal cancer. She died aged 33, ironically the same age as Jesus Christ.

From our first discussions I saw a serious problem. There is nobody in the story with whom you empathize, hardly a great premise for a successful musical. But I could see why Tim was so taken. And I loved his idea for the show's opening. A film showing the real Eva in a Buenos Aires cinema is interrupted by an announcement that she is dead. Cut to her enormous state funeral. Che emerges from the crowd as a voice of reason among the grieving – and bingo, we're away to the races.

Eva's death at such a young age of course gives the story a tragic twist. But because, at least for me, Eva had such ghastly values I couldn't see how to make an audience care about her; more importantly, *should* I make an audience care? The more I thought, the more certain I was that I needed a device which allowed an audience to remain emotionally detached from Eva, whilst understanding why she captivated so many.

It took me what seemed like ages to come up with a solution but I vividly recall when and where I did. It was on a Saturday afternoon in Bristol at a particularly low point in the *Jeeves* saga. I was humming a chorus of "How do you solve a problem like Evita?" when I remembered back in 1969 I saw one of the last-ever concerts by Judy Garland at London's The Talk of the Town. Non-perform might be more accurate, Judy was an hour late on stage and the dinner-theatre crowd, fuelled by the cheap house champagne, was restless, to put it mildly. Eventually she stumbled on, made a stab at "The Trolley Song," but was so blurred and incoherent that audience members threw coins on the stage.

What happened next was unforgettable. She motioned to the musical director and he started playing "Over the Rainbow." As she stumbled through her signature song, the booing and whistling grew louder and louder. "Over the Rainbow," her anthem, the song which is indelibly Judy's and Judy's alone, was devouring her like a vulture on a battlefield. It was like seeing a frail little sparrow crushed in an iron fist. It was heartbreaking. I hoped I'd never see such a spectacle again but sadly I did nearly 40 years later at a concert by the equally tragic and irreplaceable Amy Winehouse. If I could find an anthem for Eva and turn it on her like "Over the Rainbow" had turned on Judy it would unlock her story musically. That afternoon I wrote the slow tango melody of "Don't Cry for Me Argentina."

But that alone wasn't the solution. There had to be a dramatic context. Tim had suggested a scene where Juan Perón addresses the crowd as President of Argentina from the balcony of the Casa Rosada, the pink presidential palace in Buenos Aires, with Eva by his side as first lady. What if we reconstructed the scene so she wasn't beside him at the start? Perón makes a rabblerousing speech which goes down fine but the crowd really wants Evita and chants her name. She then makes a real star entrance before her own speech. That speech would be her anthem, her cynical love letter to her people. The crowd responds ecstatically and now she delivers her own rant. At the end of the show the anthem becomes her broken final broadcast to the Argentine nation. It has come back to bite her like "Over the Rainbow" bit Judy. I felt the balcony scene was so potentially powerful that it should close the first act, although this was not to be. I knew that its construction used music as manipulatively as you can get, but that's what a through-composed score can do and I felt good about it.

THESE IDEAS WERE ALL very well but what would Tim make of them? I felt like I was auditioning when we settled at the slightly out of tune grand piano in our jaded Belle Époque suite in L'Hôtel du Palais. Through the window I could see the relentless Atlantic surf battering the slightly sad, grey promenade. It looked a bit like my career. But Tim loved my anthem. My confidence flowed right back and immediately it was like the old days. We found a workman's cafe just off the seafront with a pinball table which we got well stuck into. There was simple real French food that you don't find now France's 35-hour week has clobbered family restaurants. One lunchtime there was unusual silence as we bagged our regular table. All eyes seemed to be on me as I viewed the menu du jour. A new dish was on offer "*cuisses des fourmis.*" The habitués knew that the more obscure the dish was the more likely I was to order it. *Cuisses des fourmis* seemed just my ticket. There was a short silence, maybe an intake of breath. Then there was an explosion of laughter, even applause. "*Cuisses des fourmis*" means "ants' thighs."

Writing went really well over the next few days and we were in high spirits when we collected our wives from the airport. Although Sarah looked dreadful, my delight at seeing the two girls together outweighed any worries. Sarah and Jane couldn't have been more enthusiastic about our writing and the four of us had a great time sightseeing and talking about the future, not just professionally but personally too. We all noticed how thirsty Sarah was but I was used to this by now.

As I look back this may have been the high point of the relationship between Tim and me. Here we were, two young, happy married couples together with a new project we were excited about and everything to play for. Sarah and Jane nattered kids. Tim and Jane's daughter had been born in February. Naturally she was christened Eva.

"How wrong was Dad about Tim and I?" I said to Sarah one night as we giggled in bed over a half bottle of champagne. "And shouldn't we have a baby too?"

Sarah turned the lights off.

BACK IN LONDON I had a meeting with Granada TV boss Johnnie Hamp about *Thomas the Tank Engine*. I first met Johnnie when Granada produced the pre-lengthened *Joseph* as a TV special with Gary Bond strutting the Technicolor robe. Johnnie completely saw the potential of an animated musical series based on the engine books and I immediately got David Land to obtain the rights. Writing music for something as simple and heartwarming as *Thomas* would be a joyous antidote to the heavy waters of *Evita*, as our story of Eva Perón was now called. I went home to Sydmonton, bubbling about the meeting to find Sarah in a very strange state.

All the stuffing seemed to have been knocked out of her. Everything she did was an effort. Beside her were a stack of empty juice tins. I immediately drove her up to London to see her family doctor for what seemed the umpteenth time. He reiterated his strong opinion that she was suffering from severe stress and prescribed valium.

Back at Sydmonton I blamed myself for her deterioration. We were living in a vast house with only a part-time, semi-retired, married couple to help with the cleaning and the huge overgrown garden. What had I done to the radiant eighteen-year-old bride I had married? It was no consolation to see the catalogue of the Victoria & Albert Museum's current exhibition *The Destruction of the Country House* among the books strewn on the kitchen table.

Next day Sarah was worse and her thirst was astonishing. I phoned Sarah's doctor and demanded he saw her again. Stress surely couldn't be the sole cause of her condition. Once again I drove her to London. Once again he said her condition was brought on by extreme anxiety. In his opinion she needed her mind taken off the ridiculous house I'd lumbered her with and I should stop burdening her with worries about my work.

When we got home I took him at his word and suggested we went for a pub supper. Sarah sat down by the kitchen table, buried her head in her hands and sobbed and sobbed. Next morning I woke to Sarah gasping for breath and moaning between gulps. She was hyperventilating. I screamed at our nonplussed part-time couple to call the local Newbury doctor whilst I carried Sarah still in her nightie downstairs and got her on to the back seat of my car. I bundled her into the doctors, bypassing a gawping queue of patients, who seemed quickly to forget their ailments once they sensed they were viewing something sensational involving a minor local celebrity. The local GP called for an ambulance whilst repeatedly questioning me about drugtaking. Time and again I assured him that neither Sarah nor I had ever taken drugs. Wine yes – me, gallons of it – but drugs were not our scene. The ambulance took us to Battle Hospital in Reading. The journey seemed to take forever. I sat in the back, holding Sarah's hand. She was fading fast. As we came off the motorway, sirens wailing, one of the ambulance men took my hand.

"Is she your sister?" he asked.

"No, my wife," I mumbled.

He turned his head away. I heard him say, "Sorry, son."

IT MUST HAVE TAKEN half an hour to reach Battle Hospital. A team was waiting to rush Sarah into intensive care. Voices kept going on and on about drugs and I kept repeating that neither of us had ever touched them. Sarah disappeared on a trolley, I remember a female voice shouting, "I have an idea," and suddenly I was alone. I was in an empty lobby. At one end was a phone box, at the other a newsstand. There were a few empty formica chairs. It was a modern hospital. That's all I registered. I checked my pockets. In my rush I had forgotten to take any money and I had left my wallet behind too. The clock on the wall said 9:20 am, in ten minutes my new PA should be in our London flat. I went outside to a sort of garden courtyard. At the other end was a chapel. I didn't go in – I don't think my head was clear enough to pray. At 9:30 I made a reverse-charge call to my flat from the phone box I was to get to know well over the next few hours.

My new PA was called Biddy Hayward, a powerhouse of a girl who became a big part of my life over the next few years. She sounded highly surprised when asked would she accept the charges for my call, breezily saying, "I suppose so." I tried to explain what had happened but was pretty incoherent. I didn't know what was wrong with Sarah and nobody had appeared to tell me anything. I just asked Biddy to head to Reading as soon as possible and to contact Sarah's and my parents plus Vi and George in Brighton. Biddy was reminding me that Sarah's parents were away in Yorkshire when there was a frantic tap on the phone box door. It was a young female doctor in a surgical outfit. When she spoke I recognized the voice that had shouted as Sarah was wheeled away.

"Your wife could be diabetic," she said. "Quickly tell me any symptoms that might help us. We don't have time to wait for the bloods." I told her about Sarah's chronic thirst. "Thank you," she called out as she ran down the corridor, "that's all I need to know."

Then I remembered that I had arranged to meet Tim at Sydmonton at 11 am. I reversed the charges to Biddy again. Would he believe that I was cancelling out because my wife was dying? He was growing immune to my drama queen antics. This would take the biscuit. After ages the young doctor emerged and sat beside me. "Sarah is diabetic," she said. She had never seen diabetic poisoning go so far. She had put Sarah on intravenous insulin on a hunch even before I had told her about her thirst. That gamble might just save her life but her blood was so toxic that she had to tell me the chances of pulling through were way less than 50/50. She was worried that there was nowhere for me to wait. Would it be an idea to go home? I said that home was a 90-minute round-trip. Unlike A&E in hospitals today, Battle Hospital was pretty deserted. I would wait at least till Biddy arrived. My next thought was to phone Sarah's doctor. Now I was growing really angry. There was no way he would accept a reverse-charge call, so I borrowed some coins off the newsstand. The prat's arrogance was mindboggling.

"Listen here, laddie," I remember his words distinctly because of the patronizing way he said "laddie," "there is no way your wife is diabetic. She is overstressed. Has she taken drugs?"

I wanted to say, "You pompous bastard, you have probably killed my wife," but I was too shell-shocked. I went to the chapel and did what you do in chapels when you don't go for architectural reasons.

BIDDY HAYWARD TURNED UP. There was still no news of Sarah. A matter-of-fact lady in the A&E office said the doctors were all doing their best and absolutely could not be disturbed. Biddy had found a phone number for Sarah's parents so I called them and her mother promised to return home immediately. We took a walk and found a local greasy spoon. I don't remember our conversation though I do recall a congealed fried egg. I poured my heart out to Biddy. Maybe it was a defining moment in what became a long, personal and professional relationship.

Back at the hospital we were met by the young woman doctor. Sarah was still in a coma. I asked if I could see her and she said that was not really her decision but she saw no harm. Sarah was in a small room, hooked up to too many tubes to count. A nurse was holding what looked like a panic button as she monitored the bleeping gadgets. I gazed at Sarah and took her hand. What had I done to this young girl? Had stress bought this on? Someone had told me that diabetes was stress-related. Then she opened her eyes, looked at me and gave me a faint squeeze. She was alive. She recognized me. Then she closed her eyes again. The young doctor motioned that it was time to go.

In the corridor I thanked her. Whatever happened now, at least Sarah had recognized me. The young doctor said Sarah was far from out of the forest, but the fact that she had slipped out of the coma was a really hopeful sign. She advised me to leave my phone number with her and go home. There was nothing I could do hanging around the hospital A&E department and Sarah would be in intensive care for a long while. I pulled myself together enough to ask her how she guessed that Sarah was diabetic. She said that she was a trainee blood specialist and Sarah was showing the classic symptoms of the terminal stage of type one diabetes. By luck she had been seconded to the doctors who greeted the ambulance when it arrived. Her name was Marilyn Croft. She was the first member of the Battle Hospital team to save Sarah's life.

VI AND GEORGE HAD driven from Brighton to Sydmonton and were waiting for me when I got home. It was a huge comfort to have them for company in that rattling empty house. The only other occupant was our Burmese cat Grimshaw.

George thought I was in no fit state to handle calls from the hospital and anyway as a doctor he was more likely to be told the truth. The rest of the day is a blank other than that it was stiflingly hot. Vi cooked some supper but even she did a reasonable impression of a Trappist as we toyed with it. Around 9 pm George spoke to the night doctor in charge of intensive care. His name was Dr Fisher. George thought he sounded very young. Dr Fisher told George that Sarah was drifting in and out of consciousness. He didn't think I should wait through the night at the hospital, but it would be good if I was nearby. I thought about going to a nearby hotel but it would be a quick drive from Sydmonton in the middle of the night and I didn't want to rely on some half-asleep hotel operator putting an emergency call through in the small hours. George gave me a pill.

I must have crashed out immediately because when I awoke I still had my clothes on. The bedside clock said 2 am. I picked up the phone. It was dead. I tried the light switch. Zilch. I found the torch we kept beside our bed and opened the door onto the staircase. We were in the middle of a massive thunderstorm. The rain was pounding the skylight so hard it sounded like a football rattle. I went downstairs to the sitting room. The curtains hadn't been drawn. Suddenly the church on our lawn was bathed in a garish white light and then the trees turned as black as the thunder that followed. El Greco would have reached for his easel. I went to the kitchen and tried the phone there. That was dead too. There was another monumental thunder-clap and the electric wiring bedded in the Tudor plaster wall lit up like a Christmas tree. Again the pill George gave me must have got the better of me.

When I awoke I was lying on the sofa opposite the kitchen TV. It was bright outside and I guessed it was around 7 am. I picked up the kitchen phone. It was still dead. I went to the sitting room, tried the second phone line but of course it was dead too. I was panicking now. Through the window I could see that the giant Wellingtonia behind the church was split down the middle. Grimshaw was miaowing. I cursed him but then I thought I should have had the little cat with me during the storm. I hoped he hadn't been too scared. I took him into my arms as Vi appeared, gave me a big hug and said, "No news in the night is good news."

I was explaining that the electricity had gone down in the storm when the power flickered back on. Almost immediately the phone rang. George picked it up before I could. The hospital had rung re-peatedly in the night. Why had nobody replied? Sarah had been on the brink of death throughout the small hours of the morning and no one had answered the phone.

Sarah was fully conscious when I got to the hospital. It was true she nearly died. Years later, Sarah still describes what she saw and felt that night as the most astonishing and beautiful experience she has ever had. She says she gets "a strange fizz" at the base of her spine whenever she talks about it. She tells of a beautiful tunnel lined with the most loved people and the happiest moments of her life combined with an overwhelming feeling of joy. Then there was a huge hole on the other side of which were people she knew who had died bidding her welcome. Suddenly she felt herself being pulled back up the tunnel and waking to seeing Dr Fisher saying "We nearly lost you at 3 am."

19

The Long Hot Summer and the Sound of a Paraguayan Harp

I was so overwhelmed just to see Sarah alive that I don't recall what we said. I only remember that her resilience was extraordinary. We had announced a cello recital at Sydmonton by my brother Julian for two weeks' time as I wanted to discover if there was a potential local audience for an annual Sydmonton Festival. Sarah said cancellation was out of the question. Furthermore she had made some pastry for after-concert quiches which was in the freezer. With Vi at Sydmonton, could I carry on with these, please? Although she was very weak, she was determined to get to grips with diabetes and its implications immediately. There were many people with type-one diabetes who lived normal lives. Sarah Jane Tudor Lloyd Webber was going to be one of them. Such was Sarah's determination that the musical evening indeed went ahead as planned. Its success spawned the Sydmonton Festival which for three decades has premiered most of my new writing.

Top priority was to get Sarah under the wing of a top diabetic specialist. George and Brian Pigott's recommendation was Dr David Pyke and a consultation was arranged immediately after Sarah's discharge. Sarah had two key questions. Could she lead a normal life and could she have a baby? The answer was yes to both, provided she looked after herself. Forty-five years ago it was more complicated for a diabetic to have kids than it is today. But everything was possible provided she followed two cardinal rules. Regular blood monitoring and no refined sugar. Refined sugar is toxic to diabetics. It wasn't the sweetest pill for Sarah's dad to swallow as a bigwig in Britain's top sugar company. I had to learn to help with her twice-daily insulin jabs. I was so squeamish and worried about my shaky hand that I discovered an insulin gun gadget that stops you seeing the needle. Sarah still thanks me for something I forced her to do out of total self-interest. I was terrified that her diabetes would mean no more eating out. Everything from the palaver of pre-meal insulin injections in public places to paranoia about the wrong sort of sugar threatened no more top nosh for yours truly.

So I doubled up on our restaurant visits. This kicked off a crash course about the ingredients in the dishes we were eating. The consequence of Sarah's diabetes was that we both ate better than ever, and far more healthily to boot. It does nobody any harm to know how much sugar there is in carbohydrates or different types of fruit. For instance, how many people realize that there is around 60% more refined sugar in Fever-Tree tonic water than there is in Schweppes?* Controlling diabetes is about balancing the natural sugar the body needs with the right amount of insulin to process it. We found that a sensible diabetic can safely eat out and enjoy wine without any danger. You just have to know what you're eating. Sarah is 64 now and we are blessed with two healthy children. She is living proof of the sugar-free pudding. If everybody followed a diabetic diet we'd all be a heck of a lot healthier.

COMPLETING *EVITA* MEANT ZERO travel so Sarah could be based at home. Most of the time Tim and I worked at Sydmonton. He wasn't yet living in the house he had bought with Jane in the Oxfordshire village of Great Milton, a village now famed as the home of Raymond

---

* Fever-Tree has 8 gm of refined sugar per 100 mL; Schweppes has 5.1 gm. (I've never tried either.)

Blanc's two-Michelin-starred Le Manoir Au Quat'Saisons. It's just as well it wasn't open in 1975. *Evita* might never have happened.

By the beginning of 1976 we were ready to play through the show to an understandably bemused David Land and his wife Zara at my Eaton Place flat. Two non-singers and my dodgy piano playing perhaps didn't entirely convey the potential of our latest epic. From the outset Tim was keen that we recorded *Evita* first. Having stumbled with *Superstar* by mistake on what people presumed was a brilliant marketing strategy, it seemed a good plan. Sadly no record company was that interested. An obvious candidate was Robert's own RSO Records who had a huge deal with Polydor. Robert told me that he had to make money for his shareholders and this story was not for him. I don't know to what extent David Land shopped *Evita* around, but eventually we ended up back at MCA. Did they feel they couldn't turn us down?

Tim was worried. The new boss was Roy Featherstone with whom he had brushed in his EMI days, Brian Brolly having long left MCA to run Paul McCartney's affairs. I was less apprehensive because of Roy's comments about my Tales of Justine arrangements. But the truth was that there had been a six-year gap between *Superstar* and *Evita* with no Rice/Lloyd Webber successes in between. It was obvious that record company honchos feared we were one-hit wonders. A double album about an Argentine dictator's wife didn't sound like fodder for instant chart success. So I had another meeting which I thought best to keep to myself. At the beginning of February I had a drink with Hal Prince at the Savoy. I even showed him some of the material. We made a pact that when the album was finished I would be his guest at his holiday home in Mallorca and play him what we had done.

AH THE ARROGANCE OF youth! From the outset I didn't want to get into Argentine pastiche. I figured no proper opera composer took on the persona of the countries their plots were set in. Puccini didn't plaster *La Bohème* with accordions because the story is set in Paris. I was pleased that the melody that would become "Don't Cry for Me" had a tango lilt, but I was going to score it my way, not give it a fake Argentine patina. Also I did something highly irrational. I loved the sound of the Paraguayan harp. For no other reason whatsoever I stuck a harp in the rhythm section. Years later when I went over the score for Michael Grandage's revival, I did some re-orchestration with tricks that Argentine cafe musicians use, like doubling the string bass with the left hand line of the piano. It certainly added local colour and probably is better. But 40-odd years ago my thinking was a country mile from authenticity.

First I tried to re-form our old *Superstar* Grease Band-based rhythm section but nobody was around. In any case as the writing progressed I realized I was moving away from the heavy rock they played so well. So I assembled a new band around a brilliant young drummer, Simon Phillips. Simon was much more attuned to modern jazz than any of the old rockers and this greatly influenced the choice of the other players. My obsession with the Paraguayan harp led me to a brilliant jazz harpist, David Snell. I'm glad it did. The harp might have nothing to do with Argentina. But by using it as an integral part of the rhythm section – rightly or wrongly – it immediately gave *Evita* its own dynamic. Joe Moretti and Ray Russell did the honours on guitar. Henry McCullough had now joined Paul McCartney's Wings but was available for a few tracks as was our *Superstar* sax player Chris Mercer, despite there being few places in the score where I could use him. Finally I was recommended a young keyboard player, Ann O'Dell, whose credits included working with Blue Mink and Roxy Music.

Olympic Studios was again our first-choice studio. Sadly Alan O'Duffy was now freelance and MCA Records baulked at the cost of hiring him – he would have cost extra – so we wound up with the equally qualified Olympic staffer David Hamilton-Smith as our man at the control desk. Finally Anthony Bowles came on board as orchestral conductor with Alan Doggett in charge of choirs.

TIM AND I HAD a big West End hit still running so this time artists picked up the phone when we called, even if a stack of eyebrows were raised at what we called about. The happening TV show was a raunchy series about three aspiring rock chicks called *Rock Follies*. All three girls, Charlotte Cornwell, Rula Lenska and Julie Covington, were singers with acting pedigrees. But it was Julie Covington who caught our eye as a potential Eva. She had been in the original London cast of *Godspell* which featured a gaggle of young actors who crossed into the pop world, most notably David Essex who soon was to premiere the role of Che in the theatre. Julie was a very of-the-moment, self-styled tomboy. She dressed like she was one of the Greenham Common peace women. I knew a fair bit about this crowd as Greenham Common air base, now no more, was close to Sydmonton. The women set up camps around the perimeter fence to protest against the base being stocked with American nuclear warheads. Since the alternative was B11 bombers – which were huge noisy brutes and would have flown over my home whilst the stationary warheads were silent – Sarah and I were massively in favour of the warheads. Sarah is a peace and quiet woman.

Julie was super left-wing so probably it was the sheer uncommerciality of the subject that overcame any qualms she had about playing the role of a fascist dictator's wife. We met at my flat and from the moment she sang Tim and I knew she was special. We made some demos at Air Studios with me accompanying on piano of "Buenos Aires," "I'd Be Surprisingly Good for You" and "Don't Cry for Me." Julie had the most extraordinary vulnerability combined with a serious rock belt voice. The demos were spine-tingling. From the moment Roy Featherstone and the MCA Records team heard them they were unstinting in their support for the project. Naturally we asked Murray Head to try some of the Che songs but this time he didn't really connect with the material and anyway he was becoming a huge star in France.

Both Tim and I had been hugely impressed by the takeover Judas in the London *Superstar* Colm Wilkinson. Colm is a wonderful Irish rock tenor, who subsequently created the role of Jean Valjean in *Les Misérables* and premiered *Phantom* for me in 1985 at Sydmonton Festival. He hugely got Anthony Bowles's vote and he became our Che. Tim had a very brilliant thought for Perón, Paul Jones. Paul had been lead singer of the sixties band Manfred Mann but had long left the pop world behind. He was now an established West End actor and accepted our enticements immediately. This left three smaller but important parts, Perón's schoolgirl mistress, Agustin Magaldi, the cheesy second-division tango singer to whom Eva hitched her star en route to Buenos Aires, and a cameo role for the manager of the Fundación Eva Perón.

Robert Stigwood had recently signed a young folk singer called Barbara Dickson to his label. She had starred in *John, Paul, George, Ringo . . . and Bert*, the Beatles musical by Liverpool writer Willy Russell, which Stigwood co-produced in the West End. I heard her in March at Ronnie Scott's club and thought her honeyed, folksy charm just right for the mistress's song "Another Suitcase in Another Hall." The "manager" cameo role fell to Chris Neil, another *Superstar* takeover who had followed Paul Nicholas as Jesus. He sang "And the Money Came Rolling In" which became Che's song come the stage show. I can't think why it wasn't given to Che in the first place.

The big question now was who could play Magaldi the tango singer? Someone had a brilliant thought. Tony Christie. Tony Christie was a mainstay of the working-men's club circuit who had a big UK chart success with songs like "I Did What I Did for Maria" and "(Is This the Way to) Amarillo." We decided to bypass the usual minefield of agents and managers and approach Tony directly. This dictated a visit to Cleethorpes, a less than salubrious seaside resort on the Lincolnshire coast where Tony was performing a summer season on the end of a pier. After an extremely slow and complicated train journey we eventually arrived in the pouring rain at the run-down pier theatre. We parked ourselves outside the stage door waiting for an audience with the star turn. As the wind howled and the waves lashed the groaning rickety steel structure, little seemed to separate us from the angry North Sea. Tim turned to me and said, "Andrew, if in 1965 someone had shown us a snapshot of where we are now, would we have written *Jesus Christ Superstar?*" Over a very pleasant dinner with Tony in a restaurant that served dishes like grilled grapefruit with brown sugar and sherry, we persuaded him to come on board.

I met with the musicians on March 1 to decide the best way of working. I wanted the harp to be integral to the band. However, I had never yet come across a harpist who didn't play from a formal written part. I feared that if I wrote formal arrangements it would clobber the musicians inventing freely. I had reckoned without harpist David Snell. We evolved a shorthand system about where we stuck to the written notes and where he could play freely. Recording was set to begin on April 4.

Before we began there was one important piece of business to get out of the way. I hadn't forgotten *Thomas the Tank Engine*. On January 15 the Really Useful Company had been incorporated as a vehicle for my *Thomas* TV project. It had a hundred one pound shares owned 50/50 between Sarah and myself. I didn't think at the time that this little company would one day grow into the worldwide production company it is today. But for now Thomas had to rest in his siding.

THE SUMMER OF 1976 was the hottest in Britain on record and co-starred Britain's longest-ever drought. At Sydmonton the effects were devastating. Centuries-old beech trees literally fried and handed in the towel. If it happened today it would be hailed as conclusive proof that the entire Antarctic had melted. Back then we just thought it was horribly hot. The heat didn't interrupt the smooth recording of *Evita*, except when the full orchestra plus Julie Covington were assembled in Olympic Studio 1 to record "Don't Cry for Me." The studio control room was in lockdown so I was not best pleased when a harassed young tape op barged in saying there was an urgent phone call for me.

"Who the hell is it?" I yelled.

"The army," he replied.

It transpired that what with the heat and the drought my tax scheme had caught fire, i.e. my forest at Pant Mawr was ablaze and would I authorize the army to extinguish the flames? I told the military bloke that I had a 70-piece orchestra waiting for me and to do what he had to do. You see what I mean about tax schemes always coming back to bite you?

Maybe the blaze explains why the first recorded version of "Don't Cry for Me" features a vintage cock-up. If you listen to the big orchestral section after Julie Covington has stopped singing, the french horns play a humdinger of a wrong note which I didn't notice at the time. I thought I had got away with it until two years later the legendary film conductor Harry Rabinowitz passed me in a corridor, loudly humming the errant horn line.

Julie did a magnificent vocal take that day. But it raised an outsized problem I was wary of broaching with Tim. The title we recorded wasn't "Don't Cry for Me Argentina," it was "It's Only Your Lover Returning." One of my beefs was that it didn't fit the melody. The word "it's" weakens the impact of the tune because it adds an extra note. It anticipates its start and screws up the melody which starts on the down beat. Surely Tim could hear what I meant? He had completely grasped the scansion when he wrote "Don't Cry for Me Argentina," the first line that Eva sings in the show. Tim came up with a new title "All Through My Crazy and Wild Days." It fitted my melody and it made sense . . . "All through my crazy and wild days / The truth is I never left you." But as a title it sucked and Tim knew it. I kept saying why not let's use "Don't Cry for Me Argentina" and be done with it, but Tim said it made nonsense of the rest of the lyric. Eventually we threw logic to the wind and went with "Don't Cry for Me Argentina."

The problem now was how to prise Julie Covington out of rehearsals for Tom Stoppard's *Jumpers* at the National Theatre. She asked us to send a discreet car so she could sneak to Olympic Studios in secret. The last thing she wanted her compatriots at the National to discover was that she was sidling out to moonlight as a fascist dictator's wife. So we hired the biggest stretch limo we could find and despatched it to the National. The twist was that we stationed the Olympic crew who worked on the album at various street corners between the National and the studio. Each in turn flagged the limo down to hitch a ride, so by the time it got to Barnes most of the Olympic's employees were heaving alongside our star in the back seat. It did the trick. Julie was well into the spirit of the occasion when she gamely dropped in the line "Don't Cry for Me" protesting all the while that the lyric made no sense. When we heard the song back it didn't matter about the sense. It sounded absolutely right.

ONCE *EVITA* WAS MIXED, we presented the work to MCA Records. Roy Featherstone's reaction was as ecstatic as Brian Brolly's had been about *Superstar* and he set a UK release date for October. We went ahead with an audiovisual presentation at the first-ever Sydmonton Festival. Tim did a great job in assembling slides to accompany a playthrough of the album. The famous wit Frank Muir was in the audience and had an issue. There was a line sung by Che Guevara about his flyspray invention "if you've got six legs, I ain't doing you no favours." Frank pulled Tim aside and said he strongly objected to its tone. "It's an unwarranted attack on the Andrews Sisters." Everyone else was overwhelmingly positive.

Next I contacted Hal Prince, who I discovered was in London en route to his holiday home in Mallorca. We met briefly at the Savoy Hotel and Hal immediately invited me to stay at his villa. Hal and his wife Judy's house was on the north of the island near Pollença in a converted former monastery that looked over the village to the sea. Sadly the view has changed today, but the north of the island felt very remote then. Franco had only just died and the journey from the airport passed through towns that seemed third world compared with the Riviera I knew through Aunt Vi.

Hal had allowed me to interrupt his family holiday with Judy and his two children, Daisy and Charlie. We all had dinner on my first night and I don't think *Evita* was even mentioned, nor the next day. I was beginning to wonder when it would be, but that evening Hal scooped me up and said we were off to the port for a drink. Over a bottle of wine Hal quizzed me about musicals, how I had discovered them, what my ambitions were, and I told him my story. We didn't talk about *Superstar* – there wasn't much point.

It seemed I passed the interview. Next day we listened to the recording. I knew that Hal's mind was whirring when he heard the opening funeral music. Subsequently he tells that the moment he heard the full symphony orchestra and vast choir that we had recorded, he was hooked on directing *Evita*. I just remember him saying that *Evita* had great moments but that he had some issues, particularly with the Che Guevara insecticide plot which he thought was irrelevant. But he was genuinely excited enough to want to contact Tim with his thoughts. We agreed it was best to say that I had sent him the recording for his comments and that he would reply to both of us, without letting on that I had been anywhere near Mallorca.

When I got home I told Tim and David that I had met Hal at the Savoy, sent him the recording and was intrigued whether he would reply. "Who is this mush?" Tim exclaimed to David Land. Of course they both knew precisely who he was. Shortly we received this letter:

Dear Andrew (and Tim),

. . . I have tried to include everything that occurs to me, without regard for your feelings . . . overall I think it's a fascinating project. You fellows deal in size and I admire that. Before I get into individual scenes, numbers and lyrics, I would like to say I had a feeling (which grew) that something is missing in the second act. That fate intervenes and levels Evita rather than instruments of her own doing. You touch on growing disillusionment within the government, but you don't describe it theatrically. There is no confrontation in which Evita (and Perón) accelerate their own downfall. The first act is structured so well that I found myself considering eliminating the intermission, which is a cop-out, and then I realized what I was missing in the structure of the second act. It's all in number sixteen (And The Money Kept Rolling In) and probably should be solved there.

. . . The opening is dazzling. I would like, for the stage, to use the movie theatre more organically. Not for multi-media sake, but because I see something similar to Citizen Kane in the piece's style and aspirations . . . I'm crazy about the idea of Che functioning in the piece, but I think – again for the stage – he should be much cooler, loose and cynically humorous. If he is to be strident, it should be after the waltz, after he is politicized.

The funeral is brilliant, as is Magaldi's song.

I think Che is too British. I think some of his recitative is corny, quite frankly below the rest of the material. I don't get a clear character as I do Eva and Perón and some of the minor characters. He seems a familiar rock performer, "Listen chum, face the fact they don't like your act," and "Which means get stuffed" also seems too British.

I don't like the way the GOU is explained. It's too easy. It interrupts, but I don't think effectively. On the other hand, I would recommend eliminating number seven (The Lady's Got Potential) entirely, which means that the GOU will have to be explained.

"She is a natural high" (Isn't this an anachronism?)

I like Eva's seduction of Perón and the scene that follows with his mistress. I think it will work well on the stage.

I'm sorry but I do not like "Dangerous Jade". I wish that you would excise it.

The last scene in Act One is marvellous (at that point "On The Balcony Of The Casa Rosada" "Don't Cry For Me Argentina") but I don't think that the aristocrats are written as ingeniously, either musically or lyrically, as they should be. I don't think they necessarily need more material but they are predictable – so I wish they were better written. It remains a question in my mind whether Evita should revert in the final speech or whether she should simply capitalise on the aria; after all the audience knows by now who she is.

. . . In "Rainbow High" I do not like the reference to Lauren Bacall (principally because it distracts.)

I think it's a mistake for Che to say "I don't think she'll make it to England now". It confuses us. Wouldn't it be clearer if we knew from Che that she eagerly awaited an invitation from Buckingham Palace, and subsequently she was snubbed? (Incidentally, I would retain the quatrain about the King of England.)

Much as I like the waltz, there are some words which I do not like. "So why go bananas chasing Nirvana" (I think it distracts because it is not up to quality.)

Tim, I am aware you may be offended by this, but "So Saint Bernadette ME!" faintly embarrasses. (Again it distracts.)

In summing up, I think the style of the piece should be abrasive – simple – raw is probably a better word. Contemporary Brecht. Bold.

Best to you both, Hal

PS Tim I wish I'd met you. It might make some of these criticisms easier to take in a more personal context.

The letter is instructive about how Hal thinks. He finds an overall concept – he calls it a metaphor – as a catalyst for a production and this is nearly always visual. This letter shows he had already identified that the cinema screen in Tim's opening scene could become an audiovisual device throughout the show.

With the record release's date set it was too late to change the writing much, ditching the insecticide plot would mean delaying the release until next year. But in August I did rework "Dangerous Jade." What a difference an orchestration makes! It was such an improvement that the sequence survived unaltered in Hal's production two years later.

Any guilt I had about the sneaky way I had introduced Hal Prince into the mix evaporated when I discovered that Tim and Jane had gone to stay with Robert in Bermuda and had played him the tapes. I knew Tim was doing a presentation to the US MCA chiefs in Los Angeles, but I didn't know – or at least I didn't realize – that he was going to see Stigwood. Apparently Robert liked them, although I only learned this in a roundabout way from David Land. I would have liked to be there, but actually I didn't really mind that much.

EVITA WAS 103 MINUTES long, considerably longer than *Superstar*, but like *Superstar* it had to be squeezed onto two vinyl albums. When you cut a vinyl album the louder the music the more the grooves physically open up. So a typically loud rock album is less than twenty minutes a side. Obviously the longer the music, the smaller the grooves have to be to pack the music in. So the side has to be cut at a lower volume which affects the sound quality and also, disastrously if you are trying to break a pop album, means it sounds quieter on the radio than its bedmates. This created a massive problem for *Evita*, especially Side 3 which is 28 minutes long and at the absolute limit of what a vinyl side can cope with. Side 3 contains the scene with "Don't Cry for Me" and it was vital for it to sound great. An additional mega problem reared its head. "Don't Cry for Me" was chosen as our first single. It was six minutes long. Most 45 rpm pop singles last three minutes or so. "Don't Cry" is scored for a symphony orchestra who play alone for a full minute before the soloist begins. How on earth were we going to get enough volume onto the 45 rpm disc for it to remotely compete on radio with its three-minute rivals?

For me sound quality is everything and successfully transferring *Evita* from tape to disc was driving me nuts. This wasn't the kind of issue Tim worried about as he figured other people are paid to sort things like this out, so it's their problem. I realized that we needed a craftsman to cut *Evita* and that it would probably take several attempts to get it right. Roy Featherstone totally understood. But now comes a perfect example of why the relationship between easy-going Tim and hypertense Andrew became stretched to screaming point.

I had arranged a listening session at Olympic to work out where to alter volume levels to work out how to make the record easier to cut. Our engineer, David Hamilton-Smith, was on holiday. So I listened to the tapes on my own, making notes about where I could make sections quieter so the important sequences could be cut louder for radio. I was really pleased with what I heard until a tape op came in and casually said that the Dolby noise reduction system was not switched on which meant the recording sounded unnaturally bright. Once the "Dolbys" kicked in the recording sounded dull and lifeless.

I was hysterical. I found David Hamilton-Smith on holiday in

Greece and told him to fly home so we could remix everything. David came back and, maybe because he had made the effort to come home but I'd like to think because he agreed there were a few things we could improve, gamely started the whole mixing process again. Tim went nearly spare, saying he couldn't hear what the problem was. We struggled through all four sides again and tempers frequently were as frayed as a worn out Persian carpet. On August Bank Holiday Monday we finished the remixes, the rain fell, the worst drought in living memory was over and *Evita* was finally ready for her close up.

THE BEGINNING OF SEPTEMBER brought Sarah and me a moment of real joy, even if for Sarah it was tinged with a touch of trepidation. She was pregnant. Blood tests showed that her diabetes was reasonably stable. However blood sugar monitoring in 1976 was not as simple as it is today and her specialists made it absolutely crystal clear that she would have to be in hospital for at least six weeks before the baby was born. Six weeks incarcerated in hospital was a big ask for a 25-year-old woman and worse the London hospital with the best diabetic care facilities was not in the centre but in the southeast suburb of Dulwich. Assuming nothing went amiss Sarah would be admitted to hospital in mid-February 1977 and the baby born on a precise date, March 31. That meant I would have to be in London for February and March, a problem if *Evita* was launched in the USA. We decided to keep the pregnancy dark for a bit, not least in case anything went wrong.

MCA launched the album at the New London Theatre, one day to be home to *Cats* and *School of Rock*. On the afternoon of the playback I once again went berserk. The playback quality in the auditorium was so appalling I threatened not to turn up to the listening. Eventually David Land calmed me down but not before David Hamilton-Smith had been hastily drafted in to sort out the sound system. The playback then went very well and the audience feedback was very positive.

But by now Tim was sick of my tantrums. The problem was exacerbated because the more laid back he was about everything the more wound up and passionate I became. My defence is that I care so much about getting sound right. Forty-plus years on I haven't changed. I have behaved appallingly in theatres because of bad sound more times than I care to mention.

20

The Song that Cleared
the Dance Floors

As with *Superstar* the construction of *Evita* was task number one. If you are not interested in the construction of musicals I suggest you skip the next few pages. We agreed at the outset where the big set pieces would be so "Buenos Aires," the song celebrating Eva's arrival in the Argentine "big apple," was written early. Likewise Eva's rabblerouser "A New Argentina," the only real rock moment in the score, was completed early. Tim's idea of opening in a cinema and segueing into Eva's huge state funeral suggested a major musical building block. His ending had Eva singing a retrospective "lament." I wrote a melody that could serve both. It was vital to portray the massive scale of the occasion. I set an adaptation of the words of the Latin Requiem Mass *"Requiem aeternam dona Evita"* for the grieving chorus/crowd and built the music to a huge climax which is undercut by Che. Using Che as a narrator meant that we could tell the story *Joseph* style. So Che fills in the Perón back story in "Oh What a Circus" which is melodically a rock tango version of "Don't Cry for Me."

After a concluding rant by Che against Eva and all she stood for, the focus shifts back to the funeral. The chorus sing a setting of the Latin "Salve Regina" to the tune of the verse of "Oh What a Circus" which is then taken up by the full orchestra. Now we hear the voice of Eva, literally from the grave, singing "Don't Cry for Me Argentina" for the first time in her own version of the chorus we first heard sung by Che. The "Oh What a Circus"/"Don't Cry for Me" melody is not heard again until it underscores Eva's entry on the balcony of the Casa Rosada much later in the story. The minute-long sequence holds because the audience subliminally associates the music with Eva.

I smile inwardly every time I hear the funeral. Ever since I saw the Zeffirelli production of *Tosca* at Covent Garden I wanted an excuse to fire a cannon off stage. Tim gave me a gift. "Ride on my train oh my people / and when it's your turn to die you'll remember / they fired those cannons sang lamentations." I grasped the opportunity. After the funeral we get down to business with an urgent 6/4 time rocky melody designed to move the story on. It was as deliberately un-Latin American as I could make it with a mildly dissonant motif that recurs in various guises. Tim has Che seamlessly darting in and out of the action so we learn quickly that Eva has hitched herself onto a second-rate tango singer called Agustin Magaldi so she can exit her backwater home for Buenos Aires. Magaldi tries unsuccessfully to talk Eva out of the plans in "Eva Beware of the City," but in a contrasting "Eva on the Move" section she makes it abundantly clear that she didn't drop her knickers for nothing.

They arrive in the capital to an explosion of the Paraguayan harps whose sound grabbed me so much back in 1976. I particularly liked this eruption because Paraguayan harpists love playing in musical tenths so the major third always features in their chords. When they play in different octaves they commit the harmony teachers' number one cardinal sin. They double the major third, but frankly it sounds great. I revelled in the opportunity to commit musical mortal sin in the most heinous way.

The set-piece song "Buenos Aires" shows off not just Eva's triumphant arrival but also the city's social make-up. Back in 1976 I wanted to keep the rhythm section rocky so I wrote a little riff with Henry McCullough and the guitarists. But over the years Latin got the better of the song and finally with Michael Grandage's production I handed in the towel and bossa nova now reigns unchallenged.

Tim's device of moving Che seamlessly in and out of the action works really well for songs like "Goodnight and Thank You," where a stream of Eva's lovers are unceremoniously given the boot. Tim compresses a long passage of time into this one song.

Next up on the original album is "The Lady's Got Potential." Musically it is a deliberately old-fashioned rocker in which Che veers away from the Perón saga to the plot Tim liked so much about Che's capitalist hopes for his flyspray. Once Hal was on the scene it was junked for "The Art of the Possible." (Alan Parker, a true old rocker at heart, reinstated it minus the flyspray for his 1996 movie.) Next Eva meets Perón backstage at a political rally to raise money for earthquake victims and hits on him with "I'd Be Surprisingly Good for You." Here, as with "Don't Cry for Me," I needed a melody that I could use again as Eva approached her death. I enjoy listening out for whether performers accurately sing the deliberate dissonance (a note that is intended to sound slightly "wrong") on the word "for" which occurs in the line "I'd be good for you too" at the end of the middle section. Many presume it's a mistake. It's not. It's about the deep cynicism of both protagonists.

"Another Suitcase in Another Hall" was deliberately written as a standalone number sung by Perón's schoolgirl mistress after she is unceremoniously egressed by the upwardly horizontal Eva. I took Hal's advice about banking the score of *Jeeves* literally. Tim opined that *Jeeves*'s worst moment was a song about a tennis match called "Summer Day." He was right. So I reused its chorus for "Another Suitcase." I suggested that we knitted the song into the structure by reprising it in what would have been a factually accurate scene where a new very young girl becomes Perón's latest item as Eva is clinging onto life. We never wrote this, although the germ lingers in a very short reprise of the "Another Suitcase" chorus at the close of the final scene between Perón and Eva.

The next scene "Dangerous Jade" is the song we re-recorded after

Hal Prince heard the first draft. The army officers who put Perón in power are juxtaposed with the aristocrats as they sing of their mutual opposition to Eva. A brief scene with Perón and Eva leads to the only real rock song "A New Argentina." I even used the old heavy-metal trick of two drummers playing identical parts. I got the idea for Eva's rabblerouser from the crowd chanting at a soccer match in the infamous, long-demolished "Shed" at Chelsea football ground. Come the stage show "A New Argentina" ended the first act but on the concept album a scene with Perón and Eva set to the "Eva on the Move" music segues straight to the balcony of the Casa Rosada, the scene which is my biggest contribution to *Evita*'s architecture. First Perón makes his maiden presidential speech to the crowd. Demagogues use similar speech patterns, so I wrote a low-pitched musical line for Perón to trot out a few nationalist platitudes which rises to a high register when he extols "the humble bodies of Juan Perón and his first lady Eva Duarte de Perón." Eva then makes her lengthy entrance.

I am still proud of my orchestration of "Don't Cry for Me." The sense of space created by the basses and four french horns in the second verse is an effect I have never bettered. The crowd reacts wildly to Eva's anthem. Those who criticize the cynicism of Tim's words are missing that the lyrics are meant to be hollow crowd-pleasers. Eva is performing her signature set piece. It is an act. Backstage an exultant Eva receives a mega putdown by an army officer – "Statesmanship is more than entertaining peasants" – commandingly sung by our recording engineer David Hamilton-Smith. The scene ends with massive block chords on the rock guitars and brass accompanying the increasingly frenetic crowd as Eva returns to the balcony with a musical expression of the type of meaningless crowd-pleasing garbage that depressingly is once again all too familiar.

I originally intended the first act to end with Eva's putdown to the aristocracy "Your despicable class is dead" and Act 2 to begin – as it does on the concept album – with a contemplative orchestral variation based on music from the Junin cafe scene. First up is a very short reharmonized version of its opening line followed by an equally short but disturbing development into "High Flying, Adored"* played on the upper strings. My idea was to start Act 2 reflectively with Che and later Eva taking stock of events before Eva gets back to business with "Rainbow High." "High Flying, Adored" contains some lines that have always bothered me. "You won't care if they love you it's been done before / You'll despair if they hate you you'll be drained of all energy / All the young who've made it would agree." As someone who's been through half a decade in a trough and come out the other side, I know the lyric doesn't speak for me.

Eva's biggest solo aria is "Rainbow High." This "world is my oyster" moment invariably defines whether you are seeing a truly great performer playing Eva or not. It is among the most demanding showcases I have composed. The bouncy Paraguayan harp tinged "Rainbow Tour" relates the saga of Eva's solo European tour with a melody that harks back to easy-going *Joseph* days. Now we get the first inkling of Eva's failing health and witness her fury at being invited by the King to Windsor Castle rather than Buckingham Palace. (I wonder if Eva realized that "Windsor Castle" is an anagram of "Ascot Swindler.") The aristocracy crow about Eva's half-successful trip before the music changes direction. Eva's retort "the actress hasn't learned the lines you'd like to hear" is one of the few occasions where I set Tim's words to music rather than the music coming first.

Although the section is followed by a short reprise of "Another Suitcase" with entirely different lyrics, I introduce elements of the whole-tone scale, an early twentieth-century musical idiom that introduces an effect of bleakness. This is developed by Che in his interruption "Forgive My Intrusion," followed by a short section or-

---

* "High Flying, Adored" is the same melody as one that was wasted in a previous Rice/ Lloyd Webber song "Down on the Farm," recorded with Leicester Haymarket's Joseph Maynard Williams.

chestrated for percussion. It is a harbinger of Eva's death and was suggested by a deserted ice-cream van parked outside Battle Hospital on the day Sarah nearly died. It was overbearingly sinister, like the cart serving apricot shandy in Bulgakov's novel *The Master and Margarita* when the devil first arrives in Stalinist Moscow. Whenever I hear the chimes of an ice-cream van I shiver. On the very rare occasions that *Evita* is performed with its full orchestration, the chime-like effect of the xylophones and glockenspiels gives me the creeps.

Che now scythes through a ton of information in "The Money Kept Rolling In" which tells of the highly irregular activities of the charitable Fundación Eva Perón. This scene was Tim's idea. He felt we needed an energetic up-tempo song before the scenes leading to Eva's death. I added a chorus to a very loose adaptation of an authentic Peronista propaganda song which I twisted into 7/8 time. The finish with its false ending, another of Tim's suggestions, is always a big applause moment, the last until the end of the show. Thus the song's function resembles "King Herod's Song" in *Superstar*. Like its *Superstar* cousin it occurs halfway through Act 2 and closes the third side of the original double album. It releases the audience's tension before the nitty gritty of the final furlong.

Another variation of "Oh What a Circus"/"Don't Cry" shows children and later a crowd elevating Eva into semi-sainthood. Now Che directly challenges Eva's values in "Waltz for Eva and Che." Tim portrays both as cynical political opportunists. I composed a bittersweet waltz which I orchestrated for full symphony orchestra. It was recorded at the Henry Wood Hall, whose brittle acoustic I thought perfect as opposed to the much warmer sound of Olympic Studio 1. This performance by Julie and Colm is still my favourite, possibly because it is the only one with my original orchestration. It does, however, contain a couplet that caused such a major issue for Tim that he often claims it sums up his take on life. "Why go bananas / chasing Nirvanas" grated with too many people for it to make it onto the stage.

The next section on the concept album is a stinker in both our departments. Che rages about his denied patent and departs the action with an Oedipus cry of "Oh My Insecticide," a Monty Python-esque moment that utterly undercuts the waltz. It now lurks where, to quote Lorenz Hart, "harps are just the thing." Discontent builds with the military moaning about Eva's increasing usurping of power. Perón maintains that it is her popularity with the *descamisados* that keeps the military regime afloat in his only solo song "She Is a Diamond," a reflective melody whose last line deliberately echoes the last of "I'd Be Surprisingly Good for You."

Now follows the final scene between Perón and Eva for which Tim wrote the words first. He was particularly pleased with Eva's "sonnet" which he wrote in strict iambic form. It contains the lines "conservatives are kings of compromise / It hurts them more to jeer than to applaud." I was sorry that the lines were axed when Hal felt the sonnet was too long for that late in the evening. Before the scene concludes, the terminally ill Eva collapses in Perón's arms. It's the one moment I allow the audience an emotional connection with Eva through a big orchestral statement of "I'd Be Surprisingly Good for You" followed by an ironical reprise of "What happens now?" from "Another Suitcase."

Next comes the Judy Garland Talk of the Town "Over the Rainbow" moment. A broken Eva sings an equally broken version of "Don't Cry for Me" in her final broadcast. This time the lyric makes perfect sense. A kaleidoscopic collection of fragments of previous scenes follows, depicting Eva's dying thoughts before her final lament. On the concept album the lament is twice the length of the stage version which lost Tim's verses where Eva mourns the child she never had. They should be reinstated someday.

EVITA WAS BILLED AS an opera on the first MCA album. Needless to say, that caused outrage among some and made it a cause célèbre with others. What else could we call it? It wasn't a "rock opera" – much of it is orchestral and anyway that sounded very dated by 1976; and it wasn't a musical in the conventional sense as it was through-sung. Personally I think it is a pointless discussion. The British reviews were polarized. Our ever-loyal Derek Jewell in the *Sunday Times* led with "Simply A Masterpiece" whilst the then pop bible of the thinking man *Melody Maker* countered with "Eva's Giant Turkey Trot" and was appalled that a singer/actress such as Julie Covington would have had any association with such garbage. This didn't encourage Julie to help us with promotion.

Unlike *Superstar*, the album of *Evita* was a massive hit in Britain and a fair bit of the world but a total bomb in the USA. The single of "Don't Cry for Me" was a slow burn on British radio, but when it did ignite it took on the aura of the epic six-minute single "MacArthur Park." DJs spoke reverentially about the daring of the one-minute orchestral introduction.

By the end of February the holy grail of a performance on the all-powerful TV show *Top of the Pops* celebrated Tim and my first UK No. 1 single. Even then Julie Covington refused to perform. She merely deigned to turn up whilst the record was played to a potpourri of Eva Perón slides. I was particularly intrigued when "Don't Cry" hit No. 1 in the disco charts. A dance hit with a one-minute adagio introduction played by a symphony orchestra suggested action on the dance floor that I didn't know about. The chart triumph was easily explained. Discos were using "Don't Cry" to clear people out last thing at night.

Evita wasn't the only thing on my horizon. Hal Prince suggested I saw a charming movie called *Shakespeare Wallah* in which a very young Felicity Kendal plays a teenage actress in a travelling theatre troupe bringing Shakespeare to Indian cities against the rising tide of Bollywood – an uphill challenge if ever there was one. I couldn't work out how it could be a stage musical and, I suspect, neither could Hal as the project never materialized. Maybe I wasn't ready for *Shake-speare Wallah*. Years later I produced *Bombay Dreams*, the first Bol-lywood musical to appear on the London and Broadway stage which introduced the brilliant subsequent double Oscar winning composer A.R. Rahman to Western audiences. London loved it, but A.R. is a Muslim and when I brought it to Broadway critics reacted as though I was in league with Al Qaeda. I lost the entire investment.

Thomas the Tank Engine was also chugging down the track. I had knocked up some songs with Peter Reeves, the narrator in the Edin-burgh Festival/West End *Joseph*. Peter was a witty writer with tons of experience in children's TV. Johnnie Hamp at Granada commis-sioned a pilot episode (recorded in January 1977). Granada bosses were excited and the laborious pre-computer era animation process steamed into action. My third project involved no collaborators. I be-gan composing "Variations on a Theme of Paganini."

At the end of 1976 several siren voices emerged to lure *Evita* away from the commercial stage. The Earl of Harewood, then chairman of the English National Opera, was the first. The thought of a premiere in a proper opera house with a full orchestra obviously was a tanta-lizing proposition, even though there was no way trained opera voices were right for the score. A more serious thought materialized from Aunt Vi's old friend Ronnie Neame. He offered to direct *Evita* im-mediately as a movie. Ronnie did have serious Hollywood street cred. Since *The Odessa File* his stock had swelled with the massive box office smash, *The Poseidon Adventure*. He had directed Albert Finney in the Leslie Bricusse musical *Scrooge*. What tempted me were his promises about the movie's sound. Cinema sound had hugely improved since *Superstar* and my stage experiences so far led me to fear that *Evita* would never be heard as I wrote it in the commercial theatre. Ronnie put pressure on us to let him hawk *Evita* around Hollywood and at a meeting in my London flat at the beginning of 1977 we guardedly let him off the leash.

Two weeks later saw MCA's almost derisory launch of the album in New York's Paris Theatre. We might as well not have bothered to turn up. At the playback someone laughed at the deliberate moment where the movie breaks down in the opening scene. MCA's publicist Lynn Kellerman even wrote to David Land that we were "hardly the local heroes in the USA that your boys are in Britain" to justify her company's lack of enthusiasm. At least Sarah was able to hold my hand. Her diabetic specialist trusted her enough to let her fly, even though she was over six months pregnant and her long enforced hospital stay was only days away.

As the year rolled on Ronnie's attempts to fire up an *Evita* movie hit ever stonier ground. I was terrified of history repeating itself and once again being manoeuvred into a theatre production with no real producer. Stigwood was well into movies by this time with *Saturday Night Fever* and *Grease* under his belt. So theatre was now small beer for him and he was already making noises about Michael White as *Evita's* possible creative producer. I was determined that someone with real creative production experience took the helm and that man should be Hal Prince. Hal was not just a superb director, his producer credits of *West Side Story*, *Cabaret* and *Fiddler on the Roof* weren't too bad either.

Although my views on Hal were deafeningly clear, the Stigwood camp was playing schtum. So I played a game. I kept saying that I was unsure whether a theatre production was wise. Tim grew so furious with me that once we nearly came to blows in the foyer of the Regency Hotel. However all the while I was in touch with Hal. In early April we had a major catch up in the Savoy Hotel. I don't think my subterfuge paid bad dividends.

21

Imogen and Niccolò

Something positive did come out of our US non-promotional trip. Two young producers Craig Zadan and Neil Meron invited Tim and me to be part of a cabaret series called *Broadway at the Ballroom*. Broadway composers and lyricists entertained for an hour or so with anecdotes, warbling their own songs with varying degrees of success. We were to be part of the second series. Craig and Neil had exhausted obvious names like *Bye Bye Birdie*'s Charlie Strouse and *Fiddler on the Roof*'s Sheldon Harnick and were forced to dig way deeper into the pile, hence us. Craig and Neil were obviously going places. *Chicago* heads a long line of their movie credits and they pioneered the recent slew of live TV broadcasts of classic musicals.*

The slot we were offered was the first week in March. Sarah was scheduled to be in week three of her hospital run but was insistent I didn't say no. Tim is never shy when it comes to grabbing a microphone and so for six days we gave our only ever public performances to an audience of a hundred or so theatre aficionados twice nightly. I loved it. I found confidence I didn't know I had. Craig directed and wouldn't allow us off script so Tim – and I for that matter – couldn't upstage the other. I felt at home among theatre people and was sad when the week whizzed to an end. I formed a real friendship with Tyler Gatchell, *Superstar*'s general manager, who was particularly insistent I put money into Charlie Strouse's upcoming show. "It's what

* Their latest, of all coincidences, is *Jesus Christ Superstar* for NBC.

we Americans do so well," he said. I heard the score and agreed. The problem was that Britain still had exchange controls so I said no. The musical was *Annie*.

By now I was desperate to get home for Sarah who was going stir-crazy cooped up in her small hospital room above a busy railway line. It seemed bonkers, she was 100% healthy. But in those days they insisted on three-hourly blood tests for diabetic pregnant mums during the six weeks before their babies hatched. I tried to visit her twice a day and organized as big a stream of friends to alleviate the tedious six weeks as I could. But Dulwich is a fair old trek from central London. Sarah was particularly touched by a visit from Julie Covington when "Don't Cry for Me" was No. 1. From then on the hospital sisters turned a slightly blind eye to the odd bottle I smuggled into the maternity ward.

MARCH 31 WAS SET for our baby to hit the deck. It was a weird feeling knowing the precise day in advance. But at least I could plan things and in between hospital visits I toyed with my Paganini variations. Soon these, along with *Evita*, finally had to take a back seat. Our baby was born by caesarean section on the planned morning of March 31. It was a gorgeous healthy girl. I was absolutely delighted. The question now was what to call her.

A bottomless crock of Pre-Raphaelite Christian names seemed ripe for pilfering. Oddly Sarah wasn't keen. I can perhaps understand that Parthenope or Aglaophemia might be a little over the top, but why she baulked at an everyday name like Proserpine is still beyond my comprehension. Reluctantly I had to settle on Sarah's grandmother's name, Imogen. I must admit it does suit her, although I sometimes wonder what a painting of a Rossetti-like Imogen taking a bite out of a forbidden pomegranate would look like. Her middle name is Annie after the musical.

Shortly after Imogen happened, something else happened that

catapulted the Paganini variations to the top of my creative pile. I lost a bet with my cellist brother Julian. Leyton Orient were as usual struggling against relegation and needed to draw at home to survive. I bet Julian they'd lose but astoundingly they pulled a goalless draw out of the bag and I had to cough up. The deal was that if I lost I would compose something for him. My get-out-of-gaol card was to write my Paganini variations for the cello. I announced the premiere in our Sydmonton Festival programme for August 6.

Niccolò Paganini (1782–1840) was arguably the most celebrated virtuoso violinist of all time. His technical ability was so extraordinary that people thought he was in league with the devil. His wild appearance did nothing to demolish this myth. He was tall and lanky with long, bony fingers and an outlandish dress sense. Audiences were mesmerized as he swayed from side to side, performing fiddling feats of unheard of dexterity. Once he made a legendary appearance dressed entirely in bright red at a concert of Berlioz's music in Nice. The entire audience thought the devil incarnate had been conjured up among them. I think this was the inspiration for Gaston Leroux's masque of the red death sequence in *The Phantom of the Opera*. Such was the belief in his supernatural powers that his body was denied a Christian burial. Instead it was exhibited in a freakshow at a fair until spirited away by friends who hid it in a spot near the rocks of the Pointe Saint Hospice on Cap Ferrat near Nice, i.e. probably in the garden of the house I used to own with Sarah Brightman. Paganini's fame today rests greatly on his Caprice No. 24 in A minor. The theme has been "varied" by over 50 composers, including Brahms and Rachmaninov.

Now I joined the party. All music has a link to maths, so the infinite possibilities created by the variation form and a theme such as Paganini's has occupied composers for hundreds of years. Essentially you take a simple melody and build your own versions based upon it. Paganini's melody is ideal because it is essentially the first note of the scale followed by the two notes called "the fifths" above and below it. This is repeated and followed by seven chord changes that end up harmonically where they started. Possibly the most famous variation in musical history is Rachmaninov's Variation 18 from his *Rhapsody on a Theme of Paganini*. He takes the original melody out of the minor into the major key and more or less inverts it. It sounds simple but is pure genius. It is pure Rachmaninov. Another reason why Paganini's theme is so attractive to composers is its inherent link to virtuosity.

Writing and recording *Variations* was one of the happiest times of my life. I can't remember a single low along the way. From the outset I conceived my variations as a showpiece for Julian and therefore intended to be performed live. They were therefore the antithesis to Mike Oldfield's humongous hit *Tubular Bells* which was the product of layers of overdubbing in the recording studio. My variations had none.

Luck had it that I overheard an album called *Electric Savage* by a band called Colosseum when I was in Roy Featherstone's office about *Evita*. Their playing sounded just the ticket for my new opus. Colosseum, a jazz/rock instrumental band, was the brainchild of the brilliant drummer Jon Hiseman. The band members were very much musicians' musicians who ticked the box of rock players who could read music, yet played together as a band. I wasn't ready to try out my efforts at Sydmonton on a full lineup, but I phoned Jon Hiseman nonetheless.

I met Jon and his beautiful wife Barbara Thompson at our Eaton Place flat. I knew I had seen her somewhere before. When Jon told me she was a tenor sax player, everything clicked. She was the gorgeous Kit Kat Klub girl saxophonist in Hal's London production of *Cabaret* and she also played the flute. Now I only needed a pianist. Once again Roy Featherstone did the honours. He sent me a single based on Satie's *Gymnopédie* No. 1 which had been arranged by ex Zombies keyboard player Rod Argent who penned their huge hit "She's Not There." I loved it. Shortly afterwards Roy sat me next to Rod at some music industry function. We clicked at once. I had found my keyboard player and a friend who was to work with me for many years. Soon we were all having kitchen table dinners at Sydmonton. Over the years many a creative team were lured home by Sarah's delicious roast chicken suppers.

WITH MY FIRST DRAFT of *Variations*, as it was now known, complete it was time to revisit *Evita*. On July 24 I flew once more to Mallorca to stay with Hal Prince and hopefully convince him to finally commit to direct the show in London. I strongly presume that Hal had already decided he would direct *Evita* but he told me my trip sealed his commitment. I was as relieved as I was excited. With Hal at the helm we would gain a theatre producer's instinct as well as a director's. Someone at the Stigwood organization must have listened to my wittering on as it seemed Robert had made contact with him and his deal parameters had already been discussed. The only issue was that Hal was unavailable until the spring of 1978 which meant *Evita* couldn't open until the summer. Despite worries that *Evita* would go off the boil by then, I was thrilled that everyone agreed that Hal was worth the wait. In fact, the reverse happened and the wait only made the anticipation greater, much aided by the announcement that Broadway legend Hal was at the helm. Anyway I had my *Variations* to think about during the gap – plus another minor diversion.

THE NORTH OF MALLORCA may have been unspoilt Mediterranean in 1977, but the south had long established the island's infamous reputation as a magnet to the lowest common denominator British tourist. All over Palma airport drunken pot-bellied lager louts and their molls were bawling the runaway holiday smash "Y Viva España." As the plane banked over Shagaluf – as their HQ Magaluf is aptly known – my love of rock-bottom pop got the better of me and I thought Tim and I could knock up a song like that. Foolishly Tim agreed. The result was "Magdalena," whose lyric was about a bloke dreaming of the local girl he'd had a holiday affair with as he headed home to damp foggy Britain.

Tim and I rarely wrote songs out of a theatrical context. The last one had been "It's Easy for You," specifically written for Elvis Presley with a plot about a married man who'd left his wife and children for a girl who subsequently dumps him. On the "jungle mix" version (much the best) the King is heard mumbling "this is a very emotional song for me." Allegedly it's the last song he recorded, which if true means we wrote the song that killed him.*

There was no question who we wanted to sing our summer smash. It just *had* to be Tony Christie. Roy Featherstone swallowed the bait. I booked a huge orchestra, Tony was in fine voice and the chorus of his erstwhile summer love was provided by no less than our former Mary Magdalene Dana Gillespie. Sadly the song never hit the spot. Could it have been a mistake that this blatant attempt at a summer hit was released in the iron wintry grip of February? However the session spawned a young man who featured in my professional life many times in the future. My father had been banging on for a while about one of his students at the London College of Music who he thought could be a musical director on one of my shows. This session seemed a good opportunity to test him out. A tall, very good looking young man called David Caddick took to the podium and having caused a major flurry in the female ranks of our orchestra (unrequited, I'm afraid) conducted his first recording session with great aplomb. David has gone on to have a major career in theatre. He is still our highly valued music supervisor of *Phantom* in New York.

---

* When The Everly Brothers recorded my song "Cold," co-written with *Bat Out of Hell's* creator Jim Steinman, in 1998 it meant I had written a song for both my childhood idols. I thought all my dreams had come true and seriously considered retiring, at least for a day or so.

MY *VARIATIONS* PREMIERED ON August 6 in the second half of a cello recital at the Sydmonton Festival. Julian was accompanied by Rod, Jon and Barbara, respectively playing piano, drums and flute doubling saxophone. They were only 20 minutes long as they were still conceived as one side of an album but the audience went wild. An encore of the final variation didn't prove enough and we had to repeat the whole piece. Melvyn Bragg was in the audience and immediately made a pitch for the first public performance to be on his new ITV arts programme, *The South Bank Show*. Roy Featherstone instantly committed MCA to make a record on one condition, that I extend my *Variations* to fill an entire LP. I jumped at it before you could say "Pagan Ninny's Keep 'Er Goin' Stomp" by Red Ingle and his Natural Seven, the title of one of the lesser-known Paganini inspired opuses. If only Auntie Vi had been in the audience. She had been complaining of feeling sick which I didn't worry about at the time.

Now was the moment to invite the other Colosseum band members, Don Airey (keyboards), John Mole (bass) and Gary Moore (guitar) on board. The expanded lineup was perfect. It gave me two top-class keyboard players so I could explore the burgeoning colours of the synthesizer. John Mole was a cracking bass player and Gary Moore is simply one of the greatest, most underestimated rock guitarists ever. Ex Juicy Lucy, Gary's DNA screamed heavy metal yet he was also the most lyrical guitarist I have worked with. He oozed the lived-in debauched good looks that personified Seventies rock guitarists. His death in February 2011 deprived rock of one of its finest and deeply musical players.

With a lineup like this I could take my composition anywhere. The theme and variations form meant that provided there was real structure there were no rules. I could mix heavy metal with classical, humour with lyricism, in other words let myself go, but at all times I wanted to write music that demanded real virtuosity. *Variations*, as I now called it, might be born in a recording studio but I was composing something theatrical and showy. Above all it was written to be performed live. Jon Hiseman suggested we record at Morgan Studios in Willesden, a colourful if then ever so slightly no-go area of northwest London, a far cry from affluent leafy Barnes, home of Olympic Studios. However the equipment at Olympic was aging, the wrong horn note in "Don't Cry for Me" still rankled and a quick peek at Morgan confirmed that it was a good bet especially when I was promised that the engineer would be their top man, Martin Levan.

WE RECORDED *VARIATIONS* IN two batches, two weeks at the beginning of October and then November after which Martin Levan and I decamped to Brussels where Morgan had a sister studio to mix the album. We rightly figured we would be undisturbed and I discovered that Martin's highly attuned "pair of ears" was unsurprising since his father had been a professional violinist with the London Symphony Orchestra. He was also adroit at sorting out cock-ups. We discovered we missed a percussive shaker off Variation 4. His solution was to close-mike me rattling a tin of Hermesetas. It was in Brussels that Martin and I cemented a professional friendship that saw him as my right-hand sound man and recording engineer for nearly fifteen years, right through *Aspects of Love* until he semi-retired to Wales during the early days of *Sunset Boulevard*.

The two-week gap in the *Variations* recording schedule found me in Chicago with Tim. The main reason for our trip was to see Bonnie Shon, an actress Hal thought might make a fine Eva. Already our camp was suspecting that Julie Covington would turn us down. I had severe reservations that the porcelain rather than the Joplin in Julie's voice would get the better of her. Frankly I couldn't see how any performer could sing *Evita* eight shows a week and I worried that she would struggle with four. Bonnie proved to be really good. But both

Tim and I had serious reservations about how casting an unknown American would go down in Britain.

Shortly after our return Julie did turn us down. Of course the press made it out to be a snub, but I'm absolutely sure she did so for the right professional reasons. I think she knew she couldn't have handled that role physically or psychologically. Years later she did agree to play the role for an Australian revival but she withdrew in rehearsals. The search for Eva was now on big time but I had to juggle my time with the sudden eruption of *Variations*.

Roy Featherstone at MCA was totally stunned by the recording. Dear David Land came round to my flat with his wife Zara and the poor man was really nonplussed. Melvyn Bragg not only confirmed *Variations* for his second *South Bank Show* on ITV but chose a version of my opening variations for his title sequence for the 32 years of its run. The music was uncredited. I wonder how many of the world's top arts luminaries who appeared in his show know where the title music comes from.

IN SEPTEMBER AUNTIE VI had taken a turn for the worse. George decided she needed care she couldn't get at home. So after a short stint in hospital it was into a nursing home in Hove. I was honestly not surprised – neither George nor Vi were card-carrying members of a Temperance Society. It's just that she was only 50. I presumed it was simply a matter of time before she recovered, even though it was a shock to see her so sallow, so listless. Perhaps I shouldn't have, but I followed Mum's mantra that my work had to come before everything. This meant I only saw Vi twice before the end of the year.

22

Variations

MCA Records released *Variations* in January 1978 to coincide with the TV performance on *The South Bank Show*. The reaction completely stunned me. Amazingly *Variations* became the talk of the chattering class and swiftly rose to No. 2 in the album charts. It would have been No. 1 but couldn't compete with ABBA's first-ever *Greatest Hits* release which today would not be eligible for the mainstream chart. Drat it.

But I wasn't complaining. I suppose the biggest change was having to do all the press and promotion on my own. I was never going to be able to compete side by side with Tim on chat shows but here I was on safe turf, talking about music. My confidence boost wasn't big enough to have me planning a one-man show but it wasn't zero either. Offers came in from ballet companies and dance troupes for the stage rights, lyricists sent me unsolicited words, Heineken pitched to use the music as a beer commercial. There was a sold-out concert at the Royal Festival Hall and Capital Radio followed with two total sellouts at the same venue.

The soccer World Cup was being held in Argentina that summer and BBC TV asked me to write its theme tune. Rod Argent and Don Airey joined me on keyboards for "Argentine Melody," perhaps not the most imaginative of titles, but under the name of San Jose featuring Rodriguez Argentina we got to No. 14 in the charts and I made my first and only *Top of the Pops* appearance dressed in a pinstripe suit, after which the single scored a first after such a mega plug. It went down.

But as ever when things are riding high, fate was lurking around a corner with a well-honed banana skin. On January 28 my beloved Aunt Vi's liver decided enough was enough. True she had been ill since she cried off going to Sydmonton. True the last time I saw her she was a colour verging on bright canary yellow but I had lost my soulmate, the woman who meant everything to me when I was a boy. I felt gutted that I hadn't seen as much of her as I would have liked over the past year. I knew I was going to miss her terribly. I do hope she didn't say "God bugger the Pope" at the pearly gates.

As if that wasn't enough, I got a phone call one early evening at home from Tim to say that he had received a suicide note from Alan Doggett. He had thrown himself under a train near his childhood home at Iver in Buckinghamshire. My immediate feeling was guilt. Alan was a gifted amateur musician but although his London Boy Singers had featured on a couple of *Evita* sessions I hadn't otherwise used him on the *Evita* album because the score demanded a far more experienced conductor. Obviously there had been no role for him on *Variations*. Had he felt passed over?

It transpired that there had been a sex allegation against him made by a young boy. It didn't add up. Everybody knew that Alan was openly gay but he had an adult partner, called Michael Stuckey who, like Alan, was a choir trainer. Julian had been taught by Alan at school, but neither he nor Tim and I in our *Joseph* days had seen the slightest hint of him stepping out of line with the kids in his charge and Julian especially would have known. True there had been an allegation against him before, but he had been completely exonerated by an enquiry which proved that at the time of the alleged incident he was in a recording session with, among others, Tim and me. If Tim and I had had the slightest inkling that there was a genuine issue, we would have ceased working with him immediately.

Having had so little recent contact with Alan, I don't know what the allegation was that caused him to take such an appalling step.

A few years later my mother told me that she had been teaching piano to the child of the chief of the Chelsea police whose force was handling the charge. He told her that there was no credible evidence against Alan and no case could have been pursued against him. I still ask myself if this tragedy would have happened if I had been as close to him as in *Joseph* days.

BY MARCH 1978 IT wasn't a question of if someone would choreograph *Variations*, but of who. I did seriously wonder if a dance troupe could find musicians of a high enough standard to play it, apart from perhaps for a one-off gig. *Variations* was written to show off Julian and was meant to be virtuoso fun.

I don't want to get too technical and over-analyse *Variations*, but I applied my theatrical construction rules to its composition so light and shade were at its epicentre. I wrote a moody version of Variation 19 as an introduction to Paganini's famous melody which is then played by Julian on the cello accompanied only by drums. The first four variations develop the Paganini tune but they remain deliberately close thematically. *The South Bank Show* title music was culled from Variation 3. Variation 5 departs significantly. It is in a major key with a modulation up a major fourth where I introduce a counter melody. When *Variations* became the second part of *Song and Dance*, Variation 5 became the full company song at the end of the show with the title "Unexpected Song." A brooding Variation 6 contrasts with Variation 7 which goes right back to my rock roots, and is heavy metal in 7/8 time. It is the devil to play. You can hear it and Gary Moore's spectacular solo in the "guitar hero" sequence in *School of Rock*.

A reflective Variation 8 has a short repeated pattern or "ostinato" on the keyboards. It becomes the heart of the music as *Variations* progresses and leads into a slightly sleazy sax solo beautifully interpreted by Barbara Thompson and written very much with her in mind. Julian then has a simple and deliberately lyrical moment developed from a melody I wrote some years earlier for which Tim did a lyric for a long-forgotten recording by a French girl called Danielle. Rock returns with Variation 11, followed by a clump of four where I had great fun playing around with time signatures. The section closes with "The Tributes" the first of which is a homage to Hank Marvin, lead guitarist of the Shadows. The second "tribute" is to Prokofiev and is my attempt to imagine what he might have done to Paganini's theme.

In Variation 16 I play around with keyboard sounds and fragments of phrases, anchored by a deliberately repetitive guitar and drum based two-bar phrase. I couldn't resist writing a short mock fugue that has nothing to do with Paganini and is illogically based on the hornpipe theme. I admit that when I wrote this variation I did wonder if one day a choreographer could make a tap number out of it. A slow puzzler in the harmony department eventually resolves into D flat major, the key of Rachmaninov's famous Variation 18 for my 18th. This lyrical melody was again designed to showcase Julian. Frankly its connection to Paganini is tenuous other than the first part of the melody repeats and it has seven chord changes. It's a re-use of the title melody of Tim and my first collaboration, *The Likes of Us* for which I was still awaiting Leslie Thomas's script. Julian had always liked the melody and thought it was a shame it was buried, so after not much persuasion I disinterred it. Unfortunately it had, unlike the others, a publisher viz Southern Music. This meant it was technically an instrumental cover version of a song with lyrics so Tim receives half my royalties which, as he says in his autobiography *Oh What a Circus*, he finds "amusing."

Variation 19 is a tribute to George Gershwin, beautifully played by Rod Argent, which leads to a new melody on the flute and high keyboards, married second time around with a simple guitar and bass variation very close to Paganini's theme. Next there is a repeat of the countermelody of Variation 5. A modulation up a fourth brings back a climactic version of the main Variation 5 melody on the cello. It's my favourite sequence. It is cut short by the rocky Variation 21 with unison lines for bass and guitar and big drum breaks from Jon. The keyboard-based Variation 22 builds to the final Variation 23 which I composed to show off Julian's phenomenal technique. It finishes with Julian detuning his cello to an "off-instrument" low C with which he alone flamboyantly ends the piece.

I AM EXTREMELY PROUD of the original recording of *Variations*. I turn to it whenever I need to pick myself up after some setback or another. It hasn't got a bone in its body that isn't about joy, melody and celebration of virtuosity. The keyboard sounds that Rod, Don and I developed were state of the art at the time, especially as we always had to remember that they had to be recreated live. It wasn't simple in those days before sounds could be pre-programmed. Despite the huge arsenal of sounds available today, I wouldn't change any of my original choices. Should you want to listen to *Variations*, try hearing it from a good-condition original 1978 vinyl pressing. Because the sides are relatively short, the sound quality is amazing. Even if you hate my piece, it demonstrates what great vinyl sound is all about.

Variations got an A star critically in the USA. We gave performances in the Speakeasy in Los Angeles and the Newman (Public) Theater in New York, but we didn't have the equivalent national TV exposure that *The South Bank Show* gave us in Britain which rendered the album a well-received curiosity. The audiences went wild at the live shows, particularly in LA where we were asked to do a residency. Something else happened that I was unprepared for. I became a bit of a magnet for girls. Mimosa, my 1971 swimming instructress, surfaced and said she could conquer my fear of putting my head underwater as she'd be under the water too which would make it worthwhile if I did. Opportunities arose that, although I was a good boy, I would be lying if I didn't say I was hugely tempted to take.

Meanwhile *Evita* was progressing in sure, rather stately fashion to the stage under the watchful eye of Robert's line producer Bob Swash. Robert decided not to risk his own money so the capitalization came mostly from private "angels," plus a large chunk from Capital Radio. David Land advised me not to invest, saying I would make enough money out of my royalties if it was a hit, wise advice that I wish I'd stuck to later in my career. The only theatre available was the Prince Edward. It was hardly the first choice. The Prince Edward is tucked away behind the Palace Theatre and had previously never had a hit. For years its name was changed to the London Casino and as such was the home of Cinerama, a sort of early version of Imax. It became a theatre again once Cinerama waned and housed two massive flops. Hal, however, liked the cinema connection because of our opening scene and thought we could make a virtue of the ugly 1920s auditorium which he draped on either side of the proscenium with huge murals somewhat in the style of the Latin American artist Fernando Botero.

In view of Hal's dictum about the crucial importance of how a production looked, I was agog to learn his choice of designer. He settled on Tim O'Brien in association with Tazeena Firth and they proved to be an outstanding choice. Tim had designed many productions for the Royal Shakespeare Company and was a perfect fit for Hal's concept. This was what is sometimes still called an "RSC black box" in which minimalist sets, like a frame containing revolving doors for "Goodnight and Thank You," propelled the action along in Brechtian style against a black background. The show began with an on-stage audience watching a giant movie screen showing a film starring the real Eva. After the announcement of Eva's death this screen soared above the stage so throughout the show contemporary slides and footage accompanied the action below. The only big chunk of scenery was a two-level gantry that could move up and downstage and served among other things as the balcony of the Casa Rosada. All the scenery was as monochrome as the opening black and white movie. The only colour came from the costumes and the huge murals on either side of the proscenium.

IT SEEMED EVERY MUSICAL theatre actress in Britain plus a fair few from elsewhere turned up for auditions. However there was one I would prefer to gloss over. My father developed, shall we say, a crush on a not over-slim classically trained mezzo soprano called Justine. Despite saying to Dad that the team ideally wanted someone small with a cast-iron rock-tinged chest voice, Dad entered Justine into the fray. Worse still, Dad decided to play for her audition. I decided to give this occasion a miss. Unfortunately the whole of the rest of the team, including David Land, who never went near auditions unless a star was involved, decided this particular audition was required viewing. What happened is beyond the scope of this volume.

Eventually the Evitas were whittled down to three: Verity Anne Meldrum, Elaine Paige and an actress whose name I can't remember. Hal couldn't choose between them. Like me he was also worried that the role would be unperformable eight shows a week. So he came up with one of his concepts. Three girls would play Evita each night. Tim and I went to a presentation at Tim and Tazeena's studio where he demonstrated on the set model how this would work. There followed a rare demonstration of Rice/Lloyd Webber unity. We said this was not our vision. Would the girls draw lots on who would sing "Don't Cry for Me"? Hal put up no real resistance. The final three, Elaine, Verity Ann Meldrum and the mystery unknown were recalled for the umpteenth time.

I was already strongly leaning towards Elaine. She was petite, brassy and sexy. Her chest voice seemed cast-iron, yet she could show real warmth and vulnerability. In short, she had star quality. But I wanted to be doubly sure. After a dazzling rendition of "Rainbow High" I asked her to sing "Don't Cry for Me" one more time.

"Oh fuck!" she said eyes blazing. We knew we'd found our street-fighting Evita.

Hal, however, now wanted us to see his American candidate Bonnie Shon one more time. The poor girl was flown to London and the entire creative team auditioned her at the Prince Edward back to back with Elaine, who must by now have assumed that our dithering was pathological. Hal still leant towards his fellow countrywoman, but agreed that Tim and I should work back at my London flat with both girls and then choose. Bonnie was technically iron-plated, but once again there was something wonderfully human about Elaine which shone through her grit and by now understandable frustration. I phoned Hal and said we wanted Elaine. All he said was "If it's all right with you, kid, it's fine by me." Bonnie Shon was incredibly gracious. I never saw her again but if I ever meet her I owe her the most humongous hug.

There is one small footnote to the three girl Evita concept. If ever you can catch Hal's production there is the tiniest vestige left over. At the end of the funeral, unlike on the original record where Eva's voice alone is heard from the grave, three girls emerge from the crowd and sing "Don't Cry for Me." One is the actress who will play Eva, the other two disappear, their raison d'être never explained. It is a staging moment Hal obviously couldn't let go.

Casting Che became a massive issue. Colm Wilkinson did not cut it with Hal and he had to wait for theatrical stardom until Trevor Nunn cast him as Jean Valjean in Les Misérables. For a while we were stumped. A breakthrough came from the Rice camp when Tim, apparently prompted by his wife Jane, suggested David Essex. David had successfully made the difficult leap from legit theatre star (he played Jesus in Godspell) to local British rock god and would be a huge catch as far as the West End was concerned. Hal met him at the Savoy and was as impressed in David as David was in meeting a Broadway legend. David only agreed to play four months, but that was more than enough for all of us. His laidback laconic style delivered Tim his dream Che. Not only that, his version of "Oh What a Circus" gave us the bonus of another Top 10 single. Joss Ackland, a veteran of straight and musical theatre whom Hal knew from the London cast of *A Little Night Music*, was offered the role of Perón. There was a massive bash at Stigwood's office to introduce a shell-shocked Elaine to the press. Robert got his two bites of the cherry with a later photo call outside the Savoy. As with Paul Nicholas and *Superstar* no interviews were allowed. That way Elaine was kept an enigma. Enigma or no, she was mega front page news.

REHEARSALS WERE AT THE Cecil Sharp House north of Regent's Park, delightfully close to the Oslo Court Restaurant. British readers with long memories may remember that for several years I was the food critic of the *Daily Telegraph*. I visited the Oslo Court in late 2016 and it was one of those occasions when I wanted my column back. Connoisseurs of time warps should head there at once. Where else will you find lobster cocktails with Marie Rose sauce, duck with cherries and crêpe suzettes served by tuxedoed waiters in a decor which features frilly curtains that look like an Edwardian granny's camiknickers? It's marvellous. Anyhow, Elaine handled herself brilliantly throughout rehearsals. She knew when to rest her voice but her work ethic was 110%. Our choreographer was another American, Larry Fuller, who had recently worked with Hal on the Comden and Green musical *On the Twentieth Century* on Broadway. I got on well with Larry so I was surprised when I was banned from choreography sessions. Hal said he would allow me in when the time was right. Eventually I was summoned and Hal took me to one side.

"Kid, I'm going to show you 'Buenos Aires' first," he said. "There's new music and you'll hate it."

Before I could bridle, Hal explained that a dance arranger had been called in to write the music for Larry's steps. I had never heard of such a person. Hal said that once I'd seen the staging I could take the new music away and compose my own to fit. Hal hadn't wanted me to see anything until he was happy with what Larry was doing. I sat down sensing an oversized rat, but was soon applauding furiously. All the choreography enhanced the action. Unsurprisingly "Buenos Aires" needed the most new music. A new sequence was inserted where Che had dialogue to describe the Buenos Aires social structure which was depicted in dance. After this came a thrilling new section offering me huge possibilities. I grasped it voraciously and had only one caveat. At one point Larry choreographed the dancers to follow Eva's moves precisely one step behind her. It was easy to illustrate musically but I worried that, if our Eva was a less brilliant dancer than Elaine, she would simply look out of time.

Hal and I developed a real friendship. One Sunday night we found ourselves guests at some record industry charity bash at the London Hilton. I was praying it would finish on time as I wanted to hook up with Gary Bond who was going to a cabaret by the new hot TV dance troupe Hot Gossip at the achingly hip Country Cousin club in the Kings Road. Hot Gossip had caused Britain's self-appointed TV moral watchdog Mary Whitehouse apoplexy for their suggestive dance routines on the early evening TV *Kenny Everett Video Show*. Needless to say, Mrs Whitehouse's protestations doubled everyone's interest in their choreographer Arlene Phillips's naughty routines which in turn awoke the British public to something hitherto well off the radar, contemporary dance.

The dinner overran but I needn't have panicked. The cabaret was Elton John. When he introduced his new piano opus "Song for Guy" the audience started talking causing Elton to have a temper tantrum, slam down the piano lid and exit, never to be seen again. I scooped up Hal and off we went to Hot Gossip. Hal and Gary Bond hit it off famously and very soon Gary was cast as David Essex's takeover in *Evita*. But the evening belonged to Arlene Phillips and her fabulously sexy dance troupe. Hal insisted on meeting her, pronounced her work as "What Bobby Fosse should be doing" and I was introduced at the bar to one of the girl dancers who said her name was Sarah Brightman and that she wanted to be a singer. I headed home, vowing Arlene Phillips was the woman I needed to choreograph *Variations* preferably with Hot Gossip. The question was how to make this happen.

THE PERIOD BETWEEN THE end of rehearsals and the first dress rehearsal is called "technicals." I advise any new writer to take a holiday during technicals. They redefine watching paint dry. Thirty seconds after you've settled back enjoying your oeuvre on stage for the first time, someone gets on a microphone to refocus a light cue. Or the set breaks down and everyone is told to come back in two hours whilst a harassed stage crew, flanked by an anguished stage manager, is shouted at by the director who in between haranguing the backstage team pronounces the producer to be the most incompetent in the business.

I was green in those days and consequently had some gruesome days in the Prince Edward when I was convinced Ronnie Neame was right and *Evita* should have been a film. It was during one of these enforced endless gaps that Rod Argent introduced me to his actress friend, Jennie Linden, best known for her role in the movie *Women in Love*. She had an idea for the Sydmonton Festival that she was developing with pianist Janet Edwards called *I Say, I Play* in which poetry was read to a musical accompaniment. She asked if I might compose something. I was intrigued. Apart from the few recitative bits in *Evita* I had never set existing words to music before. I wondered if I could, and if I could write melodies to existing formal verses. I said I'd think about it.

It was in rehearsals next day, when the Casa Rosada plus Elaine Paige in full ball-gown regalia came to a grinding halt downstage and got stuck, that I thought of *Old Possum's Book of Practical Cats*. Mum used to read T.S. Eliot's cat poems to me at bedtime when I was a kid. I myself had lectured our Burmese blue Grimshaw with "Macavity the Mystery Cat" only a few days previously after I found a rare William de Morgan vase inexplicably knocked over in the drawing room at Sydmonton. So I called Jennie and we agreed I would set four of the poems to music. I chose "The Song of the Jellicles," "Mr Mistoffelees," "The Naming of Cats" and, of course, "Macavity." I had in mind something like William Walton's setting of Edith Sitwell's *Façade*, although apparently at its premiere the author proclaimed her poems over Walton's music from behind a screen through a megaphone. This didn't go down at all well and I didn't advocate this approach to Jennie. We agreed *I Say, I Play* would be the Festival morning offering on September 9.

EVITA'S FIRST PREVIEW WAS one of the unforgettable nights of my career. Every aspect of Hal's production came together perfectly. The minimalist scenery meant the action flowed seamlessly, whilst David Hersey's lighting wonderfully conveyed everything from the warmth of the Buenos Aires streets to the starkness of Eva's hospital deathbed. All the performers were superb. Every London theatre queen, plus a few from other walks of life, was in the Prince Edward that night. The overwhelming consensus was that nobody had seen an original London production of a musical like it. I can't forget the reception to the rewritten – thanks to Hal – "Dangerous Jade." Larry Fuller had the soldiers and the aristocrats in two separate crisscrossing clumps, the soldiers marching in a tight military formation and the aristocrats gliding around the stage as if they were joined at the hip. I wrote no applause point but I needn't have bothered. The audience was applauding wildly a full minute before the song ended. Then there was the stunning staging of "A New Argentina." Eva's *descamisados* with their spectacular banners and flaming torches touched quite a nerve in 1978 Britain. The talk of private armies might have receded but the power of the trade unions certainly hadn't. There was no forced OSO* that night.

I lost count of the number of curtain calls. When finally the cast were back in their dressing rooms popping the warm champagne, an anguished stage manager had to round them up for yet another call as the audience refused to leave. The Hal Prince production of *Evita* was one of those very rare occasions in musical theatre where every creative element came together. As Hal told me, you can't listen to a musical if you can't look at it. You could sure look at this one.

That night we all went to Au Jardin des Gourmets and celebrated. Short of an IRA terrorist attack, and that was an issue, nothing could stop *Evita* now, at any rate in London. One thing struck me. There was no sign of Robert Stigwood. In truth there had been no sign of him during rehearsals either. I asked David Land if Robert knew there was a new musical in London with his name above the titles. David mumbled something about Robert being tied up with the impending release of his *Sgt. Pepper* movie in the US. Hopefully he would be in London next week. But on a night like this my question wasn't a moan, it was more of an interested observation. I spent most of the following previews at the sound desk. It was a fine place to watch any comings and goings during the performance. It was around the eighth preview that I saw Robert and an assistant sneak into the orchestra stalls towards the end of the first act.

The previews had gone so well and the word of mouth was so good that *Evita* was probably critic proof. On the day of our opening,

---

* Obligatory standing ovation.

June 21, I even appeared with the BBC TV sports panel commentating on the soccer World Cup talking about *Evita* and Leyton Orient and got played out with my Argentine theme tune. Outside the TV studio I was doorstepped by ticket touts and screamed at by some girls queuing for *Top of the Pops*. David Land detected a new phenomenon. People weren't buying one souvenir programme, they were buying three, one for themselves, one for their coffee table and one to put under their back car window to boast they had seen the hottest ticket in town. So David had stacks of brochures printed. Unfortunately as the show ran on the club became less exclusive. Souvenir programme sales reverted to normal and you couldn't move in David's office for stacks of glossy programmes which he said one day would be rare collectors' items.

None of this cured my first night nerves. Halfway through Act 1 the film and slides on the big screen got completely out of time with the stage action. I was convinced we were doomed and poor David Land had to cope with my inconsolable blues at the interval. Nobody else seemed to notice. Robert might have won Absentee Producer of the Year 1978, but he knew how to give an outsize party. He hired a big boat called the *Tattershall Castle* moored on the River Thames close to the Houses of Parliament almost in sight of where my school musicals were staged a decade and a half earlier. Austerity London had not seen anything like this for a while and certainly my parents hadn't. Gary Bond was among my gang and at one stage I noticed him in deep conversation with Hal and Robert. I had wondered whether Hal and Gary would click and it wasn't long before Hal was seriously pressing for Gary to be David Essex's takeover as Che.

Genista Streeten, our show publicist, warned Tim and me backstage on opening night that the reviews would belong to Elaine and Hal, and by and large she was right. Derek Jewell was true to his loyal self, saying *Evita* was "simply a masterpiece." Bernard Levin, the *Sunday Times* theatre critic and self-proclaimed custodian of all things opera, savaged it, but his views were by now equated with his predecessor, the up-the-wrong-tree-barker Harold Hobson and people smiled more than took notice. Shortly afterwards he opined that his idea of bliss was to see opera in any world city other than Paris because he hated the Garnier Paris opera house so much. Thankfully he wasn't the critic ten years later when *The Phantom of the Opera* opened.

23

Really Useful

Summer 1978 was a whirlwind. Ten days after *Evita* opened, Capital Radio presented *Variations*, once again at the Festival Hall. It went so well that another date was booked at nearly double the money by its chief John Whitney, a newcomer to my address book who one day would be my CEO.

David Land used to say that I had a hundred ideas a week to win the war, 99% were rubbish but you had to wade through the treacle as one might be the battle clincher. Heaven knows what was going on in my head that summer. In no particular order, I invented a board game about insurance called *Calamity!* in which players were insurance giant Lloyd's of London underwriters trying to lay off risks on other players before disasters struck. Sarah and I hosted many soirées in a vain attempt to launch this extremely prescient game. Lloyd's nearly went bankrupt in the late 1980s due to asbestos damages claims. One memorable night Richard Branson tricked me into buying his offshore oil rig risks just before a hurricane struck.

I was given a massive budget by ITV to create and record the theme tune for a big series, *Whicker's World*. They asked for something big, brash, symphonic and celebratory. I am not sure I gave them what they wanted, but at least it was unique, a TV signature tune in 7/8 time. In August the Earl of Harewood offered me a formal commission to compose an opera for the English National Opera to premiere anytime onwards from the 1980–81 season. I proposed Charles Dickens's spinetingler "The Signalman" as a possible story and his excited administrator Edmund Tracey said he would put the subject to his board. The board rejected the idea because it was a two-hander. "What shall we do with the chorus?" was the reply. I never let go of "The Signalman" and eventually incorporated elements of the story into my musical of Wilkie Collins's *The Woman in White*. Meanwhile Michael White wanted to mount *Variations* as a dance programme. I said let's wait and see. Then there was the *Evita* London cast album. David Land helpfully explained to a *Daily Express* reporter who asked why I wasn't around that "Andrew is too busy to have a wee."

Robert began strategy discussions about how to premiere *Evita* in the USA. At an à deux dinner at Stanmore he flagged that it might be dangerous to open cold on Broadway and an LA opening might be a better option. He thought *Evita* needed to be "discovered" in America and should go to Broadway via the back door. He also planned immediate productions around the rest of the world. Australia should be Hal's but some European countries would be allowed to do their own versions, provided they staged them quickly. This was Robert at his best. By 1981 *Evita* was playing in eleven territories. I thought he had a point about America. Few knew the music there and my experience on Broadway hadn't been exactly scintillating. Robert was effusive about my snaring Hal. What I found inexplicable was that he didn't mention anything about my management deal ending next year. The only overtures were the usual ones when I was on my own minus Sarah.

THROUGHOUT THE SUMMER MY lovely PA Biddy Hayward was having a whale of a time juggling requests for *Evita* house seats with David Land, who kept crowing "There's nothing that a hit can't cure" whilst playing a ridiculous record he had made of *Evita*'s opening night applause. One request had to be handled discreetly. The leader of Her Majesty's Opposition proved particularly partial to Eva's big set pieces with adoring crowds at the end of Act 1 and the top of Act 2. This involved sneaking the Right Honourable Margaret Thatcher into the back of the stalls after curtain-up, then into the bar of Wheelers opposite the theatre during the interval and back for "Don't Cry for Me" and "Rainbow High." A few years later at a dinner in her Downing Street flat she joked that I should compose her some entrance music for the next Tory party conference like Eva's on the balcony of the Casa Rosada. Well, I think she was joking.*

David Land was getting heaps of offers about turning *Variations* into half of a dance show. I started to take my settings of *Old Possum's Book of Practical Cats* rather more seriously. What if the cat poems became a "dance combined with poetry" curtain-raiser? In the meantime poor *Thomas the Tank Engine* hit the buffers. Johnnie Hamp at Granada had finished overseeing the animation of the pilot episode. His bosses loved it but animation in 1978 was labour-intensive and colossally expensive. Computer animation was still very much in its embryo. The Granada honchos felt *Thomas* was too British to appeal outside the UK and they couldn't justify spending a fortune on what they thought would only be a local children's TV series. Little did they or I think that simply filming the stories with model railway trains and a voiceover by an ex-Beatle would turn *Thomas* into an international franchise. So I did something the opposite of really useful, allowed the rights of *Thomas* to revert back to its publishers and let a no-brainer of a smash hit slip through my fingers.

However I still had the name the Really Useful Company and I wasn't about to let my singing steam trains evaporate. I had heard on a recording session a guy with a most interesting party trick. He could sing three notes at once in the exact pitch of an American steam locomotive whistle. His name was Earl Jordan. Perhaps my train story

---

* That wonderful rogue, Conservative member of Parliament Alan Clarke, has an early 1980 diary entry about Thatcher in the House of Commons after she had just given a TV interview. "Goodness she is beautiful; made up to the nines of course. But still quite bewitching as Eva Perón must have been."

should be set in America? And surely anyone who could sing three notes at once could at least front a novelty single? Peter Reeves and I wrote a song called "Engine of Love" and once again Roy Feather-stone swallowed the bait. The Sydmonton Festival was fast looming, but I promised Roy "Engine of Love" would steam away as soon as Sydmonton had strutted its stuff.

AT FIRST SIGHT THE 1978 Festival programme didn't look par-ticularly inspiring. There was no full work like *Evita* to premiere. There was a Beethoven concert by pianist Denis Matthews; and an avant-garde mime company who had studied in France and were as insufferable as only mime companies who have studied in France can be.* Robert allowed us a special late-night showing of his about to be released movie *Grease*, which was indeed a scoop. The Fauré *Messe Basse* was performed with a choir directed by Alan Doggett's part-ner Michael Stuckey at our Sunday morning church service where Alan was remembered. There was a Sunday afternoon cricket match and among our after-dinner speakers was the Conservative politician John Selwyn Gummer, now the noble Lord Deben, and Lady Isobel Barnett, the posh TV celebrity who tragically committed suicide af-ter being copped for popping groceries into a poacher's pocket sewn into her outsized fur coat.

John became a Festival stalwart for three decades and more. I caught him on TV after the first 1974 election in the small hours after the electors had chucked him out. A rather slurred anchorman Reginald Bosanquet, unaware that John was in the TV studio, com-mented "John Gummer, that's a man who in the eighteenth-century sense has no bottom" to which John replied "No, I am a man without

---

* A brilliant album was once issued entitled *Marcel Marceau's Greatest Hits*, which con-tained absolutely nothing. Richard Branson played the same trick with an album called *The Wit and Wisdom of Ronald Reagan*.

a seat." This was a fine riposte, so I tracked him down, discovered he shared my love of Victorian architecture (the higher church the better) and he and his wife Penny have remained close friends ever since. John is widely thought to have been the best British environment minister of the past few decades.

Then there was Jennie Linden and Janet Edwards in *I Say, I Play*. Buried in the blurb was "The programme will feature the first performance of four newly composed settings from T.S. Eliot's *Old Possum's Book of Practical Cats*."

In the audience was Brian Brolly, whose faith in *Jesus Christ Superstar* as chief of British MCA Records had kick-started Tim and my careers. Brian had left MCA to run Paul McCartney's MPL business vehicle which he had done successfully for five years. He was now looking for new pastures where he could have a stake in the business. With his track record with *Superstar* and his experience in building Paul's copyright empire, he seemed the right man for me. I was determined to have my own production company once my Stigwood contract was over. After all it had been my idea to bring Hal Prince into the mix and Robert hadn't seen anything of *Evita* until halfway through the eighth preview. On Sunday David Land was unusually quiet. At lunch he sidled over to me.

"Is it all over cocky?" he said. I didn't know what he meant.

"Now with your variations and these cat poems does it mean my boys are drifting apart?" he said.

I said not to be daft, that Tim was always doing solo projects which was completely true as in both America and Britain he had released several singles with himself as singer-songwriter and writing the music too. I said if Tim came up with another great idea for the theatre I would jump at it and I meant what I said. He then asked me why Brian Brolly was a guest. I replied that I was thinking about setting up my own production company. After all, I had had quite a hand in putting the *Evita* team together. Why didn't he and Robert put up some seed money and take a stake in this new enterprise? David said he'd talk it over with Robert.

GARY BOND WAS CONFIRMED as David Essex's takeover around the time my big fear for *Evita* proved all too real. Eva was too big a role for any actress to sing eight shows a week. Elaine started to miss performances and her understudy Michelle Breeze found herself propelled in front of less than merry audiences too many times for the Stigwood office not to consider an alternate. Cartoons started appearing in national newspapers. Typical was one featuring a doorman outside the theatre, captioned "I'm not the commissionaire I'm the understudy, the strain of appearing eight times a week was too much for him." Then backstage rumours circulated about a relationship between Elaine and Tim which David Land did nothing to diffuse. I didn't pay too much attention at the time. I had grown very fond of Elaine. I admired her professionalism. It wasn't her fault that she couldn't sing the show eight times a week. Nobody could.

Stigwood's man Bob Swash was in such a quandary that he even began cutting short his lunches about the overthrow of capitalism at L'Escargot. Although audiences were flocking to *Evita*, Elaine had triumphed in the reviews and was now a star. Someone needed to be hired to ease her burden. But if it was a big name it would be expensive and could undermine her confidence. Furthermore, we had scoured the country for Evitas and surely we weren't going to find one quickly now. Help came from Gary Bond. Had anybody thought of his friend Marti Webb? Marti, like Gary, was a veteran of stacks of West End musicals. They had both been in a show called *On the Level* which, although a flop, had a cast which spawned a bevy of West End musical talent. Marti had also been the leading lady opposite Tommy Steele in *Half a Sixpence* which I remembered seeing in my Westminster school days.

Gary brought Marti round to sing for me at my flat and she un-leashed a huge chest voice, effortlessly hitting notes that I frankly thought no chest singer could touch. Furthermore Marti seemed easy-going about the prospect of only performing two shows a week and being a standby if Elaine was ill. I duly reported this to Hal, who said if I was happy he was happy. I said Marti was far less feisty than Elaine and might come over as much more of an ordinary English girl, but Hal felt that if she could really sing the role we should go ahead. By November Gary was our Che and his friend Marti was his leading lady twice a week.

"ENGINE OF LOVE" CAME and went in a rather good record sleeve that showed just how an animated TV train series could have been great fun. But without a video it was doomed and an animated video would have been impossibly expensive back then. Anyway I was too busy with the *Variations* dance project to bother much. Also plans for Brian Brolly to head up my embryonic production company were eating up the hours. I suggested that we could use the name the Re-ally Useful Company which Brian rather liked. A deal was struck with Brian by my tax lawyer John Avery Jones and my accountant, a slightly old womanish bloke called Robin Ivison. Brian wanted 30% of the company but only a relatively modest guaranteed salary of £20,000 a year (today £114,400), peanuts compared with what he was getting from Paul McCartney.

Robin was opposed to Brian getting such a high equity stake. Sarah was equally opposed. She strongly felt that it might one day make me a hostage to fortune, however happy the marriage between Brian and me might look at the present. I couldn't see a problem. Really Useful was going to be a production company. I would still get my composer royalties as usual. If Brian had such a stake, surely he would want to build the company into a successful organization that could also produce other people's shows, not just mine? Also the company might do what it said on the ticket, be "really useful" and nurture all sorts of exciting non-theatrical projects. Sarah gave up the fight. Little did I realize how on the button she was.

Brian Brolly was reared at the altar of copyright ownership. He had observed in his Paul McCartney days how Paul's father-in-law, the New York lawyer Lee Eastman and his son John who I of course knew through the *Superstar* illegal performance saga, had bought copyrights for Paul. The Eastmans steered Paul into the Buddy Holly and Carl Perkins publishing catalogues plus the Frank Loesser, Meredith Willson and Jerry Herman copyrights which means today Paul has a stake in big musicals like *Guys and Dolls*, *Hans Christian Andersen* and *The Music Man*. The Eastmans also bought him Harold Arlen's songs like "Rockabye My Baby with a Dixie Melody." MPL is today the world's largest family-owned rights organization. It is ironical that whilst Paul owns so many of other people's copyrights he doesn't own The Beatles songs. Paul could have bought them when Sir Lew Grade's ATV put them up for sale but felt he shouldn't buy them without John Lennon, who wasn't interested or maybe couldn't afford them. So the greatest pop catalogue of all time was sold to Michael Jackson, from whom it was bought in dribs and drabs by Sony as Jackson's fortunes evaporated in medication.

I learned from Brian the importance of keeping the underlying ownership of my compositions. What I didn't fully grasp at the time was that if Brian owned 30% of Really Useful, de facto he would own 30% of my future copyrights. It would be a highly valuable stake if I was successful and I didn't think through what would happen if he wanted to sell it. The deal with Brian was agreed by the end of October, a few months before my Stigwood contract ended. I was thrilled. Although Brian could not officially join me until spring 1979 there was a ton of background knowledge to catch up on. He introduced me to Michael Simkins, a show business lawyer who took a highly dim view of Robert's activities as our manager, particularly him selling Tim and me to himself as producer. We saw a barrister who advised that Tim's stint as a trainee lawyer plus both our educational backgrounds would mean a judge would conclude that we had the nous to know what we were doing. I told Michael Simkins that Robert had been the right man for us in the right place at the right time. Furthermore, if anybody could build on *Evita*'s London success it was Stigwood. Let's not rock the boat.

Come November, railway trains had been replaced by cats big time. Michael White was now sold on *Old Possum* being the curtain-raiser to *Variations*. We both agreed that we needed to snare the choreographer of the hour, Arlene Phillips. Arlene and I had lunch with Brian Brolly at the Savoy Grill. Quite why we chose the staid old Savoy as the venue totally eludes me but I remember time and place vividly. Arlene was really keen to choreograph although she was far more certain about *Variations* than *Old Possum*. Brian had to leave for an appointment with Paul McCartney but Arlene insisted I stayed. Then she eyeballed me. "There's a girl in Hot Gossip that's going to change your life. She has a voice from heaven. Her name is Sarah Brightman." I was non-plussed. This was the girl I had briefly met in the bar of Country Cousins. She was also the singer of Hot Gossip's big summer hit "I Lost My Heart to a Starship Trooper." Now I love pop, but to say the voice on that track was a voice from heaven was arguably a stretch too far.

"Oh, ah," I said articulately.

NEXT UP WAS LUNCH with Faber & Faber boss Matthew Evans. I needed a nod that *Old Possum* in the theatre was a possibility. Though neither of us knew it at the time, Matthew's assenting nod changed both our lives. His only caveat was that other composers had wanted to set Eliot's cat poems to music and he couldn't let me have the rights exclusively. I wasn't bothered. *Variations* was what the public really wanted to see. As David Land would have put it, the cat poems were the warm-up act. Come December Michael White proposed a co-production with me as composer and creative producer, Arlene as choreographer, Tim Goodchild as set designer, David Hersey as lighting designer and two actors to read or sing *Old Possum* to be mutually agreed. Julie Covington and Paul Jones were top of our wishlist. The as yet untitled dance extravaganza would preview in a tryout at the Oxford Playhouse from April 2, 1979, opening on April 19.

I was glad when Gary joined the *Evita* cast. He had become a close friend of Sarah and me, and now I had a lifeline to the goings on backstage. I needed it. The backstage plot at *Evita* was thickening like chickpea soup. As is the way during rehearsals, extravagant luvvy promises had been hurled around like confetti in a helicopter landing. So Elaine and David Essex started to believe that Broadway beckoned and after the euphoria of the London opening Tim and I assumed their Broadway casting was a formality.

My first inkling that perhaps it wasn't had been at a solo dinner with Robert. The next hint that America might prefer homegrown leads came in a phone call with Hal in mid-November. Meanwhile there was growing tittle tattle about Tim's affair with Elaine Paige. This made things very awkward, particularly for Sarah. Tim and Jane had hardly been married long. They had their lovely daughter Eva and we were both very fond of Jane. However I had nothing but respect for Elaine professionally and really liked her. Tim's affair with Elaine unfortunately played straight into the hands of the Stigwood camp's crescendoing dictum that *Evita* would risk a USA backlash with British leads.

David Land started a softening-up process by phoning me with "You'll never guess what happened with Elaine at the theatre last night" stories. On one occasion she was supposed to have had a four letter temper fit in front of the children coming off stage after the "please gentle Eva" sequence. In September Robert proposed a firm plan. *Evita* would open in Los Angeles on May 9 next year for a two-month run at the Dorothy Chandler Pavilion under the umbrella of the LA Civic Light Opera, a clear ploy to add respectability to ensure an American soft landing. Broadway was planned for the following September, theatre to be announced.

Not I suspect for the last time in this tome, I am going to claim a senior moment. I have absolutely no clue when or from whom I first heard the name Patti LuPone. I remember being asked to listen to a recording of her singing a song called "Meadowlark" by Stephen Schwartz from his hapless musical *The Baker's Wife*. Three things struck me. First the song was brilliant. This was hardly surprising as Stephen was the composer/lyricist of *Godspell* and *Pippin*. This latter musical had been produced in London by Stigwood and, unlike on Broadway, flopped but through no fault of Schwartz. Some blamed its director Bob Fosse, who failed to turn up at the press conference telling its publicist, my friend Anthony Pye-Jeary, that he was shagging Liza Minnelli in the Savoy and would be until further notice.

The second was that Patti LuPone definitely seemed to have the chops. "Meadowlark" is a showpiece tour de force for a woman. Her performance suggested my score was well in her range. The third was that she must have had a stinking cold when she recorded it or had a bad problem with adenoids, which I assumed was a temporary issue. I reported back via David Land that I was keen to audition her. Due to my senior moment I don't remember if that happened when Sarah and I went to New York in early December for preliminary auditions. But I do remember meeting Craig Zadan who was most complimentary about her.

Meanwhile Tim was understandably getting twitchy about the way casting was going. Maybe I still perceived myself as junior partner in our relationship. But I felt really awkward about raising the Elaine issue directly with him and Tim certainly never talked frankly about it with me. So we never had a joint strategy to at least discuss the by now universal mantra that Americans must play *Evita's* lead roles. To this day I wonder if Tim and I had held a united front we could have insisted on getting Elaine cast, although bulldozing David Essex through as well would probably have been an ask too far, especially as he had played Che for such a short time. But with David Land doing nothing to defuse the gossip that Tim wanted Elaine cast for personal reasons and people whispering how highly convenient it would be for Tim to have Elaine on the other side of the Atlantic, I found myself in an impossible and rather grubby situation.

Now it was dredged up that Elaine couldn't do eight shows a week. I quickly countered that objection. However I was finding myself increasingly regarding *Evita* as a work I would always be professionally proud of but from which I was emotionally detached. My work ethic and my pride in what I had composed meant that I would do all I could to make *Evita* an American success. Yet one thing was blindingly obvious: I had to write something new. I needed an antidote to Mrs Perón or I would go stir-crazy.

Enter lyricist Don Black.

24

Tell Me on a Sunday

Any forebodings I had about 1979 and *Evita* in the US evaporated with the wonderful news that Sarah was pregnant again. Once more we had the curious experience of being given a date for the birth. July 24 was duly blanked a no-go zone. Sarah had to prepare herself for another long hospital stint. Thankfully *Evita* would be open in LA by this time and wasn't opening on Broadway till September. So I told Sarah that I would plan whatever was happening workwise around her hospital incarceration. At least that's what I promised her.

I first met Don Black at a dinner given by the Society of Distinguished Songwriters (SODS for short) at the Dorchester Hotel. I had just been elected to this exclusive group which was in those days an excuse for grown men to behave badly, there being no female songwriters in the club. All the members were backstage boys, people like Tony "Downtown" Hatch, Geoff "Winchester Cathedral" Stephens, who has the distinction of being among the first to import Turkish Van swimming cats to Britain, and Tony "Don't Give Up on Us" Macaulay gracing the chosen few. Then there was lyricist Don Black. Don was an ex stand-up comic. "Comedy is in my blood" he would say. "Shame it never made my act." He was unique in the clan as he was its sole Oscar winner for "Born Free." His hits included "Ben" for the young Michael Jackson, James Bond title epics like "Diamonds Are Forever" with composer John Barry, and the *Billboard* No. 1 from the *To Sir with Love* movie sung by Lulu.

Don was also the only SODS member apart from me to have written a musical. Again with John Barry he wrote *Billy*, the Drury Lane show that was the scene of the coat episode with Tim Rice. SODS meetings were an excuse for everyone to get pissed which suited me better than Don who I have never seen even mildly sozzled. Despite the truth that in those days I rarely declined a glass, my stint at SODS was short lived. I am not great at jolly functions. Having won a contest for Worst Performed Song by getting the distinguished members to bang out a metronomic beat and singing "I Got Rhythm" out of time across it, I thought it was time to quit. But not before Don invited me to the opening night of a musical he had written with Jule Styne based on the Jack Rosenthal TV drama *Bar Mitzvah Boy*. I was mightily impressed that Don was writing with the composer of *Gypsy* and *Funny Girl*. Although *Bar Mitzvah Boy* didn't work – it needed a much smaller theatre and production – I found the story of a boy who couldn't face his barmitzvah touching and charming. So Don and I met for lunch in the late lamented Ma Cuisine in Walton Street.

He told me that he had just been on a flight to New York and found himself next to an English girl who had yakked on for the entire journey about finding love in the greener pastures of America after a traumatic bustup back home. I told him about an English girl who had taken a shine to me when I was doing *Variations* and was coat-tailing around in search of the ideal man. What about a one-woman show about an English girl of late 20-something, trawling America for love? Everyone knows a girl who's closer to 30 than 20 and getting twitchy about being left on the shelf. It would be the perfect antidote to Mrs Perón. It also meant that I could achieve a long-held ambition of opening a show with a doorbell as the overture.

Don was excited. The question was who could perform it? I said there was a girl with a cast-iron larynx who was only doing two shows a week at the Prince Edward Theatre. I introduced Don to Marti Webb. They clicked so much that Don became her manager. *Tell Me on a Sunday* was out of the starting gate. We set ourselves a target date of the first weekend in September for a performance at the next Sydmonton Festival.

I CAN'T OVERSTATE HOW writing *Tell Me* helped me to keep a clear head about *Evita* in the US. Working with Don was so easy and refreshing. We invented an ordinary girl from the North London suburb of Muswell Hill who wrote letters home to her mum and somehow kept optimistic whatever her lovelife threw at her. It was welcome relief from Eva and her *descamisados*. However, no way was I deserting *Evita* and I reluctantly told Michael White and his sidekick Robert Fox to put "Practical Cats"/*Variations* on hold. Brian Brolly in the meantime was very keen to make a deal with Faber for the exclusive rights to *Old Possum*.

Just thinking of writing about cats was another passport to sanity as *Evita* inched towards Broadway. A febrile February dawned with the news that all hopes of British leads on Broadway had been scuppered by an unbudgeable no from American Equity. I flew over for the final auditions which were held in New York on February 18 and 19. Patti LuPone was the best overall candidate although my notes have "Diction, Warmth?" scrawled across them. I also much liked a girl called Terri Klausner, who gave a cracking account of "I Don't Know How to Love Him." Mumbling began about insisting the US Eva played eight shows a week, but I was adamant that we protect our leading actress and stick to the London six and two show regime.* Happily I was given invaluable support by our general manager, Tyler Gatchell. Hal was happy that Terri was our alternate and Patti was chosen as our number one. My concern for our leading lady's vocal cords was rewarded some years later when Miss LuPone opined that *Evita* was clearly written by a composer who hates women.

---

* That is, six shows a week with the leading actor, and then an alternate in two shows – usually one evening and one matinee.

As Elaine was written out of the Broadway scenario I felt awful for Tim and deep down I felt uneasy we were doing the right thing. But I had to make the best of where we were and my support for Patti as our leading lady was total. A superb Che emerged in Mandy Patinkin, already a veteran of the New York Shakespeare Festival, who combined something of David Essex's laidback cynical nonchalance with a great rocky tenor voice. He was very much the thinking man's Che and he even squeezed real anguish out of the part. Bob Gunton was Juan Perón whose previous credits included Ron Field's ill-fated Broadway musical *King of Hearts*, whilst the actress Jane Ohringer was given four minutes' stagetime eight shows a week playing Perón's mistress.

The first song Don and I wrote was "Come Back with the Same Look in Your Eyes." I wrote the melody after Don gave me the title. I soon learned that he had a small-sized bank of them and once we had our plot mapped, titles flew at me like balls from a revved-up tennis machine. However despite *Tell Me* now being my top writing priority I made a brief trip to LA at the beginning of March and met with Al Coury, boss of Robert's RSO Records. MCA had the rights to all the *Evita* cast albums but there was nothing to stop me producing the songs with another label. I wanted to cut "Buenos Aires" with Patti LuPone as a Latin disco track.

I didn't realize it, but RSO Records was in a big mess. It's incredible that it could have been. In 1978 the RSO label established a record that no record company major or otherwise has touched before or since: six consecutive American No. 1 hit singles and nine *Billboard* chart toppers in one calendar year. The problem was that this astonishing feat had been eclipsed by the catastrophe of Robert's *Sgt. Pepper* movie that all but clobbered the reputations of its stars, the Bee Gees and Peter Frampton. I learned later that Robert and Al Coury were on non-speaking terms which equalled me wasting my April and spending a heap of RSO's money in New York on a recording that

RSO would never release. Coury agreed to Patti voicing a version during rehearsals at the Minskoff Studios. What I didn't know was that Robert had independently commissioned an *Evita* disco album which, if Coury knew about, he didn't let on. So the Patti single was never released. The huge tensions in RSO Records soon became public knowledge. The Bee Gees' colossal 1979 hit album *Spirits Having Flown* was followed by the bitter lawsuit the brothers brought against RSO Records and Robert. In 1981 Robert ceased to have anything to do with the company and the most successful independent record label of all time was gobbled up by Polydor.

A RATHER PREGNANT SARAH joined me at the beginning of April for the start of rehearsals but began to miss Imogen so terribly that she went home on the same day Tim and my ten-year management contract ended. I stayed in New York for the rehearsal room run and the show's launch to the ticket agents before decamping to LA. It was a lousy time. Besides missing Sarah, I suppose it was inevitable that I wouldn't find rehearsals as exciting second time around. On April 29 the company moved to LA and the Dorothy Chandler Pavilion in the downtown Music Center.

The theatre was wildly too big for *Evita* with over 3000 seats on four levels and the production didn't sit at all well there. It seemed cold and with the exception of Mandy Patinkin I found the performances detached. David Land arrived just in time for the dress rehearsal. There was an odd feeling in the Brit camp as we watched our story of a woman in the man's world of Argentine politics. Two days before, one of our London VIP audience members had been elected the first ever woman leader of a European state. It was slightly surreal seeing Margaret Thatcher all over American TV a mere few hours before we saw our US *Evita* make her entrance on the balcony of the Casa Rosada for the first time.

The first preview threw everyone in at the deep end. Despite the catastrophic failure of the *Sgt. Pepper* movie, the huge success of *Grease* and *Saturday Night Fever* ensured that Robert still had the muscle to make it a black-tie charity affair, a lethal idea for a new show with a new cast since benefit nights are famous for the rich paying fortunes for tickets to a show that they don't want to see. Come Act 2 Tim and I wound up fully tuxedoed in a local bar. We had no desire to view how the great and good of LA reacted to Eva's line, "She won't go scrambling over the backs of the poor to be accepted by making donations just large enough to the correct charity." Shortly after we'd got a drink, another couple who had ditched the show sidled in, the female half wearing a most Evita-like ballgown. "Where these guys went wrong is they didn't invite the real Eva Perón tonight," proclaimed her beau to the barman.

The LA opening went pretty well. The *Times* sent their classical critic Martin Bernheimer who regarded it "like it or not" as an opera. "Evita," he wrote, "is without doubt a clever show full of effective songs." He wondered if my rock experiments of *Superstar* days had been deliberately watered down, noting that Broadway veteran orchestrator Hershy Kay had been hired to work beside me and the "pit band contains nothing more exotic than a guitar." His main reservation was the casting.

> Bob Gunton manages the minimal "Sprechgesang" of Perón with a perfect pseudo-macho point. But Patti Lupone musters a rather scrawny sound for the temperamental outpourings of the titular sinner-saint, and she finds her haunting "hit" number, "Don't Cry For Me, Argentina" something of a strain. Mandy Patinkin brings plenty of suave baritonal fervor to the music of Che Guevara, especially in a showstopping area called "The Money Keeps Rolling In" but the essential bitterness

and the brutality of this charismatic character somehow elude him.

Washington Post reviewer James Lardner remarked on the "exciting score that palpitates between Latin and English rock rhythms." But he also observed that it had been "de-rocked" on its journey from album to the stage. He noted "As Eva, Patti Lupone must deal with the shallowness of both the character and the authors. It is a losing battle. And since her singing voice is hard to understand in certain registers [I presume he meant diction] her performance comes across, perhaps unfairly, as one of Evita's serious drawbacks." He did, however, praise her version of "Don't Cry for Me." I had three worries about Patti. She wasn't caressing and seducing the audience in "Don't Cry for Me" like Elaine did. She also had a tendency to bend the timing of musical phrases. Finally there was her diction. Mutterings began about her and Broadway. So before leaving LA I wrote her this letter. I added my private phone number.

10 May 1979

Dear Patti,

I am going back to London today as there is an awful lot back home I have to sort out so I probably will not see you before I go but I wanted to congratulate you on your performance and to say that I am quite sure you will make the role of Evita your own in a very short time indeed.

My main feeling is that it is terribly important to concentrate now on the actual singing of the material. I know Hal has spoken to you about "Don't Cry For Me Argentina"; the main point of that song is that it should be sweet and seductive. I am quite sure that if you work on the delivery of the songs the whole thing will fit into place astonishingly quickly. I found in London that there is a really fine line between the shows reactions being remarkable and merely good. Every time the show has not gone down as well as it could have done, I find the music is not quite registering for some reason or another.

Please if there are any worries or problems that you have do always feel free to telephone me. I have put my number at the bottom of the letter and in London there is always the answering service. Patti, I know you are a really superb Evita and I have every confidence in you. I just think the thing to concentrate on now is to match Hal's brilliant direction with a great musical performance.

All the best to you, I hope to see you soon and I will certainly be back before the show goes to San Francisco. Also I have every hope we will be able to proceed with an American record.

> *Andrew*

Sarah had flown to LA for the opening and got a thorough bollocking from her doctors as a consequence. They moaned that it involved far too long a flight for a diabetic mum to be. So on the earliest possible day we compounded the problem and flew to Nice, having scooped up two-year-old Imogen. I had decided that the best place to write *Tell Me* was the south of France and rented a house near la capitale mondiale du parfum, Grasse which was just plain stupid but Sarah thought she could wing it with the medics and pretend she was at Sydmonton. We had reckoned without the 1979 French phone system. In the rare event that you could get a line it crackled and her doctors soon smelt un rat. But we had a lovely time. I continued composing *Tell Me* as happily as I always did in mimosaland and also got carried away writing a rock guitar concerto of which I have no recollection whatsoever.

Don Black and I were already discussing other projects. He had a huge address book of old-time stars including one of my all-time favourites Petula Clark. Back home Don introduced us and a song was born, "I Could Have Given You More." I arranged it for a small orchestra and Pet interpreted the lyric with a real actress's colour and character. It's an extraordinary moment when you first hear your own song sung by an artist you've been a fan of since you were a kid. Unfortunately no record company wanted to release a one-off single without an album. I was very pleased with the melody and didn't want it hawked around. There was no place for the song in *Tell Me*, so I told Don that this had to be one for my tune bank and he totally understood. I reworked it as my setting of T.S. Eliot's "Gus the Theatre Cat."

At the beginning of June, Robert decided we needed a US *Evita* cast album. This meant three weeks in LA, starting at the end of June, a week before Sarah went into hospital for child number two. It put me in a real spin. Although the doctors had grumpily agreed that her stay could be two weeks shorter this time, she would still be in hospital for four weeks and separated from two year old Imogen. The only phone contact was via the ward matron so with an eight hour time difference it was going to be virtually impossible to call her. On the other hand she knew I couldn't leave such an important recording to someone else. So I agreed to produce the album provided Tim came too and that it was mixed in London with David Hamilton-Smith. Robert was happy and threw in a two-bedroomed bungalow at the Beverly Hills Hotel to seduce me onto a flight.

I flew to LA via New York solely because of Concorde. The thrill of a Concorde flight never evaporated, no matter how many times you'd been on it or experienced its technical glitches which had you landing in places where you never thought there were places. There was an awkward incident this trip. Concorde was tiny, so possibly due to lack of space, mustard was dished up in sachets rather than proper pots. I was fiddling around trying unsuccessfully to open one when suddenly the entire contents shot across the cabin. Luckily the guy in the line of fire leant forward just as the missile struck and failed to notice the vaguely orange liquid dribbling down the wall opposite him. Ready-made mustard evidently is difficult to remove as next time I flew on this plane I noticed it had congealed into a sort of impasto. Or perhaps the British Airways cleaners had mistaken it for an early Damien Hirst. The guy who I narrowly missed was Cubby Broccoli.

I had had a very good time in LA with *Variations* the year before. Even if recording *Evita* during the day wasn't exactly going to be a breeze, there were the evenings to look forward to. Peter Brown was living in LA and very much a light of the "Colonial Dinners" that were held at Le Dome on Sunset Boulevard. Ex-pat Brits severed from the mother country like Dudley Moore held court into the small hours and for these few weeks I was an honorary guest. It wasn't a hopeless forum to bring the occasional girl to, especially English ones which I put down to research for *Tell Me*.

WE RECORDED ON THE Universal sound stage. Patti brought a hotter Latin flavour to songs like "Buenos Aires" but I worried about her musical accuracy in the score's more dissonant regions. I really liked Jane Ohringer's performance of "Another Suitcase," full of vulnerability and confounding the *LA Times* review which found her strident.

At one lunch with Tim, Bob Gunton and Mandy Patinkin in the commissary, I was struck that the fallout from the Watergate and Vietnam years seemed to have Americans burying their heads in the sand about politics. It was as if everyone wanted world issues to simply go away. The suggestion that the extreme left joined the extreme right in the political circle was seriously off limits. That lunch I felt my first real forebodings about how *Evita* would fare in New York.

We finished the album a day before the LA run closed on July 6. I flew home that night, went straight to our London flat to clean up, phoned Sydmonton to tell Imogen that Daddy was back and took a taxi straight to Dulwich Hospital. I felt really awful when I saw Sarah. She was cooped up in the same little room beside the railway line where she was holed up for Imogen. But it was far worse this time. It was a hot summer so either she opened the window and was deafened by the train noise or she sweltered. What sort of idiot could have designed a hospital with its inmates housed next to a mainline train route?

Also there had been fewer visitors. Sarah's family and loyal friends like the Gummers had made the trek to South London but it was amazing how many people seemed to be busy or away and of course there was no phone. So we cried a lot and hugged a lot and she asked just how long I would survive on the awful monotonous hospital food, dried-up lamb chops on a Tuesday, congealed macaroni cheese on a Wednesday and so on in soul sapping weekly rotation. That was easy to fix, I'd already smuggled in supplies, including a decent bottle of white burgundy to top up the baby's natural sugar levels. The tears really flowed when I showed her some pictures I'd taken of me and Imogen. Imo stayed at home because Sarah was worried that she'd get in a state if she came to the hospital.

OLYMPIC STUDIOS HAD OPENED a new studio near Chelsea Football Club which was slightly closer to the hospital than their main HQ in Barnes, so we mixed the US album there. Now I was free from the Stigwood management contract, Brian was keen to get motoring. I had a meeting with Julie Covington about *Old Possum*. The cat poems had been temporarily put on the back burner, but I decided I would complete my settings once *Tell Me* was finished. I was now thinking they could make a standalone album. Even today the thought of what Julie might have done with, say, "Old Deuteronomy" or "Gus the Theatre Cat" sets the blood racing. One sadness was that although Roy Featherstone loved what I played him of *Tell Me*, Brian would not do a deal with MCA Records because of his mantra that Really Useful must own everything. Roy insisted, probably following Brian's rulebook when he was the MCA boss, that MCA owned the master recordings. So Brian approached Tony Morris, the boss of Polydor, who jumped at a deal that allowed the ownership to stay with us.

On Sunday, July 22 I had lunch with Bryan Forbes, the doyen of British film directors (*The Stepford Wives*, *King Rat*) and his gorgeous wife actress Nanette Newman at their Surrey home near Virginia Water, after which I was going to drive to the hospital to see Sarah. He was keen to find out what was happening with *Evita* movie-wise and he was surprisingly interested in *Tell Me*. I don't usually accurately remember a date like this but this one is an exception. In the middle of lunch, an anguished house-help burst in saying there was an urgent phone call for me. It was Imogen's nanny at Sydmonton saying I must phone Dulwich Hospital at once. Sarah's waters had burst. It transpired Sarah's gynaecologist was also wrong-footed. When I arrived at Dulwich he was in his tennis shorts and the top half of his operating togs. Forty-five anxious minutes later and two days ahead of schedule, I was looking at a baby boy.

My first thought was if there was ever a case for calling a baby boy Isumbras this was it. This child had Isumbras written over every orifice. Once again Sarah baulked at a sensible Pre-Raphaelite name. Dante Gabriel found no favour either. Even a straightforward name like Gowther was nixed. I nearly got Gawain to the finishing line but in the end we both agreed on Nicholas. His middle name is Alastair after the uncle I never met.

Sarah based herself at Sydmonton that summer but it was a busy one for me. There was still the *Evita* album to finish off. In another development the BBC approached me about *Tell Me*. They had heard I was writing a one-woman show and not to be outdone by ITV they wanted to put a marker down. Simultaneously the Polydor record

deal came through. Brian was anxious that *Tell Me* was recorded
before the *Evita* Broadway opening once again beckoned me away.
These days I would pronounce August plus a new kid a firm n/a, but
not so in the summer of 1979. For nearly three weeks I was holed up
in Morgan Studios. All my *Variations* band turned out for *Tell Me*
with the exception of Gary Moore who was touring with Thin Lizzy.
Two guitarists, Ricky Hitchcock and Paul Keogh, joined the lineup
with Maurice Pert on percussion. It was Paul who played the twelve-
string Rickenbacker 360/12 FG on "Take That Look Off Your Face"
whose sound no other electric guitar can replicate.

THE STORY OF OUR girl's American Odyssey couldn't be simpler.
It begins with a row on British soil with an unseen bloke who can't get
a word in edgeways. Marti was perfect casting. It is impossible to stop
Marti talking. Intense sessions about musical phrasing and charac-
terization invariably end up as a one-woman show about her central
heating and no claims bonuses. Anyway, our girl leaps on a flight to
LA, where she meets a film producer called Sheldon Bloom, whose
PA's voice is played on the album by no less than Hal's friend Elaine
Stritch. Disillusioned with him, she legs it to New York and has an
affair with a younger man. She is convinced he's the one but things
go pear-shaped with him too. The title song "Tell Me on a Sunday"
has a beautiful lyric about asking a girlfriend to break the news that
her affair is doomed in an easy way: "No long faces, no long looks, no
deep conversations / I'd like to choose how I hear the news / Take
me to a park that's covered with trees / Tell me on a Sunday please."

   Tim Rice took issue with the word "covered." Up to then I'd never
wrestled with thoughts about a word for trees in a park, planted, peppered, littered, camouflaged? . . . but sorry Don, I think I'm marginally with Tim. Our girl's final affair is with a married man. "Married
man always looking at your watch / I wanted to spend more time
than twelve to two, loving you." *Tell Me* has endured because Don

goes straight for situations that women know all too well and men, if they are honest, do too.

All the while our 20-something is writing home to mum. This idea came from a working session with Marti at Sydmonton. She was banging on about loyalty cards when I came up with a sort of English minuet which I played Don on the phone. We wrote our first letter in under an hour which wonderfully encapsulated both our artist and our girl's homespun optimism. After a verse extolling her latest bloke, she's scribbling about her mum's pet dog Cassius barking and causing problems with the neighbours. The song cycle* – that's what *Tell Me* really is – ends with our girl picking herself up after her doomed fling with a married man and hopefully next time finding Mr Wonderful. We presume she does.

Tell Me premiered at the Sydmonton Festival on the morning of September 1. Marti sang up a storm and Brian Brolly found himself in the happy position of a bidding war for a TV special, although this had to be conducted behind one of the trees with which Sydmonton's park is, shall we say, covered as business is strictly forbidden at the Sydmonton Festival. BBC TV arts prevailed and the project was assigned to a producer who some years later was dubbed "The Spanker" by a scurrilous satirical magazine.

* A term for a series of linked songs used mainly by classical composers, e.g. Schubert.

25

"This Artfully Produced Monument to Human Indecency"

On the morning of September 26, Robert was a worried man. Confident that *Evita* would prove a solid hit in the USA, he had broken a cardinal theatre unwritten law by not offering any of the Broadway investment to the London angels and putting up the entire capitalization himself. *Evita* had opened the night before to some of the most excoriating reviews in Broadway history. The word on the street was that no show could remotely survive this venomous onslaught more than a few weeks. Walter Kerr in the *New York Times* was relatively mild, beefing about Tim dealing with the story through Che's narration rather than writing dramatic scenes. He was full of praise for Hal's staging and liked Patti's singing and dancing – "she sings the role well and moves with a rattlesnake vitality" – but also remarked on her "leering tongue, her firmly set jaw and the ice water that plainly runs in her veins." He might have added that her performance was frequently inconsonant. Mandy was applauded but the only other actor to get mentioned was Jane Ohringer and she only in passing. The final barb was directed at Tim and me. "You go home wondering why the authors chose to write a musical about materials they were going to develop so remotely, so thinly."

Douglas Watt in the *Daily News*, perhaps not wanting to be on the wrong side of the consensus like he was when he raved about

Tom O'Horgan's *Superstar*, didn't mince his words. The headline was "Evita equals empty and is vulgar to boot," an interesting observation on Hal's stark production from the man who found Tom O'Horgan's empty vulgar *Superstar* "Stunning, vibrant and reverent." He did find my score "melodic and musically literate," but ended his review in no uncertain fashion: "Evita is a dud."

One of the worst reviews was John Simon's in *New York* magazine. "Stench is a stench on any scale," he wrote in a revue which was unequivocal in implying that we were glorifying fascism:

> What sort of chaps are these authors who can exalt with equal enthusiasm Jesus Christ and Eva Perón? The two had nothing in common except that they died at 33. To Rice and Webber they seem equally suitable for enshrinement . . . if you want to fill the coffers of these two amoral, barely talented whippersnappers and their knowing or duped accomplices by all means see this artfully produced monument to human indecency.

Of course Tim and I exalted neither Eva nor Jesus.

After the show Robert threw a massive first night party at the then "it" club Xenon, where he posed with Gina Lollobrigida and Lauren Bacall, but once the reviews came through, Sarah and I were in no mood to celebrate. We went back to our room at the Carlyle Hotel and were joined by Mandy Patinkin and some other cast members and Brit friends who'd come to New York for our presumed triumph. A morgue would have been a jollier place. The ever loyal Tyler Gatchell ruefully said the advance would carry us through the next few weeks and then "every day would be another good day away from the reviews."

The extraordinary thing was that ultimately these appalling reviews didn't matter. *Evita* went on to receive eleven Tony nominations and win seven of them including Best Musical, Best Score and Best Actress for Patti. It wasn't a pushover season either. The other contenders were *Barnum*, *Sugar Babies* and *A Day in Hollywood/A Night in the Ukraine*. Broadway folklore has it that it was Robert who turned *Evita* around with the first ever TV advertising campaign for a musical. Now there are so many ads for musicals on American TV that the only people who take notice are the advertising agents who get commission out of placing them. But back then it was another unprecedented bold move by this great showman. Even so, despite Robert's massive campaign *Evita* was still haemorrhaging badly as Christmas approached and the naysayers were doubling their bets that the show would soon be the salt to Robert's *Sgt. Pepper*.

Then overnight everything changed. Come New Year and the first week of January, *Evita* was Standing Room Only. This in itself wasn't too unusual. The post-Christmas week is traditionally Broadway's hottest. Even a French avant-garde mime act performing the whole of Marcel Proust's *À la recherche du temps perdu* to a score by Arnold Schoenberg would have a fair chance of reasonable business. It was that the sold-out business continued through the dog days of January and February, which was so inexplicable.

Undoubtedly the sensational TV ad with its spectacular burning torches and "Evita in the ballgown moment" played a big part. But I wonder, I may be completely wrong, if something else contributed too. The zeitgeist. On December 26 Russia invaded Afghanistan. Overnight the attitude in America towards world politics seemed to change and I noticed it became far easier to have a rational discussion about *Evita* at a New York dinner table.

26

Shaddap and Take That Look Off Your Face

During *Evita*'s late October dog days I got a call from Hal inviting me to New York to meet with him and playwright Hugh Wheeler to discuss a musical based on Billy Wilder's iconic movie *Sunset Boulevard*. In fact, earlier in the year he had arranged a screening for me in London and I immediately saw why. The story of Norma Desmond, the silent movie star whom the talkies passed by and her obsession with a younger man, struck me as a brilliant subject. I even discussed it with Don Black who wrote on spec two lyrics, one for Norma Desmond's butler Max called "Madame Needs a Lot of Looking After" and another for the scene where a lot of Norma's old movie-star friends gather for a game of bridge and claim "There Are Not Enough Hours in the Day." Neither song resurfaced when I eventually did write *Sunset* with Don more than a decade later.

I was particularly excited to meet Hugh Wheeler who had written the book for *A Little Night Music*, *Sweeney Todd* and *Candide*. He was an ex-pat Brit with a slew of musicals under his belt and a major force to be reckoned with. An air ticket arrived, but something told me to pay my own way. I didn't want to be beholden to anyone, what with Brian and the new company on the go. We met at Hal's office and I was immediately a little uneasy. What I loved about Billy Wilder's movie was its *film noir* quality combined with the exotic. Hal had one of his concepts. He wanted to change the era the story was set from the 1940s to the 1950s. He was intrigued by the huge Fifties film star Doris Day who had become a virtual recluse in her Carmel Valley home. Once dubbed by a wag the oldest living virgin, she apparently now shuttered out the light from her mansion lest anyone photographed her.

I told the truth. I could absolutely see an absorbing parallel between Doris Day and Norma Desmond, but I couldn't see the point of changing the setting. I said of course I would read any treatment when it was ready. I also asked Hal if he would direct my upcoming BBC TV *Tell Me*, but he said he was too committed to his "Sondheim project" *Merrily We Roll Along*. When I got back home a thought struck me. Hal, Hugh and Stephen Sondheim had been collaborators on two definitive musicals and Hal and Steve on so many more. Why was Hal talking to *me*?

IN NOVEMBER 1979 I got a very strange phone call from Sarah's dad. Could we meet for a drink, he was feeling rather low? I of course said yes. I asked if it was anything to do with the family. He said it wasn't, but he had something he really wanted to get off his chest. We met at the Savile Club. He drank two "gin and sins," as he called gin and Cinzano, before he lowered his voice. I shall never forget what he said next.

"Andrew, there's going to be a plague and it is going to kill a lot of people. It is mainly transmitted either through sex or infected fluids. It will grow out of control in Africa where it will kill millions. It will spread to the West probably via the homosexual community on the West Coast of America. There is no known cure." With that he went silent. As I mentioned earlier, to this day neither Sarah nor I know exactly what Tony Hugill's real job was.

TELL ME ON A SUNDAY was scheduled to be filmed for BBC TV at their Television Centre on December 11. The musical director was

Harry Rabinowitz, the man who spotted the wrong horn note on the original "Don't Cry for Me" recording and sang it to me as we were passing in a corridor. Jon Hiseman, Barbara Thompson and Rod Argent were once again the mainstay of my band, Marti was on cast-iron vocal form as usual and the studio audience went nuts.

A transmission date was immediately set for February 12, 1980. But there was a glitch in the sound department. The BBC had not heard of stereo in 1979, so everything was mixed down to mono with a timecode track to synchronize the sound to the picture that was so loud it broke through into the sound system when *Tell Me* was screened at BAFTA for the TV critics. As usual nobody seemed to notice except me, but I persuaded the controller of BBC TV, Bill Cotton, to risk a total union walkout and let me smuggle the soundtrack out of the hallowed corporation into Morgan Studios where Martin Levan fixed the problem by "phasing it out."

Marti was set to launch *Tell Me* at the 1000 seat Royalty Theatre on January 28 and the demand for tickets from the media was so great there was a repeat performance the following day. Astonishingly most of the mainstream theatre aisle scribblers turned out, including the then arbiter of musicals, Jack Tinker of the *Daily Mail*, who wrote "Marti Webb stakes an indisputable claim to a role which I prophesy every musical actress from Streisand down may soon be begging to sing." Incredibly, perhaps out of a sense of *Evita*-inspired guilt, the *New York Daily News* pronounced, "Superstar strikes again! This is a stunning collaboration between three enormous talents, lyricist Don Black, composer Andrew Lloyd Webber and Marti Webb . . . Marti's voice is a warm, feminine and wide ranging instrument of enormous personality. It's Lulu, Olivia Newton-John and Mary Hopkin rolled into one." How fortunate we were that Marti had agreed to take over from Elaine Paige as Evita just before Christmas.

It was a win win situation all round. After the TV premiere Norman Jewison pitched to direct a movie version and Trevor Nunn, then the boss of the Royal Shakespeare Company and whom I had never met, was among several mainstream directors who wrote to me intrigued by *Tell Me*'s future. To cap it all we had a big hit single with "Take That Look Off Your Face" which got to No. 3 with the album peaking at number 2. Three-year-old Imogen begged to be allowed to stay up to watch Marti on *Top of the Pops*. Imogen had a hand, or more precisely a small finger, in *Tell Me*'s title song creation. I was writing away at Sydmonton and wrestling with the last verse when Imo sidled up to the piano and prodded a note on the keyboard. She ran away, fully expecting to be rounded on for interrupting my creative flow. Instead she got a massive hug. She had solved a melodic conundrum that had occupied me for a good three days.

The following Saturday Imo was repeating like a demented parrot about going into our local town to buy the record about "your face." I was touched by such an early show of loyalty. We joined a queue of other parents and their kids all wanting the single about "your face." When we got to the counter the smiling salesman said to Imo, "You're a lucky young lady, this is our last copy," as he handed Imo Joe Dolce's No. 1 single "Shaddap You Face" to the beaming up-to-then apple of Daddy's eye.

Shortly after the other face song denied us a number 1, I took Marti to the Belgravia Funfair, a now defunct annual must-be-seen-at-posh charity bash which used to parade its swanky dressy self in Belgrave Square. There was a gypsy fortune teller charging a fortune to read Sloane Ranger palms. Marti and I thought we'd give her caravan a whirl. Marti's future was pronounced a breezy speed-bump free zone. Not so mine. The soothsayer's expression gave new meaning to the lyrics of "The Gypsy Cried." "You must change your profession at once," she anguished, flashing a central casting gold tooth that just possibly might have been painted in for the evening. Unsurprisingly I was a bit rattled. There was a gaggle of black tie Belgravia types lurking around the caravan so I ashenly explained my plight.

"Should the cost of my gypsy visit be a tax charge against closing down my old profession or a start up cost of my new?" I concluded.

A be-souped-and-fished fellow stepped forward.

"I might be able to help. I'm the senior tax inspector of the Belgravia district."

THE PROBLEM WITH *TELL ME* was that everyone thought I had a game plan for a fully blown musical and I hadn't. It had already expanded from Sydmonton. Over the years there have been various attempts by producers to turn it into a full-length show which I should have resisted, as attempts to make more out of it never worked. One of the most persistent believers in a rethink was Shirley MacLaine. This was deeply flattering; I was a huge fan. Don recalls that during one of our NY trips to meet her, Jack Rosenthal came round to his apartment and asked how life was going. Don didn't reply. He merely smirked and turned on his answerphone where there was a message: "Hi Don, it's Shirley MacLaine. Do you never return calls?"

Don and I met Shirley a few times. She talked about her various previous lives and, as Don puts it, how being guillotined in the fifteenth century explained her latest summer cold, but discussions with the delightful Shirley ultimately led nowhere. Quite simply *Tell Me* was never meant to be expanded.

27

Mr Mackintosh

Exciting as the launch of *Tell Me* was, there is one 1980 date that is indelibly inked in my brain. January 24, 1980 is when I first met Cameron Mackintosh. Before you say miaow, it must be stated that omens for our meeting were far from propitious. Cameron had let it be known in the West End that he wanted to kill me. The trouble sprang from the 1978 Olivier Awards. They weren't known as the Oliviers in those days, rather they were monikered the SWET Awards since they were imparted by the Society of West End Theatre. As the SWET Awards is a rather unattractive name, this year the society decided to call them the Wedgies after a Wedgwood pot that was temporarily dispensed. Finally the society came up with the rather better notion of calling the gongs the Oliviers and bronze statuettes of a young Olivier playing Henry V became the coveted trophies.

That year the ceremony was held after a dinner at the Cafe Royal and was an unmitigated shambles. Hal Prince was in America so when I picked up *Evita*'s Wedgie for Best Musical I said how grateful we were to Hal and what a shame it was that he wasn't around to direct the proceedings. I thought I heard a bit of a hurrumph from somewhere in the room but it was the last award of the night and Sarah and I headed to the Oscar Wilde Bar with our Wedgie pot whose finial fell off. Next morning David Land was on the phone in high spirits. The producer of last night's ill-starred fandango wished me to be hung, drawn and quartered and my various bits to be displayed the length of Shaftesbury Avenue as a warning to other ungrateful theatrical upstarts. This producer turned out to be Cameron Mackintosh.

The various modes of my death were tossed back and forth between David Land and Cameron Mackintosh for well over a year. David savoured every minute. Come 1980 I thought it time to make peace with this Mackintosh guy before David got so over-excited that his hernia caused him problems again. So I asked him to lunch. The problem was where. I didn't know anything about Cameron Mackintosh other than he had produced touring revivals of classic old shows, one or two of which had come into the West End. I concluded he was an old-timer and frightfully tetchy, so I built up a mental picture of the ancient codger.

He was almost certainly in his mid sixties, rather thin and wizened, spoke in a broad Scottish accent, wore tweed jackets with leather patches under the elbows and very probably sported a bow tie, possibly pink but more likely yellow to prove he had theatrical connections. I even wondered if he had a moustache. Then there was the matter of where to take the old boy to lunch. What if he was a strict teetotal Presbyterian? His broadsides against me suggested he might be no stranger to blood and thunder sermons. Then again what if this Mackintosh were partial to a wee dram of whisky and got frisky with chorus girls come Burns Night? He might be a closet raver. Anyway what with him obviously being a senior out-of-town type I figured the odds were he'd want a quick lunch and be safely on board a train up north to Aberdeen or wherever by teatime. So I played really safe and booked up the staid men-only dining room of the Savile Club, telling Biddy and Brian that I'd be back by half past two.

When I finally rolled up slightly worse for wear at around 6:30 pm it was to tell them that I was writing a full-length musical about cats.

WHEN YOU MEET A soulmate you forget time and place. Well, perhaps not the place, but I don't think time has ever passed so quickly as it did that afternoon with Cameron. I had met the only Brit who loves musicals as much as me, in fact, Cameron is more obsessed with them than I. There is the odd other younger producer these days, but no way was there back in 1980. Folklore has it that we got so stuck in that we consumed four bottles of burgundy. This is untrue. It was three bottles and two kirs. Nonetheless by 6 pm and the umpteenth anguished phone call from Biddy asking where my dead body was we had sorted out the future of British musicals for several generations.

The first thing that struck me was Cameron's boyish, bouncing, giggly, girlie enthusiasm. I have never come across such a passionate force of nature or anyone so sure of himself. Cameron has a wicked infectious sense of humour, mostly at the expense of those of us who have had legendary musical disasters. This led to a tit for tat that embraced my *Jeeves*, his revue *After Shave* plus a string of joyous turkeys from Peter Hall's *Via Galactica* to John Williams's *Thomas and the King*. I learned that Cameron started out as a stage manager on *Oliver!* and he revealed a deep affection for Julian Slade and his musical *Salad Days* about which I deemed it wise to shaddapa my face.

Cameron didn't seem to have rock on his radar. I sensed he didn't really think it belonged in a musical and I wondered if he really liked *Superstar* or the rockier bits of *Evita*. That's the big difference between us and I think Cameron would agree. But we did have a joint passion for all the classic American musicals. He was a massive Sondheim fan, having staged the highly successful revue *Side by Side* for the great man, and I was intrigued that he was mounting another revue based on Tom Lehrer, as well as a new production of *Oklahoma!* In fact this production replaced *Jesus Christ Superstar* at the Palace later that year.

I was intrigued by how Cameron financed his productions. His West End *My Fair Lady* which opened around the same time as *Evita* was no cheap corner-cutting affair. He told me that he had a small pool of loyal "angels," but the bulk of his finance was public money from the Arts Council who, he had persuaded, would be supporting high-quality touring shows that brought first-class theatre to the regions. He beamingly described this as a brilliant wheeze. It was halfway through the second bottle that I mentioned T.S. Eliot's cat poems. I told him about my idea of setting them as a curtain-raiser to *Variations* and where I was with Michael "Chalky" White which wasn't very far.

Soon the cat project overtook our lunch. We both had clocked how dance was becoming hip in Britain – you could hardly miss the Pineapple garbed kids hanging around Covent Garden. We talked about Arlene Phillips but Cameron thought that it was vital any choreographer had real theatre experience. He suggested I met Gillian Lynne. I was taken aback. Of course I knew of Gillian. She had choreographed virtually every British musical from the 1960s onwards anyone had heard of, from the Bricusse/Newley *The Roar of the Greasepaint – The Smell of the Crowd* to *Pickwick* via the film of *Half a Sixpence* – everything, that is, except my shows. I associated her with an old-school style of dance, miles away from what Arlene was up to with Hot Gossip. Prancing cockneys with their hands in their braces were more her line than sinuous pussycats, or so I thought.

Cameron asked me if I had seen the Royal Shakespeare Company's razzle-dazzle version of *The Comedy of Errors* which Gillian choreographed with RSC honcho Trevor Nunn directing. I hadn't, nor had I seen his production of the Kaufman and Hart classic *Once in a Lifetime* which Gillian also staged. But I could see where Cameron was headed. He wanted to snare Trevor Nunn. It was one thing to be talking about setting the existing poems but to turn *Old Possum* into a full-length musical would involve reworking and possibly rewriting the poems. This would need T.S. Eliot's widow, Valerie's, permission. If we had a heavyweight director such as Trevor Nunn with his RSC background on board it would reassure her that we would respect her husband's work.

Cameron was obviously very close to Gillian. She was about to direct his Tom Lehrer revue. Gillian could be our conduit to Trevor. We both agreed to sleep on it – and after that lunch we needed to. I shook hands with Cameron and promised that if I developed the cats musical it would be with him. Then it was back to *Tell Me*.

THAT LUNCH TURNED OUT to be a turning point in both our lives. I had to say something to Michael White who immediately wrote to me saying he didn't think a full-length *Old Possum* would work. I also toyed with two other possible projects. One was a one-act idea which had no takers. It was to write the story of how the opera *La Bohème* came about – or rather the two operas. I got the idea from reading Mosco Carner's biography of Puccini. Both operas are based on Henri Murger's novel *Scènes de la vie de Bohème*. Puccini's *La Bohème* is arguably the most popular opera ever written. The other by Leoncavallo is now a seldom performed curiosity.

It didn't start out that way. Although Leoncavallo was a composer, his career began as a librettist. He co-wrote the words of Puccini's *Manon Lescaut*. Next he adapted the Murger novel as an opera for Puccini to compose. However Leoncavallo in the meantime had a smash hit as a composer with *Pagliacci* so he decided he wanted to compose *La Bohème* himself. There followed a massive public falling out which resulted in both Leoncavallo and Puccini announcing their own versions. Leoncavallo's opened first to rave reviews. Puccini's opened to some stinkers. Carlo Bersezio wrote in *La Stampa*, "Puccini's La Boheme, just as it leaves no great impression on the mind of the spectator, will leave no great mark on the history of our opera." Another wrote, "Boheme shows a deplorable decline, written in haste [a reference to the race with Leoncavallo] and with little discernment and polish often lapsing into the empty and sometimes the puerile." (A nugget here culled from Mosco Carner's biography. Puccini thought of and rejected *Oliver Twist* and *Les Misérables* as subjects. What else did he turn down?!)

My idea was to write the backstage story of the operas, the rivalry, the tension, the bitching that led to the reception of the operas being what they were. I had one huge conceit. Puccini would go into his publisher Ricordi's office and play him a melody that Ricordi says is rubbish. After the lousy reviews of his opera, Puccini says to his wife "If only that tune Ricordi rejected was in *La Bohème*, I'd have a hit on my hands." With the arrogance of slightly fading youth I composed a tune which was deliberately Pucciniesque. I was really pleased with it, so pleased that I did something I had never done before. I played the tune to Dad. My father was an acknowledged expert on Puccini and, although my offering was obviously a Puccini tribute, I needed a frank opinion on whether it was original or not. After he heard it he asked me to play it again. When I'd finished second time around I nervously asked him, "Dad, does it sound like anything to you?" He pondered for a moment.

"Andrew, it sounds like a million dollars, you crafty sod."

The Puccini/Leoncavallo idea was soon forgotten, although I did mention it once over lunch in London with Stephen Sondheim. The melody, however, was not. This was one for the tune bank if ever there was one.

THE OTHER PROJECT WAS top priority, a new show with Tim. He had mentioned several times in the past year that he had an idea based around a grandmasters' chess tournament. The main protagonists would be Americans and Russians and it would feature their backstage machinations and illicit romances set against the menacing background of the Cold War. The musical possibilities inherent in the maths of chess immediately struck me. Naturally I was intrigued to read what Tim had in mind. I can't remember exactly when I received Tim's synopsis, probably around the end of 1979. But I do remember reading and re-reading it and worrying that it lacked a coherent storyline. I phoned him from my old refectory table desk at Sydmonton and told him that I thought the idea had real potential but maybe this time we needed to get a dramatist involved. I suggested it lacked a John le Carré-type suspense ingredient and maybe we needed a writer like le Carré or Frederick Forsyth to help fashion a strong plot.

Tim immediately countered that in the past we'd always done every aspect together. Why change a winning formula? I don't remember exactly how we left it, but I do remember thinking that he sounded slightly surprised and, maybe, put out. But I didn't think too much more of it and presumed we'd pick things up later. There was *Evita* opening in Australia and now that you could talk about *Evita* in New York, Robert wanted us there for the Tony Awards in June. Meanwhile I confirmed that the next Sydmonton Festival in July would feature the first performance of *Old Possum*.

So somehow in between *Evita* in Adelaide, *Tell Me* in the USA and sudden demands from Polydor for a follow-up album for Marti Webb, I composed the rest of *Old Possum*. I discovered one of the joys of setting existing poems to music is that you don't have to hang around for lyrics. It makes them ideal material for composers on long haul flights. I still had not abandoned the idea of *Old Possum* being the curtain-raiser to *Variations*, I also still wondered if its future was as a concert piece, but I was beginning to explore the wider body of T.S. Eliot's work. I decided to sound out Hal about directing and the Adelaide opening provided a great opportunity.

Adelaide was a whirlwind of events, mainly about Hal and Robert. Hal had a *This Is Your Life* devoted to him which took place on the theatre stage after the first preview which meant everyone plus a knackered cast had to stay on after the performance to pay their exhausted respects at God knows what in the morning UK time. Rupert Murdoch held a massive bash for his fellow countryman Robert at which Robert's mother demonstrated that alcohol did nothing to attenuate the Stigwood clan's life expectancy. Tim and I weren't noticed much. But next day I did get some time with Hal about what we called the T.S. Eliot project. Just before the Tonys, Hal wrote to me at the Carlyle Hotel.

> 2 June 1980
>
> I thought some about the T S Eliot and, much as I think the area in which we were talking makes sense – an all-over structure that suggests Eliot and you have more on your minds than just an appreciation of cats – I can't do it.
>
> I want to get the Sondheim thing completed and I want to get into something more totally involving from my point of view. In the meantime, I have to approve scenic and costume designs for the Carlisle Floyd opera that I'm doing next spring, for TURANDOT in Vienna 83 and, my God, a Mascagni* at the Met! And I consider those diversionary, but time-consuming.
>
> Let's find a project.

He wasn't the only Broadway name to say no. I played the score for choreographer Twyla Tharp who was less than enthralled by the piano playing and singing. Craig Zadan and Neil Meron had me play for Joe Papp who fell asleep after I got to "The Naming of Cats." Cameron didn't seem worried by these setbacks. He was insistent on my meeting Gillian Lynne and I could see his logic about ensnaring Trevor Nunn.

My meeting with Valerie had to wait until after the Tony Awards at the beginning of June. Sarah and I didn't know what to expect

---

* Actually Gounod's *Faust*.

after the disastrous initial reception, but when Tim and I won Best Score, Hal won Best Director and Patti Best Actress in a Musical, it dawned on us that we might just win Best Musical. When we did, it completed what must be the biggest volte face of the media elites in Broadway history. The Broadway production ran for 1567 performances and spawned three US national tours. Its numerous US revivals included a return to Broadway directed by Michael Grandage in 2012.

28

"All the Characters Must Be Cats"

I finally met with Valerie Eliot at the end of June in her Kensington flat in the heart of Mungojerrie and Rumpleteazer territory. She was a tall, good-looking woman with very blonde hair and from our first firm handshake it was clear that she was a fierce custodian of all things T.S. Eliot. I was very nervous but I think she was too. Almost the first thing she said was, "You aren't going to turn Tom's cats into pussycats are you?" which I thought was hopeful. She then dropped a bombshell.

"Tom turned down a huge offer from Disney for *Old Possum*."

This sounded ominous. Before I could ask why she lectured, "Tom hated *Fantasia*. Did you like *Fantasia*, Mr Lloyd Webber?"

I muttered something about not really remembering what *Fantasia* was like, although I liked it a lot when I was small.

"How do you see the cats?" she said, boring into me with her gorgonlike clear blue eyes.

I thought I might as well come clean. "Have you seen a dance troupe on TV called Hot Gossip?" I faltered.

"Are they the ones who Mary Whitehouse made all the fuss about?" Valerie asked, becoming rather animated.

"Yes, but they really are good dancers and what they are doing is breakthrough stuff. The great Hal Prince said that Bobby Fosse . . ."

Valerie cut me off. "Tom would have liked Hot Gossip," she smiled.

Stage one of "The Wooing of Valerie," as we came to call that meeting, was complete. She agreed to come to the Sydmonton Festival and then we could take things further if she liked what I had done.

"PRACTICAL CATS," AS MY setting of the T.S. Eliot poems was billed, followed a performance by the new kid on the block, punk violinist sensation Nigel Kennedy who dazzled the 1978 Festival audience with a virtuoso display of Bach, Messiaen and a touch of jazz. It was a tough act to follow. My performers were Gary Bond, Paul Nicholas and Gemma Craven, with my now stalwart musical musicians Jon Hiseman, Barbara Thompson, John Mole and Rod Argent. "Practical Cats" went pretty well, but it wasn't an obviously complete piece like *Tell Me* or *Variations*. Although the audience loved Paul's "Magical Mr Mistoffelees" and Gemma's slinky "Macavity," it came over as the sort of fun anthology that would raise a smile at genteel music festivals rather than having a theatrical life.

That was until ten minutes after the performance. Valerie had come as promised with Faber boss Matthew Evans. Cameron had brought Gillian Lynne. Gillie was already doing sexy cat movements on the lawn when Valerie gave me a large envelope.

"I've brought some of Tom's unpublished poems," she said in a warm but matter-of-fact way. "Andrew, I think you should look at the story of Grizabella first. Tom thought it was too sad for children."

I remember truly going cold when I first read:

> She haunted many a low resort,
> Round the grimy road of Tottenham Court.
> She flitted around the no man's land
> From The Rising Sun to The Friend At Hand
> And the postman sighed as he scratched his head
> You really would have thought she ought to be dead
> And who would ever suppose that that
> Was Grizabella The Glamour Cat.

And that was not all. There was a letter from Tom Eliot to his publisher Geoffrey Faber about an event which brought all the Pollicle Dogs and Jellicle Cats together who then ascended to the "Heaviside Layer" in a great big air balloon. There was even a couplet to go with it: "Up, up, up, past the Russell Hotel, / Up, up, up, to the Heaviside Layer." So Eliot himself had an idea for a bigger structure for these poems, very vague, but it was there. I knew then that I had the bare bones of a stage musical.

Most importantly Grizabella the Glamour Cat gave me a tragic character, a character who you would really care about. I asked Cameron and Gillie to join Valerie and Matthew, and the excitement was tangible. There were other poems too, the story of a parrot called Billy McCaw, who lived on the bar of an East End pub. There was the saga of a Yorkshire terrier called Little Tom Pollicle, which was apparently Eliot's nickname, and a long poem about a man in white spats who meets a casual diner in a pub called the Princess Louise and starts talking about "this's and thats and Pollicle Dogs and Jellicle Cats."

I asked Valerie what the words "Pollicle" and "Jellicle" meant. She explained it was Eliot's private joke about how the British upper class slurred the words "poor little dogs" and "dear little cats." She also revealed that Eliot intended the "Princess Louise" poem, as we came to call it, to be the preface of a book about dogs and cats, but in the end cats prevailed. "The Awefull Battle of the Pekes and the Pollicles" was the sole survivor of his original scheme.

Eliot's letter to Geoffrey Faber suggested another building block, an event that brought the cats together. "The Song of the Jellicles" is about a Jellicle Ball. Could this have been the event that Eliot was proposing? If so "Practical Cats" would have dance at its centre. Dance was now sweeping Britain, albeit about six decades behind America.

Brian Brolly reluctantly accepted that Cameron would co-produce with the Really Useful Company. "Practical Cats," the musical, was born.

ALTHOUGH I ONLY HAD a sense of the overall structure I began setting the crock of unpublished T.S. Eliot gold. I kicked off with the "Princess Louise" for which I created a chorus using the words "Pollicle Dogs and Jellicle Cats" as a nonsense word chant which eventually became the chorus of "Jellicle Songs for Jellicle Cats." Next came "Grizabella the Glamour Cat." I added the "Little Tom Pollicle" section to "The Pekes and the Pollicles" and earmarked "The Ballad of Billy McCaw" the dancing parrot, as a possible song for the "bravo" pirate cat Growltiger to sing to the Lady Griddlebone in the poem about his epic last stand. I remember being struck that, as with the *Old Possum* poems, Eliot had written "Billy McCaw" with a defined verse and chorus almost as if he were writing lyrics. Here Eliot betrays that he was American. I don't believe any British poet wrote at the time like this. Years later Valerie told me that Eliot invariably had a hit tune of the time in his head when he wrote what she called his "off-duty" poems.

I wrote an overture, composed "The Jellicle Ball," constructed a running order and made a demo of the whole lot in my studio at Sydmonton, with me singing a guide interpolated with the best performances from the Festival. From the outset I wanted the cats to live in their own soundscape. I created the miaow sound on my mini Moog, which is still used in the theatre today. Then I orchestrated the overture and the Ball with various sounds programmed from the Prophet 5 synthesizer plus a few more generated on the Moog. A real piano provided the percussive glue. All of this survives in the final orchestration, both the overture and "The Jellicle Ball" sound remarkably similar to the present-day theatre version although my pre-choreographed version of the Ball was a lot shorter. The final sequence starting with "Skimbleshanks the Railway Cat" followed by "Macavity," "Mr Mistoffelees" and "The Ad-Dressing of Cats" was exactly the same except that at this point there was no "Memory" and no ascent to the Heaviside Layer.

Although the material Valerie gave me changed the direction of "Practical Cats," Cameron and I soon realized that to make a musical out of such a potpourri a writer would have to come on board. Faber boss Matthew Evans was extremely nervous and thought Valerie would find the idea difficult. It was now blindingly obvious that without a director with a pedigree like Trevor Nunn's she could veto "Practical Cats," at least as a musical.

Cameron began wooing Trevor. It wasn't easy. It was a big deal for Trevor to plunge from the Royal Shakespeare Company into the wicked world of commercial theatre, especially with such a bonkers-sounding project. Musicals were not accepted by the subsidized sector like they are today when no National Theatre season seems complete without one. Another big issue was moonlighting from the RSC. Today the prospect of a bumper box office would have the RSC jumping through hoops to develop a project like "Practical Cats," but in 1980 it was unthinkable. It took *Cats* to be a smash before the RSC governors considered that a musical of *Les Misérables* was the sort of enterprise to nurture under their roof.

Meanwhile Gillie made a pitch to direct as well as choreograph. She sent Cameron and me a treatment that made us exceptionally queasy. It began with the curtain rising on the exterior of a row of Kensington townhouses. It is evening. A maid opens one of the front doors and puts out a row of empty milk bottles. From the side of the stage a cat emerges who sniffs the bottles. Now the feline action begins.

Ouch, Gillie! For openers, the minor problem posed by humans playing both cats and maids is that they are both the same size! I told Cameron that since he was the one who knew Gillie, he would have to deal with this. Gillie's treatment rammed home how essential Trevor was to our project. But it was equally clear that Gillie was vital to the team. Not only did Trevor rate Gillie's choreography but their past working relationship on *Once in a Lifetime* and *The Comedy of Errors* would provide Trevor with the crucial security blanket to make him say yes.

Before Trevor committed he expressed serious concerns in a lengthy letter he wrote to both Cameron and me. In it he writes of Cameron "dreaming of a show which sweeps away all barriers of class and taste and predilection, appealing as much to the devotee of Covent Garden as to the football fan who would never dream of going to the theatre." Trevor was unequivocal about what needed to change.

> I cannot think of any show, opera or play or work of fiction or film or dance that had wide and popular appeal if it did not tell a story. An anthology entertainment, be it Facade or Ain't Misbehavin' has a limited life ultimately restricted to the aficionados of the world they celebrate. I believe we have a simple choice. Either we retain the form of Eliot's anthology and work towards an entertainment of high quality but limited appeal; or we use the poems and Andrew's musical settings as a basis of a narrative in which cat characters become identified and developed towards a conclusion to which Eliot would have been sympathetic. I believe all the characters MUST BE CATS [I had gone along with Eliot's suggestion there was a human narrator]. Cats introducing us to other cats, cats telling us what only cats can ever possibly know; cats divulging secrets, cats arguing, cats of different classes, cats sexually or romantically involved with each other . . . and finally cats remaining mysterious, inscrutable, unknow-

able and (need it be said?) inhuman . . . Some real talking
seems to me to be vital.

Trevor's vision was a far cry from maids and milk bottles.

AFTER TONS OF MEETINGS in coffee shops between rehearsals
for season two of Trevor's eight and a half hour stage adaptation of
Dickens's *Nicholas Nickleby*, the length of which should have been
more noted by Cameron and me, Trevor was on board. He had three
conditions. He wanted Judi Dench in the company. No issue here.
Apart from her obvious acting credits I thought she was marvellous
as Sally Bowles in *Cabaret*. With a serious actress like Judi on board,
people might just think we knew what we were doing.

Secondly he wanted *Nickleby* designer John Napier on the team
and David Hersey to light. This too was a joyous no-brainer. John
designed the sets and costumes of Peter Shaffer's *Equus* and we figured he might do for cats what he did for humans into horses. David
Hersey's work on *Evita* meant he got both thumbs up from me.

The third was a potential deal breaker. He wanted it made unequivocally clear that he was the director, i.e. that he really *was* the
ultimate boss. This was an issue for Gillie. She had twenty years of
musical theatre experience ahead of all of us and had just successfully
both directed and choreographed *Tomfoolery* for Cameron. Cameron
had to deploy every ounce of his considerable persuasive charm to
convince Gillie to accept this. He painstakingly explained that Valerie Eliot's consent was the key to this musical. Without a director
at the helm with serious literary credentials Valerie Eliot might well
scupper the show. Eventually Gillie agreed to the title Associate Director and Choreographer which Trevor just about accepted. Now we
had to present the team to Valerie and broach that we might need a
writer to fill in a few gaps. Trevor suggested himself. He also wanted
permission to delve into all Eliot's work as the show evolved.

Matthew Evans told me many years later that Valerie's decision to say yes was a very close call and that unquestionably she would have said no if Trevor had not been in sole charge. Matthew confided that Valerie had taken soundings from her many friends in the literary and theatre worlds and this is what she found.

My theatre successes had all been with Tim Rice and produced by Robert Stigwood. *Jeeves*, my sole effort without Rice, had been a triple gold-plated bummer. Cameron Mackintosh had never had a commercial hit with a new musical. Trevor Nunn had never worked in commercial theatre before, let alone on a musical. There had never before been a successful British dance show and conventional wisdom was that British musical theatre performers had two left feet. To top it all this show was seriously asking audiences to watch actors dressed as cats for over two hours.

Small wonder that Valerie came so close to saying no. It's impossible to overstate my gratitude to Matthew Evans. He tipped the balance.

NOW CAMERON AND BRIAN BROLLY had the unenviable task of raising the £450,000 budget. (Today £2,097,000.) Three inflation ridden years later it was still £50,000 less than *Evita*. But *Evita* had massive hit records behind it and people begging to invest. There was an additional negative: the lethal sounding combination of the Royal Shakespeare Company's boss making a musical out of a dead highbrow writer's poetry. We had no theatre, no script and an unfinished score. But somehow that insane, incurable, blinkered optimism that overtakes reason and leads otherwise normal men to stage musicals had wormed far too deep into the minds of Lloyd Webber and Mackintosh for us to do the sensible thing and ditch the nutty project.

To the unbridled glee of connoisseurs of vintage theatrical car crashes we announced "Practical Cats, the Musical." The press release was all about every dancer in the land coming forward to audition for our groundbreaking confection. Cameron and I were on the musical theatre equivalent of the Cresta Run.

None of the pitfalls ahead worried me. I was on an exhilarating crusade and the thought of trawling the nation and auditioning lots of pretty girl dancers didn't seem too bad either. But looking back, a hell of a lot was based on a wing and a prayer and blind belief in Trevor's track record, even if none of it was in the commercial theatre. Also it looked increasingly likely that the investment would not be raised and I would have to plug the hole. This caused Sarah and me to agonize deeply. What if the team merely shrugged when the show flopped and left Sarah and me holding the bedraggled baby? Trevor would simply return to his safe job at the RSC. Cameron could fall back on producing shows funded by the Arts Council.

Looking back, I am amazed we didn't abort "Practical Cats." No way would I announce a musical in such an unready state today. However we blithely cracked on. Cameron and I saw nearly more dance shows than we had hot dinners together. By far the most exciting was *Dash*, starring pint-sized ex Royal Ballet dancer Wayne Sleep. Wayne was getting huge audience reaction with this show, and Cameron and I thought it vital to snare him. Thankfully we did; a minor miracle since we had no specific role to offer.

Cameron worried that Trevor, having said yes, seemed to have receded into his RSC bunker. In a letter to Trevor, copied to me, Cameron wrote:

> I have absolutely no worries about your single-mindedness and organisational abilities, I am just concerned that when you are ready and able to devote your mind and energies to our show the rest of the team won't be available or the type of performer we are after (a very rare animal indeed) will not be ours for the asking.

Cameron was also growing anxious about how much seemed to depend on miracles in the rehearsal room. What was new to both of us was the very different attitude of subsidized theatre animals. There the safety net of an infrastructure and facilities like swish rehearsal rooms are taken for granted. As there is no need to raise money from investors, you can indulge in long, improvisational rehearsal processes, something impossible in commercial theatre without suicidally deep pockets. Back then British commercial theatre shows rehearsed, and often still do, in church halls or community centres where you are lucky if there is more than one lavatory, let alone luxuries like in-house canteens. Invariably you share your space with the local youth sports club come the evening, limiting the scope for meaningful experimentation. Cameron and I also didn't realize then that Trevor has tunnel vision about the project he is currently working on. This is why we found it so hard to get his attention. It would of course be counterbalanced by his dedication once he was fully on board. But Cameron and I didn't know this that autumn.

SEASONED THEATRE INVESTORS, apart from that increasingly rare breed of "angels" who back shows on a hunch and for the opening night invitation, want to read scripts and hear scores. Cameron and I had only a few songs we could play. Brian Brolly became increasingly concerned that there was no proper budget or breakdown of running costs. With nothing definite there couldn't be. The one department that was firming up was John Napier's.

John had made a major breakthrough with the look of our cats. As so often with John it was triggered by something happening in the big city. Every wannabe dancer was wearing woolly leg warmers and most of them sported wild punk wigs. Add both to a cat body stocking and presto! With leg warmers you break the line of the human body and hint at something furry. With wigs you eliminate human hair. Trevor took a cue from T.S. Eliot's *The Waste Land* and proposed the set should be a giant rubbish dump. That way all manner of human detritus could become props. John suggested that the design should be three times human scale. By October one thing was agreed by all: the design, at least, was on the right track.

But it was becoming clearer that Trevor was right, we needed a story. A very basic structure was agreed. Once a year Jellicle Cats hold a Jellicle Ball where their leader Old Deuteronomy chooses a cat who will be reborn to a new life in the Heaviside Layer. So only one cat would make the journey Heavisidewards, not the whole tribe as Eliot suggested. John Napier reconceived Eliot's big air balloon as a giant car tyre that rose up to the heavens like something out of *Close Encounters*. The minor snag was we had no theatre for John to design for.

John and Trevor both passionately felt that our audience had to be close to, almost a part of, the action and therefore ideally the staging should be partially in the round. Gillie had understandable worries. Most dance is conceived to be staged behind a conventional proscenium which acts like a picture frame. But Trevor was insistent the action should at the very least be able to come forward by building over an orchestra pit. This severely limited the West End theatres we could play in. Almost all have sight lines that make it impossible to build a stage forward like this which made Trevor increasingly sure that we needed an unusual space where we could create our own environment.

Cameron and I scoured London for, as John Napier put it, "four walls and a roof with flexible seating," but spaces like that didn't exist. The Roundhouse at Camden Town had the right feeling but had a policy of short runs only. We had another thought. The National Theatre had built a temporary theatre-in-the-round within the old Lyceum for a well-reviewed season of medieval mystery plays. The theatre had been converted into a dance hall during the Second World War with a vast flat floor created by levelling the stage and auditorium. This, combined with the crumbling architecture, could be magic for a show set in a rubbish dump. The Lyceum was owned by the Greater London Council who bought the theatre in 1938 to demolish it for a road-widening scheme. War scuppered this disgraceful plan. We offered to lease the theatre but the GLC wanted to be rid of it permanently. Furthermore the building was so run-down it was deemed unsafe for long-term use. It was nearly two decades before it was restored and reopened, ironically, with my production of *Jesus Christ Superstar*. So come November "Practical Cats" was still homeless. Salvation was to come in a most bizarre way.

NOVEMBER WAS BLANKED OUT for me and Gillie to audition up and down the country for that impossibly rare breed in 1980s Britain, dancers who could sing and act. That's how I first properly met Sarah Brightman. It was a surprise that she wanted to audition as she was a pop name with a big hit with "Starship Trooper" under her belt. A private meeting was arranged at my London flat. She arrived wearing a blue wig which may be the reason why I played "Don't Rain on My Parade" so appallingly for her. I thought she had a nice voice and that was about it.

Two days later it was up to Glasgow and Newcastle, in the middle of which I had a glorious half day off which I planned to spend squinting at architecture. I couldn't understand why Biddy, my sanguine PA, kept crazily scheduling an audition in London between the two northern casting dates. No matter how many times I said she was a congenital idiot either Cameron or Sarah insisted the London auditions were etched in granite.

I discovered what was behind this nonsense in the middle of the night. My poor wife was worried so sick about my suicidally stupid musical that she had taken to pouring out her angst in her sleep. One night I woke to hear her burbling on about a big secret that "Andrew mustn't know about." Naturally I took advantage of her semiconscious state and asked in my best soothing psychiatrist tones what it was. After a lot of incoherent drivel about relatives, she mumbled the words "This Is Your Life."

So that was the reason for my ludicrous schedule. It was that old chestnut of a TV show where ancient relatives and so-called friends were wheeled out to the surprise and shock of all too often B-list celebrities. Next morning I gave a virtuoso acting performance about knowing nothing which caused Sarah to fear the polar opposite.

I remember little about the TV programme nor the parade of relatives and friends who were dredged up. That was because my mind was entirely somewhere else. I had found our cats' home. The TV programme was recorded in the New London Theatre. During the endless procession of cousins I never knew I had, my eyes wandered around a perfect pussydrome. Built on the site of the old Winter Garden, the New London opened in 1973 as the "theatre of the future." It was designed by Sean Kenny, the man responsible for some of the most revolutionary sets ever, as both a proscenium theatre and theatre-in-the-round. Whilst kissing some long-lost great-aunt I remembered that this was achieved by a giant turntable in the floor.

The moment the show was over I told a disbelieving Sarah that I'd found a cats' home. Could she keep my various relatives and wellwishers at bay in the green room whilst I phoned Trevor Nunn? Luckily I got straight through to the RSC's HQ at the Aldwych Theatre and begged him to sprint the few hundred yards to the New London. Sarah did a brilliant covering job for me at the party by saying I was at the other end of the room when I wasn't, so for ten minutes Trevor and I had free rein of the empty theatre.

What happened next rendered us speechless. I don't think two theatre animals could ever have mouthed "eureka!" so instantly. The building manager had wandered in and I asked him if the turntable that changed the audience configuration still worked. He said sure, would we like to see it? Next Trevor and I were looking at 300 seats moving to make a perfect theatre-in-the-round. We clutched each other. Not only had we found our cats' home, we could physically move our audience too! Trevor said it was the most exhilarating moment he had ever had in a theatre.

Unfortunately the New London owners were considerably less exhilarated. In short, they said "piss off." Their reasoning was understandable. The New London had failed as a theatre. Even *Grease* with Richard Gere had flopped. So they had turned it into a conference centre/TV studio. They were building a successful business. If the New London became a theatre again and failed they would have cancelled a clutch of conference and TV bookings and would have to rebuild their new business all over again. So no dice, especially with a musical about cats. We were desolate. Trevor's enthusiasm was so huge that John Napier had even started to design for the building. We had combed every weird space in London for our cats' home. No New London, no "Practical Cats."

Rescue came in the form of Bernard Delfont. Bernie had followed my career ever since he told me never to get involved with a football club. He was on the board of the company that owned the New London and he came up with a typical Bernie solution. If as expected "Practical Cats" was a total disaster we could hire the theatre with no penalty as the conference business could continue with barely any interruption. The problem for the owners arose if we were a small hit and ran for a bit. This would mean the building would be off the conference/TV circuit for long enough for them to have to build the business virtually from scratch. So Bernie proposed this deal. If "Practical Cats" was a flop we paid a normal rental for the time we were in the theatre and that was that. If we ran beyond three months and closed any time within two years, we paid the owners a £200,000 penalty. (Today £932,000.) After that it would be the normal theatre deal.

This was a nightmare Catch 22 situation. It was just possible that "Practical Cats" could be the sort of show to limp through a year. Of course Cameron hadn't got the money and obviously nor did anybody in the creative team. All eyes turned to me. I too had nothing like that in raisable cash. I was already underwriting the investment. I would have to take a second mortgage on Sydmonton. To Sarah's horror I agreed. So we went into December with still no script to show investors and realistically nothing concrete we could offer them other than a wing and a prayer. But we did have a theatre.

AT THIS POINT, HOWEVER, Trevor had disappeared once more into the PA-protected bowels of the RSC. We had set up auditions with key performers that it was vital he should see, but were informed a change of schedule had made him unavailable. I wrote to him pointing out how much I personally was at risk and suggested we abort. Everyone around me was now literally begging me not to sign the papers that could gamble away my home. Cameron went ballistic with Trevor and insisted that our principal casting was done by Christmas. Finally Trevor freed himself up. His initial idea was to create an ensemble where cast members played multiple roles, so Judi Dench would double as the Gumbie Cat and Grizabella, the actor playing Old Deuteronomy would play Bustopher Jones, Gus would play Growltiger and so on. With only limited access to Trevor, our whittling down process had so far been a balancing act between Gillie's need for real dancers and mine for singers. Now Trevor added acting, plus feeling it was vital that our performers were real characterful individuals. In short they had to be like cats.

At last, with the aid of a few extra Eliot cat names that Valerie unearthed, we began a proper cast breakdown. Final auditions were scheduled for December 10 and 11 at the Royal Academy of Dance in Battersea, just a hop, skip and a jeté away from the fabled Battersea Dogs Home. Three new cast members were added to Judi Dench and Wayne Sleep: Paul Nicholas, Brian Blessed and a staggeringly beautiful girl dancer, Finola Hughes. Casting Finola was a no-brainer. Gillie and I both wanted a moment that defined the strange, other-worldly beauty of the cat and the now iconic "white cat" section had already been choreographed for Finola come that December. Finola was no singer, but she soon became the untouchable, intangible essence of what our show was about. Brian Blessed was neither untouchable nor intangible. Trevor described him as "an agricultural actor." But his authoritative if rumbustious quality, plus strong baritone voice, made him a natural for Old Deuteronomy, who in our developing story had become the leader of the Jellicle tribe.

There was a tussle about Paul Nicholas. Gillie, Cameron and I thought he was a natural Rum Tum Tugger. Paul's single of "Magical Mr Mistoffelees" was already hitting the airwaves, if not the charts. Trevor found his laid-back, lived-in charm irritating. Paul had seen some of life's more colourful offerings, having had fifteen years' experience with Stigwood, not to mention backstage at *Superstar*. Eventually Trevor capitulated. With Paul, Brian Blessed, Wayne Sleep and Judi Dench, we at last had four very solid marquee names to grace our playbill.

FINAL AUDITIONS DAWNED. SOMETHING I find extraordinary about musical theatre actors is that time and time again when you offer them a part, often after several gruelling auditions, they turn you down. They either transpire to be unavailable or have another job offer they infinitely prefer. I often wonder if the only reason they audition is to find out as much as they can about an upcoming show and then bitch about it.

One such auditionee that day was Sharon Lee Hill, a very sexy girl whom Trevor much fancied as one of the cats who, in our slip of a plot, was under the mesmeric spell of the dreaded "Hidden Paw" Macavity, Eliot's answer to Professor Moriarty. Sharon said how honoured she was to be offered a part, but thank you, no, she was signing up to *The Best Little Whorehouse in Texas*. I was deputed to ambush her and talk her out of it. I burbled on about how "Practical Cats" was a game-changer for the British musical which didn't cut much ice as she was Australian. Melodramatically I said that joining our cast would change her life. She did, and five years later she was Mrs Trevor Nunn. Trevor, John Napier and I all married "cats" – maybe some of the girls were auditioning us?

Come day two lunchtime we still had major gaps to fill. But we'd found some great talent to join our headliners, not least the lithe leggy singer/dancer Geraldine Gardner as a Macavity girl plus former child star and brilliant all-rounder Bonnie Langford as Rumpleteazer. Bonnie had made her name as Baby June in *Gypsy* on Broadway and she'd also played the little girl in the musical *Gone with the Wind* of which Noël Coward said "Cut the whole of the second act and the child's throat." Most unfair. Bonnie is the ultimate musical theatre pro. Also on board were Jeff Shankley, who played Pilate in London's *Jesus Christ Superstar* and whom Gillie dubbed Thunderthighs, plus the wonderfully funny character actress Myra Sands and Sue Jane Tanner, a dancer who could act out a real story and whom Trevor wanted as Jellylorum, Gus the Theatre Cat's friend. Also cast were Ken Wells, a real Gillie ballet stalwart who danced brilliantly and could just about sing, plus a truly eye-catching black boy called Donald Waugh who I thought was destined to go far.

Finally nabbed that day were John Thornton as Mungojerrie, ex-*Superstar* Judas, Stephen Tate, in the dual role as Growltiger and Gus the Theatre Cat and Sarah Brightman, whose role no one could decide. I still have my audition notes for Sarah. It was how she looked and danced that really grabbed me. It was a full two years before I clocked how good a singer she was.

WE HAD NO ONE else to see that day and Trevor, ignoring Cameron's asides about the RSC's financial crisis being explained by the size of his tummy, was making noises about lunch. He also dropped a mega bombshell. "Practical Cats" lacked an emotional centre. He passionately yearned for a new song that defined our show and it should be sung by Grizabella. He reckoned the kernel of its lyric could be found in Eliot's writing but after Christmas I had to come up, no pressure, with our show's answer to "Don't Cry for Me Argentina."

There was silence. Then everyone started yabbering at once. I led Trevor to the grand piano in the corner of the rehearsal room and tentatively played him the tune that Dad thought sounded like a million dollars. When I finished Trevor rolled his eyes and summoned everyone to gather round. He quietly coughed which, as I was discovering, he always did before pronouncing something portentous.

"Andrew is about to play. I want you all to remember the date, time and place when you first heard this melody."

When I'd finished and played it twice more, any lingering thoughts of a Puccini/Leoncavallo mini opera were a memory.

29

Growltiger's Last Stand

In between the cats shenanigans I hadn't forgotten about Marti Webb. The BBC devoted a TV special to her, based on her new album, *Won't Change Places*, the title of a song I wrote with Don Black. It was meant to be one of those cabaret numbers where the headliner star adopts a rictus grin and warbles that there is no place on earth they'd rather be. It wasn't too bad an effort of the "thank you very much you've been a wonderful audience God bless" genre, although my arrangement was not my most inspired. Despite a repeat of the TV special, the album didn't echo the success of *Tell Me*.

My instant New Year task was to get a lyric written to the tune that Trevor had made such a fuss about. I explained the saga of our fallen glamour cat to Don Black who met with Trevor and patiently listened to an analysis of Eliot's central belief in new lives. Soon we had:

> *Good times only live in the memory*
> *Like a tune from the old days*
> *But the words don't belong.*

They didn't. Next we had:

> *Good times, don't despair of the good times*
> *At the end of the journey*
> *To the heaviside layer.*

It will be your time, and all you have to do is believe
And the good times will be there.

The Grammy for Best Song didn't seem automatic with this one either.

As there was no lyric imminently in sight, I played the tune to Tony Morris at Polydor who had reluctantly agreed to finance the "Practical Cats" cast album. I suggested he released it as an instrumental single. Tony was not like Roy Featherstone at MCA. He was a corporate bean counter who would have been equally as happy selling widgets as records. Nonetheless I thought Tony's reaction would be euphoric like everybody else's. Instead when I'd finished he looked so lugubrious that I thought he was about to administer the last rites. No way was there any money for this. He told me the American company were extremely unimpressed by the "Practical Cats" demos, let alone the script. Only the success of *Tell Me* had forced them to stump up for the cast album. If I wanted to record the tune he supposed he would have to release it, but I must pay the recording costs myself.

When I got home I wrote him a passionate letter. I pointed out that I had put my home on the line for the show, that I had a double gold record for my instrumental album *Variations* and I believed this melody to be the most commercial I had ever written. No dice. In desperation I called Roy Featherstone. Maybe it was for old times' sake, but he happily stumped up the cost of the single and suggested that like *Variations* it was issued under my name. He wondered if we could reunite our *Variations* band with Gary Moore on lead guitar.

Everyone minus Gary Moore and Don Airey was on board "Practical Cats" anyway, but Gary was now a star with Thin Lizzy. You can't be told no if you don't ask, so I tracked Gary down. He was only too pleased to help out. So the first incarnation of "Memory" was a gorgeously lyrical guitar version by one of heavy metal's greats. As

Tony Morris predicted, the single did absolutely nothing. But very soon it paid for itself big time.

WHILST THE LYRIC CRISIS rumbled on, John Napier, Trevor, Cameron and I had heated meetings about the design. Trevor wanted the orchestra to be out of sight. He had a good point. If the orchestra was in vision you would see musicians at the same time as you saw actors as cats which Trevor vehemently argued would destroy all sense of illusion. I was worried about how the orchestra would sound if it was boxed in. Memories of *Superstar* in New York haunted me. Also I feared that the audience might think the music was pre-recorded.

Abe Jacob had put himself forward for the sound job and on the "better the devil you know" principle Cameron and I had offered him the gig. Trevor got his way about the band and it was enclosed behind some three-times-real-life-scale rubbish bins stage right below a walkway. Meanwhile the investment continued to dribble in horrifyingly slowly. I must have auditioned the score half a dozen times that month. One afternoon Brian Brolly had me play for a bigwig from Warner Bros. After I finished, the guy intoned in a West Coast drawl, "The problem with this show is half the world hates cats." I did an Elton and slammed down my piano lid. "That's exactly right!" I shouted, "and the other half of the world is a plenty big enough audience for me." Brian looked horrified. As I showed the twerp the door, he drivelled, "There's no money in poetry." I borrowed a line from Robert Graves. "There's no poetry in money either."

However, the twit's reaction rubbed home just how unready the show really was. Cameron and I kept delaying announcing the opening night, but come early February the theatre owners wouldn't wait any more. Then just two days before our press release was due to go out, Trevor dropped a bombshell which by any standards was a corker. He wrote me a four-page, closely typed letter (which was short for him), not even copied to Cameron. It ended up:

I think we are facing one inescapable reality. We have to give the writing task to somebody professional enough and free enough to come up with the goods. I have said several times that I feel like an imposter to be fiddling about with the writing responsibility and as time is flowing fast away, to quote Mr Eliot, it is staringly obvious that we need somebody who isn't me to get on with it . . . I think the time has come to take essential preservationary action.

I was aghast. Cameron and I had been agitating about the lack of a proper script weeks before Christmas and although we were uneasy we thought Trevor had been making some progress. I had just signed the £200,000 theatre guarantee. With rehearsals a mere few days away Trevor was proposing that we found a first-class writer "with the wit that I can't provide" to take on T.S. Eliot and pass the Valerie test at the very eleventh hour. Who on earth was available who could fit that bill at such short notice? Brian Brolly and I again seriously discussed aborting the show. I would have to shoulder a big cost but at least the theatre guarantee could be got rid of and my house would be safe.

STILL WE PRESSED AHEAD. Our publicist was the famously laconic Peter Thompson. If Peter didn't like a show he was puffing up he would stand in the foyer on its opening night and drawl to passing critics, "It's a stinker." He announced that previews would begin on Wednesday, April 23 (typically he got the date wrong, Wednesday fell on the 22nd) with opening night set for Thursday, April 30. Tickets went on sale from February 16, priced at £3.75, £5.50, £7.00 and £9.50. Our show was now simply called *Cats*.

The new title emerged out of meetings about the poster. Cameron had engaged the new theatre advertising agency Dewynters, owned by "mad major" Robert De Wynter, a tall, dapper cove who invariably sported a cigarette in a holder and spent every waking hour trying to live up to the character he had created for himself. His marketing ideas man was Anthony Pye-Jeary, my old friend from Stigwood days.

The creative designer was Russ Eglin who was to come up with the iconic logos still irrevocably associated with the big British musicals of the 1980s. Loads of ingenious graphic options were dangled in front of the creative team. However, we all had a different idea of what a cat on a poster should look like. After a month's indecision Anthony had had enough and asked for a week to come up with a completely new angle. We were then all summoned to mount the four sets of stairs to Cameron's office above the Fortune Theatre, where for the first time we saw the poster that revolutionized theatre advertising for all time.

Against a jet black background were two yellow cats' eyes with human dancers as their pupils. Underneath were simply the words "Practical Cats," no billing, nothing else but the theatre in small letters at the bottom. We were all blown away. If ever the eyes had it, it was now.

But something was wrong. The title screwed up the image. After we had all endlessly shunted it up and down the poster, Trevor took away the word "practical." Russ stared at the result for about thirty seconds. Then he moved "cats" to where a real cat's mouth would be in relation to those mesmeric eyes.

Game over. We had the title of our show and our theatre poster. In a few months that image adorned the world's number two best-selling teeshirt second only to the Hard Rock Cafe.

YOU WOULDN'T HAVE GUESSED this on March 9, day one of rehearsals. Everyone gathered in a bright modern church hall in Chiswick, West London, a suburb on the way to Heathrow Airport, an address that I was more than once tempted to grace over the coming weeks. The atmosphere reeked of the usual fake camaraderie that masks that unique combination of fear, nervous anticipation and "what the hell am I doing here?" feeling that thespians who mostly don't know each other experience on day one of rehearsals of a new musical.

They weren't about to be enlightened. After Trevor had got everybody to sit in a circle and introduce themselves, he then talked about T.S. Eliot for hours. Then the plan was for the musical director Chris Walker to play through the score – or more precisely what we had of it. My task was to help him out and meaningfully convey just how groundbreaking everything truly was going to be. Chris Walker was Cameron's choice. He had been Musical Director on several of his recent revivals such as *My Fair Lady*.

Things started out OK. We gave a reasonable account of the overture and I glossed over that we had no words for the opening number nor anything to set up "The Naming of Cats." The cast seemed to buy my trancelike setting of the poem – either that or their glazed-over expressions masked disbelief – so things seemed to be going OK. Then came "The Old Gumbie Cat." Chris's playing got slower and slower. We just about got through "The Rum Tum Tugger," Paul Nicholas knew it from Sydmonton anyway, but "Mungojerrie and Rumpelteazer" drew to a grinding halt. An ashen Chris slumped onto the piano keys and said he couldn't play any more. I took over and got through the score as best as I could. Before lunch Cameron told me that poor Chris felt he could not go on and had resigned. Now we had no musical director as well as no writer.

Luckily Gillie had planned enough choreography to keep the terpsichores off the streets for decades and most of the dance music was written. I reckoned I could fudge for a couple of days, but then it was imperative that we had a musical director if only to teach the cast the songs. That lunchtime I called Harry Rabinowitz for advice. Harry was not a musical theatre animal, his world was film where he was widely considered to be the go-to conductor in Britain, but his work on the *Tell Me* TV special had been outstanding and he had got on famously with my loyal key musicians, all of whom had agreed to open *Cats* for me. I told Harry everything, truthfully where we were, how we lacked a proper story, how we lacked a writer, how Valerie Eliot might object to one anyway but I also said that I had blind faith that *Cats* would turn out to be something thrilling. Could Harry suggest somebody to help us out whilst Cameron and I found a permanent MD replacement?

Staggeringly Harry said that *Cats* sounded so exciting he would extricate himself from a major film and take over as musical director himself. I gulped. I never dreamed it was even worth sounding out Harry about coming aboard a West End show. But by the end of day one we had the safest possible pair of musical hands at the helm of my score. Miraculously that evening we also acquired a writer.

Pre his bombshell Trevor and I had spent a lot of time during late January and early February on the structure and order of the poems and had agreed on the simple storyline. Here in a nutshell is the plot as it stood on March 9, 1981 . . .

This is the night once a year when Old Deuteronomy, the Jellicle leader, chooses a cat who will be reborn to a new Jellicle life. Unfortunately Macavity, the evil mystery cat known as the Hidden Paw is out to hijack the proceedings, presumably to become the chosen cat himself. In the end all is well and Grizabella, the rejected outsider, redeems herself thanks to her rendition of a big lyricless tune and ascends to the Heaviside Layer, leaving Old Deuteronomy to sum up with Eliot's poem about learning to understand a cat well enough to "address" it. To be fair Trevor had also proposed a paraphrase of Eliot's poem "Rhapsody on a Windy Night" for Grizabella's cri de coeur.

Every street lamp that I pass
Beats like a fatalistic drum,

And through the spaces of the dark
Midnight shakes the memory
As a madman shakes a dead geranium.

Half past one,
The street lamp sputtered,
The street lamp muttered,
The street lamp said "Regard that woman
Who hesitates towards you in the light of the door
Which opens on her like a grin.
You see the border of her dress
Is torn and stained with sand,
And you see the corner of her eye
Twists like a crooked pin."

Then later:

The street lamp said,
"Remark the cat which flattens itself in the gutter . . .

This poem would provide not just the core of the lyric that be-came "Memory" but the backbone of our Grizabella story and the heart of the show itself. By simply changing "woman" to "cat" we had Grizabella the fallen Glamour Cat's opening lines. The last verse of the poem is not used in the show but it encapsulates *Cats'* central message:

The lamp said,
"Four o'clock,
Here is the number on the door.
Memory!
You have the key,

> *The little lamp spreads a ring on the stair,*
> *Mount.*
> *The bed is open; the tooth-brush hangs on the wall,*
> *Put your shoes at the door, sleep, prepare for life."*
> *The last twist of the knife.*

Trevor also unearthed another Eliot verse which he strongly felt reinforced the show's heart. It comes from "The Dry Salvages" and is one of many messages in the main body of Eliot's work about memory and our need for the past. This is what Trevor edited and I set to music for Old Deuteronomy to sing at the start of Act 2:

> *The moments of happiness . . .*
> *We had the experience but missed the meaning*
> *And to approach the meaning restores the experience*
> *In a different form, beyond any meaning*
> *We can assign to happiness.*
> *The past experience revived in the meaning*
> *Is not the experience of one life only*
> *But of many generations*
> *Not forgetting something that is probably quite ineffable.*

It was not lost on Trevor that the word "ineffable" is played on by Eliot at the end of "The Naming of Cats":

> *When you notice a cat in profound meditation*
> *The reason, I tell you, is always the same;*
> *His mind is engaged in a rapt contemplation*
> *Of the thought, of the thought, of the thought of his name;*
> *His ineffable effable*
> *Effanineffable*
> *Deep and inscrutable singular Name.*

Imo and Nick in the world's number two bestselling T-shirt, second only to The Hard Rock Café.
Photo: personal collection

Trevor Nunn's vision of *Cats* was a far cry from maids and milk bottles.

On March 22, my thirty-sixth birthday, Sarah B and I quietly got married at the registry office in Kingsclere, the village next to Sydmonton. We'd hoped to keep it secret until after *Starlight's* first night. *Photo: personal collection*

BOTTOM RIGHT: Me plus the *Daisy* girls on school opening day. *Photo: PA Images*

The well known Cotswold-set composer Beryl Waddle-Browne with two of her charges. Daisy (left, Hannah Yelland) and Trixie (right, Katherine Heath).
Photo: John Swannell

Outside the Paris Opera House – appropriately for *Phantom* – with Michael Crawford, Sarah B, Cameron Mackintosh, Baz Bamigboye, Nick and Imo.
Photo: personal collection

BOTTOM RIGHT: Did he know that my parents were called "Billie Jean"? Michael Jackson backstage at *Starlight*.

With Sarah B on the opening night of *Starlight Express*. HM The Queen said she'd enjoyed the show, although when someone asked if she preferred horse racing to actors racing on roller skates, she didn't demur.

In Tokyo on a visit to see *Cats*.
Brian Brolly, Cameron Mackintosh and Michael Le Poer Trench. *Photo: personal collection*

With Sarah B in Tokyo. Guests were not supposed to acknowledge geishas so I put my foot in it when I asked one if they served at lots of bashes like this. "I'm your Gumbie cat," she replied. So the geishas were our female cast.
Photo: personal collection

In rehearsal for *Requiem* with Placido Domingo. It was his enthusiasm and belief that I could pull it off when I first told him about the project that encouraged me to have a go. *Photo: Clive Barda/ Arena Pal*

HMV was the recording label for *Requiem,* and "Pie Jesu" was the first and only pop single on the HMV Angel label so I particularly relished receiving my His Master's Voice award (pictured here with HMV boss Peter Andry). *Photo: personal collection*

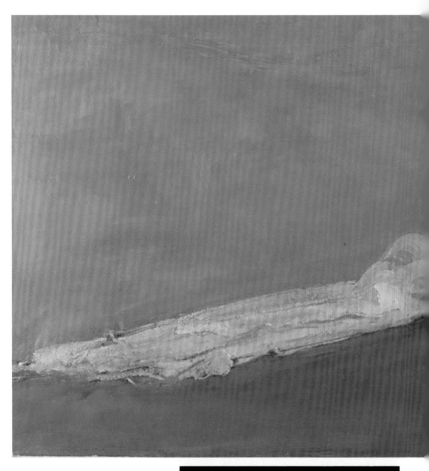

The End of Innocence by Robert Heindel who painted a series from the original London production of *Phantom*. *Photo: Robert Heindel*

Sarah Brightman and Michael Crawford on stage. When Michael sang "Sing once again with me our strange duet," the preview audience were witnessing one of the biggest changes of an actor's persona in theatre history. *Photo: Clive Barda/ Arena Pal*

In rehearsal for *Requiem* with Lorin Maazel, the only person who ever laughed at my joke in *Phantom* about 7/8 time. *Photo: Clive Barda/ Arena Pal*

Trevor talking T.S. Eliot, Gillie being feline.

David Land, my wonderful
warm-hearted manager in
Stigwood days. *Photo: courtesy
of the family of Mr. Land*

The New York premiere of *Requiem*, February 25, 1985. Placido Domingo, Sarah Brightman, Lorin Maazel and me, with Paul Miles-Kingston in front. *Photo: Clive Barda/Arena Pal*

BOTTOM RIGHT: *The Phantom of the Opera* is here. Taking bows at the premiere, with Hal Prince, Michael Crawford and Sarah Brightman.

The three principals of *Phantom*: Steve Barton, Michael Crawford and Sarah Brightman in London. I was as wiped out as the audience: never had I had more at stake. *Photo: Clive Barda/Arena Pal*

Prince Edward had pulled off a reunion that had defied top theatre producers for almost a decade: the Rice/Lloyd Webber musical *Cricket*. Left to right: Prince Edward, Ian Charleson, Tim Rice, HM The Queen, me, Trevor Nunn, HRH Prince Philip. *Photo: Clive Barda/ Arena Pal*

Margaret Thatcher at the *Requiem* premiere. At dinner in her Downing Street flat she joked that I should compose her some entrance music for the next Tory party conference like Eva's on the balcony of the Casa Rosada – well, I think she was joking. *Photo: Malcolm Crowthers*

The sad, sorry exterior of the Palace Theatre on the day that I bought it. Note the neon obscuring its gorgeous terracotta exterior. *Photo: PA Images*

And the exterior as I restored it. *Photo: courtesy of Really Useful Theatres Group*

However none of this had made it into the rehearsal script. On the first day of rehearsals we were still no closer to finding a writer than we were when Trevor lobbed his grenade in mid-February. We wouldn't have been on day two, had fate not intervened the previous weekend. On the Saturday night before we went into rehearsals I was scheduled to appear on the Michael Parkinson TV chat show. I badly wanted to postpone because I didn't feel I had anything definite enough to talk about. Thank goodness I went ahead.

The *Parkinson* show was a Saturday night British TV institution, pre-recorded in the afternoon of transmission day. Unusually this time two shows were recorded back to back and I was on the second. One of the guests on the first was Richard Stilgoe. Richard had become a local big name for his performances on the BBC TV's *That's Life*. He would sit at a piano (he is a first-rate musician too, damn him) and instantly write a lyric about any topic the studio audience threw at him. The result was invariably witty and extremely dextrously rhymed. He repeated this act on the *Parkinson* show before mine.

I don't think I've ever made a beeline to a green room faster. Could he be our *Cats* saviour? Richard was intrigued. He agreed to meet Trevor, Cameron and me in Chiswick on our first day of rehearsals. After a lengthy explanation of what we needed, Trevor handed Richard all his "doodling" – minus, Cameron and I noted, his thoughts on the big song. Next evening we had a fistful of lyrics from Richard for our opening number "Jellicle Songs for Jellicle Cats." Trevor ummed and ahhed and wanted several tweaks and the incorporation of a lot of his "doodles," but by the end of day three we had an opening number.

I thought this moment of minor celebration was the moment to tackle Trevor about Grizabella's song. Adapting a famous Eliot poem like "Rhapsody on a Windy Night" was going to be highly sensitive with Valerie. The work would have to be done by a name she respected. Trevor had said he could no longer "fiddle around with

Eliot." Cameron and I had talked upwards and sideways around the problem that afternoon and both concluded the same thing. It was worth asking Tim Rice if he would have a go. Trevor thought for an unusually long while, even by his standards. Eventually he said he wanted a chance to adapt the poem himself. We could go to Tim if we hated his efforts. This seemed reasonable enough. He had, after all, identified the poem in the first place. But looking back, I am pretty sure that Trevor had already decided no one would adapt the poem other than himself.

COME THE THIRD WEEK of rehearsals, Gillie began agitating that Cameron and I went to hear her husband Peter Land give an early evening recital of Kurt Weill songs at the Cottesloe Theatre on London's South Bank. Chiswick is a good few miles away, but if we hoofed it we could just about make the concert after rehearsals finished. Gillie had a small two-seater sports car. Cameron offered to make his own way so I wound up in the hot seat. Only once in a Ferrari driven by Rowan Atkinson with Kiri Te Kanawa as a fellow passenger have I been so terrified. Gillie drove like a fiend on a route that embraced parts of London few had seen so I wasn't the coolest cucumber when we screeched to a halt outside the Cottesloe stage door. Cameron was nowhere around so we went in without him.

It all started fine. Peter gave a good account of himself. The problem was that the audience contained a lot of schoolgirls. I can't say I go to a concert of Weill songs every night out of choice, but even his most stalwart supporters might agree that a whole programme of his stuff is a bit of an ask for restless adolescent females.

Peter began a song that took him into a register rather too high for him. The most benign word to describe the general tone in the theatre was tense. Just as Gillie turned to me saying how wonderful it was that Peter dared to extend himself like this, from high up at the back in the theatre I heard a high-pitched giggle. I knew that giggle. The sound was all too familiar. Unfortunately it fell on receptive ground. Waves of schoolgirl titters erupted all over the building. I, as is my way, got frightful hiccups. Naturally I led the standing ovation, vowing to throttle whoever initiated this disrespect for Weill music.

Standing in the corridor outside the exit was Cameron, beaming beatifically and radiating the innocence of a choirboy about to sing "Once in Royal David's City."

"It was lovely, Gillie dear, absolutely lovely, Peter was divine, now let's all go and have a drink."

"You bastard," I whispered to him as we headed backstage.

CLEARLY IT WOULD BE elasticating the truth to claim that re- hearsals were an unmitigated joy with everybody bonded, secure in the knowledge that they were changing the course of theatre history. But equally the residents of Chiswick weren't dodging flying fur, at least most of the time. There was, however, the continuing undercur- rent of a power struggle between Gillie, who was determined that *Cats* should be a dance musical like no other Britain had seen, and Trevor, who was equally determined that he was the director and the show had T.S. Eliot at its centre.

Relations were odd between Cameron and Trevor too. Trevor was used to being his own boss, having been at the helm of the RSC for over twelve years, and at times it was obvious he tolerated Cameron at best. Gillie was also used to ruling the roost, having directed *Tom- foolery* for Cameron. The power struggle meant that dance rehearsals frequently took place behind closed doors and in practice it meant that Trevor had nothing to do which Cameron took as an excuse for him being away a lot of the time.

In fairness to Gillie the rehearsal period was short for so much dance. But come the Friday before we moved into the New London, twelve days before our first preview, I wrote to Trevor and Gillie saying that I and "my hastily formed music team's opinion is that

much of the show can't be sung as choreographed" and that music
had been arbitrarily changed to fit the dance steps. I worried that
I had been deliberately excluded from run-throughs and that the
show would collapse in "a British musical sea of blame." I begged
that "the team will knit together . . . and the vital work on text, nu-
ance and music is done urgently which means that the staging must
be completed."

I typed the letter myself to keep it confidential. There was no reply, probably because a very serious crisis overtook everything. Judi
Dench was rushed to hospital, having taken a terrible fall rehearsing
"The Old Gumbie Cat." She was diagnosed with a snapped achilles
tendon. It was touch and go whether she could return; if she was allowed to it could only be as Grizabella, dance was out of the question.
Now we all pulled together. Trevor believed he could work round the
issue; Myra Sands was given the role of the Gumbie and, with that,
Trevor's plan that the cast played multiple roles ankled for good, the
only vestige being Brian Blessed doubling Bustopher Jones and Old
Deuteronomy and Stephen Tate doubling Gus and Growltiger.

Cameron had to take a horrendously difficult decision. If we postponed previews everyone would believe the show was in dire trouble.
The word around town already was that Judi's accident was an excuse
for her to jump a sinking ship. An uneasy compromise was cobbled
together. We would preview as planned but the opening night would
go back to May 11. That way Judi could be eased into the show as
previews progressed.

At the end of a week we all wanted to forget, Harry Rabinowitz
and I took the first band calls. I had shared the orchestration load
with David Cullen, thus beginning a working relationship that has
survived many a high and low over three decades. Harry was a true
rock. We got ahead with my trusted band far enough that we were
even able to make a start at the instrumental bits of the cast album

whilst technicals began in the New London. The spirit of the Blitz overtook us all.

I HAVE ALREADY OPINED that technical rehearsals are when writers should take a holiday out of reach of all known means of communication. Cameron and I were co-producers. No way could we escape together and lurk under a banyan tree. I can't speak for Cameron but the week beginning Wednesday, April 16, 1981 is a week I hope I dodge reliving if ever I am reborn to a new Jellicle life.

It began with me phoning Tim Rice. No complete Grizabella lyric had emerged from Trevor – the poor man was up to his eyes – so Cameron and I decided the clock was ticking too fast to wait for him any longer. Tim asked me if the missing song was "that pretty tune that was on the radio." My instrumental single had scored its first bullseye. I showed him Trevor's "doodlings" as I thought it might save time. By Friday Tim had completed a first draft. Cameron and I agreed that at least we had something to work with, but we held off putting the words into the score until Trevor passed the lyric.

Judi was at last out of hospital. That morning she had recorded an interview with Trevor and me for the BBC radio programme *The World at One* where she gamely said that although she was on crutches she would be back rehearsing at the New London that very night. In fact the plan was for her to walk around the stage and assess how much of the show she realistically could do. Tensions were obviously running high so Cameron and I thought it best to park the lyric issue until the next day.

Trevor and I were exchanging notes in the auditorium when Judi arrived. The new theatre manager Nick Allott (soon to be Cameron's right-hand man which he remains to this day) escorted Judi into the theatre. It was his first day in his new job and he still recounts why he thought it would be his last. He was helping Judi up the left ramp from the auditorium to the stage when she fell badly in full view of everyone. I have never seen Trevor act so decisively. Judi was shaken but she hadn't damaged herself further. However Trevor emphatically and publicly stated that she could no longer be a part of our show. The risks were unacceptably high. There was nothing for Cameron and me to do that night but sleep on it. We knew that the odds against us opening at all, let alone making the first preview, were shortening by the minute.

I remember driving ashen-faced with Cameron back to my flat. The reality was that half of our investment was still missing and now we had no leading lady. As we rounded Hyde Park Corner he touched my hand and said, "Andrew, you shouldn't have to shoulder all this." I was hugely affected by what he said. But it brought home to me the inescapable fact that if Cats went under then so would I and Cameron didn't have the wherewithal to do anything about it.

I don't remember if it was Cameron or I who thought of Elaine Paige first, I rather think we both did separately. But I knew I'd read somewhere that she was "resting" at the moment. So on Thursday morning we agreed that Cameron would phone her to ask if she could help us out, if only for a short while which was probably all the show would run for anyway. Elaine's version is that she had heard the Gary Moore "Memory" single on Radio 2 and thought the melody was somehow destined for her. As Cameron rang, a cat jumped on her window. Whatever, that evening found me at my most persuasive with Elaine in a Covent Garden wine bar, explaining the history of the tune, how Trevor had found an Eliot poem which he thought should be the basis of the lyric, that I'd shown his "doodles" to Tim, who'd had a crack at a lyric. I told her what we were attempting with the show, in short the whole story. Elaine said that if it was the tune she had heard on the radio she would do the show. That single had proved to be worth its weight in gold.

What I didn't know was that Elaine was once again having a raging affair with Tim.

GOOD FRIDAY DAWNED AND London was gloomy and empty. A dress rehearsal was slated for early evening. Gillie went into meltdown in the afternoon about the Jellicle Ball costumes. John Napier had designed some extraordinary creations that the cats were supposed to have made themselves to celebrate the occasion. The girls had elaborate costumes made out of three-times-human-scale discarded Christmas crackers. All manner of over-scaled detritus had become costumes for our exhausted cast to wear. All of them were truly breathtaking. They cost almost £45,000 or 10% of the budget and John regarded them as his finest hour. (Today £209,700.) Unfortunately they were completely impossible to dance in. Gillie said she would resign and take her dancers with her if they were made to wear them. Cameron had to say Gillie was right, the costumes would have to go, and John went berserk. He rounded up the whole lot and kicked them into the filthy gutter outside the theatre. Cameron retrieved some bits and used them as set decoration. The rest were never seen again.

The dress rehearsal progressed in stygian gloom. David Hersey had been given hardly any lighting time and was soon dubbed POD or Prince of Darkness by Cameron. Likewise Abe Jacob had zero time to work on the sound and you were lucky to hear one word in three. All the Grizabella moments were skipped, yet by 10 pm we were still only two-thirds of the way through Act 1. Then we hit "The Pekes and the Pollicles." That did it. The chaotic sight of our cats donning cardboard boxes as footwear to resemble dogs reminded Cameron and me of British amateur theatre at its worst. We were about to become the laughing stock of London. Cameron and I agreed that *Cats* could go no further.

We decided to tell Trevor at the end of the dress rehearsal that night and then tell the cast and crew at the start of rehearsals the following day. We hoovered him up and walked through a deserted Covent Garden. The only place open that Good Friday night was Joe Allen's and that too was almost empty. I can't say the usually upbeat waiters were overpleased to see us. Cameron spoke first. We had thought long and hard. But what we had seen was not fit for a stage. There was too much disunity in the team, too much unhappiness and with Judi's accident too much uncertainty. We were pulling the show. I nodded vociferously.

Trevor rolled his eyes, looked heavenwards then calmly outlined tomorrow's rehearsal schedule and a few things he needed Cameron to sort out by lunchtime. And that was the end of that.

Come Saturday evening I drove home to Sydmonton. Sarah didn't bother to ask me how things were. I took a sleeping pill and all I vaguely remember was her kissing me good night. I didn't wake till Sunday lunchtime. That afternoon I went for a walk and bumped into our next door neighbour Anthony Montague. Anthony ran Abingworth Securities, a highly successful investment company. The Judi Dench story had broken in the Sundays and he asked me how things were going. I told him the truth but added that Elaine Paige had taken Judi's place and that there was one song that I would stake my career on. He asked if he could come round after tea and hear it. Next Tuesday I banked a cheque for £50,000. (Today £233,000.)

By Wednesday we still hadn't seen a run of the show that hadn't broken down. On Monday night Elaine ran through "Memory" with Tim's lyric. Cameron, who had perked up a bit, whispered to me that it was the end of Trevor's royalty cheque. Trevor, however, had other ideas. In his opinion Tim's lyric ended not with an affirmation of life but in gloom bordering on suicide. It ended "As I leave you, a shadow of the light I once was, may my memory sleep at last." This was emphatically not the message Trevor wanted for our show. It was obvious Trevor wasn't going to discuss Tim's lyric or give him a chance to do a rewrite claiming his schedule made it impossible. Cameron and I had no alternative but to give way. It was still touch and go whether we would go up on Wednesday anyway.

Elaine tried "Memory" at the Tuesday dress rehearsal, clutching a piece of paper with a hybrid Rice/Eliot/Nunn lyric that Trevor had cobbled together. There wasn't time to rehearse her Act 1 entrance and she was understandably resistant to learning anything new. So it was agreed that "Memory" would stay as it was at the dress rehearsal. At that final Tuesday run, the less said about "Growltiger's Last Stand" the better.

Cameron and I began counting down the hours to the first preview as if they were our last before our execution. I went through a sound call as best I could. At least the orchestra, fired up by Harry Rabinowitz and buoyed by Jon Hiseman, Rod Argent et al. sounded great, although they were invisible. John Napier had calmed down and was delighting in how his set moved on the giant revolving turntable. Truly it was like nothing anyone had seen in a theatre before. The audience entered the auditorium to find the best seats faced the back of the scenery. They didn't know that during the overture, the set plus the stage and everyone sitting on it would revolve in the dark so when the lights came up the space resembled a classical Greek theatre. Not for nothing could we boast in our classified ads "Latecomers will not be admitted whilst the auditorium is in motion." But Cameron and I knew this moment would be over all too quickly. No one comes out whistling the sets, revolved or not.

30

Body Stockings, Leg Warmers and Meat Cleavers

Wednesday dawned. The first preview was at hand. I tried to think of Aunt Vi and happy days at La Mortola. As the day wore on Cameron and I met at the Zanzibar, a then hip bar round the corner from the New London, where we talked about the best bits of our careers and how on the whole we had enjoyed our time in a profession from which we would be barred for all time in a mere few hours. Sarah joined and gallantly said she would sit through the impending debacle or at least the first act. Cameron and I were in no mood for such punishment. We would stand by the sound desk which was nice and close to the door to the private room where Nick Allott had stiff drinks at the ready and which in turn connected to the fire escape for our antici- pated early exit. Being British and made of sterling stuff, I suggested to Cameron that we should go round to the New London before the show and wish the cast good luck. That way they'd know we'd been in the theatre and it wouldn't look so bad if we skipped the end due to being halfway down the M4 to Heathrow Airport.

When we got to the theatre the cast was already lined up back- stage. A peek into the auditorium revealed a packed house of vultures excitedly anticipating the rich pickings of theatrical catastrophe, even if they were somewhat wrong-footed by having the entire back of the set in their faces. I heard a queen shriek "Darling this is taking im- mersive theatre a bit too far!" before dissolving into hysterical giggles. I looked at our line of cats. How young they all seemed. Some were still in their teens and looked horrendously vulnerable in their skimpy body stockings. Somebody said, "What are we doing here?" Over the tannoy, the stage manager said, "Overture and beginners." In three minutes Sharon Lee Hill, the girl to whom I had promised a life-changing experience, would run on stage as a cat caught in a car headlight and instigate one of the greatest moments of bathos in theatre history. Instinct brought us all together in a huddle just as Harry started the overture. I thought, *Please God let the turntable work*, and then we all said "Good Luck" and I think Cameron added, "Do your best, dears," and then the pair of us were alone.

How long that overture seemed! Has there ever been such an agonizing wait for an executioner's blow? Cameron and I clutched each other as the final big "cat theme" thundered out and waited for the debacle. Instead there was a massive round of applause. Sharon Lee Hill ran out and there was silence. There were no hoots of helpless derision when the other cats joined her. "Jellicle Songs" built better than it ever had. It was as if our cast had switched a gear from self-preservation to exhilarated elation. At the moment when Jeff "Thunderthighs" Shankley as Munkustrap interrupts to introduce "The Naming of Cats" there was another huge round of applause where there wasn't meant to be one.

Furtively Cameron and I tiptoed round to the front of house. The audience was loving the show. Paul Nicholas's "Rum Tum Tugger" brought the house down. "Mungojerrie and Rumpleteazer" went down a storm too and the arrival of Old Deuteronomy seemed to touch the audience in the requisite spot. Now came "The Pekes and the Pollicles." Asking an audience to lap this one up was an ask too far. Cameron and I headed for the private room and waited for the heady balloon to be punctured. But over the speakers came gales of laughter and occasional bursts of applause. Were they laughing *at* or *with* us? They were with us.

Cameron and I embraced. To quote *The Producers*, "Where did we go right?"

We didn't go so right in the second half. The slow start surprised the punters and "Growltiger" was a mess. Things picked up with "Skimbleshanks," and just as at Sydmonton the sequence through "Macavity" and "Mr Mistoffelees" won the crowd back. Wayne wowed everyone as Mistoffelees, showing off all his crowd-pleasing dance tricks. I wrote all the dance music specifically for them. It makes me smile hearing that music and seeing someone aping his tricks nearly 40 years later as if they were holy writ. Both of them were cobbled together one afternoon in the big studio at Olympic Studios in Barnes.

"Memory" didn't hit the spot that night. Elaine was understandably tentative. So the second act didn't top the first. But no matter. We'd more than got through it and it was a very relieved Sarah who joined us at the Zanzibar later that night.

PREVIEW NUMBER TWO WAS the reverse. Act 1 was ho-hum. The performance lacked the adrenaline that swept through everyone the previous night. Elaine Stritch walked noisily out at the interval loudly shouting "Cat-astrophe!" Gillie gave the cast a team talk and Act 2 went far better. "Memory" took the roof off the building, even though Elaine was still singing the Rice/Nunn hybrid lyric. Cameron told Trevor this obviously could not go on much longer, but Trevor firmly countered that he had to prioritize rehearsing her into the rest of her role. He didn't want to give her lyric changes this side of the weekend but promised to have his new lyric by Monday.

There were no changes scheduled for Friday. So Sarah and I took a night off from the show and had our first à deux dinner for months at Boulestin in Covent Garden. Then we walked round to the theatre, only to find that the audience was going absolutely nuts.

Standing ovations weren't compulsory in London in those far away days except on first nights, but after that performance the audience must have stood for a good three minutes and we hadn't yet had time to stage a curtain call. After the show, Sarah and I went for a glass of bubbly at Annabel's. The old one, not the new effort. It wasn't the done thing to go to Annabel's on a Friday; Fridays are strictly for foreigners and out-of-towners. That is, unless you are being illicit. We sat in the little room at the back, next to a guy in his mid fifties and a very pretty girl of about eighteen. Opposite was a boy of around twenty-one and a girl of similar vintage. The boy kept eyeing up the older bloke, rather oddly I thought. The older bloke reciprocated with the occasional strange look but was far more occupied with the girl's thigh. Suddenly the boy erupted from his seat, threw his arms around the older bloke and cried "Pater!" A discussion ensued about the relative attributes of their youthful companions. Then the older bloke turned to me.

"I say, old boy, there's no chance of four tickets for that new show of yours is there?"

A few minutes later, whilst Sarah was collecting her coat, the legendary gatekeeper at the club asked me for a private hotline for seats. That night I realized we just might have something extraordinary on our hands.

TIM RICE WAS IN the audience that Friday night. Immediately after, a telex appeared saying that "he understood that he had failed the audition" for the "Memory" lyric and demanded the removal of his words from future performances. I was hugely embarrassed. I didn't intend Tim to "audition." I had approached him in the genuine hope that he would write the lyric for our new song. Now it looked as if I had used him as a stalking horse. It was impossible for Cameron and me to argue the point with Trevor. The past few days had seen his vision for *Cats* vindicated, even if it had been through a hairy rehearsal process way outside Cameron and my experience. Also Trevor vehemently insisted that Tim's take on Eliot's poem was at odds with his.

I replied saying that Elaine had a huge amount to learn very fast and it had been impossible to alter her song on top of everything else, something he surely must have known anyway through his relationship with her. But obviously we would remove the lyric as soon as possible. I didn't say it could only happen when Trevor completed his version. Come Monday he hadn't. To Cameron and my huge embarrassment, Elaine still sang the hybrid version that night.

David Land used to say, "Where there's a hit there's a writ." Now Tim was about to follow his mentor. He sent another telex. "Understand some of my lyrics still in show despite your assurances to the contrary. Demand removal by tonight or legal action follows." Trevor didn't seem or maybe didn't want to be bothered by the problem. There was a lot of bitchy muttering that maybe the money a lyricist might make out of "Memory" had a bearing on the situation. I had to bring everything to a head. So I told Trevor that Polydor urgently needed a single. Elaine and I were going into the studio immediately and would record the best lyric we could cobble together. Trevor and I met in the rehearsal room at the Theatre Royal Drury Lane and armed with Trevor's "doodles" and the Eliot poem two versions of a lyric were agreed, one for the recording and one for the theatre. The reason for the two versions is musical. The melody is written for a female "chest" singer. This means that a composer is limited to a range of about ten notes, even with a great performer like Elaine. A well-trained singer can "blend" a gear change into soprano which extends her range but "the money notes" which give an audience the hair-on-the-back-of-the-neck moments lurk in the upper end of the chest voice.

The construction of "Memory" is unusual. I deliberately change key three times to keep the song in a chest singer's best range and achieve the full emotional impact of Grizabella's passionate cry "Touch me, it's so easy to leave me." The single version has the soloist go very low with a lyric based directly on Eliot: "burnt out ends of smoky days, the stale cold smell of morning." This low register works fine if the singer is close-miked but in a live theatre without a hand mike its low pitch means that it would be lost. So in the theatre it's sung by a kitten an octave higher. This also gives us a great visual juxtaposition of the innocent and the fallen and provides the springboard for Grizabella's "money notes." However, female kittens aren't supposed to sing about burnt out ends of smoky days which explains why in the theatre we use the lyric "sunlight through the trees in summer" instead. The first person in the role of the innocent kitten was Sarah Brightman.

Writs and hostilities from a former collaborator having been averted, *Cats* settled into previews and was fast becoming not just the talk of London but Broadway. A week after the first preview the missing investment was oversubscribed. If I'd been smart I would have held on to the whole lot myself, but Sarah and I both worried that we were in some weird honeymoon period that couldn't last. I got an encouraging note from Hal Prince although he had a caveat which I knew was down to the sound rather than the performers. There was an ongoing problem with body mikes failing due to being covered in sweat.

> Saw Cats and the work is first rate. Permit one caveat. We did have difficulty in understanding the names of the cats in question. Being unfamiliar with the source poems it was occasionally frustrating. Otherwise – Bravo! Hal

May dawned and Cameron and I wished we hadn't pushed the opening night back so far. Whenever something gets the kind of buzz *Cats* got there's a backlash. I first felt it on BBC Radio's *Start the Week* on the Monday morning of our opening. The acerbic Kenneth Robinson had a go at me and the show saying, among many other things, that he had never seen such unattractive girls on a West End stage. I replied almost tearfully that everyone involved had put their careers on the line for *Cats* and that we thought we were doing something original and brave. Although it earned me a tidal wave of press support later in the week and Robinson apologized to me after the programme, it heightened my nagging fear that the *Cats* bubble had burst. Sarah and I had thought we would spend that Monday anticipating a triumph. Here's to you, Mr Robinson. You put paid to that.

CATS' LONDON OPENING IS still legendary and not all for the right reasons. In Britain at that time the critics invariably reviewed on the first night, unlike on Broadway where press night is usually two days earlier. It was therefore extremely unhelpful when a loud cry of "rubbish" emanated from the circle after "The Jellicle Ball." It transpired it was a drunk observing the set who had somehow bought a single ticket. But it did nothing for the nerves of all of us in the green room at half time.

During Act 2 Sarah and I were thinking more about the forced sale of our home than the forced first-night applause. It was during the OSO* that the big sledgehammer struck. Old Deuteronomy/Brian Blessed came on stage and raised his arms. The audience thought it was to egg the OSO on further when he bellowed, "Ladies and gentlemen, please leave the theatre at once! We have been informed there is a bomb in the building!" Everyone looked at each other in disbelief.

"I ask you to leave at once!" Old Deuteronomy had now removed his wig and all cat illusion was in the mortuary. "Please leave the theatre now."

Sarah and I headed for the stage door, where we beheld the bizarre sight of our dazed cast in their body stockings and full cat make-up rudely jolted out of the maximum adrenaline high of their first-night performance. It wasn't the location to say "you were wonderful, darling." Somewhere in the crowd an American voice said "It's like

---

* For the last time, obligatory standing ovation.

when *Genghis!* was playing the Alhambra [I've deliberately changed the name of the show and theatre]. Someone called saying 'there's a bomb in the house' and they cleared the theatre when the caller meant 'you're housing a turkey!'"

The bomb warning was a hoax and it wasn't long before the cast was allowed back inside. But a wet blanket had smothered our opening big time. I tried to cheer Sarah up by saying at least it didn't happen before "Memory." At the after-show party everyone did their best to be jolly. After all, it had been as good a performance as anyone could have hoped. But there was no euphoria. Tyler Gatchell had pitched up from New York and said he honestly couldn't see a life on Broadway. But that night, along with everyone else involved with the making of *Cats* and a good few others as well, my life changed for ever.

CATS WAS A VAST tinderbox waiting to explode and it only needed a tiny spark to ignite it. A couple of rave reviews did the trick. John Barber in the *Daily Telegraph* pronounced it "Purr-fect," Jack Tinker in the *Daily Mail* called it "A marvellous piece of rubbish" and the paper ran a big sympathy news story about our night of triumph being wrecked by the bomb scare. It didn't matter what the Sundays said. *Cats* was a smash. Within days ticket touts were brazenly taking newspaper ads for seats and a new phenomenon emerged that we'd only seen a glimmer of before. Merchandise. Merchandising had never played a big part in London musicals before, so only one person manned a small kiosk during previews. Before long there was as big a queue for *Cats* teeshirts as there was at the box office. Likewise for interval drinks.

None of this was lost on Cameron or De Wynter's chief, Anthony Pye-Jeary. A vast merchandising stand appeared manned by gorgeous "Dewynterettes" several of whom became intimate with the management and creative team in the post-show drinking sessions at the New London bar. The drinks drought was solved by "Catpacks" which contained a miniature gin and tonic or vodka and whatever plus a plastic glass. Soon invites to the post-show soirées in the New London bar were a tad hotter than tickets to the show itself.

Thank goodness this was the age before social media. Back at Sydmonton we had a huge jacuzzi that once held a record 30 people. The cast thought nothing about heading my way on high days and holidays and the Sydmonton jacuzzi parties became a minor legend. The jacuzzi was discreetly and thank goodness flatteringly lit and nobody batted an eyelid about stripping off. It was much more about fun and loud music than a bacchanalian orgy. But I ruefully think of *temps perdu* when I look at the brick edge that is all that remains today of my magnificent vast hot tub.

THE CELEB FEST THAT erupted that summer kindled enough stories for a mini-series. There was a serious diplomatic incident when the Tugger/Paul Nicholas ruffled an Arab prince's bald head. His bodyguards drew guns. The prince's sidekicks were held under arrest until their boss told the Home Secretary Britain might run short of oil for the next few years. One night we were joined by the Prince and Princess of Wales. When Prince Charles wondered how the dancers accomplished their feats, Diana, Princess of Wales, responded by demonstrating the splits. Unfortunately she had a wardrobe malfunction and displayed more intimate royal parts than is usual for members of the House of Windsor. That was the night Princess Diana developed her crush on Wayne Sleep. When he revived *Dash* she regularly watched him from the wings, doey eyes akimbo. Another night a rather overdressed woman brought the show to a standstill thanks to a pre-show curry at the Indian restaurant opposite in Drury Lane. Her messy exit via the walkway over the band caused our trumpet player to remark "I've been shat on by the management before but never by a member of the audience." There was the night a hideous bug swept our company. So many of our cast were sick it was touch and go whether we could do a show. As Cameron arrived to sort things out the "S" fell off the big *Cats* sign.

But nothing compared to the drama of Barbra Streisand's state visit. La Streisand had let it be known that she might possibly record "Memory." But before that she needed to see the show and she absolutely had to be incognito. Now it is difficult to sneak someone into a darkened theatre when its auditorium is in motion, especially when there are actors running around with flashing cats' eyes. It isn't helped if that person happens to be one of the most famous people on earth and is wearing an outfit that Sarah Bernhardt might have thought over the top.

Nick Allott somehow slunk her into the front row next to Sarah just out of the Tugger's grasp whilst I got things ready for interval drinks in the green room. As Act 1 ended I opened a bottle of champagne which exploded all over my hair, soaked my shirt and drenched the canapés that I had bought at Harrods. The nearest bathroom was miles away. Just as I was wiping my sopping sticky hands on the carpet Nick ushered in the World's Greatest Living Superstar. There was nothing for it. I explained what had happened.

"Would you like some . . . er . . . champagne?" I ventured, nervously eyeing up the less than half glass left in the bottle.

"Milk," she replied.

This wiped a burgeoning smirk off Nick Allott's face. Let's face it, where do you find a glass of milk in the average theatre bar?

Nick muttered, "It will be with you in a moment, Miss Streisand," leaving me to busk about how Tim and I saw the first night of *Funny Girl* and that I hoped she'd enjoy the big version of "Memory" in Act 2.

Moments before the Act 2 bell rang Nick returned triumphantly bearing a glass of milk at which point she announced she had claustrophobia in the theatre and needed to leave.

Once again Nick was on the spot. She had sent her car away. He hastily found a taxi driver in a nearby pub and that, I thought, was the end of Barbra Streisand and "Memory," although I attempted a rescue operation by sending her a letter apologizing for having an audience in the theatre that night. I asked Nick in the bar later where on earth he had found the milk. He said he'd got the Dewynterettes to help him open a stack of UHT milk capsules and empty them into a glass. Nick hasn't been Cameron's right-hand man for over 30 years for nothing.

Placido Domingo was one of the charming repeat visitors. We had several meetings in London and New York which ultimately led us to work together on *Requiem* three years later. Another visitor was Milos Forman, the Oscar winning Czech film director of *One Flew Over the Cuckoo's Nest*. He was making the movie of Peter Shaffer's *Amadeus* and was hugely keen we met about it. I thought this was curious. *Amadeus* is, of course, about Mozart. What sort of music could he possibly want from me? "Memory" is Pucciniesque. But surely he wasn't after a big hit song in the style of Mozart?

I went to our lunch meeting baffled. There was a bit of small talk, I said I'd seen his movie of *Hair* one afternoon in New York with Hal Prince and we both liked it. He said we were the only two people who did. Then he hit me with it. He wanted me to play Mozart in his movie.

Andrew Amadeus Webber? A prawn nearly went down the wrong way. I burped and said tremulously that I was a hopeless actor.

"Oh no," he said. "I hear you've got a foul temper. You've just burped brilliantly and you are a hot-headed perfectionist who can be extremely obnoxious. I want you to play yourself."

I muttered about being busy with worldwide *Cats* productions and a possible movie of *Tell Me on a Sunday* which I suggested he directed instead. But he replied that I would get a massive fee for my starring role and it would turn me into a global superstar. I left the restaurant quaking at the thought not just of being a burping global superstar but the grimmer prospect of Cameron plus assorted well-wishers wafting into *Amadeus*'s first screening gleefully anticipating my public humiliation.

This was one I hoped would go away. It didn't.

ALL THE WHILE THE *Evita* movie was festering. Robert Stigwood wanted the director to be Ken Russell, who had shocked and delighted with his movies about composers like Delius and Tchaikovsky and brought home The Who's *Tommy* for Robert. I got on very well with him, we had the Pre-Raphaelites in common and the long-forgotten composer Ketèlbey, so I thought things looked averagely promising. I also hoped my enthusiasm for an *Evita* movie might put my relationship with Tim back on track. *Cats* might be a hit but T.S. Eliot wasn't exactly around for a follow-up. I still clung on to the hope that Tim would remain my long-term writing partner.

But *Cats* was overtaking my life. By the end of May every major American theatre owner and producer wanted a piece. David Merrick offered to "move *42nd Street*" for it and the top Broadway theatre owners the Shuberts and the Nederlanders offered all manner of blandishments to lure us into one of their buildings. So Cameron and I thought we'd audition Broadway. Before we did I decided to do a Stigwood. On the "when you've got it flaunt it" principle, I arrogantly placed a *Cats* ad in the *New York Times* for the London show to run the weekend before we graced Manhattan.

An ocean liner seemed far more stylish for a grand arrival than Concorde, so we took the two top suites on the mid-June sailing of the *QE2*. Sarah and I wanted to bring four-year-old Imogen plus baby Nick, so we added another for the kids and their nanny. I got a nasty feeling that "style" was the wrong word for the Cunard Line's flagship as we sailed from Southampton to Cherbourg in France where the last passengers were picked up before the big Atlantic crossing.

Lunch in the exclusive Queens Grill was a lacklustre affair. The menu was a duplicated sheet. The food was 1960s posh British seaside hotel. We told each other that this was a reduced price preview of a meal; after Cherbourg the Queens Grill would acquire a glamour and opulence that would make *The Great Gatsby* look like an out-of-town touring show.

How wrong we were. That night the menu was the same duplicated sheet, the food the same duplicated shite. Cameron, a serious foodie, selflessly offered to man the kitchen himself but was repelled by a giant Scottish chef brandishing a meat cleaver. Fortunately the menu offered unlimited servings of anything we liked. For the rest of the crossing the three of us lived on caviar. Next the nanny ran off with the captain's mate and a purser had to prise the girl from the depths of the crew's quarters. Theatrical entertainment was no better. This was provided by the aptly named "Theatre at Sea" who impossibly rendered Neil Simon's comedy *Plaza Suite* without a single laugh from start to finish. Even the Statue of Liberty was shrouded in fog. Once decanted from Cunard's flagship, I whisked Cameron to Le Veau d'Or for a proper lunch. Rather as happens if you've been in hospital for a while we were in severe danger of forgetting what real food tasted like.

OUR AUDITIONS OF THE New York theatre luminaries were illuminating to say the least. The first time we met legendary theatre owner Jimmy Nederlander was a case in point. The must-see show in town was Lena Horne's one-woman bravura effort *The Lady and Her Music* which had triumphantly opened in his organization's recently acquired theatre on then desperately unfashionable 41st Street. Cameron and I asked him for house seats. He buzzed his PA. "The boys want tickets for Lena Horne. Do we own that theatre?" I will always have a soft spot for Jimmy. How can you not for the man who said "There is no limit to the number of tickets you can't sell to a show that no one wants to see"?*

Unlike the family owned Nederlander business, the Shubert Organization's theatres are vested in a charitable foundation. Their then operating officers Bernie Jacobs and Gerald Schoenfeld were true theatre greats. But, boy, did they operate their charity on commercial lines. They invited us to lunch at Sardi's. As we sat down, the legendary agent Manny Azenberg sauntered over, pointed at the bread basket and said, "See that brown roll, it was white before Bernie looked at it."

Cameron and I dutifully traipsed around theatre after theatre. It was a blazing hot 90°F and soon we yearned for home. Nonetheless it was a unique opportunity to size up Broadway's musical houses. Since we knew Trevor would reject most if not all of them we got the search broadened to a few long-lost sleeping beauties. We crawled around the New Amsterdam on pre-Disney cleaned up 42nd Street where we accidentally had a porn movie projected on ourselves, causing the few jaded audience members to remove their hands from their trousers in disgust. We dodged falling debris from the roof of the old Hammerstein Manhattan Opera House on 34th Street. Oscar Hammerstein I's ill-fated opera house was being used as a truck saleroom.

On the afternoon of our third heat stroke we wound up in a cafe on 51st Street next door to the Winter Garden Theatre. Both of us were tired, homesick and losing the will to live the New York life much longer. Cameron was the lowest I've ever seen him. He told me that he only wanted to produce in Britain. It was in that cafe that I rammed home to him what Robert was doing for *Evita* – thirteen productions now running globally within three years of the London opening plus

---

* Michael Riedel attributes this to former Shubert Organization boss the late Bernard Jacobs.

a US national tour. Even now Robert wanted me for a Washington opening later in the year. If Cameron yearned to be a global force he must take a leaf out of Robert's book right now. It wasn't a conversation that I needed to repeat. No one has embraced Robert's mantra more fervently than Cameron Mackintosh.

UNSURPRISINGLY I DIDN'T HAVE anything to offer at the Sydmonton Festival that year. The main new offering was *Masquerade*, a musical by Rod Argent but the guest list took on a decidedly American hue as the theatre owners continued their wooing. Cameron now firmly came down on the Shuberts' side, observing that at least their theatres had seen a lick of paint in the past few years. The rights deal was negotiated by the ever-vigilant Brian Brolly who had seen to it that every aspect of the copyright from T.S. Eliot to the cats' body stockings was buttoned up by Really Useful.

Brian was still only earning £20,000 a year from Really Useful and there was no prospect of the company being able to pay him more until *Cats* was way in profit. So I gave him a percentage of my composer's royalty from any production that began whilst he ran the company. He did extremely well out of this and he certainly did not repay me when he sold his interest in my company to, of all people, Robert Maxwell without any reference to me. But I reckon his tireless protection of not just *Cats*, but all my rights made the gesture worthwhile, at least at the start.

The Shuberts now laid off half the investment on David Geffen. Neither Cameron nor I had any "skin" in the show but we had a share of the profits as original producers. The pecking order in New York was clear. Although the Shuberts would listen to Cameron and me, they were the bosses. It was going to be their production in their theatre. The billing rammed this home. The Shubert Organization and David Geffen took poll position with Cameron and Really Useful firmly on the second line. There was one unheard of concession that

Cameron got: a percentage of the interest on the advance in the box office – something which meant a lot in the 1980s when interest rates were running sky high.

Once the Shuberts took the helm they started putting on the pressure about changing *Cats* for the USA. Typical was a letter to me from Bernie Jacobs in August.

> I hope that you will continue to exert pressure upon Trevor Nunn to see to it that the work that should be done to make Cats an historic musical is accomplished during the London run of the show. . . . I know that we (!) have an enormous hit but we must combine to see to it that the work is done.

It wasn't only me who Bernie nobbled. There were mumblings that Gillie's choreography was "too darn British" which led her to have a mega rethink of "The Old Gumbie Cat." Cameron had gone away leaving me at the helm. I had one change I wanted to try which was straightforward; moving "Grizabella the Glamour Cat" song's position to earlier in the show's running order. Originally it followed "The Jellicle Ball." I figured that both audience and actors wanted to get to the bar asap after this terpsichorean epic so I shifted it to after Grizabella's first entrance halfway through Act 1, where it lives to this day.

Less straightforward was Gillie's new Gumbie. Since some of the reviews said that its tap dance was amateurish, Gillie now conceived something she thought would make *42nd Street* look like clog dancing. She also devised a huge mouse ballet with our kittens donning icing piping cones on their heads to render them more rodentlike. It took days to rehearse and our dancers, exhausted by doing eight shows a week, were not gruntled by being put through the paces of something they thought was entirely pointless. Mutiny was in the air.

Things were not helped by the first performance. "The Old Gumbie" was received in almost total silence apart from a lone shoot of "Bravo Gillie" from her husband. The audience resembled the shot in *The Producers* after "Springtime for Hitler." With Trevor, Cameron and Brian on holiday, I had to take charge. Grizabella's move stayed, but "The Old Gumbie" went back to its original. Even that I cut down. I seized the chance to excise the mice. So the result was three minutes exited the show that night. An exhausted Myra Sands who played the Gumbie resigned but calmed down when I told her all mice references were henceforth banished. To this day Cameron blames me for cutting the new Gumbie before he had a chance to relish the new staging and cut it himself.

BERNIE AND GERRY'S PARANOIA about the choreography rumbled on to such an extent that at the end of August they dispatched Michael Bennett to meet Cameron and me and see the show, presumably in the hope that he'd take over the dance. As the director and choreographer of *A Chorus Line*, Michael was, of course, American musical theatre's new god and rightly so. As far as the Shuberts were concerned the Pope was considerably less infallible than Michael. Unfortunately his London trip didn't produce the result our American producers hoped for.

Michael adored Gillie's choreography. After the performance Cameron and I took him back to my flat where the giggly conversation turned to disaster musicals we had seen and loved. Cameron and I had developed a particular passion for Irving Berlin's last musical *Mr President*. This saga about an ordinary couple occupying the White House contained such gems as the President's lament "It Gets Lonely in the White House" and a sibilant song for his daughter "The Secret Service Makes Me Nervous" (second line "When we are dating they are waiting to observe us"). The show opened to the then biggest advance ever on Broadway and ran exactly its length. It transpired Michael had not only seen it but had total recall of every detail. Every stick of furniture in my main room was moved so that Michael could re-enact the entire show. I don't think I've ever laughed so much as when this Broadway legend performed "Doing the Washington Twist, this is a twist with a twist."

When he got home Michael wrote to Gillie (blind copied to me):

> While I was in London I saw Cats and wanted to tell you that I loved, loved your work. . . . I'm in rehearsals in New York on a new show (Dreamgirls) call me when you get to New York and we'll get together. In the meantime, congratulations on your enormous success.

"Sincerely" had been crossed out and replaced with "love Michael." The tailspin across the Atlantic was ginormous. The Shuberts refused to believe Michael was the missive's author. As late as October 27 Bernie wrote to me referring to "the unfortunate letter" and claiming "The letter was not drafted by Michael as he crossed off the 'sincerely' and wrote in his own hand 'love.'" It therefore was a fake!

Away win to Gillie.

31

Song and Dance, and Sleep

Early summer 1981. This is how things stood. I was 33. Sarah and I had been married almost exactly ten years. We had two kids, Imogen four and Nick, two. We half-owned Sydmonton Court, the rest was borrowed money, but the horrendous second mortgage to cover *Cats* closing early had sailed out of the window. We owned our London flat and thanks to the top tax rate being reduced by the Thatcher government I could keep something meaningful out of my earnings, the bulk of which still came from *Evita*. I had a big local UK hit album with *Variations* notched on my belt and had followed it with *Tell Me on a Sunday*. Now I had an even bigger hit in London than *Evita* with every major global theatre producer wanting it. The lyrics were mostly by T.S. Eliot so I'd done it without Tim Rice. I was still as shy as hell, but Eliot was dead so whether I liked it or not I was the centre of attention. The truth is I liked it.

Sarah had made a real home of Sydmonton which since the Festival had taken on a new dimension. The Church of England decided the box office was not great at the church on our lawn. So they sold it to me for £1 which both parties thought was a good deal. It became my little working theatre.

Sarah's supermum role with the kids left me free to grasp every career opportunity thrown my way. Unfortunately it wasn't the only opportunity I grasped. Whatever else money can't buy, it can buy you freedom and with freedom comes the chance to play. I was now the feted centre of a smash hit that happened to feature some of the most attractive girls in London, something not lost on my RSC collaborators. Trevor, who was married to the actress Janet Suzman, started secretly dating our Demeter Sharon Lee Hill, whose life I'd vowed would change. John Napier redefined the cat who got the cream. His twinkly-eyed dishevelled artist's charm had our female cats' chorus purring big time. Despite the "Memory" debacle, even Tim Rice was once discovered by Nick Allott in Elaine Paige's dressing room. I loved having fun with our gorgeous-looking kittens but it wasn't with them that I strayed.

During the summer I began an affair with a girl who was teaching at, of all places, Westminster School. She was a distinct improvement on the master who had taken a shine to me years ago. I wasn't in love and I truly hope she wasn't with me. It never crossed my mind that I would leave Sarah. She found out about it, of course, and I was devastated not so much for myself as about what I had done.

Cameron at last had a hit with a new musical. He was about to have another one, albeit not quite a musical. Its birth showed Cameron at the top of his producer's game. One late summer morning he kicked off our usual breakfast phone call in an unusually excited way even by his standards.

"Morning dear, I've got a brilliant wheeze, let's package up *Tell Me on a Sunday* and *Variations* and call it *Song and Dance*."

Song and Dance. It seemed so blindingly obvious. I said let's do it. When *Cats'* future was still uncertain I had mooted *Variations* being the second half of Wayne Sleep's dance show *Dash*. Wayne and I had talked about resurrecting the idea when he left *Cats*. Why not involve Wayne in Cameron's scheme? The joy of Cameron's "wheeze" was that both pieces kept their identity. *Variations* would be music and dance. *Tell Me* would remain a one-act-one-woman show and not stretched into something that it was never meant to be.

Marti Webb was quickly on board. Wayne, Cameron and I were highly impressed with Kate Bush's choreographer Anthony Van

Laast. Wayne agreed to co-headline if Anthony was hired so Cameron and I met him, liked him and another piece of the jigsaw fell in place. Trevor's RSC's nine-hour marathon *Nicholas Nickleby* was co-directed by John Caird. Cameron was curious to find out more about John and what precisely he had contributed to the partnership. So he proposed John as overall director. I had no objection, John was delightful and he grasped what we were up to. I was particularly intrigued that his father was a theologian and the principal of Mansfield College, Oxford. A few years later, after John strayed from subsidized theatre and become yet another commercial theatre scalp, he married the roller-skating dining-car Frances Ruffelle from my *Starlight Express*. I wonder what his dad made of it.

Now Cameron and I needed a theatre. His revival of *Oklahoma!* was inexorably a-clipping and a-clopping to its exit from the Palace Theatre so we went to see its owner, Emile Littler, in his apartment above the theatre. Here 78-year-old Emile lived surrounded by serious Impressionist paintings in particularly cosy circumstances. He charged the producers who hired his theatre a weekly fee for him living there saying that he was the nightwatchman and fireman. We explained that we proposed to announce *Song and Dance* as "a concert for the theatre" and not claim it was a fully fledged musical. Cameron added that although we had high hopes for a run of maybe a year, initially we wanted to announce it as a twelve-week season. Emile's first question was how many girls there were in the show. We assured him that there would be lots and when we told him that our white cat Finola Hughes had agreed to join the cast the deal was done. *Song and Dance* would move into the Palace in March 1982. Incredibly, for a short time at least, I was going to have three shows in London.

IN LATE AUGUST BARBRA Streisand must have got over her claustrophobia because her people called my people saying she wanted to record "Memory" in London with me producing. We settled on a mid-September date with Harry Rabinowitz conducting an orchestra of London's top symphonic players: it seemed everyone wanted to play for La Streisand. I chose Studio 1 at Olympic for the big day, not just because it had been so lucky for me but I figured that the leafy informal Barnes atmosphere might just loosen things up a bit. Barnes would feel like a village miles from London if it wasn't for the Heathrow-bound aircraft passing overhead.

I had been told that Barbra had to be completely isolated from the orchestra during recording and that the most I could expect was a "guide" vocal. Then she would revoice the song, taking as much time as she needed to achieve a perfect performance, line by line or even word by word if necessary. I had my doubts. "Memory," of all my songs, requires real emotion for a great performance rather than technical perfection. It's not locked into a fixed tempo; a definitive version could only happen if the conductor, orchestra and singer were as one, something Harry Rabinowitz knew better than anyone. The session was booked for the afternoon of Tuesday, September 15. It was cool and sunny. After Barbra had listened to the orchestra in the control room a couple of times I suggested she came into the studio and stood beside Harry so that he could gauge the ebb and flow of her performance. I gambled that if Barbra heard 80 of London's finest orchestral players live in the room it might just inspire her to agree to give us one sensational take.

As she walked to the podium these hardened musicians gave her a round of applause. Harry raised his baton and electrifyingly, if a bit tentatively, Barbra began to sing. By verse two she was no longer tentative: one of the great voices of our time was clicking into gear. Come the big key change into "Touch me," Barbra was singing her heart out. There can't have been anyone in the room with sedentary hair on the back of their neck. Now the applause was astonishing. Barbra Streisand had performed live for the first time in years and earned the approbation of Britain's top classical musicians. I was told later that this moment was a big factor in her decision to give live concerts again.

Of course we spent the next day revoicing with her constantly finding some tiny fault or other. I wondered whether I dared say that what made Maria Callas great was her passion which overrode any technical vocal imperfections. There was one moment where a stupid joke bonded us. Barbra was sitting on a stool in the vocal booth. Just before she had yet another go at the big "Touch me" verse Barbra asked if she should stand for the big key change.

"Barbra," I flashed back, "most artists kneel when they record my songs."

We got the best version that take. I left Olympic ecstatic that she had given me the finest recorded performance of any of my songs in my career so far. Two weeks later CBS sent me the final version that she'd approved. All the tiny vocal imperfections had been smoothed out. Technically it was a flawless. I figured Barbra knew her audience and I am sure her vocal sounded better on radio stations than the one I produced. Unfortunately I don't have it any more. I would love to compare it with the astonishing version Nicole Scherzinger recorded after she appeared in *Cats* in London in 2015. This, as of writing, is ridiculously unreleased.* The only time it was played on British radio it literally stopped the traffic.

ALL THE WHILE *CATS* was emerging, Stigwood was egging along the *Evita* movie with Ken Russell still at the helm. Come October, Ken organized screen tests at Elstree not just to find Eva but for the other key roles as well. Intriguingly my files show that Sarah Brightman tested for the mistress and I wrote "no" by her name. David Essex and Paul Nicholas also entered the fray but the fireworks erupted about who played Eva. Several actresses were tested, including the

* Happily it was released in 2018 on my 70th birthday album.

wonderfully exotically named lead from the Spanish *Evita*, Paloma San Basilio, the slightly less exotically named Elaine Paige and a new face to me, Karla DeVito, a fiery singer/actress who went on to play a big part in Meatloaf's stage act. I was closeted in *Cats*, recasting, when I was handed the following memo, dated October 13, from Ken Russell.

> Good afternoon, gentlemen. Now that the team have seen the tests I would like to announce my verdict, with which I hope you will concur. For me there is no contest. Whatever merits the other contestants may claim as stage personalities only Miss DeVito means anything on the screen. The camera loves her and I am sure audiences will love her too. So far as I am concerned, the search is over.
>
> This girl has screen magic. Further tests are simply a waste of time and money. . . . she is dynamite. Gentlemen, we have discovered a star.

On October 15 Tim Rice replied as follows:

> In response to Ken's memo my comments are

1. I would have appreciated some sort of discussion before such a violently positive commitment on paper from one of our number. I could have made equally positive comments about Miss Paige but refrained from doing so in the belief that there would be a chance for unemotional discussion.
2. It was agreed that Elaine would be able to have a second test with some of the advantages that Karla had on her second test and it is a pity that this now seems to have been forgotten about.
3. I think it is disgraceful that the only successful writers of British musicals are considering an unknown American for such an important role.

4. I think Karla DeVito is an extremely talented singer and actress, who is good enough to achieve stardom through Evita. However, I was not particularly moved by her screen test. I am not sure she would be the Evita I had in mind when I wrote the part.

No way was I gracing this hornet's nest. I was due back in New York on October 20, so I dictated a rather feeble memo to the team in which I said "Based on the tests I have seen, I have to agree with Ken, but I do feel Elaine should be given a chance to prove herself musically again." I made the point, "We have taken a great deal more money out of America for Evita than we have from Britain . . . I think it is an extremely unconstructive approach to think of casting along purely British lines." My Vicar of Bray mode continued: "I do not have any particular favourites and I am not wholly convinced we have found our ideal Evita." Robert must have calmed everything down as Ken still seemed to be on the project when I got home.

THAT FALL TREVOR NUNN, John Napier, Cameron and I scoured New York for a *Cats* home. The venue we wanted was the old Rose-land Ballroom on West 52nd Street. Although the Shuberts paid lip service to Trevor, who was passionate about the building, they didn't own it and it was blindingly obvious that we would be manoeu-vred into one of their theatres. The Shuberts argued Roseland was doomed to be imminently demolished. The issue soon came down to which Shubert house was the least inappropriate.

The standout by far was the Winter Garden. This curiously shaped auditorium is not every producer's favourite. It owes its amphitheatre shape to its original incarnation as the American Horse Exchange. It was remodelled as a theatre in 1911 when the Shuberts leased it for a Jerome Kern musical *La Belle Paree* which kicked off Al Jolson's career. Subsequent revamps have not totally disguised its origin. The proscenium is abnormally wide and low which is not ideal for many shows. But the semi-circular shape of the auditorium makes it possible to bring the stage forward in full sight of the whole house which Trevor insisted on as a condition of it being our cats' home. He also demanded that the auditorium was painted black which caused the occasional gnashed tooth in the Shubert camp as it had just been sumptuously redecorated in its original pink and gold colour scheme. Although *Cats* in the Winter Garden would never be as intimate as it was in the New London, at least there would be some semblance of our semi "in the round" staging. I had a side bet with Gerry Schoenfeld when the deal was signed that the Roseland Ballroom would still be going strong when *Cats* closed. Eighteen years later I won my bet: Roseland didn't close until April 2014. The last artist to perform there was Lady Gaga.

With the deal now done, there was huge pressure from Bernie and Gerry to adapt our show for, as they put it, a Broadway audience. Frankly they wanted *Cats* to become a spectacle. They also wanted rewrites and cuts and they still muttered about the choreography, despite their god Michael Bennett's high opinion of Gillie's work. I could live with the cuts but not all the rewrites. Trevor batted away discussions with a vague promise that we would try out some changes in London. An opening date was heavy pencilled for October 1982. Final auditions were scheduled for February 1982 to allow Trevor the spring and summer of '82 at the RSC.

Cats wasn't my only show bubbling in New York that autumn. Two young producers, Gail Berman and Susan Rose, were in the throes of a new version of *Joseph* for a Christmas season at the Entermedia Theater off Broadway. Other than to give my blessing to the delightful British director/choreographer Tony Tanner, I had precisely zilch to do with it. This probably explains why it was so successful that it transferred to Broadway's Royale Theatre come the New Year. Tony's production featured a departure for *Joseph* that stuck: a girl as narrator. This inspired contrast to the all-male world of Joseph and his brothers was hugely cemented by Laurie Beechman, a diminutive powerhouse who was to play a major part in my professional life until her tragic premature death from ovarian cancer in 1998.

Laurie invariably brought the house down at the top of the second act with "Pharaoh Story," a new song which Tim and I added for the run. Part of the melody emanated from the doomed *Come Back Richard Your Country Needs You*. I didn't catch the production until after its transfer, but it garnered seven Tony Nominations including Best Musical and Best Featured Actress in a Musical for Laurie in the infamous 1982 Awards where *Nine* (the Nederlanders' baby) and *Dreamgirls* (the Shuberts) slugged it out for Best Musical in a most unluvvielike fashion. The Shuberts lost which made Bernie and Gerry even more mental to make *Cats* a Broadway phenomenon.

COME THE YEAR END loads of things were happening at once back home. The BBC offered me my own one-hour TV special. *Song and Dance*'s director John Caird wanted a song after the *Variations/Dance* second half to reintroduce Marti Webb in a final curtain call singing with the dancers. I suggested a melody from *Variations* would tie the two sections together and Variation 5 became "Unexpected Song." It turned out to be a great finale and one day a showcase for Sarah Brightman's phenomenal range. Don Black wrote the lyric. We also added a completely new song to *Tell Me on a Sunday*. It struck us that there was no moment where our girl sang about being head over heels in love. The result was "The Last Man in My Life" which Gerry Schoenfeld told me was his favourite of all my songs.

I had several meetings with Placido Domingo who wanted me to write something for him. I was immensely flattered but it wasn't for eighteen months that I had anything substantial to offer. He did, however, agree to appear on my BBC TV show. More serious was the dreaded issue of my movie-star career. Phone calls hotted up from the *Amadeus* producers. Brian Brolly fielded them but it was dawning on me that Milos Forman was deadly serious about me playing the title role.

In December I was slated to be a judge on the BBC's annual Nationwide Christmas Carol Competition, which was to be held in Wells Cathedral in Somerset. Since Wells and its cathedral are among my favourite places in the entire world, I was looking forward to an architectural awayday. Equally enticing was that somehow the BBC had cajoled the world's original rock chick Suzi Quatro onto the panel. I met the leather-bedecked poppet rocket for the first time in the cathedral. We clicked immediately so I thought it might be an idea to show the bass-toting purveyor of "Devil Gate Drive" the religious architectural gems at hand. A visit to the unique thirteenth-century Chapter House via its sensational staircase went fine. So did a visit to Vicars' Close right next door to the cathedral. Chicago girl Suzi seemed impressed by the oldest medieval street in the world.

What went wrong was that we were also impressed by the pub opposite the cathedral's front door, where we hooked up with her husband guitarist Len. Soon we were swapping stories about Gary Moore and serious motorbike songs. We didn't drink that much but enough to put pint-sized Suzi in a pretty good mood. The cathedral was rammed with schoolgirls keen to enter the Christmas spirit and arguably a tad unenthusiastic about the rather staid carols. Halfway through the judging Suzi cut to the chase, pronounced the carols boring and said what we wanted was some real rock'n'roll. Next she dumped me in it by announcing to huge schoolgirl cheers that I was a rocker underneath my posh trimmings and I should "tell it like it is." Neither of us was invited back next year. I repaid Suzi by suggesting she starred as Annie Oakley in the 1986 West End revival of *Annie Get Your Gun* in which she was mega.

MEANWHILE I HAD NOT forgotten my animated railway trains. Hal once told me that the legendary Broadway producer George Abbott invariably held a meeting about his next show the morning after his latest opened. I can't claim to strictly follow his advice but in the early 1980s I had a go. I ushered in the New Year by announcing that the 1982 Sydmonton Festival would feature the premiere in concert of *Starlight Express*, a Cinderella story about an American steam engine called Rusty. I had railroaded Richard Stilgoe into writing the lyrics and soon July 10 was etched for the first performance of an epic that Richard Stilgoe wanted to call "The Magic Toot."

Just as *Starlight* hit the tracks, Robert Stigwood was all over me again about the *Evita* movie. It dawned on him that with *Cats* scheduled for Broadway he could no longer count on me to drop everything if Paramount green lit the picture. After the shenanigans of last October it seemed sensible to test the temperature of the water with Tim and David Land. So in mid-January a lunch was scheduled at Harry's Bar. I added Brian Brolly to the guest list as thermometer. Maybe the movie was discussed at lunch, but I remember it for an entirely different reason. For the first time I saw the flip side of Cameron.

Anyone who knows Cameron, particularly the Cameron of those days, knows what a ball of bouncy infectious fun he can be, albeit often at someone else's expense. Michael White had announced that he was bringing Joe Papp's hugely successful Broadway production of Gilbert and Sullivan's *The Pirates of Penzance* to London, opening at the Theatre Royal Drury Lane the coming May. It was a big deal. Linda Ronstadt had starred on Broadway with Rex Smith and Kevin Kline. "Chalky" had put his head on the block to get the UK rights and it was the talk of the 1982 season.

In December 1981 Irish producer Noel Pearson opened his own version of *Pirates* in Dublin to rave reviews. Cameron thought that he'd have some fun and bring Pearson's version to London to rival Michael's. He proposed we produced it together. Egged on by Cameron's bumptious enthusiasm and a feeling we could do no wrong,

I went along with the scheme like a naughty schoolboy. Cut to the lunch at Harry's Bar with Tim, David and Brian about the ongoing *Evita* movie saga. Afterwards Cameron and I were booked to fly to Dublin, see *Pirates* and then do a deal with Noel Pearson. Thanks to a particularly giggly phone call with Cameron I was late. I said I was sorry in a starry cocky way, blaming everything on our cast-iron wheeze to "get one over Chalky" as if what we were doing was totally innocent sport.

When I'd finished, David Land looked at me sadly. "This isn't you, Andrew. Why would you do this to Michael? This isn't the Andrew Lloyd Webber I love."

I wanted to dig a hole and crawl in. I was silent in the car en route to the airport, I simply did not begin to know what to say to Cameron. When we got on the motorway we came to a standstill. There had been a massive pile-up ahead of us. We were stuck in the jam for hours and missed our flight. I have never been so grateful for a traffic jam in my life.

ENVIRONMENTALISTS MAY DEMUR, BUT all I can say as far as my 1982 was concerned is thank God for Concorde. It made travel between NY and London as easy as hopping on a train for a short commute. My diary couldn't have happened without the supersonic bird. Nor could it without my PA, Biddy Hayward, who not only had to juggle my manic diary but Brian Brolly's as well.

Final Broadway *Cats* auditions were scheduled for the end of February whilst *Song and Dance* went into rehearsal in London with opening night March 26. Finally I squeezed in my BBC TV special. My Wells Cathedral new best friend Suzi Quatro joined Placido Domingo on the show which famously featured Suzi and me on claves accompanying Placido singing Elvis's "It's Now or Never." Suzi and I also sang "Hey Paula" to each other which inexplicably the BBC cut.

Back in New York Tyler Gatchell had agreed to be *Cats'* General

Manager despite his London first night misgivings which was a vast help. Initially everyone thought that Broadway would offer a huge pool of actor/dancer/singers compared to the tiny field back home. Instead *Cats* proved just as hard to cast for entirely the opposite reason. The performers were too professional. Andy Blankenbuehler, *Hamilton*'s choreographer who re-staged the 2016 Broadway *Cats* revival, makes a big point that today's American dancers have far more individuality and character than they did back in those *A Chorus Line* days. Back then you could not fault the performers who auditioned for us in their training and professionalism. They could sing and dance up an absolute storm. Gillie was demented with excitement. But we all agreed with Trevor that too often their sheer professionalism meant they had acquired a veneer that masked anything individual or quirky. It was as though they were performing behind clingfilm. Trevor kept reminding us that all-round skills weren't enough: all our cats had to have real personalities. So the auditions were marathons and there was a lot of head shaking when Trevor let some brilliant people go.

SONG AND DANCE OPENED in London on April 7 and both the reviews and audience reaction soon saw the twelve-week season transform into an indefinite run. Anthony Van Laast's choreography proved a big crowd-pleaser and a live double album cast recording cemented the success. Cameron had been right about the pairing of *Tell Me* and *Variations* but what surprised even him was the immediate interest worldwide. Neither piece had been a hit outside Britain and historically double bills are not mega box office.

I was happy to leave all this to Cameron and Brian. I was enjoying myself. My name was splashed above the *Song and Dance* titles across the West End's biggest advertising hoarding. So I did something unusual. I spent April at Sydmonton with the children whilst I worked on and off on *Starlight Express* with Richard Stilgoe. It was huge fun writing off-duty songs with lyrics that came fast and furious. They were invariably funny and Imo and Nick were great guinea pigs.

We had a simple silly Cinderella plot. A famous prince wants to show his beautiful bride America. He decides to cross from East to West Coast on the railroad. Which engine will pull the Royal Train? There is a big engine contest. Rusty the clapped out steam engine is barred from entering by the ugly modern diesel and electric engines Greaseball and Electra. Poor Rusty is left alone in his yard sadly contemplating his fate when he is visited by the Starlight Express who transforms him into a gleaming new powerhouse of an engine. The deal is he must be back in the yard to pull the morning milk train. Rusty enters the competition and of course wins it. As he races home to his dairy duties he drops a piston . . . you can guess the rest. With people in America taking notice of *Cats* and the Royal Wedding of Charles and Diana a worldwide TV smash, I hoped a Sydmonton Festival debut would lead to my animated train movie finally chugging out of the marshalling yard.

AROUND MIDSUMMER NIGHT THE *Evita* movie erupted once again. My life had moved on. If I hadn't got on so well with Ken Russell, I would have parked it completely. Robert's recent movie track record had been catastrophic. *Sgt. Pepper* had been followed by *Times Square* and John Travolta's *Moment by Moment* in the golden gallery of epic flops. I doubted if any major studio would back Robert, particularly with the maverick Ken at the helm.

Come June the two contenders for Eva were once again Karla DeVito and Elaine Paige. My office, i.e. Biddy Hayward, was dragooned into finding some ace musicians for a new round of screen tests. Enter Liza Minnelli. Liza was a good friend of mine. We had a few mates in common like Leslie Bricusse and she and her then husband Mark invited Sarah and me to dinner during the Cannes Film Festival. It transpired she desperately wanted to test for *Evita*. Next Ken called me and said that Robert had given instructions to block Liza testing, it was either Elaine Paige or no movie and he was thinking of resigning. I immediately contacted Robert who grudgingly allowed Liza to test which she did in a blonde wig that my notes refer to as "remarkable." I was *Evita*'d out. I did a Trevor Nunn and told Biddy to say I wasn't around. Biddy's office diary has an entry for the following week: "Don't take any movie calls, Andrew rehearsing his railway trains."

32

"The Most Obnoxious Form of 'Music' Ever Invented"

On July 10, 1982 the Sydmonton Festival audience was hit with these opening lines from Smuts and three railway wagons called the Hip Hoppers:

> *I'm willing to bet that you take for granted*
> *That the engine's in the front and the cars get planted*
> *In the middle while the brake van's at the back*
> *And the whole thing faces down the track*
> *You don't see trains with the engine in the middle*
> *The diner at one end and the brake at the front*
> *Going in the wrong direction.*
> *Okay you do see trains like that*
> *Nobody achieves perfection.*

OK, this lyric didn't make it into the final *Starlight Express*, but it begs the question: was rap first introduced to musical theatre by Richard Stilgoe?

Charles Spencer, the feared critic of the *Daily Telegraph*, blamed me. When the show was rebooted in November 1992 he opined that I had "added insult to injury with a rap number, the most obnoxious form of 'music' ever invented." Whatever, *Starlight Express* at Sydmonton was a small, warm-hearted entertainment, peppered

with trademark Stilgoisms. Three engines in a train wreck had a song
about three heads being better than one.

> *Three heads gave the Andrews Sisters*
> *Three harmonies ethereal*
> *Three heads meant three bears so*
> *Goldilocks could have a choice of cereal*

There were questionable jokes purveyed by our cast of *Cats* stal-
warts Elaine Paige, Paul Nicholas and Bonnie Langford, and a country and western spoof "Stand by Your Engine" sung by Bonnie:

> *Though his breath smells like old stogeys*
> *And he has disgusting bogeys*

It was not a song for 1982, let alone for today's politically correct
times. But everyone thought *Starlight Express* was well meaning, if
schoolboy fun. Two songs stood out, the title song and "Only He
Has the Power to Move Me" and the omens for a cartoon film looked
promising. I miscalculated. The Festival guest list was becoming a
theatre industry shindig, so there was lots of chatter about *Starlight*'s
fate. I guess it was inevitable that after the success of *Cats* people
would see in *Starlight* something different and rather bigger than
I did.

BERNIE JACOBS WAS AGITATING about "making *Cats* work for
Broadway." The music changes boiled down to a new version of
"Mungojerrie and Rumpleteazer," on balance a plus, and a coarse cod
Italian aria replacing "The Ballad of Billy McCaw" as Growltiger's
wooing song for the Lady Griddlebone. This definite minus was written to the Italian translation of a chunk of "Growltiger's Last Stand"
and was deemed essential to give Broadway audiences a moment of

slapstick fun. I resisted it in vain. My fear that the Shuberts didn't completely understand *Cats* was hardly calmed when the first use of the artwork featured the dancers in the cats' eyes upside down.

Rehearsals dawned. Cameron and I decided that a vast run-down duplex atop the now torn-down Mayflower Hotel on Central Park West would make an ideal base for our New York sojourn. The apartment needed serious kitting out and the Mayflower was pretty much in its death throes. But the sight of Cameron buying kitchen aprons was alone worth the price of admission. There was a giant terrace which we eyed up for a massive Brits-only party the night before we opened.

Sarah decided to bring the children over to New York so after rehearsals began we could slope off and explore New England. A highlight of our trip was the Valley Railroad, not far from the Goodspeed Opera House in Connecticut. *Starlight Express* was all over the kids' minds and the joy in their faces when they saw a real working steam engine made me even more convinced a cartoon of *Starlight* would be a perennial winner.

Rehearsals began on August 9. It was a bemused cast who listened obediently to Trevor's marathon opening day address about T.S. Eliot, *The Waste Land* and new lives, topics not normally discussed by Broadway hoofers. Trevor had succeeded in casting a spectacular diverse group. Nobody could have been more opposite than tiny Cynthia Onrubia as Victoria the white cat and six foot muscle powerhouse African American Kenneth Ard as Macavity. There was lanky, sexy Donna King as Bombalurina, destined shortly to be Mrs John Napier, cheeky rocker Terrence V. Mann as the Tugger, and a definitive frail Gus the Theatre Cat in Stephen Hanan who morphed into a fearsome Growltiger and won a Tony Nomination in the process plus of course Betty Buckley with her Tony-winning performance as Grizabella. No cast could have been more varied.

Cameron and I had been a bit dazed by Trevor's opening epic, but not half as dazed as we were when we tiptoed late into Gillie's session after lunch. Gillie had got all the cats writhing in sensual positions on the floor when she suddenly addressed our hunk of masculine virility Kenneth Ard as "my little chocolate box" whilst telling the girls to thrust out their . . . actually I'm not going to go there. We slunk out sideways.

After a couple of days Betty was singing "Memory" magnificently, in fact there was little more that I could ask for and that was the beginning of Betty's problem. Betty is one of those actresses who agonizes about everything. She seriously got it into her head that Trevor and the rest of the company were ostracizing her. This she concluded was Trevor's brilliant method acting way of emphasizing that Grizabella is an outsider. The reason for Betty's isolation was rather more mundane. Grizabella doesn't have much to do apart from deliver her big song. Not so the rest of the cast. Trevor and Gillie were preoccupied with the colossal task of rehearsing the massive amount for everyone else.

Sheer time pressure meant it was hard to find the right moment to argue my corner about the new cod pastiche Italian aria. Unfortunately everyone seemed to find it wildly funny. More worryingly "Growltiger" was becoming a spectacle in a way the London production wasn't. Because the sequence is in Gus the Theatre Cat's imagination, John Napier had been encouraged to step outside the rubbish wasteland and create a colossal pirate ship. The costumes took the show nearer Vegas than Kensington Gardens and more than made up for those original Jellicle Ball outfits he kicked down the New London stairs.

Just as the set design was scaled up for Broadway so was the orchestra. This was due to the "house minimum," i.e. the number of musicians that the New York musicians' union insists are hired based on the size of the theatre, 23 musicians in the Winter Garden's case. The union is more flexible now but in those days there were ludicrous consequences. Producers of plays had to pay musicians to do nothing. David Merrick once famously insisted that the musicians he was forced to hire performed in the bar during intermission. The point is *Cats* wasn't orchestrated for 23 musicians. David Cullen did a fine job in rescoring the show. But inevitably real instruments replaced many of my keyboard electronic sounds which anchored the score in the real world. Normally I hate it when economics dictate keyboard samples replace real instruments. But not so with *Cats*. *Cats* gains when the sounds are not quite real.

Orchestral rehearsals went well until we got into the theatre, where memories of the cottonwool-clad *Jesus Christ Superstar* orchestra surged back. Abe Jacob had installed the orchestra in a purpose-built padded room. The sound was so dead there was no way the musicians could interact. Abe argued that he could create all the presence we needed by adding echo on the sound desk. He seemed to miss the point that musicians need air to perform properly.

The padded cell was one straw too many. There had been sound issues with *Cats* in London – reviews had commented that the voices too often came from speakers high above the stage. I told Cameron that I needed help from Martin Levan, my recording engineer on *Variations* and *Tell Me*. Cameron agreed. Martin flew to New York and immediately clocked the problem. He tactfully suggested removing the sound absorbent cladding cocooning the orchestra, whereupon Abe rose theatrically to his inconsiderable height, pronounced dramatically "gentlemen you no longer have need of my services," and exited stage left or right, I forget which, perhaps because it was neither.

By the end of the day the padded cell was in a skip. Martin took over the sound in New York and subsequently redesigned the *Cats* sound in London. I had him listen to *Evita* in New York. The Shuberts were worried about the sound as the *New York Times* critic Frank Rich had recently written it was terrible. What Martin found was astonishing. The main speakers had been wired the wrong way round and were "out of phase." One of the bass speakers was completely disconnected.

THE *CATS* HYPE WAS now huge and the flames were brilliantly fanned by our publicist Fred Nathan who managed to get more cover stories than I had fingers. During dress rehearsals I got some seriously bad news. Milos Forman discovered I was in New York and wanted me to meet the *Amadeus* film honchos to clinch my starring role as Mozart. I put the problem to Trevor who stroked his beard, sighed and admitted the problem was indeed knotty. I said surely as director of the Royal Shakespeare Company he could find a cast-iron reason why I was not cut out for screen glory. He promised to try.

Previews went well. The new Mungojerrie setting definitely worked. The spectacular "Growltiger" looked to me like spectacle trying to buy us out of trouble but there was no doubt the new Italian aria was a crowd-pleaser. The Shuberts loved it. I was snookered. One night Cameron and I thought we had seen "The Jellicle Ball" a few too many times so we sneaked around the corner to Mövenpick, a perfect hideaway as it was extremely dimly lit. We were muttering about the bar looking like David Hersey's lighting in technical rehearsals when gingerly the object of our smirks tiptoed in, furtively looking left and right to check he was alone. Once reassured, he ordered a drink and settled in a particularly stygian booth.

We were about to say gotcha! when John Napier slithered in ever so tentatively, performed an identical routine and ensconced himself behind a column. Next up was Trevor. He had his coat collar so high that he might just have got away with it if his trademark ancient gym shoes and faded denim jeans weren't protruding from the coat's lower end. He'd just about stage-whispered his bar order when Cameron erupted with "Hello dears!"

One serious problem appeared to be becoming intractable. The "alienated" Betty Buckley for some reason continued to sing "Memory" in every way conceivable other than give the audience the big notes. Placido Domingo saw the show one night and was incredulous in his low-key charming way. For the second time I lost it. Trevor was huddled with Betty in one of what were now becoming endless sessions about outcasts and past and future lives. I communicated Placido's honeyed advice in my own way. "Just sing the fucking song!" That night she did and the roof of the Winter Garden was raised at least two inches.

FIRST NIGHT DAWNED AND Cameron and I fussed about our Brits-only party. We plumped for pre-opening night. Now to get rid of *Amadeus*. I agreed to meet Milos and the film studio mob at 6 pm at the Essex House just before our party started. Finally this hydra would be knocked on its various heads. Come our final afternoon rehearsal Trevor had still not come up with an exit strategy and I was panicking. I paced the theatre contemplating Cameron's shrieking mirth at *Amadeus*'s first screening. How could Britain's top Shakespearean director let a colleague down like this in his hour of need?

Four o'clock clicked by; any minute I had to leave to change for our Brit party then it was across the park to the slaughterhouse. At 4:18 Trevor tapped me on the shoulder. He coughed in pre-momentous utterance fashion.

"Ahem, Andrew, here's what you do. You say you are honoured to accept the role."

I looked at him as if he'd lost his marbles.

"However . . ." Trevor always says "however" just before he demolishes an argument he has just put an unarguable case for. "However, you say that there is a problem: you can't live with the music being Mozart's – the music must be yours."

I gasped in admiration. This was laced with genius. Not even the crassest filmmaker would swallow this, let alone an Oscar-winning film director from Prague. I was walking on air when I entered the Essex House lobby. It was a five-minute walk from the Mayflower, my parents had just arrived from London and soon I would be at my party. I was mere minutes away from a joyous two hours on our terrace and a dinner with Sarah and the old folks round the corner at the Cafe Luxembourg.

Milos met me at the door and ushered me into a sunlit room with a big window looking onto the park. In the near distance I could make out the tables being set up for our bash and the occasional early guest clasping a glass. The room was packed with movie types, all of whom had bated their breath far too eagerly for my taste.

Milos was beaming. "Look at him, he's just as I told you, he's just right."

Someone suggested I should read a scene. It was time to play my ace. Smiling broadly I trotted out Trevor's coup de grâce.

There was silence. Then somewhere someone said, "I think we have a deal!"

I resembled the aftermath of a gorgon's stare. Through the window I could see the Mayflower terrace seriously filling up. I imagined Cameron gleefully shrieking, "Welcome dear. No Andrew's not here, he's auditioning for a movie . . ."

I imagined I saw Trevor. Just as I was about to curse him in a most foul Mozartian way which probably would have clinched the part, Milos came to the rescue.

"I think Andrew is saying he doesn't want to play the role."

I thanked God for Trevor, England, St George and anyone else who had a hand in my great escape.

IT WAS GREAT HAVING Mum and Dad in New York to keep my mind off the first night. I hate the day of opening nights almost as much as I hate openings. Sarah and I took Dad to Steinway's cathedral-like HQ where he toyed with a brand new brute of a full sized concert grand piano whose tone combined steel and cream in equal measures. Then Dad played the great Rachmaninov D flat

Paganini variation. It was an extraordinary moment. Here was this most reserved of men playing with a passion I'd never heard before and in a New York public showroom. I didn't know it at the time but I would never hear Dad play again.

Lunchtime passed with him downing a couple of cocktails and burbling on about Rachmaninov being an exile in New York. There was zero point in showing Mum any normal shopping haunts like clothes shops. In any case she'd heard of a pet emporium on Third Avenue that had rare Abyssinian cats so that took up the early afternoon. Sarah, Dad, Mum and I went to the Winter Garden together. I sat behind Bernie and Betty Jacobs and Gerry and Pat Schoenfeld who already had a good idea of what the critics had in store. It's odd watching an audience raising the rafters, ignorant of reviews that are already out there if you know how to find them. Bernie told me that the all-powerful *New York Times* review was OK except for the choreography. I wondered when "The Jellicle Ball" quite rightly stopped the show whether it would get the same reaction tomorrow.

Once past "Growltiger" (the audience loved the pastiche ballad) the show was magic. I forgot time and place and wallowed as Skimbleshanks, a cat I always have a soft spot for, brought the house down. The Macavity girls Donna King and Wendy Edmead had every red-blooded male roaring, but it was Betty Buckley who was astonishing that night. When the song ended the audience rose as if welded together. My father clutched me and said, "I told you, Andrew," and then a man ran down from behind and threw his arms around me.

"I love you Andrew, I'm so very proud of you."

I knew that voice. It was Robert Stigwood. Tears were rolling down his face. I am not sure if I replied. But I can say that this was one of the most precious moments of my career.

THE REVIEWS WEREN'T GREAT. In truth Frank Rich's review in the *New York Times* was one of the better ones. It was well considered and I was rather pleased he provocatively singled out "Gus the Theatre Cat" as "the show's best ballad," especially as Streisand's version of "Memory" was already a US chart hit and the song was driving me nuts at every bar with a piano.

I had a debrief with Dad before I left. He too thought the show had lost some of its charm during its Atlantic travels and thought the Italian aria was cheap. But he found the dancing a lot slicker. The Shuberts were probably right to add spectacle and I was probably wrong to worry about the changes, at least in commercial terms. Despite the mixed reviews, *Cats* turned inexorably into a phenomenon. The profit to the producers and investors (the Shubert Organization, David Geffen, ABC Entertainment and Metro Media Corporation) at *Cats'* height has rarely been equalled.

Nonetheless, despite the Shuberts taking theatre rental and investors' and producers' profits, the moment *Cats* showed any sign of the box office slightly weakening the authors and creative team were asked to take royalty cuts. It was with *Cats* that Cameron first went even further and created the "royalty pool" where creators give up their royalties for a share of the show's running profits, if any, plus a small weekly guarantee. This has now become the theatre norm. Wearing my producer's hat, running costs have risen so much that it is hard to see an alternative, particularly in the heavily unionized theatre of the USA. But the consequence is that today creators can only make real money out of a monster hit. This is making it more and more difficult for young creatives to make a proper living out of the theatre. Not every show is a *Hamilton* or *Dear Evan Hansen*. But *Cats* was a phenomenon and I cannot complain. Brian Brolly had kept all the underlying copyright for Really Useful despite much pressure from Cameron to participate in its ownership. *Cats* went on to play 7485 performances and became the longest-running Broadway musical in history until overtaken by *The Phantom of the Opera*. It is still the fourth-longest-running Broadway show. But despite the astonishing success, I never went to the Broadway production for the sheer joy of it like I did so many times in London.

During previews I produced the American cast album with Martin Levan as engineer. Our publicist Fred Nathan made a rather unusual request. Would I mind the *New York Times* critic Frank Rich bringing his son to one of the sessions? He would not disturb us. He arrived when I was urging Donna and Wendy to give a real Broadway burlesque version of "Macavity," something not far from their second nature. He sat at the back and after half an hour or so said thank you and left. Afterwards I wondered if I had been very rude in not introducing myself. It's not every day that the most powerful theatre critic in America asks to come to your recording session. Today I would have jumped up to say hello, but I honestly thought that I should keep my distance, that somehow it would be wrong to make personal contact. I was also very nervous – there was no Fred Nathan or Cameron to ease the way. Cameron took a very different view and it's an open Broadway secret that he has enjoyed a good relationship with Frank Rich over the years.

ONE FINAL WORD ON *Cats*. I am often asked how Judi Dench would have fared with "Memory." The answer is: I don't know. She had left the cast before I had a finished lyric. But I do know, based on a session with her round the piano, that it would have been a very moving performance and I would have orchestrated it far more in the style of Édith Piaf than I did for Elaine. It's worth remembering that Elaine went on to play Piaf on the stage herself.

SHORTLY AFTER SARAH AND I got home I received a handwritten letter from Ken Russell explaining that he was finally resigning from the *Evita* movie. He said there were several reasons – "first and foremost was the choice of the lady in question" (i.e. Elaine). He continued that "you always backed out when you saw the screen tests. I can't blame you – they were for the most part disappointing. It's unfortunate you were unable to see past them to the REAL THING [sic]."

I was baffled by this; with *Cats* on the go I had been practically out of the loop. But I wonder if this was the real reason.

Stigwood double crossed me as he has done before – but will never get the chance again . . . it's silly trying to make friends with a rattlesnake. Apart from not paying me the $50,000 he owes me for work on the project – a year of it, he led me into believing that he detested Paige and was just going along with it for Tim Rice's sake. When the truth finally dawned it was too late. What really gripes me is the fact that he told Fox that he had taken the project away from Paramount because I insisted on Elaine Paige and that they wanted no part of her and that he, Stigwood, was right behind me. . . . what hypocrisy! I heard all this from Sherry Lansing's "own lips."* She was appalled at Stigwood's duplicity. It was nice knowing you. Ken.

Immediately Biddy was fielding urgent phone calls about new *Evita* film deals and lawyers were running up huge bills picking over the contracts of a movie that evidently was a corpse. More importantly it was around this time that I got a call from Mum saying that Dad was going into the King Edward VII hospital for an operation, but there was nothing to worry about. To this day I am unclear what it was for. Julian thinks it may have been for a prostatectomy which I thought was the name of a Pre-Raphaelite girl stunner until I had one myself.

The day after Dad was hospitalized I lunched with Tim at the Neal Street restaurant. We discussed the movie situation but Tim wasn't very illuminating. In fact he was pretty schtum about every-

---

* Sherry Lansing was CEO of Paramount and went on to become the first woman studio head at Fox.

thing, particularly when I asked him if he had any ideas we could do together.

Back home Mum rang to say Dad's operation had gone well. I went to the HMV store in Oxford Street and bought Dad a Walkman plus a few cassettes including Rachmaninov's first piano concerto. He was sitting up perkily and genuinely seemed excited by the Walkman, particularly when he eyed the Rachmaninov cassette.

Dad donned the headphones and was thoroughly enjoying the first movement when he suddenly said, "Andrew what key is this in?"

I said G flat minor.

Dad shook his head. "Have you still not learned the difference between G flat and F sharp?"

These were the last words I remember him saying to me.

Next morning Mum rang in tears saying he had died from a blood clot. He was only 67. All the Harrington Court clan went to the funeral, John Lill, Julian, Tim and Mum of course. Mum cried out "No" as Dad's coffin descended towards the crematorium fire. Afterwards she was incredible. She proclaimed she would be making psychic contact with Bill any time soon. But that cry said it all.

She may have had her crush on a Gilbraltan tenor. She may have let her obsession with John Lill get out of hand. She may have found Billy's lack of ambition infuriating. But she truly loved him.

In November, I learned that Tim had taken his chess musical to Björn Ulvaeus and Benny Andersson, the brilliant force behind the phenomenal ABBA. I was on the way to the opera with the writer and broadcaster Paul Gambaccini who had teamed up with Tim on *The Guinness Book of British Hit Singles*. Paul innocently asked what I thought of the *Chess* collaboration. My body language must have said it all; I hadn't heard the news. Paul said that Tim, Björn and Benny had held a press conference that afternoon. He assumed I must have known. I was shaken. I always hoped that Tim and I would collaborate again when he was ready to work on a major project. Of course I was proud of the successes I had achieved without him, but all three had started out as left-field ideas to satisfy my workaholic desire to compose. It wasn't as if T.S. Eliot was a living lyricist. Now after Dad's death I was burning more than ever to work on a mainstream project. This news meant inevitably that if the right subject came up my collaborator wouldn't be Tim. I couldn't see him taking on two major projects at once. Dad's prophecy was coming true.

IN DECEMBER BIDDY HAYWARD resigned as my PA. She had become very close to both Sarah and me. I suspect she sensed that tectonic plates were shifting in my private life and it was a question of when something happened rather than if. It happened sooner than she thought. Just before Christmas a review appeared in the *Evening Standard* for Charlie (*Annie*) Strouse's children's opera *Nightingale* at the Lyric Theatre Hammersmith. What flabbergasted me was the headline, "What a marvellous singer!" because the singer was Sarah Brightman.

Sarah had been under my nose for over two years. I knew her not just from *Cats*, but also from Rod Argent's *Masquerade* when it moved from Sydmonton to the Young Vic. Yet for me she was just the "kitten" who began "Memory" and sang the set-up for my key change trick. This review was a eulogy to a new star and I sure as hell hadn't spotted her.

It was December 23. Hammersmith is on the way to Sydmonton. I thought I'd take in the show, probably just the first act, conclude the reviewer was one of Sarah's relatives and then head home for Christmas. I was ushered into a seat next to the then most powerful critic for musicals, the *Daily Mail*'s Jack Tinker. I was poleaxed, poleaxed not only because I kicked myself for never having clocked that Sarah Brightman had a captivating soprano voice, but also that she had magnetic stage presence. Jack hated the show but loved Sarah. I said to Jack, why not forget reviewing the show, it was Christmas and it was only doing a short run. Let's both go backstage and take Sarah out for a festive drink? He did the professional thing and demurred, but I aimed for her dressing room.

Sarah was sharing a room with a hamster she was looking after for some sibling or other. The other occupant was Mike Moran, a highly sought after keyboard player and producer/songwriter who had big hits in the 1970s–80s with songs like the unpromisingly titled "Rock Bottom" (a Eurovision Song Contest runner-up) and "Snot Rap" for Kenny Everett on whose TV show Sarah had appeared in Hot Gossip. They were clearly an item and were going back into town to the Zanzibar close to the New London Theatre. Sarah suggested I joined them. I really don't know why I didn't head home. Instead I followed them back into central London. It was a split-second decision that changed my life.

At the Zanzibar I discovered that Sarah's real ambition was not to dance but sing. She had been a boarder at Elmhurst Ballet School where she was a contemporary of performers like Maria Friedman. She was the eldest of six children and had been raised in Berkhamsted in Hertfordshire just north of London. Her father, Gren was a successful property developer and her mother, Paula had been a dancer. What she had kept under wraps was that she was married to the son of an eminent brain surgeon. Her father-in-law had taught her how to expertly fillet fish. However this bit I knew: her marriage hadn't stopped her having an affair with one of the *Cats* keyboard players. Sarah was fondling Mike's hand; clearly she liked keyboard players with flying digits. I asked what she was up to next. She was working through the Rachmaninov song cycle with her singing teacher Ian Adam. For the second time that night I was poleaxed, not by her studying with one of London's top vocal coaches although she'd kept that secret too. The Rachmaninov songs were Dad's greatest love. I once found him practising them with his muse Justine, the woman who auditioned for *Evita*. What on earth would Dad have made of Sarah? It was time to go.

33

Miss Sarah Brightman

1983 dawned. *Cats* was on its way to being the kind of global hit you only dream of. What happened next in my private life would lead to a musical that would eclipse *Cats* and change not just my fortune but the fortunes of the vast battalion of theatre creatives, theatre owners and producers, city financiers, shysters, lawyers and executives who have profited handsomely out of *The Phantom of the Opera*. Yet this is one of the parts of my life that I have been dreading writing about the most. What you are reading is the umpteenth rewrite. This is the best I can say.

If I hadn't gone back into London on the night of December 23, 1982 and driven home to Sydmonton, *The Phantom of the Opera* would never have existed and a lot of people, me included, would be a good deal poorer.

I suppose it was inevitable that I was going to have a serious affair at some point. Sarah and I were so young when we were married. With all that was happening it was as if I was going through my adolescence aged 33. But whatever the reason, come March 1983 I was in love with Sarah Brightman. Some friends counselled that I was an incurable romantic who poured affairs of the heart in double measures and that this was a passing blip. Almost everyone was appalled by what I did next. In mid-April I publicly confirmed that I was leaving my wife of nearly twelve years and my children for Sarah Brightman.

Looking back, I am amazed I had the time for all this. In January I saw a play called *Daisy Pulls It Off* at the Nuffield Theatre in Southampton, bought the production, revamped it and opened it with a big new set in the West End at the Globe, now Gielgud, Theatre that April. Arguably Sir John might not have appreciated a play whose almost entire cast were schoolgirls, but *Daisy* ran for 1180 performances, toured for two years and is still staged all over Britain. I've even seen a production in drag at Eton College which Sir John might have quite liked.

A particularly gloomy January was also brightened up by a right royal hissing match between Trevor and Cameron. Trevor started it by writing to Cameron, copied to the entire management and creative team, that the London show gave the impression of being "abandoned by the management . . . something needs to be done urgently or our show will go down and deserve to go down from neglect and criminal self-satisfaction." Cameron opened his reply "I'm glad to note that you have been making your regular quarterly visit to the theatre though I would have preferred it not just to have been on a Sunday when the theatre was shut." He continued, "Your report . . . is ill timed, ill informed and above all ill mannered." To Trevor's complaint that the front of house looked awful, Cameron replied, "The FOH is a constant problem for us . . . the building being of concrete and glass and very high, causes even more wind than some of your company addresses . . . your memo seems to totally disregard the amount of time we have all put in to the show while you have been involved with your other projects. Many of the cast think you are Macavity."

DESPITE *CATS* BEING THE smash of the Broadway season, Cameron vented his frustration with Trevor on the issue of the Gumbie Cat which still rumbled on,

> "As to problems 'like the Gumbie,' these are problems almost entirely of your own making. I would add to them your record with 'cuts.' As Director, only you can force them through.

Andrew, you and I and Gillie usually come to some agreement eventually, but then it is up to you to force them through. We can, and will, back you to the hilt but unless you stand over Gillie and force her or her assistant if necessary to do what WE want, we end up wasting time and getting nowhere, and causing unnecessary problems.

The Gumbie Cat should have been choreographed by a tap expert in America. You said so then chickened out on forcing a decision. And Kim should do it in London. You must make it happen.

I suggested to you a year ago that we needed a visible American choreographic presence on Broadway to satisfy the critics. I also told Gillie; if we had insisted we might not only have helped the show but also perhaps saved Gillie from having her career nearly destroyed in America."

Of course both Gillie and *Cats* survived this outpouring.

March was dominated by a workshop production of *Starlight Express*. It came about thus. Just after *Cats* had opened on Broadway, Trevor told me that John Napier had come up with a way of staging my singing railway trains. Zero was happening on the animation front so I listened. John had been walking in Central Park and had been nearly knocked over by roller-skaters. This gave him an idea. Trains have wheels. So do roller-skaters. QED its actors could be on roller skates. However, Trevor thought the Cinderella story made *Starlight* far too twee. So, with Richard Stilgoe, we hatched a slim plot about an engine race that was destined to be the basis of *Starlight Express* the musical.

We rehearsed and performed Act 1 of the now embryonic stage show at the Notre Dame Hall near Leicester Square. Tracey Ullman played Pearl and I finally got the chance to work with Arlene Phillips who was now our choreographer. It was Arlene who four years earlier prophesied that Sarah Brightman would change the course of my life. Not that she knew anything about our burgeoning affair. Arlene had been too busy finding a cast. If we thought it hard to find performers who could sing, dance and act for *Cats*, adding roller skates to the mix took casting to uncharted recesses. Consequently Arlene put together a group that would celebrate diversity today let alone in 1983.

On the first day of the workshop Trevor got our bemused cast to describe the first memory they had of a train journey. After two hours of cathartic revelations of close encounters with rolling stock, it was Tracey Ullman's turn. "My granny told me never to lean back on the headrest in a railway carriage as it could give me nits."

The *Starlight* workshop went so well that it sealed its fate was theatrical. Most of our cast wouldn't have known what the inside of a theatre looked like. This converted me to Trevor's vision. Our show could reach audiences for whom theatre was a no-go zone; not just the *Joseph* children's audience but street kids who might relate to *Starlight* and then graze on more grown-up fodder. I could have fun writing out and out pop for a show that would sit way outside the mainstream theatre box. It was later, when the suits shoehorned it into conventional theatres that *Starlight* spun off the rails, or at least some of the productions did.

Now the search began for an off-the-wall venue. Meanwhile Brian was on the sniff of another venue for a completely different reason. He wanted Really Useful to diversify into bricks and mortar, i.e. to buy a West End theatre, but as of that April he wasn't ready to tell me about it. He wanted to keep my decks clear to concentrate on creative work, thereby unintentionally freeing my time up for affairs of the heart.

MY RELATIONSHIP WITH SARAH was sealed on a brief trip together to northern Italy. After a couple of days in Milan we stayed at the empty Splendido Hotel in an equally empty Portofino. I love out-of-season tourist destinations. I could write chapters on deserted fairgrounds. Fairgrounds are at their best on damp dank November days. Portofino that March was like a gorgeous girl stretching and yawning after a deep slumber. Tables and chairs stumbled from bleary-eyed cafes. Fishing boats glinted like freshly scrubbed up sirens, poised barnacle-free to lure us to sea-locked San Fruttuoso. Sarah wore a white miniskirt that elicited whistles from windows of houses that I swore were uninhabited. I was somewhat embarrassed, even more so than I had been by the astonishing white fur coat that she had worn on the outbound plane which *La Bohème* aficionados might conclude was more Musetta than Mimì. But I loved talking music with Sarah and yes of course I loved the vicarious looks I got from the waiters in our deserted hotel and of course I loved the sex.

Cupid beckoned on an autostrada in the pissing rain. We were driving from Milan to the coast and I planned to stop off for a decent lunch in Pavia. But the rain was so gruesome that the autostrada was virtually closed and there was nothing for it but to hoof it to a motorway cafe where the congealed chicken cacciatore was Italy's answer to a highway greasy spoon.

The rain dictated an extremely long lunch. It had to be 4 pm before we left but neither of us noticed time pass. We talked and talked about music. I told Sarah about Auntie Vi and the oddball set-up at Harrington Court. She told me about her husband. It seemed to me her marriage must have been over pretty much as it began. Her father Gren was a property developer. Her family was not rich but well off enough that she and her two younger brothers and three sisters were educated privately. Her main home had been leafy Berkhamsted, a semi-suburb 25 miles north of London, but the Brightmans had clearly changed houses a bit, presumably following Gren's fortunes. Now her parents had a big flat in Bournemouth, the seaside resort crammed with Victorian goodies on the Dorset south coast.

Sarah's mum Paula had been a dancer. She once graced the stage (properly clothed I stress) of Murray's Club, today remembered as the Soho haunt where Stephen Ward of "The Profumo Affair" fame met Christine Keeler. Apparently she kept baby Sarah in a carry-cot backstage. Sarah had been through theatre and dance school and recorded her first hit single aged eighteen masterminded by Jeff Calvert, a songwriter who steered her early recording career. His other claim to fame, according to Sarah, was flying a light aircraft down Regent Street. Hot Gossip were involved because Sarah had joined the dance troupe and chucking their name on the record label guaranteed the single promotion on *The Kenny Everett Video Show*.

By the time we got to the Splendido I knew there was no alternative. I was in love and I proposed to Sarah – well, in truth it wasn't so much a proposal as a "we're in love, we're both married, what the fuck do we do about it?" We decided that Sarah would meet my mother, I would meet her parents and if we survived that test I would break the news to my first Sarah. I don't think my mother was surprised. Ever the bohemian, I suspect she thought homespun family life had overtaken me too young and that a bit of turmoil would keep my creative juices pumping. Most importantly Sarah liked cats which meant she had to be all right. Sarah Brightman's parents were a bit nonplussed but I guess resigned to the fact that their eldest daughter might get up to anything. I liked her parents immensely. Her mother Paula made a big impression. Small and petite with black hair and flashing gypsy eyes, it was hard to believe she had borne six children. There was Nicki, whom I met a while later, Claudia, a spitting image of her mother, Jay and Joey and, a lot younger than the others, Amelia, on whom Sarah doted like she was her own kid. I soon learned that Sarah was terrific with children; she'd have made a great Maria or Mary Poppins.

1984 SAW BRIAN BROLLY take the reins of my business life completely away from me. He wanted to build the Really Useful Company into a serious rights-owning entity. Although Cameron was the producer of *Cats* in London, Brian was adamant that Really Useful owned every aspect of the original production. So although Cameron had a profit interest, it was Brian and Really Useful who licensed the show around the world. From get go Brian was hugely protective of *Starlight Express*. Understandably Cameron had been curious about *Starlight* and wanted to establish a position were he to be involved. Brian was at pains to point out that a railway train project had been noodling around my skull for over a decade; that's how my company got its name. Who knew if the workshop would produce a theatre show and no way would he allow Cameron aboard automatically. Anyway *Starlight* was fast accelerating into rock and pop territory, far from Cameron's natural habitat. Also he was already busy planning a London production of *Little Shop of Horrors*, the off-Broadway show about a luxuriant plant whose pituitary gland had packed up. This was the musical he had discussed cultivating with me as co-producer and then grown me out of, possibly because Brian was so zealously guarding the *Cats* rights. Whatever, Cameron was becoming so possessive about *Little Shop* that Bernie Jacobs had to reassure me that if Cameron tried to move it onto Broadway "for the hell of it" in the same Tony Award season as *Cats*, he would scupper it.

AFTER TWO FALSE STARTS I told Sarah I was leaving her. If someone can be both devastated yet resigned at the same time, that's what Sarah was. There were moments when I wavered. Sarah even suggested that she turned a blind eye and let me lead a double life to keep the marriage intact. But I couldn't lead my life like that. I'm not the sort of person who can duck and dive. Besides I was head over heels in love with Sarah B, as my friends now called her. I decided against everyone's advice to come clean publicly. I decided to openly take Sarah B to the post-opening party of *Daisy* and let a press statement hit the fan.

The *Daisy* party was what I hoped Robert Stigwood would have done if his proclivities had embraced young actresses playing school-girls. In the 1980s the big block of serviced apartments known as Dolphin Square housed a destination restaurant. It lurks on the River Thames near the Houses of Parliament and therefore has long been a haven for the trysts of Britain's elected and unelected polit-ical elite. It also boasts a vast swimming pool. I thought this was a God-given venue for the *Daisy* party. Chuck a few 1920s swimming costumes in the girls' direction and we could be away to racy shots big time. My wheeze worked. Never had so many nubile West End actresses become so amphibious. The PR was massive and I had a big hit on my hands.

There was another bonus. I had managed to persuade the dis-tinguished composer Beryl Waddle-Browne to write *Daisy*'s school song. Older residents of the Cotswold countryside around Chipping Norton have celebrated Waddle-Browne for years. She was locally fa-mous long before the area became trendy thanks to ex-prime minister David and Samantha Cameron, Soho Farmhouse, Jeremy Clarkson and the Daylesford Farmshop. *Time* magazine's reviewer was quick to praise her anthem. *Daisy* would not have been complete without the woman whose photograph graces certain schoolroom stage sets to this day. Notwithstanding Waddle-Browne's outrageous fee, *Daisy* recouped its entire investment in under ten weeks.

THANK GOD I HAD the seemingly unflappable Brian Brolly and his cool head at the helm of my company. Time and time again I hear people who are about to get divorced say it's all going to be very ami-cable – "I'm still best friends with my ex" and so on – yet months later there are court hearings and terrible tales of intransigence and unrea-sonable behaviour spun with the kind of anger you can only have for a partner you once loved. A good divorce lawyer should be firm but sympathetic. Mine turned out to be a right pig.

It was a horrible year. Sarah 1 stayed at Sydmonton with the children whilst Sarah B moved into the flat in London. It really got to me that I couldn't go to the home which had been my creative centre for nearly ten years. Sarah let me have access to the children for one weekend in three, so I now structured my life around seeing them. Imo was just five and Nick three; Imo certainly understood something of what was happening. She remembers me telling her that nothing altered my love for her. Thank goodness Imo never blamed herself for what happened as some children do when their homes are smashed. Sarah B was great with the kids; we broke the ice by taking them to a Chinese restaurant where they made Peking duck pancakes which they found a huge excitement.

Out of the blue I was contacted by Michael Crawford. He wanted to introduce me to ice skaters Jayne Torvill and Christopher Dean. We met at my flat where they asked me to write the music for their forthcoming Olympic games routine. I hadn't got it in me to compose; they won the Gold Medal anyway. I smiled my way through the Tony Awards where thankfully *Cats* won Best Musical and me Best Score. I went to Budapest in Soviet Hungary to see the first home-grown production of *Cats* where I was shat on by a pigeon during an open-air awards ceremony in which the Minister of Culture droned on about which bank of the Danube was Buda and which was Pest. Afterwards, during a hastily convened hair-washing ceremony, his sweet little girl asked me which bank of the Thames was Lon and which was Don.

I went through the motions of seeing a load of off-the-wall spaces for *Starlight*. In the end we came down on the New Victoria, a conventional theatre albeit in a then non-West End theatrical wasteland which John Napier thought he could fill with his roller-skating train tracks running round the entire auditorium.

In August Sarah and the kids moved to London to a house I bought in Belgravia and I was back home at Sydmonton. Sarah B strongly felt we must continue with the Festival which was scheduled for September. She then showed two polar opposite sides of her personality by intensely studying Rachmaninov songs for a seriously ambitious recital whilst buying such ridiculously revealing outfits for first nights that I had to get Arlene Phillips to tell her she could not possibly be seen in them. Arlene informed her they were "costumes not dresses."

A MONTH EARLIER, BRIAN had told me he had pulled off a property deal that was mine if I wanted it. He had agreed a purchase price of £1.3 million for the Palace Theatre in London's Cambridge Circus with Emile Littler. (Today £4,225,000.) It was, of course, a no-brainer but I thought a tricky one to square with divorce negotiations in full flight, until Brian pointed out that I'd have to borrow the money divorce or no. By the end of August I was the owner of the building that John Betjeman described in *First and Last Loves* (1952) as "more impressive within and without than The Royal Opera House . . . the only theatre architecture of the last 60 years which climbs into the regions of a work of art." The Palace Theatre started life as the Royal English Opera House in 1891. Designed by the underestimated Victorian architect Thomas Collcutt (coincidentally the restorer of Cameron Mackintosh's house Stavordale Priory), it was the *folie de grandeur* of Richard D'Oyly Carte, the impresario behind Gilbert and Sullivan. It opened with Arthur Sullivan's "serious" opera *Ivanhoe*, a vast flop that nearly bankrupted D'Oyly Carte who had to sell the theatre which promptly became a variety house.

Buying such an important building as the Palace was a huge respite from domestic drama. It was, as a leader in the *Daily Telegraph* pointed out, the first time a West End theatre had been owned by a working theatre artist and it gave me the opportunity to lure back Biddy Hayward as its administrator. The magnificent building was in a sorry state. The terracotta decoration had been stripped from its facade and its statues removed, apparently to Emile Littler's garden.

The auditorium and staircases had been desecrated with a job lot of army surplus plum-coloured paint whilst the foyer was wallpapered over with a pattern rarely seen outside Indian restaurants. A vast swag neon curtain obliterated the Cambridge Circus facade. Not for nothing was the Palace described in the theatre manual *Curtains* as "one of the saddest sights in Britain." Things were so run-down that the holes in the stair carpets had been coloured in with magic marker.

The first thing I did was remove the vindaloo wallpaper. Underneath was solid Siena marble. I held my breath when we started stripping the paint. The columns would certainly be marble – if it was porous the paint would have wrecked them. They had survived unscathed. However all this was cosmetic. Restoring the terracotta exterior and auditorium was not. The reason for the seemingly bargain purchase price soon became clear. A report confirmed the cost of properly restoring the Palace was way beyond my resources. Brian wondered if we needed a commercial property partner. He began exploring a possible deal with Bernie Delfont's First Leisure, the public company he ran with property developer Max Rayne.

SEPTEMBER 9 WAS SYDMONTON Festival time. It was a baptism by fire for my new personal assistant Sue Knight who, like Biddy, soon became much more than just a PA. Most of the Festival audience stayed loyal. Divorces are horrible for friends who are fond of both sides and a few made excuses about not being able to come to Sarah's Rachmaninov recital. I understood. To so many of my theatre colleagues my marriage had been a rock of stability in a flakey thespian sea.

Not writing Torville and Dean's Olympic music wasn't the only casualty of my bumpy 1983. Perhaps I regret even more turning down being the Christmas special guest on *The Morecambe and Wise Show*. In Britain at that time no TV show was bigger. Eric Morecambe and Ernie Wise were two comedians who had become national treasures. To be the Christmas guest was an honour almost bigger than a knighthood. Previous guests had been the likes of Shirley Bassey, André Previn, Elton John and Glenda Jackson. I had several meetings with Eric and Ernie and of course the sketch was about them being in a musical that went horribly wrong. It was hysterically funny.

But I said no. The British press was having a real go at Sarah B and I wanted to keep my head down. It was an asinine decision. Nothing could have done more for me than showing I was human via a good-natured ribbing on the top-rated TV show of the year. As it happened I would have had to nix it anyway. Come December I broke my left big toe. One evening I had a bath, chucked on a dressing gown and went down to the kitchen to cook some supper. I opened the freezer door and a load of pork chops fell on the defenceless digit. Don't do this, it's agony. I couldn't walk without crutches for weeks.

ON DECEMBER 17 THE IRA exploded a car bomb outside Harrods in Knightsbridge, killing six people. It was the first time the IRA had murdered in Britain for a while. What really hit me was that they had killed someone I knew. Among the dead was a young Oxford graduate journalist called Philip Geddes. I only met him once. He was a diarist on the *Daily Express*'s William Hickey column and it was at some party where I was an obvious target for a story. I hazily recall rabbiting on to him about the Burne-Jones windows in the chapel of his Oxford college, St Edmund Hall. It's hard to explain why such a tenuous connection unleashed a cauldron of creative frustration. Although I was doing my best for *Starlight*, I never intended it to be anything other than a left-field fun project. Now it was growing like Topsy and I needed an antidote.

I was still confused personally. I felt really guilty about my kids. Dad's death had affected me much more than I realized. I truly was in love with Sarah B and of course her voice enthralled me. But the best I'd done for her was a couple of pop singles that went nowhere.

I wrote a song for her with a Trevor Nunn lyric about a girl having an affair with a married man. It was potent stuff but in reality it was a long-winded version of what Don Black had written in "Nothing Like You've Ever Known" in *Tell Me on a Sunday*. No record company would touch it, so I locked the melody secure in my tune bank.

As I invariably do when I am depressed I turned to architecture. I hobbled on my broken toe into Winchester Cathedral for Advent evensong. I don't remember what the choir sang but I do recall my tears and they weren't only about my toe. The combination of uniquely English architecture and the equally unique English choral tradition overwhelmed me with a combination of inadequacy and a burning need to compose something that would really stretch me.

Back at Sydmonton I read the headlines about the senseless carnage at Harrods. I suppose it was my theatrical instincts that led me to wonder if I could compose a plea, a shout for compassion that would somehow include a reading of a news story of the day. But I couldn't make that work.

We spent Christmas Day with Sarah B's family in Bournemouth and Boxing Day with Imo and Nick at Sydmonton. It was a no man's land of a day, with Imo trying to cope with the home she knew without Mum around. However there were presents under the Christmas tree. Imo and Nick were excited about the imminent *Starlight* opening. They remembered the day on the Valley Railroad and we had a great time round the piano singing the songs. But the day made me even more certain that I must compose something that really challenged me. I also felt I must prove that I was right about Sarah B's voice. Whatever I wrote next would include her.

Come New Year 1984, I decided to have a stab at setting music to that most theatrical of texts, the Latin Requiem Mass. I had never remotely tackled anything like this before except in the Latin sections of the opening of *Evita*. A fully blown setting of the requiem would mean writing for a choir and classically trained voices, musical forces of which I had practically zero experience. At the beginning of January Sarah and I were guests of Placido Domingo in *Die Fledermaus* at the Royal Opera House. Afterwards at dinner I told Placido that I was thinking of composing a requiem. I also explained that I knew I would be punching way above my weight. It was his enthusiasm and belief that I could pull it off that encouraged me to have a go.

Mid-January saw us in full-blown rehearsals for *Starlight* at the deliciously run-down Tropical Palace in Willesden where the highlight of the lunch menu was goat curry. The cast was pretty wondrous with Stephanie Lawrence as Pearl, the brand new girl carriage on the tracks, Ray Shell as Rusty, our gallant Cinderella of a steam train, and veteran blues singer Lon Satton as Ramblin' Poppa McCoy, the ancient steam locomotive who'd seen the light at the end of the tunnel.

Trevor gave his usual lengthy opening speech. The sight of Trevor lecturing Arlene Phillips's body poppers about the "moral, emotional and metaphysical centre" of our railroad show was alone worth the price of admission. Add me mooning around rehearsals struggling with the Latin text of my Mass muttering *"requiem aeternam dona eis,"* and you will grasp why the Hip Hoppers were wondering whether they should have signed up. One afternoon, rehearsals were in full flight when Sarah B turned up with something she wanted my OK about. The director/writer Ken Hill had contacted her to offer her the role of Christine in a production of Gaston Leroux's *The Phantom of the Opera* which was scheduled to run in spring at the Theatre Royal, Newcastle, followed by a season at the Theatre Royal Stratford East, the East London theatre irrevocably associated with Joan Littlewood. It would be a jukebox musical of famous opera arias.

Sarah didn't want to commit to something out of London, but she just wanted to run it past me. Would it be something for me to produce? I was intrigued. It obviously wasn't a project for me as a composer, it sounded jokey and anyway Ken Hill had his own ideas for the music and I was set on composing the requiem. Instinct told me to call Cameron. The three of us saw the Lon Chaney silent movie and immediately thought that with some famous opera hits and a fun script there could be a *Rocky Horror Show* type musical in embryo. So Sarah declined Ken's offer explaining that she couldn't accept it for personal reasons, but said Cameron and I very much wanted to be kept in the loop about the show's progress.

MEANWHILE JOHN NAPIER WAS pacing round his gargantuan train set at the Apollo Victoria with a fixed grin. Once the cast hit the theatre they fearlessly raced all over the auditorium and over a death-defying industrial iron girdered swing bridge that could swivel through 360 degrees, tilt and rise up and down all at the same time. It was a far cry from the Rev. Awdry's *Thomas the Tank Engine*. But no one could deny that John's American railroad was unlike anything ever seen in any theatre. You'd be forgiven for thinking Trevor and John were more at home in a theme park than with Shakespeare.

I too was having fun. The divorce clouds were lifting as the lawyers ground towards a conclusion. I parked a real steam engine outside the theatre on which the cast and I posed for press shots. I started looking for new shows to produce again. *Daisy* was still happily playing at the Globe so when its director David Gilmore offered me first dibs on a new musical he was trying out at the Nuffield where *Daisy* started, I was keen. *The Hired Man* by Melvyn Bragg and composer Howard Goodall was English to the core. It wasn't an obvious crowd-pleaser but I liked it a lot and offered to produce it in the West End.

Michael White asked me to co-produce a revival of the Rodgers and Hart musical *On Your Toes* with ballerina Natalia Makarova in the lead which we slated for my new theatre, the Palace. I was an obvious sucker for this. I love the score which features the great Rodgers set piece *Slaughter on Tenth Avenue* and who can resist a lyric like "Two of them wrote symphonies and one wrote psalms / Bach, Beethoven and Herr Johannes Brahms"? So I agreed to co-produce, provided my role was completely passive. Both shows cost me my shirt. Cameron dubbed the Bragg/Goodall musical "The Tired Man." Some callous bastard sent me a first night telegram c/o the Palace that read, "Break a toe."

BY MID-MARCH 1984 BOTH Sarah B and my divorces were finalized. On March 22, my 36th birthday, we quietly got married at the registry office in Kingsclere, the village next to Sydmonton. Our plan was to get through *Starlight*'s first night a week later and then break the news. There was a particular reason for keeping schtum. That night HM The Queen, Prince Philip, Prince Charles and Princess Diana were all coming to a charity gala of *Starlight Express* in aid of the Centre for World Development Education, a charity I have never heard of before or since. We didn't want anything to screw up this event; to have both the Queen and the heir to the throne come to the theatre at once was virtually unprecedented.

Afterwards the Queen said she'd enjoyed the show, although when someone asked if she preferred horse racing to actors racing on roller skates, she didn't demur. Sarah B was with me in the pre-show line to be presented to the royals and someone had put it around that mistresses couldn't be presented to the Queen. When the presentation took place, two plus two made five. By the end of the show rumours of our marriage were swilling around backstage. The front page tabloid stories wallpapered the star dressing room.

Starlight's opening night went really well until the last fifteen minutes when the BBC outside broadcasting unit covering the opening began transmitting across our radio microphone frequency. This all but destroyed Stephanie Lawrence's big number "Only He Has the Power to Move Me" and caused huge mirth in the finale when Lon Satton hit the lines, "There are dark days ahead when the power goes dead." When Martin Levan our sound designer realized what was happening, the BBC astonishingly refused to turn their transmitter off. Since they were only there for live audience reaction after the performance, "saboteurs" is the tamest word I can muster.

So a pall hung over the first night party as it had at the *Cats* celebrations thanks to the bomb hoax. Even though David Land hadn't managed me for five years, the lovely man still worried about me like his own bubbeleh and told me not to be too upset if the critics had a go. He needn't have worried. Amazingly, *Starlight*'s reviews were better than *Cats*'. Typical was John Barber in the *Daily Telegraph* whose gist was that *Starlight* might not do a lot for the creative team's reputations but it's huge fun. "Another Express that is rolling to a super success," announced the *Daily Express*. "First Class to success" was Jack Tinker's headline in the *Daily Mail*.

Quite a few scribes noted the rap at the top of Act 2. Arlene Phillips's body-popping choreography was rightly hailed for bringing street theatre into the West End. I smiled at how seriously some critics took the show. Irving Wardle in the *Times* wrote:

> The heart of the show comes in the three races during which the roller-skated company zip vertigiously round the loops and slopes of the course to a pounding "perpetuum mobile" more exciting than Lloyd Webber's Paganini variations . . . what reconciles the styles is the central sound of the steam engine itself, the sound that first carried the blacks away from the plantations and reverberates through all forms of urban jazz . . . from the first number with its growling boogie bass line interspersed with discordant whistles that take you back to Meade "Lux" Lewis there is no resisting Starlight's rhythmic grip.

So there. *Starlight* ran for 7406 performances. It is still running in Bochum, Germany and in 2018 will celebrate its 30th birthday having broken the world record for continuous performances of a musical in the same theatre. Some theatre critics found it way too much. I am not surprised. AC/DC sung by Jeff Daniels was transgender electro-pop over 30 years ago. The opening of Act 2 really *was* a full-blown storytelling rap.

Starlight passed its most important test when Imo and Nick liked it nearly as much as *Cats*. Imo wanted to be Dinah the dining car because of her pale blue outfit almost as much as she'd wanted to be Victoria, the White Cat.

Starlight was reworked for its 30th birthday in Bochum after I stripped it back to its roots and tried it out in concert with no sets or costumes and absolutely no roller skates. Watch this space, there just might be a new *Starlight* near you.

34

"Brrrohahaha!!!"

I started work full-time on the Requiem Mass. I say "full-time" advisedly. I am incapable of concentrating on any one thing exclusively. But at least the business decisions were now all Brian's although how he rolled out *Starlight* eventually led to our first big disagreement. Brian was diligent about following up any daft idea I had – with hindsight maybe too diligent.

Certainly there were several people who were uneasy about the next scheme I had for Sarah B. *Song and Dance* was coming to its end at the Palace. The "concert for the theatre" that was announced for twelve weeks was handing in the towel after 781 performances and four leading ladies – Marti Webb, *Pennies from Heaven* star Gemma Craven, the incomparable Lulu and Liz Robertson who was Alan Jay Lerner's eighth and final wife. Liz met Alan when she played Eliza Doolittle in Cameron's revival of this great lyricist's *My Fair Lady*.

BBC TV offered to film the show as a special. They wanted Wayne Sleep but because they already had aired Marti in the original *Tell Me* canvassed that another artist could play her role. I said it should be Sarah. Cameron was not keen. I also got a surprise call from David Land worrying that I was pushing Sarah forward too much and that it would backfire on her as surely as Tim Rice's championing hadn't helped Elaine Paige. I replied that, like Tim, I was championing Sarah because of her talent.

I should have listened. I don't think the TV of *Song and Dance* did Sarah any harm, but she was too young for it and it was never written for a soprano. There again she got an all-out rave from John Barber in an op-ed in the *Daily Telegraph*. And her huge range meant "Unexpected Song" could be shoehorned into *Tell Me* and not just sung by the company as the finale although it was nearly cut when Richard Stilgoe dubbed it "Unexploded Bomb" at the dress run and Sarah got the giggles. John Barber rather accurately summed up our status quo. He wrote about Sarah's three-octave range and quoted her saying "Andrew has great fun with my voice. . . . no he hasn't talked about a musical for me. Maybe one day there'll be one he's doing and I'll be exactly right for it." Barber closed his review:

> It is hard to see where so much talent (Sarah's) is going,
> but her instinct is towards the classics. The same is true
> of her husband currently working on a Latin Requiem.
> Just as he has extended the musical scope of the popular
> theatre, Sarah Brightman's unique voice could extend the
> musical range of pop singing. Whether or not they work
> together, I shall watch her future with as much fascina-
> tion as I do his.

Thanks once again to Concorde I went with Trevor to see the *Cats* tour close in Boston and re-open in Washington. On the way back in mid Atlantic there was an almighty bang. All the engines had stalled. The pilot came over the PA system and said there was no reason to panic, this was averagely normal, the jet streams at 60,000-plus feet often caused this sort of thing. I remembered a story David Frost told about being in a helicopter over Central Park whose rotor failed. The pilot said, "I'll steer the bird – you guys in the back do something religious." Sure enough our man restarted the engines one by one, but I thanked the good Lord that I was well stuck into the Puligny-Montrachet at the time and hoped my requiem jottings at Sydmonton were vaguely decipherable.

Possibly prodded by the supersonic drama, I cleared April for the requiem. I found it impossible to set the Latin words sitting at the piano. Thanks to my elementary school Latin and a good English translation I puzzled over the text and its meaning during long walks and days when I gorged myself on the wealth of church architecture that is Britain's most undervalued asset. I would go over phrases time and time again in my head, take them to the piano, conclude they were rubbish, go and see another building and try again. The English choral tradition with its unique dependency on boy "treble" soprano voices was my bedrock. Latin obviously is not the language of the Church of England but that's never been a bother in the Victorian Tractarian incense-toting Anglo-Catholic churches I love.

At the end of April my work was going fast enough to announce the Mass's first performance at the tenth Sydmonton Festival that July. Sydmonton is not far from Winchester which has one of Britain's finest cathedral choirs. I contacted its musical director Martin Neary to see if his choir could undertake the Festival performance. It was a huge ask. A cathedral choir performs two completely different programmes of music for morning and evening services on a Sunday, plus daily changing programmes for evensong every day of the week. The children do normal school around all this music. Learning a new work for a performance that might well be its last would not be the easiest thing to ease past the Bishop of Winchester. Nonetheless Martin agreed to meet and a date was set to go through the first draft of my score.

AT THE BEGINNING OF May, Ken Hill's *Phantom* opened in Stratford East and on a very hot night Cameron, Sarah and I caught up with it. It was what we expected. The Phantom did a lot of leaping from behind flimsy Victorian scenery spouting "Brrrohahaha!!!" causing Christine to emote arias like Puccini's "Oh My Darling Daddy." It was nowhere near ready for the West End but there were the seeds of a campy fun night out. Sarah was dubious, at least as a vehicle for her. She had her sights on mainstream opera, however small the role, and was spending Olympian hours on vocal training under the guidance of her voice teacher, Ian Adam.

When the trilling had to stop she was busy furnishing our new London flat in Green Street, Mayfair, on top of a tall thin house that overlooked the glorious garden of a long vanished mansion. Our stay there was short lived. Despite, or maybe because of, having the Dorchester and the Connaught as neighbours the area was seriously dodgy. One cold damp night I was walking home down Park Street. There, shivering in a doorway, was a miniskirted girl who looked barely sixteen. A beige minivan drew up beside her, the driver threw open the back doors and shouted "in!" and shoved the kid onto the floor where she joined two others. He then sped off towards Oxford Street yelling, "I know who you are" and hurling dire threats at me if I reported anything.

Despite Sarah's doubts about Ken Hill's *Phantom*, Cameron and I announced we would develop his *Phantom of the Opera* later in the year. We didn't plan to alter the show's campy fun tone and the music would remain an operatic mash-up. I suggested that the show would need a title song which I could write, but that would be the extent of my musical involvement. With that I forgot about Ken Hill's *Phantom* and it was back to the Latin requiem.

IN MID-MAY I WAS the subject of a major feature in *Time* magazine. The story hung its hat on the *Starlight Express* opening which meant I had the record of three shows on Broadway and four in London. It was written by its respected music critic Michael Walsh and headlined "The Musical's Superstar. Britain's Andrew Lloyd Webber is the unchallenged King around the world." It was as close to a eulogy as I could have asked for. My American PRs thought several birthdays and religious festivals had come at once. I was less certain.

The thrust was that I a total outsider had taken over that most uniquely American of forms the Broadway musical and kicked its inhabitants into the long grass. It also contained some serious analysis of my writing. Walsh talked about "the harrowing, almost atonal sections of both the Superstar overture and the opening chorus of Evita." He continued "Even that most 'learned' of musical forms, the fugue, makes an appearance in Cats, both in the overture and in the Jellicle Ball ballet." He noted "The technical aspects of Lloyd Webber's – the syncopations, the unusual 13/8 [did he mean 7/8?] time signatures – are meant to be heard not noticed."

He even gave a nod to the disastrous Jeeves: "Jeeves contains some typically winning Lloyd Webber tunes, as slick as the pomade on Bertie Wooster's hair." I am quoted re the technical stuff. "These things are the solid base on which you start to hang your hat. If the scores did not have something central, a basic strength, you couldn't begin the other things people notice, the melodies." Tellingly I am quoted, "If I had a master plan I wouldn't have written Starlight now. What I should have done is to write a three handed opera entirely accompanied by a string quartet to play for two performances to ecstatic reviews. But I don't plan to that degree."

My master plan would emphatically not have included this seeming dream of an article. Of course I was deeply grateful that Walsh took my music seriously. It was great he understood the importance I attach to construction. But I saw the article as flashing amber rags to the bulls of Broadway. Back then I was still very much an outsider. I hadn't paid my dues in workshops and piano bars around the Great White Way. Ronald Reagan and Margaret Thatcher may have cherished "the special relationship" but British musicals didn't figure in it.

The more I thought about it, the bigger I feared a backlash could be. How could I expect American theatre critics to understand the genesis of Starlight? To them it would be just another manifestation of a composer obsessed with spectacle. OK, Evita was set in a black box but that was thanks to Hal Prince, never mind that it was I who got Hal on board. *Jesus Christ Superstar* on Broadway was all glitz, *Cats* on Broadway was hardly shy of it and now this guy who's usurped exclusively American turf has followed it up with a gargantuan specfest featuring body-popping rappers dressed as railroad trains. To top it all he says he's writing a Requiem Mass! The guy's clearly a shyster. That's how I thought critics might see things and I wasn't totally wrong.

On the other hand Broadway producers were keener than ever to grab my shows. A tussle began over *Song and Dance*, despite its non-theatrical origins. Cameron saw the amber light too. He strongly felt that an American creative team should take it over as insurance particularly against American critics' jibes at British choreography which seemed, despite Michael Bennett's fulsome praise of Gillian Lynne, to be holy writ. Frank Rich had already had a go at Anthony Van Laast's work on *Variations*, although he found my music "delightful."

I thought getting *Song and Dance* to Broadway would be nice if it happened, but it could wait. However I vehemently told Brian that *Starlight* should never go anywhere near the Great White Way. I was much helped that Robert Stigwood reared his head with a plan for a US arena tour. This sounded more the ticket as did a plan for legendary record producer Phil Ramone to produce a concept album with American acts. I left Brian to get on with all this and got my head down for the requiem's performance which was set for July 13.

I HAD COMPOSED FOR full choir, four soloists, boy soprano, soprano, tenor and bass. Sarah B was the soprano and the others were culled from Winchester Cathedral choir including the boy soprano Paul Miles-Kingston who, alongside Sarah, premiered the requiem both in concert and on record. At this point the requiem was scored for organ and five instrumentalists. Jon Hiseman played percussion this time whilst his wife Barbara doubled on tenor saxophone and flute. David Caddick and David Cullen joined on keyboards, so the musicians were almost family. Winchester's choirmaster Martin Neary manned the podium.

Maybe it was the dreamy summer night, maybe the simple country church setting wove some special magic – there was something wonderful about hearing birdsong in the musical gaps – but the audience seemed genuinely moved by what they heard and the reaction was hugely positive. Almost immediately Brian Brolly had offers to record the requiem from both EMI Records' classical label HMV Angel and Philips Deutsche Grammophon. The former's boss, the urbane Peter Andry, was something of a living legend. Andry was a veteran of EMI classical, having joined in 1956 and had worked with every major name in serious music. Not for nothing was his autobiography subtitled *Working with Callas, Rostropovich, Domingo, and the Classical Elite.* Instinct told me he would be my best guide through the classical music minefield, so HMV it was. Obviously the first person I wanted to ask aboard was Placido, but before that Peter demanded to go through the score in detail. He was extremely insistent that I expanded the orchestration to full symphony orchestra size. I think he felt this would secure the endorsement of a heavyweight conductor.

His first thought was André Previn. The *Superstar* film saga was long forgiven when I met André. He really liked the opening section which at that stage began with the boy soprano from the first beat. He was really pleased with the "Requiem Aeternam," praised the "Offertorium" through to the "Pie Jesu" and liked the end. He had doubts about chunks of the rest. I said that this was my first draft, but in the end his dates didn't work out. Although he was principal conductor of the Royal Philharmonic Orchestra he was in the middle of moving from the Pittsburgh Symphony Orchestra to the LA Philharmonic. But I suspect he could have juggled commitments around if he'd really wanted.

Peter Andry immediately turned to another major conductor coincidentally with Pittsburgh connections, Maestro Lorin Maazel. After two lengthy meetings Lorin said yes. I shall forever be grateful that I worked with this extraordinary musician. His was the antithesis of the grand gesture Leonard Bernstein style of conducting. A slight hand movement was all he needed to engage his orchestral troops as he conducted the most complex musical scores, very often from memory. Lorin remained a friend until his death in 2014. We had lunch together very shortly before he died to discuss my composing for his Castleton Festival.

First we decided I should eliminate the bass soloist and adapt his music for the tenor. This helped enormously with the logic of my setting. I wanted the boy to represent uncorrupted childhood, that no child was born to hate, any more than a child is born with a specific religious faith. We may have Jewish, Muslim, Protestant or Catholic parents – we can't change our ethnicity – but we are not born Jewish, Muslim, Protestant or Catholic. I visualized the soprano as an idealistic young woman repelled by violence committed in the name of religion, and the tenor as a world-weary everyman who had seen it all. Combining the bass and tenor parts made this simple concept much easier.

IN LATE AUGUST SARAH and I went to Venice for a few days where I stumbled on what I still think could work as an off-the-wall evening, although Cameron and I screwed it up first time. We were having coffee in St Mark's Square when the cafe band struck up with an astonishing arrangement of hits from *La Bohème*, scored for piano, accordion, two violins and bass. It was masterly stuff. The bandleader told me that the cafe arrangement was by Puccini himself. I wanted to know more. Were there any others?

Apparently Puccini, anticipating that his operas would get filthy reviews, blitzed the cafes around Italy with highlights from his next opera weeks before they were staged. In short, Puccini was way ahead of concept albums, radio promotion, trending on Spotify, you name it. The Milan offices of his publishers Ricordi were bombed to pieces in World War Two, so the only copies of these medleys left are with the families of a very few old-time cafe bandleaders. This *La Bohème* arrangement had been my bandleader's great-grandfather's copy. When we got home I suggested to Cameron that we recreated these arrangements and set a show in a cafe whose waiters acted out Puccini's life story. Cameron engaged the witty classical music commentator Robin Ray as writer and we earmarked it for Sydmonton, 1985.

Having set yet another hare running, we both headed to New York for *Song and Dance* meetings. Even more importantly, I was slated to go with Peter Andry to see Placido in *Lohengrin* at the Met. The plan was to meet him afterwards and confirm we'd record and premiere hopefully some time in the coming year.

The surefire way to get howls of anguish from Wagner nuts is to opine that his overtures are the best bits as you get all the hits compressed into a few minutes and don't need to wade through eight hours of the rest. Another corker is to say that you've heard that the Reduced Shakespeare Company, who memorably condensed all the bard's works into two hours, have spawned a new arm called the Reduced Wagner Company and are performing the entire Ring Cycle in one act. A third, for cognoscenti only, was to say how much you liked Paul Nicholas's portrayal of Wagner in Ken Russell's *Lisztomania*.

The first sentiment struck me forcibly soon after the *Lohengrin* fabulous overture. Maybe due to jetlag I found it hard to get into the story of Telramund, Elsa and the shining knight in a boat drawn by a swan. I remembered Anthony Bowles saying that you have to admire Wagner for writing all this stuff down. When finally Act 1 ground to a halt, Peter Andry leapt up and said, "Now we go to dinner," I was baffled. Was the custom with Wagner that you had a long dinner between acts, like at Glyndebourne? If so brunch would be at 8 am the following morning and we'd still have Act 3 to go. Peter swept me into a restaurant opposite the opera house. "Our boy doesn't do anything in the second act and half the next," he said, "so we'll eat and come back when he does."

I was speechless. These were the words of the revered chief of EMI's classical repertoire. I sat back politely and ate my food.

THE TWO PROJECTS WERE now progressing in New York at the same time. Cameron was convinced that we should use an American choreographer for *Song and Dance* so we met with Peter Martins who I pointed out was Danish. I was reassured that he was now an honorary American, having been principal dancer at the New York City Ballet under George Balanchine since 1970 and had become its balletmaster. On the same day we lunched with Richard Maltby.

Cameron thought that with Peter and Richard we had a team Broadway would respect. I knew I could work with both. I also drooled over Richard's suggestion that we approached Bernadette Peters for *Tell Me*. Bernadette began her career on Broadway and was the star of shows like *Mack and Mabel*. But she had wisely moved into TV and film with movies like *The Jerk* and *Pennies from Heaven* in which she co-starred with Steve Martin. So she had avoided the trap so many young musical actresses fall into of being pigeon holed as "musical theatre." I thought she was an inspired choice.

My niggling worries were twofold. First, were we changing the London creative team to an admittedly talented American one solely to pander to the New York critics? Secondly, this double bill had been a British theatre hit particularly due to both *Variations* and *Tell Me* having been massive chart hits. They hadn't been in the USA. Would *Song and Dance* be mistakenly seen as my follow-up musical to *Cats*, not "a concert for the theatre" of two hit albums? But then Bernadette said yes and how could I say no? Cameron's bouncing enthusiasm had once again swept all before it.

Placido also said yes. It's incredible how people whose diaries are chockablock for years suddenly find gaps when they want to do something. Soon *Requiem*, as we were now calling it, had recording dates in the week before Christmas in Studio 1 at Abbey Road. Next Peter Andry proposed the premiere should be in America followed by a performance in London. I liked this plan. I thought it would show America my serious side. I suggested St Thomas Church on Fifth Avenue as a venue. It operates exactly like an English cathedral with a full-time professional choir and a boys' choir school that is virtually unique in the USA. Before I could blink, the world premiere was confirmed there for February 24, of next year – 1985.

It was all incredibly exciting but the speed everything came together allowed me little time to re-orchestrate *Requiem* for a full symphony orchestra. So I enlisted David Cullen to work alongside me on the score. Next I asked my father's star pupil David Caddick to be my right-hand man.

I ALSO HAD TO delegate one other project, recording the title song for Ken Hill's *Phantom* opera potpourri. Someone suggested Mike Batt as producer and lyricist – it might even have been me. It was a good idea. Mike is best known as the man behind "The Wombles of Wimbledon" but he also wrote "Bright Eyes" and the score for the movie of *Watership Down*. I had been offered this movie, but the gig had been speedily withdrawn after the fiasco of *Jeeves*. Mike and I soon had something we were very excited about and at the beginning of November he laid the track down at Air Studios. Sarah suggested her old flame Mike Moran to play keyboards.

Although the song ended completely differently, the rhythm track arrangement is the basis of the theatre orchestration. We also laid down an instrumental version; Mike Moran's virtuoso organ part was recorded at half speed to make it playable. Ultimately it became the first section of the overture. But that was a while off, because

Cameron and my involvement with Ken Hill's *Phantom* came to a resounding full stop.

It happened on a trip to Japan. Although I had jettisoned everything I could to concentrate on *Requiem*, I simply couldn't ditch going to see *Cats* there with Sarah, Brian and Cameron. I discovered that Jim Sharman, the London director of *Jesus Christ Superstar*, was going to be in Tokyo. Jim had subsequently directed *The Rocky Horror Show*. Talk about serendipity. Who better to direct the Ken Hill *Phantom* than the man who had helmed the coolest cult musical of recent time?

We arrived in Tokyo to a banquet given in our honour by the warlord of Japanese theatre, local producer Keita Asari whose Shiki Theatre Company were presenting *Cats*. A particular delicacy was aged tuna sushi. I had no idea you could age fish for sushi, much as you age meat for steaks. Instead of being hung in a cold room the fish is stored in little wicker baskets, rather like the ones used for dim sum, the difference being these have ice in the bottom. This delicious discovery was served by the most demure looking geisha girls, who bowed and scraped to the male, apart from Sarah, diners like extras in some ancient Hollywood oriental movie. Guests were not supposed to acknowledge them so I put my foot in it when I asked a geisha if they served at lots of bashes like this. "I'm your Gumbie Cat," she replied.

So the geishas were our female cast. You can imagine how Sarah felt. I was torn between being shocked and, I admit, smiling. The idea of sexy soon to be Mrs John Napier Donna King in full geisha garb dishing up sushi to us lot was delightful.

The next shock was a tent. Cameron, Brian and I had agreed to a reduced royalty in Japan because we were told there was nowhere that *Cats* could play in the semi-round in Tokyo other than in a temporary tent. This tent would have to frequently make costly moves because of planning issues, hence the royalty cut.

The tent resembled a city. There were restaurants, state of the art physio facilities, the biggest sound system I had ever seen in a theatre amid thousands of seats and a lighting rig that necessitated a small power station. We also learned that Japanese productions rarely stay in one place for more than a few months anyway.

We hadn't exactly been had, but equally we hadn't exactly hadn't.

WE HAD A VERY pleasant lunch with Jim Sharman. It was great to see him after almost ten years. But it was clear he'd moved a country mile from the transvestite world of Dr Frank N. Furter. He was now into serious opera, having recently directed Britten's *Death in Venice* at the Adelaide Festival Theatre and Berg's *Lulu* at the Sydney Opera House. A campy romp was no longer his bag.

"You should do it," he said as we hugged goodbye. "You should write *The Phantom*."

I was unimpressed. The last thing I wanted to write next for the theatre after *Starlight* was a few incidental songs for a jokey book musical.

So Cameron and I decided that was the end of the road for the *Phantom* idea. I had enough on my plate with *Requiem* and he had found a French arena *spectacle* based on Victor Hugo's *Les Misérables* that he was trying to persuade Trevor to direct at the Royal Shakespeare Company. Cameron told Ken Hill that without Jim Sharman we couldn't see a way forward. Brian Brolly thanked Mike Batt. Perhaps the *Phantom* song could be a novelty single for Sarah one day. Not before time I could devote my full energy to *Requiem*.

35

Requiem

I don't know how many composers have cried "my kingdom for a hearse" after a run-through of their requiems, but I sure as hell did after the first orchestral rehearsal of mine.

It was at the beginning of December at the Henry Wood Hall in South London. Lorin Maazel was atop the conductor's podium. It seemed every classical bigwig in town had turned out to hear the masterpiece unveiled and it was a disaster. The leap to full orchestra had turned my six piece lean and mean score into an oversized blancmange. The recording plans should have been postponed a couple of months there and then and *Requiem* rescored, but the sessions were booked and the BBC had committed to film the New York premiere. The director was the BBC's top serious music producer/presenter Humphrey Burton. He was closely associated with Leonard Bernstein and had no peer in classical music broadcasting. There was no way back.

Next day I met with Lorin. David Cullen hadn't done a bad job – he had kept all my motifs and choral writing – it was simply that scoring for a full symphony orchestra had taken the rawness away. Lorin proposed a quick fix. Cut the violins. As a quick fix it was a good suggestion. It meant at a stroke that nothing interfered with the pitch of the voices. David Caddick and I spent a week reworking the score and David Cullen did a stalwart job of incorporating our notes at breakneck speed.

. . .

WE RECORDED AT ABBEY Road in five sessions the week before Christmas. Placido was in superb voice, the only section he had a struggle with was the strict time in "Hosanna." Because it was recorded with a classical orchestra set-up rather than close-miked the drums were not screened off so they echoed everywhere which didn't help. I was fascinated by how John Kurlander, EMI's top classical recording engineer, handled the orchestra and choir. Everything was recorded through a "tree" which is a cluster of directional microphones bunched together and raised high above the conductor's podium. Consequently the musical forces are recorded balanced exactly as the conductor wants them. Only the soloists had individual microphones. I learned that old-fashioned classical musical editors really did edit by gauging the length of tape a section of music was recorded onto and substituting a similar length from the "take" the producer thought was better. I was staggered that such a crude process worked every time – a skill entirely lost in the digital age. I was very excited and a little proud when I heard the finished recording for the first time. I thought I really had taken a major leap into the unknown and come out well. Certainly everyone around me was buoying me up. Today I am not so sure – in fact, one day I want to rework *Requiem*.

I am happy with my original concept, the world-weary tenor, the questioning young girl soprano and the innocent child. I am happy with the beginning, "Requiem Aeternam." But today I would axe the orchestral opening and open *Requiem* with the child unaccompanied. I am also happy that the section repeats at the end of the Mass. Its simple E–B–E melody is meant to suggest "*lux perpetua*" or infinite light which is why I have the child repeat unaccompanied the word "*perpetua*" at the very end through and after the monumental organ chords based on my setting of "*Judex ergo cum sedebit*" ("so when the judge is seated").

I wish I hadn't set the next section "Kyrie Eleison" to the same music as the opening. There has to be a separate "Kyrie." My "Dies Irae"

("Day of Wrath") is rubbish and I have a *dies irae* whenever I hear it. A "Dies Irae" should be a spectacular moment for a composer. Mine is tame and has to be dumped. I do have a complex new setting in my head but whether I have the technical skill to pull it off is another matter. If I ever do rework the Mass it's here I will start.

The *"Tuba mirum spargens sonum"* ("the trumpet's wondrous call") isn't hopeless. With a bit more wit in the orchestration I could work it up into something. I need to feature a naughty tuba dancing as if it had strayed into a bacchanalian orgy. I am also happy with the *"Mors stupebit et natura"* section. I very much had the words in mind "Death and nature shall stand amazed when creation rises again" and the music anticipates the setting of the "Pie Jesu."

"Rex tremendae" ("King of awesome majesty") is a grand setting of the words with *"salva me"* ("save me") used as a pathetic plea. It's passable, just. The next two sections "Recordare" and "Ingemisco" are composed as solos for the soprano and tenor respectively. I tried to echo the meaning of the text with varying success. I wanted to find a floaty melody for the soprano "recall dear Jesus that I am the reason for your journey into this world." I am only half pleased with the result. The words of the tenor solo which translate as "I groan like one condemned, my face blushes for my sins" aptly describe the way I feel about my setting. Like the "Dies Irae" it is simply not up to it. It has, unlike the latter, a pretty tune but it's a melody that belongs elsewhere and is not a proper setting of the words. I have time for the melody of the *"Lacrymosa dies illa"* ("that day will be one of weeping"), although this too is a section that is way under-developed.

The "Offertorium" is not theologically part of the Requiem Mass. But I like its words and its plea for salvation – "allow them to pass from death into life." I am much happier with this setting. I like how it builds to a unison statement from the full choir when they sing *"Fac eas Domine de monte transpire ad vitam"* ("allow them to pass from death into life"). I added the *"sanctus"* section as a coda in order to suggest the mood of the Mass is becoming optimistic. This leads to a premature celebration from the "adult" tenor "Hosanna" ("Hosanna in the highest, blessed is he who cometh in the name of the Lord"). He is duly interrupted by the angry young soprano who punctures the mood with the words of the "Dies Irae" section set to the music of the "Recordare." I like the "Hosanna" melody but I hate the brass writing and might very well cut it completely.

"Pie Jesu" follows. It was one of those moments where I read the words and the melody came instantly, as did the idea that it should be a duet. Regarding this, I have a confession – and sadly it involves a wish that can never come true. I would have loved it to have been recorded by the Everly Brothers. I played around with the liturgical order in the last sequence "Lux Aeterna" and "Libera Me" and added a repeat of the "Dies Irae" text to lead to the child closing the Mass with the "*requiem aeternam*" section with its suggestion that the child sees infinite light – "*lux perpetua*." But the repetition of the word "*perpetua*" implies that the needless violence that was the catalyst to the requiem will never go away.

REQUIEM'S FIRST PERFORMANCE IN St Thomas Church on Fifth Avenue in New York was on February 25, 1985. The BBC's decision to film it turned it into a big deal. All the artists on the recording joined forces with the St Thomas Choir and the great and the good of New York and Broadway turned out in full force. Former Prime Minister Edward Heath was in the audience – it was that sort of occasion. Even the boys of the Winchester Cathedral choir were flown over. Liberated from the cloisters of a prim English cathedral town, they fell on their hotel porn channels with such vigour that their antics nearly wound up in the *New York Post*. The premiere was doubly nerve-racking for me. I wasn't so much petrified about *Requiem*'s reception as fearful for my young wife Sarah up there with Domingo and Maazel.

Lorin was a rock. One afternoon during a break I asked him to explain what minimalism and Philip Glass were all about. Lorin began talking about repetition, how it all started with some symphony that had a 20-minute sustained chord followed by 20 minutes of silence. Abruptly he stopped and looked me in my glazed over face. "Andrew, there's no point in my explaining this. You are a maximalist."

I could not have asked for a better premiere. Placido was on his finest form and Sarah not only looked stunning but handled the fiendishly high notes I had written for her effortlessly. The low point was a lengthy cringe-making though generously intended speech by the BBC's Humphrey Burton about the genius work the audience was about to hear. I went beetroot with embarrassment. Surely this speech would only add fuel to last year's *Time* magazine article. I was right. There were a few chinks of light but most critics dismissed *Requiem*. Many accused it of being derivative, citing examples by composers I had never heard of, let alone heard their music. But "Pie Jesu" was grudgingly acknowledged as a standout and has become one of my best-known compositions. I sometimes wonder how many of the people who ask for it at their weddings realize that the words "*Dona eis requiem*" mean "Grant them eternal rest." Charlotte Church, who for a while adopted it as her signature aria, used to have enormous problems. She turned down singing it at Rupert Murdoch's wedding to his previous wife Wendi, explaining it just might send the wrong signal.

In May I got an approach from the legendary Russian ballet dancer, Mikhail "Misha" Baryshnikov, who was now artistic director of the American Ballet Theatre. He asked if *Requiem* could be performed by ABT as a ballet at the Met. Not only that, he proposed the legendary Sir Kenneth MacMillan as choreographer and himself as co-lead dancer with the brilliant Italian ballerina of the moment, Alessandra Ferri. I gulped. Sir Kenneth had choreographed some of the finest Royal Ballet offerings over two decades at Covent Garden including a personal favourite *Romeo and Juliet*, not to mention Cliff Richard in *Expresso Bongo*. It was a dream team come true. Performances were to begin in spring 1986 with Sarah wanted as soloist as she was an integral part of Sir Kenneth's vision. I arranged to meet Kenneth as soon after *Requiem*'s Westminster Abbey British premiere as possible.

BACK HOME THE RECEPTION was far better. The influential *Gramophone* magazine suggested *Requiem* would become the successor to Stainer's *Crucifixion*. The critic Edward Greenfield echoed this view in the *Guardian*. Sir Edward Heath wrote a eulogy in the *Financial Times*. Much against EMI's will, I persuaded them to issue "Pie Jesu" as the first and only pop single on the HMV Angel label. Ken East, boss of the pop side of EMI, was so opposed I had to do a "Stigwood," offering to underwrite the cost of pressing 50,000 copies. Aided by a performance on top TV show Esther Rantzen's *That's Life* and a brilliant video directed by Stephen Frears, the entire stock was sold in a week.

"Pie Jesu" went to No. 3 in the singles chart and No. 1 in the 7" chart. Irritatingly 12" extended disco versions of chart hits were all the rage and counted towards the total singles chart position. It was hard to stick a drum machine on "Pie Jesu" and this time disco owners didn't use it like "Don't Cry for Me" to clear their dance floors. But it did give me my second chart hit in Latin (David Essex used the "Salve Regina" section in his "Oh What a Circus" hit from *Evita*). All proceeds of the single were donated to Save the Children.

Requiem premiered in Britain on April 25 in Westminster Abbey. All the original performers took part and Prime Minister Margaret Thatcher was among the guests. Performances followed all over Britain and Ireland, Sarah giving as many as three in a week. *Requiem* was also immediately performed all over the world. It was very well received in Russia which, because of my love of Russian music, was really gratifying. But after its initial burst, *Requiem* now only gets performed occasionally. The upper-stringless orchestration and the difficult eccentrically written soprano part mean it is a tricky work to programme. No orchestral manager wants to pay thirty violinists not to be on the platform. Plus I know it could be far better. I must try someday to revise it into something other than a curiosity from which one section, "Pie Jesu," survives in the mainstream.

36

Epiphany

One sunny afternoon during *Requiem*'s rehearsals in the Big Apple I found myself at a loose end. Sarah had gone with her mother to get her dress fitted for the premiere. I was meandering past a bookstall on Fifth Avenue when my eye was caught by a copy of the original English translation of Gaston Leroux's *The Phantom of the Opera*. I had nothing better to do, so I parted with 50 cents, headed back to the Ritz-Carlton where we were holed up and got stuck into the tome. I had an epiphany.

The Gaston Leroux is a very confused confection – sometimes a faux history story, then sporting a touch of George du Maurier's novel, *Trilby*, next a horror story, then it's French detective time, now and then it's spiced with *Beauty and the Beast* with a dash of satanic Paganini. In truth it betrays its penny-dreadful origin from get go.

But one thing poleaxed me – the very end. The Phantom's body is exhumed years after his death and on his sinuous finger is the ring he had given his beloved Christine Daaé.

The Phantom of the Opera could be a passionate story of unrequited love.

That evening I had another thought. The moment everyone re-members from the Lon Chaney movie is when the Phantom drops the auditorium chandelier. What if the show began with an auction of the contents of a doomed opera house? All my days schlepping around disused theatres when I was a boy came flooding back. And then could it be that the last lot of the auction was a smashed chandelier that rose phoenix-like from the stage and hovered over the auditorium like a living sword of Damocles? The audience would know at some point that the chandelier would come crashing down. And when did Christine give the Phantom back the ring? It's not in Leroux's novel.

Here was the plot I could fashion into the high romance I had been longing to write. I didn't say anything to Sarah until we returned to London, but when I did I had already thought of another plot twist. The Phantom has composed his own passionate opera for Christine to perform. Come its performance, the Phantom acts out his wildest fantasy by taking the lead opposite her himself. Christine publicly shames him by unmasking him in front of the entire opera house.

THE IDES OF MARCH had found me my dream subject. But as tends to be the way with Ides they also dealt me the worst mistake of my career whose expensive consequences still haunt me today. I agreed to let Brian Brolly float the Really Useful Group on the London Stock Exchange. There were two reasons. Negotiations to find a partner to finance the work on the Palace Theatre had got nowhere. Brian had given up on a partnership with Bernie Delfont. By selling shares via a public flotation, money could be raised, we could restore the theatre and be free from debt. Also Brian and I would raise a few bob for ourselves. I would have a contract with the company that specifically protected my controls over creative matters.

In reality, despite what my contract said, I was about to sell myself to the City and Wall Street. All financial analysts care about is next year's profits. Woe betide you if artistic decisions get in the way of what money men think is right. But at the time I had no clue of the problems I was bottling up for myself. I thought I would be even freer creatively, the Palace's restoration would be paid for and by being a public company Really Useful could develop areas unconnected with me so it wouldn't be entirely dependent on my writing. I hadn't a clue then that I had taken the most disastrous decision of my career. Brian began looking out for "names" as directors to come on our board. One of the first people to be offered a directorship of my company was Tim Rice.

WITH THE LAUNCH SETTLED I naively felt a huge weight lifted off me. I took a meeting with Kenneth MacMillan. Then I plunged into *The Phantom of the Opera* feet first. Never before or since have plot and music fallen into place so fast. Not everything was initially right but the structure I sketched is what is performed today. These are my notes for Act 1.

An auction in an about to be demolished opera house. Various plot related items are being sold. Among the bidders an old lady and old man Mm Giry and Raoul, Vicomte de Chagny. The items sold include a music box which Raoul buys (music note – start in dialogue and the first music should be from the music box, the first sung lines should be from Raoul). The final item sold is a broken chandelier from "the famous disaster." Magically the chandelier leaps into life. Before our eyes the opera house returns to its glory days with the shimmering chandelier hovering above us. (Organ chords, overture of Phantom theme played on pedals of vast organ with demi-semi quaver obbligato above.)

A rehearsal is taking place. New managers M Andre and M Firmin have just bought the opera house. The departing owner and the mysterious ballet mistress Mme Giry tell them that a Phantom haunts the building watching every opera from Box 5 which must be "kept empty" for him at all times. If not "a disaster beyond their imagination" will occur. (This scene should mostly be in dialogue to get through the plot asap but we must hear the opera they are rehearsing. Meyerbeer?) The

Phantom is obsessed with a young ditsy chorus girl Kristine Daae whose best mate is Mm Giry's ballet girl daughter Meg. The Phantom has been teaching Kristine to sing. He causes a piece of scenery to fall, narrowly missing the leading soprano La Carlotta. She flounces out plus the leading tenor Signor Piangi. She is replaced by Kristine who, after a nervous start, nails it with her aria (cue for big set piece song) and is immediately the talk of Paris. (We should also hear Carlotta sing this aria earlier.)

Next scene is Kristine's dressing room. Kristine explains to Meg that her strange teacher is her Angel of Music (important song tune in 3/4). Next post show wellwisher is a childhood friend, Raoul Vicomte de Chagny. He has fallen for her big time. (NB. weird stuff in the novel about Raoul and Kristine's childhood. Dark Nordic stories, gift for music!) This is overheard by an irate Phantom who lures her through a magic mirror and rows her across a lake beneath the opera house (organ chords, title song) to his subterranean lair.

There is a vast organ on which he composes. (NB He should be writing in a style outside the 19th century. . . . whole tone scale? also in the novel he's called Erik! no way — "Erik!" The Musical, bad title). The Phantom tells her that music irrevocably bonds them (cue for big song about being united in love through music etc). Night passes (have they been up to anything?!) Next morning the Phantom is composing. She pulls away the Phantom's mask to reveal that half his face is deformed. The Phantom goes tonto but then begs Kristine to see through his face into his soul (cue for major musical motif).

The Phantom returns Kristine. The opera managers are frantic that their young star has disappeared, as is Raoul. La Carlotta is overjoyed. However Kristine, to La Carlotta's irritation, reappears and in parallel the Phantom sends a note (find a motif that instantly identifies the Phantom), instructing that Kristine will again replace Carlotta in the next opera. The managers wave two fingers at this. (Not sure how to do all the above, lots of plot. Song about Box 5?) Carlotta performs in defiance of The Phantom and is humiliated as she ends up croaking like a toad. (Fun number, style Mozartian opera.)

In the bedlam that follows a stagehand Buquet, who knows too much, is found hanged. Raoul scoops Kristine up to the opera roof where the frightened girl spills out about the terrifying mesmerising figure in her life. Raoul says he will protect her. (Chance to write a big love duet! Precede by instrumental to show beauty of Paris from the rooftop.) Kristine is now in love with Raoul and agrees to leave Paris. This is overheard by the Phantom who in a heartbroken devastating rage causes the opera house chandelier to crash to the ground (repeat of love song and Phantom title song chords . . . where's Kristine – not sure). Act 2 to follow . . .

The question now was who could knock this into shape? Cameron and I approached Tom Stoppard who politely declined. Another thought was heavy metal god Jim Steinman. We met him over a fabulous lunch at Le Grand Véfour in Paris. The man who gave us *Bat Out of Hell* is a serious foodie and wine buff. He also has a serious restaurant ordering disorder. Years later when I worked with him on *Whistle Down the Wind* I discovered its full extent. One warm New York night six of us went to a Mexican restaurant. Jim studied the menu, then beckoned the head waiter over and drawled "We'll have one of everything."

The head honcho was perplexed. "Are you sure you mean one of everything, sir?"

Jim slowly pondered. "You're right," he mumbled. "We need six of everything."

Cameron and I were half an hour late when we arrived at Le Grand Véfour. Laid out in front of Jim was a row of decanters. Behind him was a line of bottles in ice buckets. "I couldn't decide which vintage of Latour to choose," said Jim.

I discovered Jim lived for Wagner, which figured. But he clearly observed rock'n'roll hours and our daylight meeting was probably a rarity. Cameron, having observed that Jim's milk white skin had obviously never seen the sun, wondered if we could install him in the cellar at Sydmonton and tell him it was night whenever we wanted to work. But Jim's commitments to *Bat Out of Hell* and our dates were never going to fit. Nevertheless I had made a loyal friend with whom I was to write "No Matter What," one of my biggest songs of the 1990s.

NEXT I CALLED RICHARD STILGOE. Richard is a serious opera buff and I figured his wit would keep the show from becoming turgid. I slated Act 1 for the 1985 Sydmonton Festival on Friday, July 5. One act should be enough to judge whether *Phantom* really had serious legs.

By now Cameron wasn't making the running. He had found another French fish to sauté. A year or so before someone had played him the French concept album of a short-running musical based on Victor Hugo's *Les Misérables* which had opened in Paris in 1980. Cameron spotted some strong songs and thought that Trevor, combined with the RSC's imprimatur, could be the right combination to rework it for an English speaking audience.

He first mentioned "*Les Mis*" at a lunch at Le Caprice and was bubbling over about approaching the one-time *Sunday Times* theatre critic and poet John Peter as lyricist who had found the last song of *Cats* particularly nauseating. He had even begun negotiations with Biddy Hayward about *Les Misérables* transferring to the Palace after its RSC run. Despite *Les Mis* we had been very much arm in arm on both *Song and Dance* and developing *Café Puccini* and once again Cameron realized how excited I now was about the *Phantom* idea as a subject for myself. When he heard the embryonic score he was unsure about Richard writing the words. But we agreed there was no harm in trying one act at Sydmonton which I slated for Friday night. *Café Puccini* would take the main full-length Saturday morning slot.

Cameron had one major suggestion. With John Napier busy on *Les Misérables*, he proposed Maria Bjornson to help with design and costumes. She had just done a magical production of *Camille* at the RSC. It was an inspired thought. He also volunteered the cast of the upcoming *Les Misérables*. I was thrilled. Colm Wilkinson, my original Che, had at last been cast in a lead theatrical role as Jean Valjean. He would play my Phantom. Although Sarah B was flying all over Europe giving *Requiem* performances she, of course, would be my Christine. May was taken up with writing. It poured out of me.

June dawned and it was time for a break. I had been invited along with composers Julie Styne and Cy Coleman to play at the Tony Awards. Unfortunately the 1985 season for musicals was not a vintage crop, some of the categories were even dropped and the pre-Tony nominees' party at the Plaza Hotel didn't promise a blast. Another downer was that there was an all-out strike of New York hotel staff.

To get to the party you had to brave an extremely hostile picket line. Something told me this was not the right forum to discuss the homilies about striking miners which Margaret Thatcher had imparted to me at a private Downing Street dinner the previous week. So narrowly avoiding a passing egg, I entered what can only be described as a rave for mortuary lovers. In a corner I spotted Hal Prince. He had been nominated as Best Director for a musical called *Grind* which even in this dire season had as much chance of winning as I had converting the pickets outside to Thatcherism. I suggested we leg it to somewhere marginally less lifeless. Before too long I found myself saying, "Hal, I guess you'd never think of directing a high romance?"

fully expecting the man who helmed *Company* and the minimalist *Evita* to change the subject to how the lemon crop was faring in Israel.

Instead he said, "You bet, kid, any ideas?"

I told him about *Phantom*, how the idea had come my way, how I had never thought of it as something for me and then by chance found the book. Hal said he was going to be in London in the last week of June. We made a date to meet at Sydmonton.

BACK IN LONDON I was gung-ho enough to book the Royal Philharmonic Orchestra to record backing tracks for the Festival at Olympic Studios. On June 23 Hal heard the first act score. He got the chandelier moment the first time he heard the organ overture which to this day is precisely as I played it to him on that summer day. To say he understood what I wanted to achieve was an understatement. The only sequence he thought was way below my best was "Box 5" which was rewritten after the Festival and became the Act 1 scene with the managers that ends with "Prima Donna."

Hal's other issue was that Richard's libretto had too many jokes, for instance the Mozartian spoof opera was called *Don Nero* which translates as "Don Black," a typical Stilgoism that Hal thought juvenile. We hugely agreed that Gaston Leroux was right to have the Phantom born with his hideous deformity. Some movie versions have strayed from this plot, for instance the Claude Rains has him disfigured by having printer's acid chucked over his face which utterly changes the tragic dynamic.

We parted company with a hand shake on Hal becoming *Phantom's* director. Cameron, however, had reservations. He was, of course, deeply dependent on Trevor and his team at the RSC with Trevor very much in the *Les Misérables* driving seat. So he strongly felt that Trevor should at least be considered. Furthermore Cameron was nervous that Hal had lost his way citing his most recent shows *Merrily We Roll Along, A Doll's Life* and *Grind* which had all been flops.

Immediately I was in an awkward position. My gut told me that Trevor would have problems with the story. His intellect would demand explanations where you have to take a dollop of hokum as a given. Hal is a master showman and a showman was what I passionately believed *Phantom* needed. Anyhow Trevor was up to his eyeballs in *Les Misérables*. But not quite enough to prevent him checking out *Phantom* at Sydmonton.

37

"Big Change from Book"

Three musicals were performed at the 1985 Sydmonton Festival: *Café Puccini*, *Phantom* and Howard Goodall's *Girlfriends*. The Festival theatre lives in the tiny former St Mary's Church in our garden. Inside the layout has been flipped around so the tiny 20 foot by 14 foot stage is opposite where the altar would have been. There is a small gallery above the stage where we all but suffocate our long-suffering perspiring musicians. It was from here that Maria Bjornson launched the Phantom chandelier. Not content with that, she also somehow concertina'd the Phantom's boat under the bell tower. There is no element of the finished *Phantom* production that has played the world over that Maria didn't miraculously fit on a stage roughly the dimensions of a boxing ring.

We had indeed pillaged the upcoming *Les Misérables* cast, Colm Wilkinson as Phantom, Clive Carter as Raoul with Myra Sands, our original Gumbie Cat as La Carlotta and of course Sarah B as Kristin (the "e" had been dropped from her name). The Sydmonton production was directed by Trevor Nunn's associate director Dion McHugh. I had asked Hal if he wanted to be involved but he rightly suggested that at this early stage I should plough my own furrow.

The performance started just after 10 pm with the audience very merry after an Italian themed dinner featuring a superb Barolo. Hence the auction was greeted with much merriment. Precisely the same lots were sold as in the show today; the poster of *Hannibal*, the collection of human skulls from a Meyerbeer production. There was laughter through the sale of the music box with a monkey playing the cymbals. But when the chord "cluster" began which precedes Raoul singing "A collector's piece indeed" to the musical motif that permeates the whole evening, it was as if a blast of freezing air had hit the auditorium.

The chandelier glimmered at the back of the gallery high above the stage and glided on a track towards the audience like a ship from another galaxy. The overture was exactly the same as now. The first difference was that the opera being rehearsed in the first scene was not *Hannibal* but *The Man in the Iron Mask*. This allowed Richard loose with the gags. La Carlotta questioned a gaoler about where her lover was incarcerated, to be greeted with a muffled cry of "I'm down here." Our Barolo-filled audience laughed lustily. But "Angel of Music" was the same as now (Meg beautifully played by the dancer Jacqui Harman) as was "The Phantom" title song and "The Music of the Night," although the lyric then had a completely different emphasis on the melody in the second half of the verse. Colm sang it brilliantly and almost stopped the show. Sarah showed her dancer's training and choreographed the song herself which she repeated under Gillian's eye with Michael Crawford a year later.

The managers' scene was as Hal said not up to scratch. It was inexplicably titled "Papers" and although I used fragments of its melody in today's show, the scene has been decently interred. Things looked up with *Don Nero* which was the same, except today it has the less jokey title *Il Muto*. The rooftop scene played exactly as it does now. The music deliberately continues after "All I Ask of You" to keep the audience's applause pent up until the end of Act 1. If I hadn't composed it that way the song would have been our second showstopper. As it was, they fell silent as Colm appeared high above the stage in the little musician's gallery with the Phantom's "I gave you my music" verse, another section to survive intact.

As we dropped the chandelier, the house went black. It was supposed to stop just short of the audience's heads although *Sun* editor

Kelvin MacKenzie claimed it hit his, at least he said as much when he broke the Festival rule of silence on a radio show the following week. I think he got up early to be first at the post show bar. The *Phantom* audience was strong on powerful media types that year. David Frost joined Robert Maxwell and Andrew Neil to debate "Sydmonton fears for the future of the press." The house won.

We only performed the first act – the second was yet to be written – and I can't say *Phantom* was the Festival's runaway hit. *Café Puccini* was the one everyone thought was the banker and a fair chunk of our audience agreed with Cameron's "concern," as he put it, about the depth of the libretto. But I learned what I needed to know. *Phantom* had the potential to be something special.

THE TABLES HAD HARDLY been cleared from the garden when I received a missive from Trevor Nunn. It said he had come to Sydmonton under the misapprehension that he was being sounded out as *Phantom*'s director, that Cameron had sent him the Leroux novel and that I had once suggested he looked at the silent movie so therefore he had "cancelled a rehearsal at Glyndebourne" to be at Sydmonton, assuming he had been asked to do "background research on a forthcoming project." He also said he had been told by Cameron that Jim Sharman was no longer attached to the project, which seemed curious as Jim never was, and that on Sunday "Cameron told me that Hal Prince had been approached to direct the show – and I experienced the muck sweat in which I am still covered."

This was clearly a sticky situation. I telexed Cameron to say the show wasn't even finished and please "not to take umbrage" but not to tout it around at this stage and his *Les Mis* director might need a shower. Cameron replied "no umbrage taken," that he hadn't offered the show to Trevor and that he had been "purely trying to ascertain interest in case circumstances, and indeed timing, would prove Trevor the natural choice." He also said he had "taken the precaution

as we discussed of telling Trevor that there was strong interest from
Hal Prince." Cameron also said that Trevor was taken aback that I
had used the melody for which he had written lyrics about a married
man as "The Music of the Night." I explained that I thought he knew
that no record company fancied them. I was also in the dog house
with Sarah B about this tune. I had written it for her and now I'd
given it to a masked bloke.

THE WEEKS AFTER THE Festival saw Sarah performing "Pie Jesu"
in front of Princess Diana at our neighbouring church at Highclere
Castle, nowadays better known as the TV set for *Downton Abbey*.
Carolyn, the daughter of its owner, the Queen's horse racing manager
Henry, the Earl of Carnarvon, was getting hitched to John Warren
who today performs the same role for Her Majesty. Princess Diana
was a guest of honour along with Prince Andrew – it was that sort of
occasion – but it was a joy to perform "Pie Jesu" at the wedding of the
beautiful Carolyn and the vastly entertaining John, even if the meaning of the Latin words was Greek to them. Sarah also auditioned for
the role of Valencienne in *The Merry Widow* which Sadler's Wells
Opera were performing in November and won the role. She had
achieved her ambition of performing with a proper opera company.

After *Requiem*'s Scottish debut in Glasgow, Sarah and I flew to
Sydney where *Cats* was opening. Following that we planned a few
days' holiday on the Barrier Reef. Then it was back to New York
for the opening of *Song and Dance*. We nearly didn't make it. The
helicopter we'd commandeered to speed us to our coral reef hideaway was about ten feet off the ground when its pilot cried out "This
emu's as useless as tits on a bull." Then it plummeted to earth with a
medium-sized thump. The expletives that followed – example: "This
fucking bee's dick was bought from a son of a bitch sheepshagger"
which translates I think as "this helicopter was purchased from a
New Zealander" – made me thankful that Auntie Vi wasn't born

Australian. No way were we game for a second try, so we took an equally terrifying boat trip through the enveloping windswept night with a captain who loudly sang "I Saw Mommy Kissing Santa Claus," a curious choice for July. Meanwhile his stoned daughter sucked air out of the boat's diesel pump. Fellini couldn't have filmed a better journey to Hades.

Somehow we made it to our fivestar hostelry where we were shown into a sort of corrugated iron shack which we were informed was our private resort villa. Sarah and I were knackered, so we hit the sack only to be awoken by a violent banging noise. I am well known for being quick and brave under duress so I sent Sarah out to investigate. Our private resort villa was being butted by a medium-sized goat.

Next morning Sarah threw back the curtains and we got the first view of our Barrier Reef paradise. I don't know if you've ever seen the mud flats around Foulness on the Thames Estuary, but add a touch of unrelenting sunshine and you've pretty much got our panorama. To be fair once the tide turned things looked up considerably. Sarah sunned herself on the beach and practised scales with a voice-coaching tape on her cassette machine.

I sat under an umbrella and sketched Act 2 of *Phantom*. I had already written the moment when the Phantom substitutes himself in his own opera and written the melody that became "The Point of No Return." Leroux's novel suggested the subject of the Phantom's opera, *Don Juan Triumphant*. Now I had to construct the storyline up to it. What better way to begin the second act than a glamorous masked ball to celebrate the installation of a new and improved chandelier?

At the celebration's climax the Phantom makes his Paganini-inspired "red death" entrance and delivers the score of the opera he has composed for Kristin. By this time she is happily engaged to Raoul and refuses to sing it. Raoul clocks that if Kristin performs the Phantom is bound to watch her. With Kristin as bait he will be ensnared. Kristin's dilemma is huge. She knows once she hears the Phantom's music again she will be inexorably drawn to him. His music touches her soul. Yet her head knows that she must resist its power.

I now had the moment for Kristin's big second act aria and what became my favourite section of all of *Phantom*, "Twisted Every Way." It is derived from the secondary "counter melody" of the last verse of "Prima Donna." I still have a quirky superstition about it: every time I begin work on a new piano I quietly play it to myself. It's the heart of *Phantom* and for this reason I quote it in *Love Never Dies*. It reminds me of the best moments of my marriage to Sarah B. For me nobody has sung it better and nobody ever will.

I set Kristin's second act aria in the graveyard where her father was buried. The melody of "Wishing You Were Somehow Here Again" came quickly. I had already composed the Phantom's *Don Juan Triumphant* aria along with his pathetic lovelorn reprise of "All I Ask of You" which leads to Kristin knowingly publicly unmasking him, the biggest plot change from Leroux's novel. Now I had to find a discordant idiom for his "modern" opera. I decided to park this until I got home. My final notes from the Barrier Reef include the musical sketch for the "Phantom's lair" scene. The Phantom is both furious and in despair, thanks to Kristin humiliating him in front of Le Tout Paris. His rage is abated by the arrival of Raoul who has, with the aid of Mme Giry, discovered the Phantom's hideaway. The Phantom traps Raoul (my notes don't say how) and gives Kristin a choice; either spend the rest of her life as Mrs Phantom or her lover dies.

I wrote in underlined capital letters "big change from book," followed by "Kristin takes pity on POTO and passionately kisses him to an orchestral reprise of Angel Of Music. Genuine love or knowing and cynical? Or both?"

Kristin's kiss, the first taste of love the Phantom has ever tasted, causes him to set the two young lovers free. They leave but Kristin briefly returns to give the Phantom back the ring he once gave her as his keepsake. It is too much for the Phantom. He is broken by losing the only person who has ever shown him what he craves for. Love. Sarah and I returned home with my mind whirring. I wanted to plough on and finish *Phantom*, but *Song and Dance*'s opening on Broadway loomed.

AT THE END OF August Cameron and I flew to New York for the dress rehearsals. Of course *Phantom* was high on the agenda during the flight. Cameron was effervescent about how brilliantly Trevor was handling *Les Misérables* at the RSC. He told me that John Napier's design for the barricades included a stunning *coup de théâtre* and it became very clear that he wanted Trevor and John to pitch for *Phantom*. This was a nightmare. Hal was staying at Le Meurice in Paris, and I had kept him up to date with my progress. Yet I depended on Cameron and me being joined at the hip for the next few weeks in New York. I couldn't very well refuse to hear what Trevor and John had to say. So I agreed to meet them once *Song and Dance* was out of the way.

When I got to the Ritz-Carlton there was a message from Roy Disney Jr, son of Roy Sr, co-founder with younger brother Walt, of the Walt Disney Company. He wanted to meet me about composing an animated musical of *The Little Mermaid*. I was intrigued. Roy Disney brought with him his senior executive Jeffrey Katzenberg who with Michael Eisner was to spectacularly revive the fortunes of the then ailing studio. Roy gave me a huge selection of storyboards with beautifully drawn mermaids and sundry other inhabitants from the sea's lower regions.

My body language probably didn't suggest enthusiasm, what with *Song and Dance* opening and *Phantom* being my next project. But I did promise to look at the script once I had a moment. It was impossible not to be drawn to a story about a mermaid who gives up a glorious singing voice to become a human. After all Burne-Jones's most enigmatic painting is his extraordinary celebration of the mermaid's power in *The Depths of the Sea*. However Valerie Eliot's story about Eliot turning Disney down reverberated as I said goodbye. I suspected my take on the Hans Christian Andersen story would be darker than anything Disney would fancy. How stupid was I?

A few months later I wrote a song for the mermaid which I got very excited about. So I called Roy Disney and had a conversation in which I sensed he had been moved sideways. Anyway it was too late. Disney had moved on.

SONG AND DANCE WAS in good shape. A heap of work had been done by Richard Maltby on the *Song/Tell Me* half. Richard had wanted new songs from Don and me of which the best was "English Girls," whose plot was that an English accent could work wonders for a single girl in LA. The previews were totally sold out so the show played to a real audience, not the usual preview house papered with freebies. The reaction was the strongest and certainly the jolliest I can remember of any show of mine on Broadway until *School of Rock* in 2015. Cameron and the Shuberts were convinced we had a hit. I felt so confident that I flew Mum over for the opening, Sarah got time off from her *Merry Widow* rehearsals and brought her parents. We all looked forward to the happy opening of a big audience pleaser.

It was not to be. The New York critics pretty much dumped it. If it hadn't been for my head being so firmly in *Phantom* I would have hit the blues big time. What I found most curious was how the *New York Times* critic Frank Rich changed his mind about my *Variations* which he had found "delightful" in London. Not a note had been changed. The London critics had been almost unanimously positive about the music of both *Tell Me* and *Variations*, so had many of the American writers reviewing the original albums. I couldn't help feeling that my worst fears in America were coming true. Had I been right about that *Time* magazine mega story? Should *Requiem* have premiered in the Bronx rather than a ritzy church on Fifth Avenue? But it might just have been that *Song and Dance* was perceived as an attempt to capitalize on the success of *Cats*. It was, after all, merely billed in London as a limited season "concert for the theatre."

Cameron ankled back to London asap. Previews of *Les Misérables* at the RSC were days away and he needed to check what tightrope Phineas T. Nunn, as he had taken to calling Trevor, was traversing with his French baby. I followed on with my tail faintly rising between my legs because the Broadway *Song and Dance* business was OK. It wasn't going to do a lot for Bernie and Gerry's pension fund, but the show ran fourteen months, better than a slap in the face with a medium-sized fish for two albums that were never conceived for the theatre in the first place.

Eight Tony nominations ended in a win for Bernadette as Best Actress in a Musical. A sadness was that she had frightful flu problems during the cast album sessions so it's not the best record of a wonderful stage performance. *Cats'* great Grizabella Betty Buckley took over from Bernadette in the final few weeks. I love Betty to bits but I'm not sure that she was born to play a twenty-something English girl from Muswell Hill.

BACK AT HOME SARAH was gearing up for her Sadler's Wells debut. I began *Phantom* work with Richard, whilst planning how to get the music on radio. The *Phantom* title song was the obvious frontrunner, especially as we already had Mike Batt's great track up our sleeve. Mike suggested Cockney Rebel lead singer Steve Harley to duet with Sarah. I understood where Mike was coming from. Steve made no secret that he had polio as a kid and had triumphed over its consequences by becoming a huge Seventies glam rock star. He hadn't had a hit for a while but Mike had recently worked with him and was adamant he could strut the stuff.

Polydor loved the single and wanted a crazy video to go with it. Who better for such a task than Ken Russell? He duly outdid himself with serpents, graveyards and sundry appropriate Gothic paraphernalia. Meanwhile Cameron was pressuring me to talk once again to Trevor who had found time during *Les Misérables'* birth pangs to discuss *Phantom* with John Napier. They proposed that the set should be a sideways cut-away profile of the opera house showing the stage, orchestra pit and auditorium complete with its chandelier.

It was a radically different take on how to stage the show from mine. I wanted the chandelier to rise up and hover over the audience as it had at Sydmonton. I was going to have to say no to the two friends and colleagues who had brilliantly brought my cats to life and I am hopeless at this sort of confrontation. What made it worse was that *Les Misérables* had opened at the RSC to largely negative reviews. Of course it is theatre legend that the public quickly proved the critics wrong. Indeed what now happened with *Les Mis* demonstrated how clever Cameron had been. If *Les Mis* had opened cold in the West End the reviews probably would have knackered it. But the RSC has an inbuilt audience no matter what, enough to ensure that word of mouth counteracts a critical mauling if the punters like the show. Cameron had brilliantly harnessed a subsidized theatre not only to provide production facilities but also an audience as insurance against pissy aisle scribblers.

However when we met the future of *Les Mis* looked dicey. I feared that both Trevor and Cameron would think it was the reviews that were the reason for my insisting the director must be Hal. Cameron seemed curiously disturbed when I stood my ground. Years later I discovered the reason. Although I still presumed that Hal was to be our director, in fact he had been stood down. I also learned that Hal blamed me for this and I was appalled. It's best left at that. Anyway, the circumstances meant that Hal was able to extract a killer deal from Cameron for *Phantom*. Come early November he was installed at the Savoy, Maria Bjornson was confirmed as designer, Gillian Lynne was under instructions to deliver a Degas vision of ballet girls and the Mackintosh/Webber duo was back in business.

38

Year of the Phantom

1985 bowed out gracefully. *Merry Widow* critics concluded that Sarah B could sing and dance the can-can at the same time. We had Imo and Nick for Christmas plus the Brightman clan which was great. Sydmonton leapt into life; there were carols at midnight, Christmas presents under the tree and a disaster involving Sangster the tailless Manx cat and the turkey. On Boxing Day we were back in London to launch the Ken Russell video of *Phantom*'s title song on the primetime TV Terry Wogan show. On December 28 Polydor reported the single was selling.

I spent the dying days of the year with David Caddick, by now my full-time musical right-hand man, and Biddy Hayward who had joined the board of the imminently "public" Really Useful Group. "Group" had been substituted for "Company" because the name abbreviated to RUC which also stood for the Royal Ulster Constabulary, the Northern Ireland police force. With the "troubles" in Ireland far from over, city analysts thought this was undesirable. They feared headlines like "RUC Chief in Record Ransom Kidnap" would do little for the share price.

RUG's flotation was scheduled for January 6. Apart from grinning inanely for the City press, this was Brian Brolly's turf. Grey, Earl of Gowrie became chairman. I had suggested him which the City loved. Grey was formerly the Tory Arts Minister who resigned from government saying he couldn't afford to live in London on a minister's pay. He subsequently exercised his consummate diplomatic skills as

Sotheby's highly successful chairman as well as being really useful. Brian Brolly was CEO. Biddy Hayward became an executive director with responsibility for theatre production and the Palace Theatre. I became a non-executive director alongside Tim Rice who now formally joined the board with a preferential share deal and access to privileged information about what I and the company were up to. The lineup was completed by Richard Baker Wilbraham, a professional city board member who was there to reassure shareholders everything was kosher.

The production slate David, Biddy and I chewed over was formidable. First up was Kenneth MacMillan's *Requiem* with American Ballet Theatre which kicked off in Chicago on February 7. It then pirouetted via Los Angeles around America until it landed in the Met in New York in early May. Sarah was booked for key performances between *Requiem* premieres in Vienna and Stuttgart and promotion of the *Phantom* single. David was deputed to supervise whilst I was left with an alarming amount of press and TV that I had stupidly agreed to do.

Obstacle B was that I was producing a farce written by American writer Ken Ludwig about a famous opera tenor failing to turn up for a sold-out performance of Verdi's *Otello* and a nobody standing in for him. Then the famous tenor *does* turn up with awkward consequences. Its title was *Opera Buffa* which I hated. So it was renamed *Lend Me a Tenor* thanks to Richard Stilgoe. Amazingly, considering the extremely un-PC mistaken identity plot involving two performers "blacking up" and even more surprisingly since the play was produced by me, when the comedy made Broadway it elicited a rave review from the *New York Times*'s Frank Rich as "one of the two great farces by a living writer."

I took the first meetings with Ken Ludwig and its director David Gilmore of *Daisy* fame and left rehearsals to them, planning to interfere when the cast was ready for a run-through. The West End opening was March 6 at the Globe Theatre to follow *Daisy* which I was closing after 1180 performances to begin a UK tour.

Item 3 was *Café Puccini*. I had taken my eye off this one which Cameron and I had slated to open in the jewel box Wyndham's Theatre the week after *Lend Me a Tenor* opened. Cameron's office was running the production and our writer Robin Ray and director Chris Renshaw had been at it since Sydmonton. They seemed to know what they were doing, rehearsals were going well, so I let it be.

ON JANUARY 2, 1986, Sarah and I had a quiet dinner at the Greenhouse round the corner from our flat. We had a lot to think about. We were sanguine about Really Useful going public. Both of us naively thought the suits could run the business whilst I wrote whatever whenever I liked. The flotation augured well and Brian and I would take some dosh out of the business, although the lion's share was earmarked for restoring the Palace Theatre. We talked a lot about *Phantom*. We guessed the single would be a medium-sized hit. In fact it turned out better and was a solid Top 10 entry peaking at No. 7. We talked about how Sarah's ambitions fitted with us having children but decided kids had better wait.

I remember thinking Sarah's professional dedication was staggering. She had doubled her singing lessons and spiced them up with twice daily dance classes. There was a lot of holding hands as we talked about how great Christmas had been with Imo and Nick. Imo would be nine next March and was forming a real bond with Sarah. I took a deep breath and said I wanted to buy my first Sarah a house in the country. It was a gesture I really wanted to make. *Cats* was doing far better around the world than I had thought at the time of my divorce. Sarah B totally agreed.

Over coffee I pined for my Mediterranean days with Auntie Vi. Sarah, who doesn't drink, said I always did in January after a bottle of wine and that if I really missed the Riviera I should buy a house there and stop wittering. Sarah looked ravishingly Pre-Raphaelite that night and I suddenly felt very protective of her, yet I also felt slightly scared. Sarah's work meant she was increasingly away from home. Less than two years into our marriage there was often no one to come home to. Sarah's stint in *The Merry Widow* had shown me how hard it is to be married to someone whose day job is in the evenings. Also we were spending less and less time at Sydmonton. Was it that Sarah B would always associate Sydmonton with my previous marriage? The countryside was hardly her natural habitat. What if we bought a home together in France? Maybe she would feel it was hers. That's exactly what we did and three days later we were on a flight to Nice.

THE HOUSE WE BOUGHT was called La Chabanne on the Pointe Saint Hospice of Cap Ferrat. Unlike the local grand Riviera villas, it was a modest stone built farmhouse that had been fleshed out in an endearingly unsuccessful bid to keep up with the neighbours. It needed totally rebuilding but it was slap on the sea with a staggering two hectares of flat land.

There we caught the last days of the Golden Riviera with neighbours like Harding Lawrence, the maverick titan of the aviation industry and his wife Mary Wells. Mary was the first lady of advertising who dreamed up the brightly painted tailfins of her husband's Braniff Airways. Famously she was the first woman CEO of a US quoted company. We made friends like Roger Moore, Michael and Shakira Caine, Maurice Saatchi and his late wife, the glorious eccentric Irish author Josephine Hart and Leslie Bricusse, the songwriter who has composed more hits than anyone I know but nobody realizes, plus his glamorous wife Evie, of whom we were in awe because she had co-starred in the movie *Double Trouble* with Elvis Presley under her stage name Yvonne Romain.

Twenty years ago the Riviera completely changed. It seemed to happen overnight. We never used to lock a door but suddenly there were horror stories of burglars putting gas into the air-conditioning, kidnappings and worse. I sold La Chabanne to a fellow Brit who flipped it two years later for about five times what I sold it for. I'm told La Chabanne has been torn down and the land redeveloped. I can't bring myself to go back and look. I had some of the best times of my life there.

I CAUGHT UP WITH Kenneth MacMillan's *Requiem* in Chicago. Mikhail Baryshnikov had been forced to pull out through a recurring injury but Alessandra Ferri was astonishing even to my untrained eye. Kenneth had amplified a story that had deeply affected me during *Requiem*'s composition about a Cambodian child forced to choose between killing his sister or himself. He cast a brilliant young boy dancer, Gil Boggs, now director of Colorado Ballet, to dance to the singing boy soprano. I found many of the sequences with the gorgeously lissome Alessandra curiously disturbing as was the Daliesque set and costumes by Yolanda Sonnabend, Kenneth's frequent collaborator who shared my devotion to Burmese cats.

But truthfully I never could get my head round *Requiem* as a ballet. The soloists were mired invisibly with the orchestra in the pit and I found watching the dancers mirroring their singing very discombobulating. There were some powerful moments but for me it didn't gel, despite achieving far better reviews for the music when it got to the Met than it had received the previous year.

JUST BEFORE *CAFÉ PUCCINI*'S dress rehearsal I got a call from Buckingham Palace. The Queen's youngest son, HRH Prince Edward, wanted to meet me. We fixed a date at the Green Street flat. It was the Queen's 60th birthday in June and he wondered if I could compose something special which could also celebrate his father the Duke of Edinburgh's 65th. He had a pageant in mind at Windsor Castle. Edward was charming. It was obvious he was stagestruck and hadn't a clue what to do about it. We discussed what the pageant could be about and the usual thoughts about highlights of the Queen's reign were tossed around. Edward needed a quick answer. I explained I had two West End openings over the next few days but I'd come back to him within a week. I also suggested he met Biddy Hayward. It wasn't long before Biddy had Prince Edward working in my theatre department.

Lend Me a Tenor opened well and ran for a year, not as long as *Daisy*, but it spawned a Broadway production. *Café Puccini* was a disaster. Shoehorned into a conventional proscenium theatre, it lost its charm: the audience was observing the goings on in a cafe rather than being in the cafe and being part of it. Cameron and I knew we had screwed up and consoled ourselves with the thought that London doesn't have spaces where you can stage this sort of theatre. We closed the show immediately.

Phantom was accelerating fast by this time. Hal was getting on famously with Maria Bjornson so the design was moving on apace. Hal had done some work with Steve Harley and wasn't averse to him playing the Phantom. The single was now in the Top 10 and picking up massive radio play. Abetted by the Ken Russell video, some press pundits had already presumed Sarah and Steve were our stars.

I got Steve to sing "The Music of the Night" on the unreleased orchestral track of "Married Man," the song I had originally written with Trevor Nunn. We were really pleased with his vocal in the studio, but back home I had doubts, particularly about his diction. Cameron and David Caddick were also seriously worried whether Steve could sustain eight live performances a week. One evening I picked Sarah up from her vocal lesson with Ian Adam. Ian had already coached Steve and had a lot of time for him. But he too knew how operatic the score was and worried that Steve would be out of his depth. Suddenly Ian cut to the chase. "You need Michael Crawford."

I was taken aback. Michael Crawford was best known in Britain as Frank Spencer, the gormless high pitch voiced rather effeminate star of the BBC's smash hit comedy series *Some Mothers Do 'Ave 'Em*. True in 1969 he had co-starred with Barbra Streisand in the movie of *Hello, Dolly!* and was currently the lead in *Barnum* at the Victoria Palace. I had seen him walk that famous tightrope a few years before at the London Palladium. It was a charismatic bravura performance but nothing suggested Michael had the vocal chops to handle what I had written nor had his vocally bantamweight performance in *Billy*, Don Black and John Barry's musical based on *Billy Liar* which I had seen with Tim Rice on the night of the coat saga.

However I also recalled seeing Michael in the late Seventies in a musical by Charles Strouse, the composer of *Nightingale*, called *Flowers for Algernon*. Michael played a mentally retarded man whose only friend is a pet mouse. There was a staggering scene in which a mouse ran all over his shoulders. Years later Michael did a variation with a rat when he played Count Fosco in my *The Woman in White*. Although *Flowers for Algernon* had been a disaster on both sides of the Atlantic, I found Michael's performance intensely moving. Ian offered to discreetly get me a tape of Michael singing opera. The moment I heard it, I had to meet Michael. It took a bit of doing. Michael was paranoid about secrecy. He insisted the venue for our tête-à-tête was the Angus Steakhouse right next to the Victoria Palace – a bit too close to the stage door to my view, but Michael's reasoning was that nobody we knew could possibly go there. Michael was right. It was deserted, apart from a wizened Polish couple in a corner who I was quite certain were spies. He agreed to meet me again to hear the score.

Come early February the *Phantom* team was seriously anxious about the libretto. So Cameron went to see Richard Stilgoe at his BBC TV dressing room in Lime Grove Studios having sounded out his old friend Alan Jay Lerner about collaborating on the lyrics. I don't precisely know how the meeting went, but very soon afterwards

Cameron arranged lunch with myself, Richard and Alan to listen to Alan's observations. Richard was understandably uncomfortable but it was hard not to hear out the lyricist of *My Fair Lady*. Cameron suggested that Alan took the libretto, worked with me for a while and then we'd all discuss the revised version.

I had my first solo meeting with Alan at Cameron's top-floor flat in Montagu Square. Alan had great difficulty climbing the long flight of stairs. He had to sit down on a half-landing to get his breath back and I remember his colour was alabaster. But he had become passionate about our project and had a lot of time for Richard's material. He particularly liked many of the song titles, but did think there was much work to do. He was adamant we first tackled the Act 2 opener "Masquerade." We blanked March out to begin, but fate had already decreed that I was not to work with this legend. A few days later Alan was diagnosed with terminal cancer. This is his letter of March 31:

Dearest Andrew,

Who would have thought it? Instead of writing "The Phantom of the Opera" I end up looking like him.

But, alas, the inescapable fact is I have lung cancer. After fiddling around with pneumonia they finally reach the conclusion that it was the big stuff.

I am deeply disconsolate about "The Phantom" and the wonderful opportunity it would have been to write with you. But I will be back! Perhaps not on time to write "The Phantom," but as far as I am concerned this is a temporary hiccup. I have a fifty percent chance medically and a fifty percent chance spiritually. I shall make it. I have no intention of leaving my beautiful wife, this beautiful life and all of the things I still have to write. As far as I am concerned it is a challenge, and I fear nothing.

But I shall be thinking of you, and Sarah, and Richard, and Cameron all the way, and I know you will have the success God knows you deserve. It is a wonderful score and I am heartbroken that I cannot get a crack at it.

I will be in touch with you over the summer just to let you know I am up and around and thinking of you, and I hope with all my heart that one day we will have a chance to work together.

Blessings always to you and Sarah. Aye,
Alan

Alan Jay Lerner died on June 14, 1986.

39

In Another Part of the West End Forest . . .

Cameron and I were now up the proverbial shit's creek. The meetings with Alan had proved the libretto needed help. We met with Herbert Kretzmer, whom Cameron had brought into the *Les Misérables* team as lyricist after he fired John Peter. It led nowhere. In desperation we eyed the entries of the 1986 Vivian Ellis Prize, a worthy but now defunct annual event to discover new musicals. I was intrigued by the lyrics of *Moll Flanders* by a young writer called Charles Hart. Cameron summoned him to his office.

Charles transpired to be a tall, dark, pencil-thin well-spoken 25-year-old. He was understandably overwhelmed but highly composed, so we asked him to do some sample lyrics to a music only tape of three songs. In a few days we were looking at three replacement lyrics. The first was for Kristin's opening aria "What Has Time Done to Me" retitled "Think of Me," then a revised lyric of the Act 1 managers' scene and a hopeless version of Kristin's graveyard aria whose lyric I have lost. I liked the simplicity of "Think of Me." Cameron thought Charlie had sharpened the managers' scene without ditching the essence of Richard's work. We showed the rewrites to Hal, who was impressed so Cameron arranged for the two to meet. Hal probed Charlie about his back story. He had trained at the Guildhall School of Music and his grandmother was Angela Baddeley, the lead in Hal's

London production of *A Little Night Music*. That clinched it with the Prince of Broadway.

Next we introduced Charlie to Richard. It was one thing asking Richard to take a back seat to Alan Jay Lerner, but this was different. Richard understandably found it much harder to accept an unknown on board and withdrew. Happily time and Charlie's work proved a great healer. There's nothing that a hit can't cure and everyone's friends now.

IN ANOTHER PART OF the West End forest a bombshell was announced. Trevor Nunn was replacing Michael Bennett as director of Tim Rice's musical *Chess*. Tim's collaboration with the ABBA writers had spawned a huge hit concept album around the world and the Shuberts were now driving the juggernaut. I had been kept up to date with the show's progress by Michael Bennett who the Shuberts had announced as director with every trumpet available within ear-bashing distance of Times Square. But although it was kept secret, AIDS was fast overtaking Michael and on January 28, 1986 the *New York Times* reported that Trevor had been parachuted into the driving seat for a May London opening.

I learned recently he wasn't Tim and the ABBA boys' first choice. According to Hal Prince, on January 23 Tim, Benny and Björn descended on the Savoy Hotel and called him in his room as he was just about to leave for a working *Phantom* dinner at the Green Street flat. Hal was obviously in London for *Phantom* pre-production but, not knowing what they wanted, he agreed to give the threesome ten minutes in the American Bar. He was astonished to be asked if he could get *Phantom* postponed so he could replace Michael Bennett as director of *Chess*.

AT THE TIME I was of course oblivious to Tim's attempt to hijack Hal. Although we had last worked together in 1976 I had asked him to be a director of my company because I still clung to the hope we'd collaborate again one day. We had edged a bit closer in the early 1980s when we bunkered up in Michel Guérard's nouvelle cuisine palace in Éugenie-les-Bains trying to musicalize David Garnett's novella *Aspects of Love*.

But I did know that Tim had not jumped at being involved in *Phantom*. The year before there had been an embarrassing incident as a result of Robert Stigwood coming to dinner at Sydmonton. I played Robert the *Phantom* score and he went bonkers about the music saying it was the most exciting I had ever written. But he was no fan of the lyrics. To my horror Robert then and there phoned Tim at home at Romeyns Court. Tim was slap in the middle of a dinner party and was understandably unkeen to be dragged out of it. Robert pronounced that he was driving over immediately with me and my *Phantom* tapes and that he didn't care a monkey's about Tim's dinner guests. He was going to listen to his old partner's greatest ever score, like it or not. We then drove over in Robert's old white Rolls, me silent, Robert saying I was about to have the biggest hit of my career and Tim was going to be part of it come hell or high water. Poor Tim was dragged out of his dinner and forced to listen to the tapes in his study. I just sat there, cripplingly embarrassed.

If I had known about that Savoy Hotel meeting I wonder if I would have invited Tim to co-write the celebration for the Queen's 60th birthday. Tim said yes before I put the phone down. We met the next day. We rejected Prince Edward's pageant idea for a short musical about Tim's favourite subject, cricket. I said horse racing was HM's passion. We agreed to a plot that featured both.

I called Edward to propose ditching the pageant for a mini-musical. He was a bit nonplussed. For openers there was no theatre in Windsor Castle. But he agreed to meet Biddy Hayward and my team and together they came up with the idea of making a temporary theatre for the royal dinner guests in Windsor Castle chapel. Somehow Edward persuaded the highly protective bosses of the Royal Household to say yes. As *Chess* had opened successfully I felt I could call Trevor Nunn. Next day Prince Edward was the producer of the new Rice/Lloyd Webber musical *Cricket* directed by Trevor Nunn, playing one night only on June 18 in the Chapel Royal, Windsor Castle. Edward had pulled off a reunion that had defied top theatre producers for almost a decade.

Cricket turned out to be a P.G. Wodehouse affair with characters like Wittering, played by Tim, and Vincent St Leger, a spivvy bookmaker given life by aging rocker Alvin Stardust. Since it was a one-off event and had to be written quickly, I borrowed a few ideas, mostly from my next show *Aspects of Love*. One that wasn't was "The Art of Bowling," sung by an intimidating fast bowler called Winston:

> *The art of bowling*
> *Is very subtle*
> *For those who doubt it*
> *Here's a rebuttal*
> *From Lords to Sydney*
> *Or in Barbados*
> *Batsmen remember*
> *When they have played us*

However there was one melody destined for bigger things . . . see if you can work out the tune from these words.

> *I'll never make another*
> *Confident prediction*
> *Except for one*
> *All said and done worth hearing*
> *That the narrow minds of morning*
> *Will be breaking out this evening*
> *A life can change in one hot afternoon*

Sarah Payne sang it as Emma Kirkstall, daughter of the Earl of Headingly. You might recognize the scansion of "As If We Never Said Goodbye."

TREVOR AND I WATCHED the performance from the chapel Gallery with the entire Royal Family gathered downstairs. The Queen and Duke of Edinburgh made polite noises. After the show Princess Diana rather obviously detached herself from the rest of the royals and moaned that she couldn't make her entrance to the upcoming ball before the Queen made hers. I didn't care that much. The cast, Tim, Trevor and I were not invited to the ball as we were staff. Instead we had a jolly dinner in an Indian restaurant on the way to Eton. When less than a year later Biddy installed Prince Edward in my theatre division, the British press dubbed him "the tea boy."

A few miles on the Thames upstream from Windsor, something was happening that had a rather more lasting effect on my life. Two days later a triumphant Hal bade Cameron and me to a mask workshop in the Thameside village of Pangbourne where he and Maria unveiled the famous Phantom half-mask. It was a major breakthrough. It made complete sense of our premise that only half the Phantom's face was deformed whilst the other was beautiful. Now our Phantom was no monster. With that mask in place he was a handsome hunk.

40

Mr Crawford

Ask anyone who knows Michael Crawford and the first thing you'll learn is that if he says yes to a challenge he will deliver it. He insisted on doing all his own highly dangerous stunts on *Some Mothers Do 'Ave 'Em*. No way was there a safety net near that tightrope in *Barnum*. So I didn't need Ian Adam's assurance that Michael could smash the role of Phantom. If Michael said he could ditch skinny Frank Spencer and become a commanding sexy high baritone come opening night, he would. The issue was to make him say yes.

I knew Michael was snared when I played him the overture. The moment when the full orchestra enters clinched it. It was a hot sunny afternoon and I had the windows open onto the gardens at the back of the Green Street flat. I described the auction scene and how the big organ chords heralded the chandelier rising high above the auditorium and the opera house bursting into life. *Sod the neighbours*, I thought as I pressed play. Michael clutched the sofa as the organ thundered and was standing next to me when the orchestra lurched in.

"Andrew," he whispered, "this is the most thrilling start to a musical I have ever heard."

I had netted the most consummate theatrical performer I have ever worked with. Negotiations with Michael were the next hurdle and at times it seemed we'd hit a brick wall. Cameron in the end had to sin against his religion and give him a piece of the profits. Since he had been forced to give away a chunk to Hal as well, it was a good twenty-four hours before he was himself again.

Michael was announced on May 27, a fortnight after *Chess* opened. The combination of a massive hit record, Tim Rice, Elaine Paige in the lead, Trevor Nunn and the worldwide army of ABBA fans had made *Chess* the biggest West End opening in living memory. *Phantom*, by contrast, sounded decidedly dodgy. The composer's wife plus the man who played Frank Spencer as the star? "Now we get it," the theatre Rialto muttered, "here comes a glossed up version of the Ken Hill show with Crawford swinging on chandeliers and saying 'boo' to La Brightman between comedy routines."

The only thing the Rialto couldn't grasp was where Hal Prince fitted in. Cameron and I knew exactly where when he and Maria Bjornson took us through the model. It was an unforgettable morning. We met in Maria's Earl's Court basement flat in Gledhow Gardens, literally next door to my old first flat. Was that an omen? Never before or since have I got such goosebumps at seeing a set design. I knew that it was totally at one with my music from the moment Hal demonstrated how the opera house would be reborn with the dust sheets covering Maria's decadent false proscenium flying away and its grotesque scenery rising from the stage floor after the chandelier ascended. Everything was fluid, about movement and above all gorgeously feminine.

People say that *Phantom* has massive scenery. It hasn't. All the sets are suggestions in another of Hal's black boxes. The managers' scenes are curtains with one door frame. The Phantom's lair is no more than an empty mirror frame, a bed, the small organ on which he composes and candelabra silhouetted against a black cloth. Even the masquerade sequence is only a cutaway half-scaffolded staircase. Many of the costumed revelers are fixed mannequins. What Hal and Maria did do was revive some of the Victorian machinery in Her Majesty's Theatre, our destined home. Raoul's leap into the Phantom's lake, for example, was born out of the discovery of a long-forgotten stage trap.

Maria's costumes, however, were as opulent as her design was about sleight of hand. The masquerade outfits must be among the most sumptuous and inventive ever created for a musical. There was one costume joke that got cut. At the start of the act the managers M André and M Firmin frighten the life out of each other by bumping into each other in skeleton outfits. We had written the skeleton-suit version of two women turning up to a posh bash wearing identical ballgowns. Come the costume fitting, John Savident who was playing M Firmin, refused to wear his as he said it made him look fat. So his costume was changed and the joke lost which was rather sad.

THE 1986 SYDMONTON FESTIVAL was held over the July 4 weekend. The Windsor cast repeated *Cricket* and the verdict was "fun curiosity." Our Saturday night cabaret featured the Act 2 *Phantom* songs that weren't written last year. The lyric of "Wishing You Were Somehow Here Again" alarmingly was still not cracked, its title now being "This Is Where the Story Finishes." Charlie Hart blamed this on the five repeated notes at the start of the main melody and threatened to call it "Spare a Thought for Kids at Christmastime." He still blames me that he has to have the word "somehow" in his final title. Some audience members were amused that Kristin Daaé had now become Christine. Hal thought the name Kristin was stupid.

Despite *Phantom* gathering pace Sarah managed to make an album of Benjamin Britten folk songs for EMI. They weren't her only sessions at Abbey Road that August. Two days after she'd recorded "O Can Ye Sew Cushions?," "Dear Harp of My Country" and seventeen other folk smashes she was back in Abbey Road helping to fulfil a personal dream of mine – having a song recorded by Cliff Richard. Cliff had agreed to duet "All I Ask of You." Just as it had been when Elvis and Pet Clark had warbled one of my efforts, I was in seventh heaven. Consequently Cliff recorded his vocal on the wrong orchestral take but that didn't stop the single from being No. 3 in the charts when *Phantom* opened a few weeks later.

There were two downers that summer, neither of them about *Phantom* but they were the harbingers of serious trouble in store for me thanks to Really Useful becoming a public company. First Brian Brolly bulldozed through a recording of *Variations* for EMI/HMV. The rock band was rescored for the Royal Philharmonic Orchestra by David Cullen. Lorin Maazel conducted. Although my brother Julian was once again the soloist and played superbly, I protested in vain that it was an appalling idea. If ever music was not conceived for a classical orchestra, this was it. I don't know or care what mesh Brian had got himself entangled in with EMI, but for the first time he was acting for company profit and not for me. I had a "told you so" moment when the orchestrations turned out so badly that Lorin had to call an extra day of sessions which cost a fortune.

Of course the album didn't sell much. The only good thing was that as a quid pro-quo for not publicly throwing my toys out of the pram I got my father's tone poem *Aurora* recorded as a companion piece. Due to the time it took farting about with my emasculated *Variations*, Lorin's performance of *Aurora* isn't just the first take. It's the run-through. It proves what a phenomenal musician Lorin was when he had decent material to conduct.

The second storm cloud was the withdrawal of Robert Stigwood from *Starlight Express* in America. Robert had proposed teaming up to present *Starlight* in USA arenas with rock promoter Steve Leber, who in his William Morris days had been involved with the *Superstar* concert tours. To me this was the blindingly obvious way to go rather than risking Broadway. But come midsummer both pulled out, fed up with Brian's procrastination. I didn't know then that Brian had been offered an incredible guaranteed $10 million ($22 million in today's money) by Jimmy Nederlander to shoehorn *Starlight* into one of his Broadway houses. It was a classic case of a theatre owner and a money man who thinks he's a producer treating a show as a "product" and not understanding what made that "product" tick.

Brian then used Jimmy's vast offer to leverage another deal involving producer Marty Starger. With hindsight I believe Brian was trying to get the highest guarantee for *Starlight* to bump up Really Useful's short-term profits and please the City, which of course didn't create a bad dividend for himself. Also Brian was beginning to make the mistakes of the businessman who believes he can be a creative – witness his dumb-headed classical version of *Variations*. Thank goodness I didn't grasp what he was up to or I might have taken my eyes off *Phantom*.

PHANTOM REHEARSALS BEGAN IN the third week of August in "Awful" Alford House, the community centre in Vauxhall, but nobody was complaining. It was like rehearsing a production that had been tried and tested before. Hal stuck rigidly to his mantra that scene changes would anticipate the music and vice versa so the production was always ahead of the audience.

Everything went so smoothly we were able to run Act 1 at the end of the second week and with time to spare to hear Act 2's opening song "Masquerade." The song didn't work. I remembered that Alan Jay Lerner had wanted to tackle "Masquerade" first. It was the long August holiday weekend so Charlie Hart and I took off to Sydmonton. It took a day to realize it but the problem was straightforward. We had written a conventional act opening number celebrating six months of a Phantom-free opera house. The setting was a masked ball. But masked balls are scary and exotic. They even have undertones of the occult – try the Venice Carnival for size.

Charlie rewrote the lyrics to a new musical rhythm and now the undertone was menacing. Was the Phantom behind one of those masks? I built "Masquerade" to a big choral old-fashioned staircase walkdown before the Phantom screws up proceedings in his "red death" costume. Gillian had the scene fully staged by the following Tuesday.

During that week there was what might be described as an "incident." Cameron, Michael Crawford and I were driving from Vauxhall to the theatre. As we neared Lambeth Bridge, Michael said that he wanted his performance of "The Point of No Return" to be pre-recorded because he performed the song with a hood over his face. He thought he'd sound muffled. Cameron went tonto and said for the money he was earning Michael could at least sing his big second act song live. Did he want to phone in his performance? By now we were stuck in a traffic jam. Michael yelled "How dare you!" whereupon producer and leading man leapt onto the pavement and a few astonished tourists savoured a mini bout of fisticuffs. I, being a pacifist, stayed in the car. The sight of the traffic jam clearing and the car receding with me in it mouthing "May the best man win" calmed things down. We proceeded to Her Majesty's in silence. The topic was never raised again.

Otherwise things were going well enough that Cameron's attention shifted to Her Majesty's Theatre, where things weren't. Hal and Maria's claim that the set is basically bits and pieces in a black box is true but they sure are complicated bits and "technicals" were particularly protracted. The press got hold of a story about a bathroom being specially installed in Sarah's dressing room because Michael Crawford wouldn't share his. Actually it was for Christine's ten-plus costume changes. Cameron responded with "Too loos, no treck."

Next there was a big drama about pigeons. Hal wanted pigeons to flutter over the audience at the start of the rooftop closing scene of Act 1. Apparently pigeons are attracted to light sources so two bright beams were installed in the gallery for the pigeons to home to. Not our pigeons. After too many near misses from passing bird shit Cameron declared Her Majesty's Theatre a feathered-friend-free zone.

After this Cameron and I felt we needed a night off. It was unwise. What happened led to us being banned for life from the King's Head Theatre, Islington. The occasion was *Marlowe*, the musical, the title referring to Christopher Marlowe the poet and playwright contem-

porary of Shakespeare. Steve Harley was playing Marlowe. Actually
he was really rather good. The trouble was the show. It began with a
song about a sixteenth-century man with a twentieth-century brain.
Then there was a character called Rent Boy Charlie and a song called
"Ode to Virginity." What really did it was when the dying Marlowe
handed his plume to Shakespeare with the immortal line, "It's up to
you now, Willie." I thought Cameron was going to have a seizure.
That was when the management felt our presence in the audience was
not an advantage.

As the week ended things at Her Majesty's were looking increasingly bleak. The Council health and safety people reduced the speed
of the chandelier's fall to the perambulation of a genteel old lady in
a bathchair. Michael, Sarah and I escaped to Paris where we posed
on the opera house roof for the *Daily Mail* show business writer Baz
Bamigboye. Imo and Nick came too and we were even allowed to
see the famous lake. Michael was particularly taken by an enormous
valve labelled "Eau de Seine" which he thought we should market as
a perfume.

On Monday it was orchestra rehearsal time. Our musical director was Mike Reed, a protégé of impresario Harold Fielding and the
youngest ever conductor to debut in the West End. He had worked
with Michael on *Barnum* which gave Michael enormous confidence
and he always erred on the side of pace. This made him the perfect
Phantom baton waver. We rehearsed in Sir Herbert Beerbohm Tree's
old private apartment under Her Majesty's Theatre's dome. Cameron
got into a frightful state during the first run-through of "The Point
of No Return." He bounced up and down hissing, "It's wrong dear,
it's wrong," which was maddening because I knew it was wrong and
knew how to fix it. It had been orchestrated like a Francis Lai film
score, whereas it needed an erotic, seductive undertone of menace. I
rescored it overnight, adding a military snare drum which not only
undercut the schmaltz but heightened the sensuality and tension.

We spent a lot of time examining key musical motifs. Nothing in the *Phantom* score is random. For example M Firmin's line in Scene 1, "Good heavens will you show a little courtesy?" is deliberately set to the descending musical line of the title song. The scene-shifter Buquet's "Please Monsieur don't look at me" echoes Raoul's "a collector's piece indeed," which in turn becomes the music for the Phantom's "notes." The connection is deliberate. It drives me bonkers when I hear these musical lines spoken. But important as this detail was the vital thing now was to hear the orchestrations in the theatre.

SEPTEMBER 27, 1986 WAS the night of the infamous *Phantom* public dress rehearsal. How the chandelier got stuck is still West End legend. The set may have moved like clockwork all over the world for over 30 years but it defeated our stage crew that night. I lost count of the breakdowns. Sarah was so tired when she got home that she fell asleep on the sofa in her rehearsal togs. Cameron refused to cancel the first preview. The following day was spent going over the scenery moves again and again.

By now I resembled a jelly about to enter a pizza oven. The technical shenanigans meant I lost my full music run-through in the theatre. Worse, up there, centre stage, was my wife. Whoever plays Christine is the workhorse of the show. The Phantom is only on stage for seventeen minutes! Everyone in London was waiting for Sarah to slip on a banana skin. She was still thought of as the squeeze who broke up a happy home. It was time for the new Mrs Lloyd Webber to have her comeuppance.

41

"Let Your Soul Take You Where You Want to Be!"

The audience was in joyful mood as they crammed the opulent but cramped foyer of Her Majesty's. A few queens did impressions of Michael in Frank Spencer mode saying "Boo everybody, I'm the Phantom!" They certainly were not there for an evening of high romance. I felt sick. I stood at the back of the stalls with Cameron near the sound desk. The audience was now verging on the rowdy. There was a huge anticipatory laugh when the house lights dimmed. Then the auctioneer's gavel came down.

"Sold!"

The audience fell silent. This wasn't how the punters expected the romp to start. The synthesizer chord cluster before Raoul sings "A collector's piece indeed" chilled the audience just as it had done at the Festival. When the chandelier glowed and the Phantom chords struck, the audience were like children seeing their first magic trick. The chandelier ascended, the opera house reassembled with no mishap. It was almost too good to be true.

Sarah sang "Think of Me" truly beautifully. Her voice was like cool, pure mountain water and she radiated the frailty of fine porcelain. Our Meg was a bit off-pitch during the dressing room scene but Janet Devenish's childlike beauty hit home and the bond between the two girls when Christine sings of her "strange angel" really landed.

The scene with Raoul, Christine's childhood friend and now

would-be lover, was when our audience clocked that if it was a laugh-fest they were after they'd gone to the wrong party. The "Little Lotte let her mind wander" section is sung on one musical note around which the orchestra ducks and dives harmonically with the music that eventually we identify with the Phantom. It is vital the perform-ers stay pitch perfect which Sarah and Steve Barton absolutely did. The audience shot out of their seats when a huge-voiced Michael Crawford reverberated around the auditorium with "Insolent boy." What had happened to Frank Spencer?

They soon found out. The moment when the Phantom is first re-vealed through the big dressing room mirror singing "I am your angel of music" worked technically perfectly to reveal a very different Mi-chael Crawford. No scrawny Frank Spencer he. A handsome, sexy, well built, middle-aged man stood before us with absolute command of Sarah and the stage. When Michael sang, "Sing once again with me our strange duet," the preview audience were witnessing one of the biggest changes of an actor's persona in theatre history.

THE DAY RUNNING AND re-running the sets had paid off. All the technical gremlins had miraculously vanished. Equally mirac-ulously the orchestra and performers played as one too. Mike Reed was giving a properly thought through account of the music. I can always tell if a conductor truly understands my *Phantom* score by the tempo of the first section in the lair where the Phantom sits at his organ and sings, "I have brought you to the seat of sweet music's throne." This is a development of the "Little Lotte" section and es-tablishes the Phantom's control over Christine. It is marked *"maes-toso,"* i.e. majestic.

Some conductors hurtle through the section which completely un-dermines its purpose as the climax of the "Phantom of the Opera" duet. I once asked one of our Broadway baton wavers why he was rushing this section, to be told it was because the current Phantom was tall and found it uncomfortable sitting at the organ. There was no rushing that preview night. The orchestra played the key change into D flat for "The Music of the Night" consummately. The sexual tension, the passion and the yearning in the song that night was like nothing anyone had seen in one of my musicals before. Sarah seemed like putty in Michael's hands. Never had I seen her dance training pay off like this. Michael hit the strong top A flat – "Let your soul take you where you want to be" – with true operatic power. But he never allowed his acting performance to waver. The applause would have stopped the show were it not for Hal and my instruction to Mike Reed to keep the show moving.

Still there were no technical hitches! Mike propelled the managers' scene forward and the audience was following every word. A major point of the scene is that Carlotta, the opera house's top diva, is a good singer. We smile because she represents the old way with opera but she is not a figure of fun. It's just that the Phantom hears music very differently and Carlotta is a large obstacle to his plans for Christine's stardom. Rosemary Ashe's Carlotta was bullseye, the audience smiled but savoured the song "Prima Donna" too.

I clutched Cameron during the applause, partly out of relief that the most complicated vocal arrangement I had written to date seemed to have landed, but also because the big scene change loomed into the Mozart pastiche opera *Il Muto* with its monstrous bed and elaborate drapes. No hitches. The stagehands had obviously had an epic afternoon. *Il Muto* is when Carlotta croaks like a toad and the Phantom crows "she's singing to bring down the chandelier." The nervous laughter in the orchestra stalls as the chandelier wobbled threateningly above them was all too tangible. The big pigeon-free scene change into the opera house roof went flawlessly too. "All I Ask of You," helped by familiarity with the Cliff and Sarah single, absolutely would have stopped the show were it not that the music deliberately cuts across the applause point with the "Masquerade"/music box motif sung by Christine – "I must go, they'll wonder where I am." Everything leads to the discovery that the Phantom has been watching the two lovers all along.

The whole theatre gasped when Michael emerged at the top centre of Maria's opera house proscenium which then descended midway between the chandelier and the stage floor. The pain in Michael's voice when he pathetically sang, "I gave you my music, made your voice take wing," was almost unbearable. His "Oedipus cry," as Hal describes the Phantom's despairing sound before he threatens, "You will curse the day you did not do all that the Phantom asked of you," utterly conveyed the Phantom's pain and that he was not dropping the chandelier solely in a melodramatic rage. Even if the chandelier's progress towards the stage was a lot more stately than it is today, it surely made its point that night.

THE BUZZ IN THE interval was astonishing. Now I had a career first to look forward to. My entr'acte. This was the first time in my 20-year career that I'd found a place for one. Any composer who says they don't like to hear their tunes whacked out by an orchestra in a full frontal medley is either a liar or doesn't do tunes. Mike Reed is one of those conductors who given a chance to flaunt it does so. There hadn't been an old-fashioned entr'acte like this for years and both he and the orchestra dug into it as if their very existence was at stake.

Next up was "Masquerade." Had we really fixed it in rehearsals? Someone was clutching me. It was Charlie Hart this time. He needn't have worried: "Masquerade" hit the spot. There were diction issues but nothing serious. Charlie had reflected Maria's exotic costumes in his rewrite of the lyric. The writing and design intertwined as if no problem had ever existed:

> *Flash of mauve*
> *Splash of puce*

Fool and king
Ghoul and goose
Green and black
Queen and priest
Trace of rouge
Face of beast
Masquerade
Leering satyrs
Peering eyes.

Michael's entry in his "red death" costume at the top of Maria's mannequin bedecked staircase climactically topped a costume design master class that must rank among theatre's all-time greats. When he dropped the score of *Don Juan Triumphant*, the opera he has composed for Christine, on the stage floor through which he disappears only to miraculously reappear at the top of the staircase, our audience was seeing Hal the master showman at his peak.

Mike Reed was powering through the score. Raoul's new motif as he takes charge in the Act 2 opera managers' scene, "We have all been blind," was given exactly the right amount of clout to establish Raoul as the action man who would ensnare the Phantom by performing his opera with Christine as the bait – "If Miss Daaé sings he is certain to attend." The cacophonous argument that ensues leads to the moment I shall forever associate with Sarah: "Twisted Every Way" set to the counter melody of "Prima Donna."

Maybe it was because of the exhilaration I was feeling, my pride in Sarah and the sheer emotion of seeing my *Phantom* come to life for the first time, but my first preview notebook has no entries after here. I remember Sarah's performance of "Wishing You Were Somehow Here Again" being touching and vulnerable, nothing near as valkyrie-like as I have heard it so often subsequently.

I remember my joke about 7/8 time in the rehearsal for *Don Juan*

Triumphant falling flat as it has done for 30 years with the exception of the night Lorin Maazel was in. But the point about the Phantom writing futuristically in the "whole tone scale" landed as the repetiteur M Reyer banged out the tritone that poor Signor Piangi is unable to sing.

I vividly remember "The Point of No Return" being rammed with sexual tension and how the audience gasped when Sarah ripped off Michael's mask. However cloying it reads, I was crying at my own music during the last scene and when Sarah kissed the pathetic Phantom to the orchestra playing "Angel of Music" I was as wiped out as the audience. Never had I had more at stake. It wasn't just that *Phantom* meant so much to me as a composer. Casting Sarah had put my professional integrity on the line. Hal ran up the aisle and clasped my hand. "It's the best musical I have ever seen, pal. Let's go away and come back opening night."

Not one note of music was altered between that first preview and the world premiere.

PHANTOM BECAME THE MOST commercially successful musical of my career. Depending on how you juggle the statistics, it is arguably the most successful entertainment of all time and I suppose if you inflation-adjust the total, the claim is right. Hal's production of *Phantom* was that rare moment in musical theatre when the planets Casting, Book, Music, Lyrics, Direction, Choreography and Design align to produce the kind of hit you see once in a generation. It is a reminder of how incredibly collaborative and fragile that creative process is. Just one of those planets out of kilter can bring a great show down.

Phantom celebrated its 30th birthday in London on October 9, 2016. It became the longest-running musical in Broadway history on January 9, 2006 and was 30 on January 9, 2018. The London *Sunday Times* critic John Peter had two words for it.

"Masked balls."

PLAYOUT MUSIC

I meant to cram my memoirs into one book but my verbosity got in the way so I drew a line at the opening of *Phantom*. It's not a bad place to stop. *Phantom* has been performed in 166 cities and the original production is still running on Broadway and London plus five other major cities around the world. It has changed the fortunes of everyone involved in a way that I could never have remotely dreamed of when I exchanged fifty cents for a secondhand copy of Gaston Leroux's "penny dreadful" on Fifth Avenue back in 1984.

My life up to *Phantom* was charmed by any standard – a few bumps and disappointments, but nothing like the bumps I will have to write about if ever there is a remote interest in a Volume Two. On the other hand I have been blessed with an extremely happy 27-years-and-counting marriage to my wonderful wife Madeleine who has given me three great children, Alastair, Billy and Bella, to join my elder brood of Imo who now lives and works in New York, and Nick who has made me a proud grandfather with his daughter Molly. I met Madeleine Gurdon in 1989 through mutual friends when my marriage to Sarah Brightman had got rocky. There had been publicity about Sarah's affair with the original *Phantom* keyboard player and, hugely fond of her as I still am, things weren't the same for me after that. Sarah was shattered when I said I was leaving her for Madeleine but we continued to work together. As late as 2016 I composed a song which she would have performed on the Space Station were her plan to be the first person to sing in space not aborted through no fault of her own. Sarah Brightman's voice will always be very special to me.

Madeleine is the daughter of an army brigadier and was coming to the end of a career as a professional equestrian when I met her. She supported her horse-riding career by founding a successful country clothing business and has a mind like a razor. She is an active board member of my companies and has stood by me like a rock through some grisly career moments and four missing years thanks to health problems. Happily I recovered from them in early 2015 but in 2014 I was in a pretty dark place and it is no secret that most people assumed I would not compose again. Then I turned the corner.

There was much to catch up on. I decided to give up alcohol, sold my wine cellar and went back to my roots with *School of Rock*, based on the Jack Black/Mike White movie. It is the first of my musicals to world premiere on Broadway since *Jesus Christ Superstar*. I produced it myself as well as composing the score and it is my first Broadway show to go into profit since *Phantom*. Only three of my seven shows since *Phantom* have made Broadway, my small "chamber" musical *Aspects of Love*, *The Woman in White* and *Sunset Boulevard* which despite winning the Tony for Best Musical and Best Score and receiving some of the best reviews of my career, failed to recoup due to circumstances that would take up a fair chunk of any continuation of my saga.

In some ways I am glad this book stops where it does. When things are not going your way you discover who your true friends are. I have found some toe-curling truths about so-called friends and colleagues and I really don't relish the thought of raking over them. But then what's the point of an autobiography if it isn't truthful at least from your own perspective? Not that it's all been bad. In 1991 I succeeded in buying back the shares in my company and it is now the family-owned business it always should have been. In 2000 I was able to buy the Stoll Moss group of London theatres. Among the seven I now own are two of its most famous, the Theatre Royal Drury Lane and the London Palladium. I am proud that every cent of profit goes back into these wonderful buildings.

In 1992 I was knighted by HM The Queen for services to the arts and in December 1996 I had the honour of being created a life peer and member of the British House of Lords.

In the fall of 2017 I resigned as an active member of the House. The character of the House has changed profoundly during the last twenty years. It has become far more political in character and its numbers have soared. The previous Prime Minister, David Cameron, made scores of party political appointments with 295 new peerages created since 2010, which increased the size of the House by over 40%.

I won an Oscar in 1997 with Tim Rice for "You Must Love Me," the new song in the movie of *Evita*. In 2017 a combination of *School of Rock* bedding in on the Great White Way with *Phantom*, a revival of *Cats* and a season of the incomparable Glenn Close in *Sunset Boulevard* meant that I had four shows on Broadway, equalling the 1953 record set by my heroes Rodgers and Hammerstein.

I am very proud of some of the music and subjects that I have chosen for my less successful shows of the past few years. The story of how young people were politicized and became terrorists in Northern Ireland told in *The Beautiful Game* is almost more relevant today than it was in 2000. It is my only musical to have won the London Critics prize. I am particularly proud of the *Phantom* sequel *Love Never Dies*. The production was not right in London despite some hugely talented people being involved. But in Australia everything came together and this is the production that is now playing in the US. Since I have been back in full throttle health wise I have considerably revised it. It may never equal *Phantom*'s phenomenal success but there are parts of its score that I feel are my best writing and I make no secret that it contains my two favourite melodies. Its opening night in Detroit is one of the most treasured moments of my career.

Someday I will sort out *Stephen Ward*, the story of the man at the centre of the sex and spy scandal known as "The Profumo Affair."

The files on the enquiry into its ramifications are considered to be so explosive by the British Establishment that they will not be revealed until 2046. Even if I never get to rework *Stephen Ward*, someone should tackle this story. The cover-up is too important an issue to be forgotten.

I am hugely proud to have produced the great Bollywood composer A.R. Rahman's musical *Bombay Dreams*. It was a big hit in London and enticed a very new audience to the theatre. Unfortunately Broadway was unready for such a show in 2004. One major critic suggested I had lost my grip completely. Rahman won an Oscar for both Best Score and Best Original Song for *Slumdog Millionaire* five years later.

What drew me to A.R. Rahman's music was his remarkable melodic gift. I was determined that Western theatre audiences should experience it. Melody fascinates, even obsesses me. There isn't a moment when it isn't somewhere in the back of my mind. I can't be specific about where it comes from. Sometimes a tune simply arrives. It can be in an airport, a car, a restaurant – even in the interval of a show! Sometimes melodies hit me complete. At other times I work on them for ages. Sometimes a song title can be a trigger, or I doodle at the piano and hear a phrase that I have extemporised which sticks. From *Cats* onwards, I have frequently set existing verse.

But almost invariably it's a story that inspires my melodies. I rarely have written a song outside of the theatre. Of course, like most melodists, I have the odd tune up my sleeve but I have one overriding imperative. The right melody has to be in the right place in the right story for it to work in the theatre, witness Richard Rodgers's revelation to me about the tune of "Getting to Know You" and its aborted beginning in *South Pacific*. I reckon more than 95% of the music in my shows has been composed after I have found the story. I hope my music has always been my story's servant.

As I approach my 70th birthday I look back and think again how lucky I have been. You are very lucky if you know what you want to do in life. I am doubly lucky that I not only have made a living out of my passion but a hugely rewarding one. I thrive on taking risks both with subject matter and occasionally producing other writers. Most importantly I hope through my Foundation and the restoration of my theatres that I am able to give something back to the profession that has been so good to me. I am a passionate believer in the importance of the arts in schools, particularly music, which transcends all languages, shades of politics, race and creeds. In our increasingly dangerous and fractured world, the arts have never been as vital as they are today.

As I write this I haven't found a subject for a new show. But I'll find it. I have to get back to workshops and rewrites, out of tune rehearsal pianos and sweaty rehearsal rooms, dodgy previews and the blind panic of opening nights. I am having dire withdrawal symptoms. Even if I haven't got near to writing "Some Enchanted Evening," I hope I've given a few people some reasonably OK ones. I'd like to give them some more.

EPILOGUE

After my doorstop was published, 2018 proved an eventful year.

Aside from my seventieth birthday and all that went with it, including a fantastic party that Madeleine threw in the Theatre Royal, Drury Lane, a highlight was the brilliant NBC live telecast of *Jesus Christ Superstar*, produced by Craig Zadan and Neil Meron, my old friends from Broadway at the Ballroom days. Their production not only saw *Superstar* presented in the way that I had hoped it originally might have been on Broadway, but it also led to Tim Rice and me winning an Emmy and becoming "EGOTs." The joy was punctured by the sad death of Craig Zadan in the late summer. I was honoured to be able to pay tribute to Craig when the lights were dimmed on Broadway in his memory.

Another sad passing was Gillian Lynne, our indefatigable *Cats* choreographer. Happily, she lived to see me rename the New London Theatre the Gillian Lynne in her honour at a ceremony in which she was borne on a litter onto the stage by four boys dressed only in loin cloths. This pleased her enormously.

In June I was presented with a lifetime achievement Tony Award as well as being given a gala evening by the American Theater Wing. But rather than taking this firm hint that it was high time I was put out to pasture, in 2018 I started work on two new musicals. I don't want to tempt fate by saying what the subjects are, but hopefully by the time this appears, it looks as if one will be fully in the works.

A very big surprise was the announcement by Universal Pictures that, after thirty years' contemplation, they were making a movie of *Cats*. The director Tom Hooper has assembled a fine cast: Judi Dench, Taylor Swift, Ian McKellen, and Jennifer Hudson for openers. I await the result with suitably feline curiosity.

Amazingly my verbal diarrhea seems to have been pretty much received OK, but I will forever cherish one of the less complimentary reviews. Its main thrust was that all too often in my autobiography I reverted to writing about myself. I shall be more careful if there is a next time.

ALW
November 2018

ACKNOWLEDGMENTS

This book would not have been possible without the help of Robin Barrow, Peter Brown, John Eastman, John Goodbody, David Harington, Sue Knight, Martin Levan, Julian Lloyd Webber, Nick Allott, Martin Noble, Alan O'Duffy, Mark Fox and Victoria Simpson, Jan Eade and Louise Burns in my personal office.

Thanks to Sir Cameron Mackintosh, Hal Prince, Sir Timothy Rice, and Sir Trevor Nunn for allowing me to quote from their correspondence.

Special thanks to Jonathan Burnham and all at HarperCollins, Sarah Norris, Ed Victor and of course my wife Madeleine who has tirelessly read the manuscript even though she doesn't feature in it.

APPENDIX

As Composer

*Joseph and the Amazing Technicolor®
    Dreamcoat*
Lyrics: Tim Rice
First performed at Colet Court School
    London, March 1968
UK Premiere-Edinburgh International
    Festival: 1972 (as second half of
    Bible One)
West End premiere: February 1973,
    Albery Theatre
Director: Frank Dunlop
Original cast: Gary Bond (Joseph);
    Peter Reeves (Narrator)
Broadway premiere: January 1982,
    Royale Theatre;
    Director: Tony Tanner
Original cast: Bill Hutton (Joseph);
    Laurie Beechman (Narrator)

Jesus Christ Superstar
Lyrics: Tim Rice
Broadway premiere: October 1971,
    Mark Hellinger Theatre
Director: Tom O'Horgan
Original cast: Jeff Fenholt (Jesus);
    Ben Vereen (Judas); Yvonne Elliman
    (Mary Magdalene)
West End premiere: August 1972,
    Palace Theatre
Director: Jim Sharman
Original cast: Paul Nicholas (Jesus);
    Stephen Tate (Judas);
    Dana Gillespie (Mary Magdalene)

Jeeves
Lyrics and Book: Alan Ayckbourn
West End Premiere: April 22, 1975,
    Her Majesty's Theatre
Director: Alan Ayckbourn
Original Cast: David Hemmings
    (Bertie Wooster);
    Michael Aldridge (Jeeves);
    Gabrielle Drake (Madeline Bassett)
Choreographer: Christopher Bruce
Design: Voytek
Lighting: Robert Ornbo

Evita
Lyrics: Tim Rice
West End premiere: June 21, 1978,
    The Prince Edward Theatre
Broadway premiere: September 25, 1979,
    Broadway Theatre
Original Cast: Elaine Paige (Eva);
    David Essex (Che); Joss Ackland
    (Perón); Siobhan McCarthy
    (Perón's Mistress); Mark Ryan
    (Magaldi)
Director: Hal Prince
Choreographer: Larry Fuller
Set & Costumes: Timothy O'Brien
    and Tazeena Firth
Lighting: David Hersey
Sound: Abe Jacob

Variations

First performed at the Sydmonton
    Festival 1977
Released: November 22, 1978
Julian Lloyd Webber: cello
Don Airey: grand piano, synthesizers,
    Fender Rhodes electric piano
Rod Argent: grand piano, synthesizers
Gary Moore: Gibson Les Paul,
    Rickenbacker electric 12 string,
    Fender Stratocaster, Guild acoustic
    guitar
Barbara Thompson: flute, alto flute,
    alto & tenor saxophone
John Mole: Fender Precision Bass,
    Hayman fretless bass guitar
Jon Hiseman: Arbiter Auto-Tune drums,
    Paiste cymbals & gongs, percussion
With additional performers
Andrew Lloyd Webber: synthesizers
Dave Caddick: piano
Bill Le Sage: vibraphone
Herbie Flowers: bass
Phil Collins: drums, percussion

Tell Me on a Sunday

Lyrics: Don Black
First performed at the Sydmonton
    Festival 1979
BBC TV Special 1980
West End premiere: March 26, 1982,
    Palace Theatre as one half of *Song
    and Dance*
Broadway premiere: September 18, 1985,
    Royale Theatre as one half of *Song
    and Dance*
Original cast: Marti Webb (The Girl)

Cats

Lyrics: T.S. Eliot, Trevor Nunn
West End premiere: May 11, 1981,
    New London Theatre
Broadway premiere: October 7, 1982,
    Winter Garden Theatre
Original Cast: Elaine Paige
    (Grizabella); Stephen Tate
    (Gus the Theatre Cat/Growltiger);
    Sarah Brightman (Jemima);
    Wayne Sleep (Quaxo/
    Mr Mistoffelees); Brian Blessed
    (Old Deuteronomy/Bustopher Jones);
    Paul Nicholas (Rum Tum Tugger);
    Bonnie Langford (Rumpleteazer)
Director: Trevor Nunn
Choreographer: Gillian Lynne
Set, Costumes, Makeup: John Napier
Lighting: David Hersey
Sound: Abe Jacob

Song and Dance

Lyrics: Don Black, with additional lyrics
    by Richard Maltby, Jr.
West End premiere: March 26, 1982,
    Palace Theatre
Broadway premiere: September 18, 1985,
    Royale Theatre
Original Cast: Marti Webb (The Girl);
    Wayne Sleep (principal dancer);
    Jane Darling (principal dancer)
Director: John Caird
Choreographer: Anthony Van Laast
Set & Lighting: David Hersey
Costume: Robin Don
Sound: Andrew Bruce and Julian Beech

Starlight Express
Lyrics: Richard Stilgoe
West End premiere: March 27, 1984,
    Apollo Victoria
Broadway: March 15, 1987, Gershwin
    Theatre
Original Cast: Ray Shell (Rusty);
    Jeff Shankley (Greaseball);
    Lon Satton (Poppa);
    Jeffrey Daniels (Electra);
    Stephanie Lawrence (Pearl);
    Frances Ruffelle (Dinah);
    Chrissy Wickham (Ashley);
    Nancy Wood (Buffy);
    P.P. Arnold (Belle)
Director: Trevor Nunn
Choreographer: Arlene Phillips
Set & Costumes: John Napier
Lighting: David Hersey
Sound: Martin Levan

Requiem
Premiere: New York: St. Thomas
    Church, February 24, 1985
Performed by:
Placido Domingo
Sarah Brightman
Paul Miles-Kingston
The Saint Thomas Choir
Winchester Cathedral Choir
The Orchestra of St. Luke's
Conductor: Lorin Maazel

The Phantom of the Opera
Lyrics: Charles Hart and additional lyrics
    by Richard Stilgoe
West End premiere: October 9, 1986,
    Her Majesty's Theatre
Broadway premiere: January 26, 1988,
    Majestic Theatre
Original Cast: Sarah Brightman
    (Christine Daaé); Michael Crawford
    (The Phantom); Steve Barton
    (Raoul, Vicomte de Chagny);
    John Savident (Monsieur Firmin);
    David Firth (Monsieur André);
    Rosemary Ashe (Carlotta Guidicelli);
    Mary Millar (Madame Giry)
Director: Hal Prince
Musical Staging & Choreography:
    Gillian Lynne
Production Designer: Maria Björnson
Lighting: Andrew Bridge
Sound: Martin Levan

Aspects of Love
Lyrics: Don Black and Charles Hart
West End premiere: April 17, 1989,
    Prince of Wales Theatre
Broadway premiere: April 8, 1990,
    Broadhurst Theatre
Original Cast: Ann Crumb
    (Rose Vibert); Michael Ball
    (Alex Dillingham); Kevin Colson
    (George Dillingham)
Director: Trevor Nunn
Choreographer: Gillian Lynne
Designer: Maria Björnson
Lighting: Andrew Bridge
Sound: Martin Levan

Sunset Boulevard
Lyrics: Christopher Hampton and
    Don Black
West End premiere: July 12, 1993,
    Adelphi Theatre
Broadway premiere: November 17, 1994,
    Minskoff Theatre
Original Cast: Patti LuPone
    (Norma Desmond); Kevin
    Anderson (Joe Gillis); Daniel
    Benzali (Max von Mayerling);
    Meredith Braun (Betty Schaeffer)
Director: Trevor Nunn
Choreographer: Bob Avian
Production Design: John Napier
Costume: Anthony Powell
Lighting: Andrew Bridge
Sound: Martin Levan

By Jeeves
Lyrics: Alan Ayckbourn
West End premiere: July 2, 1996,
    Duke of York's
Broadway premiere: October 28, 2001,
    Helen Hayes Theatre
Original Cast: Steven Pacey
    (Bertie Wooster);
    Malcolm Sinclair (Jeeves)
Director: Alan Ayckbourn
Choreographer: Sheila Carter
Set: Roger Glossop
Costume: Louise Belson
Lighting: Mick Hughes
Sound: Richard Ryan

Whistle Down the Wind
Lyrics: Jim Steinman
Book: Patricia Knop
US premiere: December 12, 1996,
    National Theatre, Washington DC
Original Cast: Davis Gaines (The Man);
    Irene Molloy (Swallow)
Director: Hal Prince
Choreographer: Joey McKnelley
Projections: Wendall K. Harrington
Costumes: Florence Klotz
Sound: Martin Levan
West End premiere: July 1, 1998,
    Aldwych Theatre
Original Cast: Marcus Lovett (The Man)
Lottie Mayor (Swallow)
Director: Gale Edwards
Choreographer: Anthony Van Laast
Set: Peter J. Davison
Costumes: Roger Kirk
Lighting: Mark McCullough
Sound: Martin Levan

The Beautiful Game
Lyrics: Ben Elton
West End premiere: September 26, 2000,
    Cambridge Theatre
Original Cast: Frank Grimes (Father
    O'Donnell); Michael Shaeffer
    (Thomas); Jamie Golding (Daniel);
    Dale Meeks (Ginger); Ben Goddard
    (Del); David Shannon (John);
    Josie Walker (Mary); Hannah
    Waddingham (Christine); Alex
    Sharpe (Bernadette)
Director: Robert Carsen
Choreographer: Meryl Tankard
Set: Michael Levine
Costume: Joan Bergin
Lighting: Jean Kalman
Sound: Martin Levan

The Woman in White

Freely adapted from the classic novel by Wilkie Collins

Adapted by: Charlotte Jones

Lyrics: David Zippel

West End: September 15, 2004, Palace Theatre

Broadway: November 17, 2005, Marquis Theatre

Original Cast: Maria Friedman (Marian Halcombe); Michael Crawford (Count Fosco); Angela Christian (Anne Catherick); Martin Crewes (Walter Hartright); Jill Paice (Laura Fairlie)

Director: Trevor Nunn

Movement Director: Wayne McGregor (Broadway)

Production & Video Design: William Dudley

Lighting: Paul Pyant

Sound: Mick Potter

Love Never Dies

Book: Ben Elton, Glenn Slater, Frederick Forsyth and Andrew Lloyd Webber

Lyrics: Glenn Slater

West End premiere: March 9, 2010, Adelphi Theatre

Director: Jack O'Brien

Choreographer: Jerry Mitchell

Set & Costumes: Bob Crowley

Lighting: Paule Constable

Sound: Mick Potter

Original Cast: Ramin Karimloo (The Phantom); Sierra Boggess (Christine Daaé); Joseph Millson (Raoul); Summer Strallen (Meg Giry); Liz Robertson (Madame Giry)

US premiere: October 25, 2017, Fisher Theatre Detroit

Director: Simon Phillips

Choreographer: Graeme Murphy

Set & Costumes: Gabriela Tylesova

Lighting: Nick Schlieper

Sound: Mick Potter

Original Cast: Gardar Thor Cortes (The Phantom); Meghan Picerno (Christine Daaé); Sean Thompson (Raoul); Mary Michael Patterson (Meg Giry); Karen Mason (Madame Giry)

Stephen Ward

Book and Lyrics: Christopher
    Hampton and Don Black
West End premiere: September 19, 2013,
    Aldwych Theatre
Original Cast: Alexander Hanson
    (Stephen Ward); Charlotte Spencer
    (Christine Keeler); Charlotte
    Blackledge (Mandy Rice-Davies)
Director: Richard Eyre
Choreographer: Stephen Mear
Set & Costume: Rob Howell
Lighting: Peter Mumford
Sound: Paul Groothuis
Video & Projection: Jon Driscoll

School of Rock

Lyrics: Glenn Slater
Book: Julian Fellowes (based on the Para-
    mount movie written by Mike White)
Broadway premiere: December 6, 2015,
    Winter Garden Theatre
West End premiere: November 14, 2016,
    New London Theatre
Original Cast: Alex Brightman
    (Dewey Finn); Sierra Boggess
    (Rosalie Mullins); Spencer Moses
    (Ned); Mamie Parris (Patty)
Director: Laurence Connor
Choreographer: JoAnn Hunter
Scenic and costume design: Anna
    Louizos
Lighting: Natasha Katz
Sound: Mick Potter

As Producer

As well as producing or co-producing many of his own shows including *Cats* and *The Phantom of the Opera* Andrew Lloyd Webber's producer credits include:

Daisy Pulls It Off
Written by: Denise Deegan
"Grangewood School Song" by Beryl
  Waddle-Browne (ALW)
West End premiere: April 18, 1983,
  Globe Theatre
Original Cast: Alexandra Mathie
  (Daisy Meredith); Helena Little
  (Trixie Martin); Adrienne Thomas
  (Monica Smithers); Kate Buffery
  (Clare Beaumont)
Director: David Gilmore
Design: Glenn Willoughby
Lighting: Brian Harris

On Your Toes
Music: Richard Rodgers
Lyrics: Lorenz Hart
Book: Richard Rodgers, Lorenz Hart,
  George Abbott
West End opening: June 12, 1984,
  Palace Theatre
Original Cast: Natalia Makarova
  (Vera Baronova); Tim Flavin (Junior);
  Siobhan McCarthy (Frankie); Kevin
  Owers (Sidney Cohn)
Director: George Abbott, recreated by
  Peter Walker
Choreographer: George Balanchine,
  recreated by Donald Saddler
Set & Costumes: Zack Brown
Lighting: John B. Read

The Hired Man
Book: Melvyn Bragg
Music and Lyrics: Howard Goodall
West End premiere: October 31, 1984,
  Astoria Theatre
Original Cast: Paul Clarkson (John
  Tallentire); Julia Hills
  (Emily Tallentire); Billy Hartman
  (Isaac Tallentire); Gerard Doyle
  (Seth Tallentire); Richard Walsh
  (Jackson Pennington); Clare Burt
  (May Tallentire)
Director: David Gilmore
Choreographer: Anthony Van Laast
Design: Martin Johns
Lighting: Chris Ellis
Sound: Rick Clark

Lend Me a Tenor
Written by: Ken Ludwig
West End premiere: March 6, 1986,
  Globe Theatre
Original Cast: Denis Lawson (Max);
  Jan Francis (Maggie);
  Ronald Holgate (Tito: Il Stupendo);
  John Barron (Saunders)
Director: David Gilmore
Design: Terry Parsons
Lighting: Michael Northern

Café Puccini
Written by: Robin Ray
Director: Christopher Renshaw
Musical Director: William Blezzard
First performed at Sydmonton Festival
  (1985)
West End premiere: March 12, 1986,
  Wyndham's Theatre
Original Cast: Lewis Fiander
  (Puccini); Nichola McAuliffe
Charles West; Terence Hillyer;
  Jacinta Mulcahy; Maurice Clarke
Design: Tim Goodchild
Lighting: Jenny Cane

La Bête
Written by: David Hirson
Director: Richard Jones
Broadway premiere: February 10, 1991,
  Eugene O'Neill Theatre
West End premiere: January 30, 1992,
  Lyric Hammersmith
Original London Cast: Alan Cumming
  (Valere); Jeremy Northam (Elomire);
  Simon Treves (De Brie); Timothy
  Walker (Prince Conti)
Steven Beard (Rene Du Parc); Linda
  Spurrier (Marquise Therese Du Parc)
Designer: Richard Hudson
Lighting: Jennifer Tipton, recreated by
  Scott Zielinski

Bombay Dreams
Music: A.R. Rahman
Lyrics: Don Black
Book: Meera Syal
West End premiere: June 16, 2002,
  Apollo Theatre
Broadway premiere: April 29, 2004,
  Broadway Theatre
Original Cast: Preeya Kalidas (Priya);
  Raza Jaffrey (Akaash); Ayesha
  Dharker (Rani); Dalip Tahil (Madan);
  Ramon Tikaram (Vikram)
Director: Steven Pimlott
Choreographer: Anthony Van Laast
Production Design: Mark Thompson
Lighting: Hugh Vanstone
Sound: Mick Potter

The Sound of Music
Music and Lyrics: Richard Rodgers and
  Oscar Hammerstein II
Book: Howard Lindsay and Russel
  Crouse
West End premiere: November 15, 2006,
  London Palladium
Toronto premiere: October 15, 2008
Original Cast: Connie Fisher
  (Maria Rainer); Simon Shepherd
  (Captain Georg von Trapp); Lesley
  Garrett (The Mother Abbess);
  Sophie Bould (Liesl); Ian Gelder
  (Max Detweiler); Neil McDermott
  (Rolf Gruber)
Director: Jeremy Sams
Choreographer: Arlene Phillips
Set & Costumes: Robert Jones
Lighting: Mark Henderson
Sound: Mick Potter

The Wizard of Oz

Music and Lyrics: Harold Arlen and E.Y.
    Harburg

Additional music and lyrics: Andrew
    Lloyd Webber and Tim Rice

West End premiere: March 1, 2011,
    London Palladium

Original Cast: Danielle Hope (Dorothy);
    Michael Crawford (Wizard/Professor
    Marvel); Hannah Waddingham
    (Wicked Witch of the West);
    Edward Baker-Duly (Tin Man);
    David Ganly (Lion); Paul Keating
    (Scarecrow); Emily Tierney (Glinda)

Director: Jeremy Sams

Choreographer: Arlene Phillips

Set & Costumes: Robert Jones

Lighting: Hugh Vanstone

Sound: Mick Potter

Projections & Video: Jon Driscoll and
    Daniel Brodie

INDEX

ABOUT THE AUTHOR

ANDREW LLOYD WEBBER is the composer of some of the world's best-known musicals including *Cats, Evita, Joseph and the Amazing Technicolor Dreamcoat, Jesus Christ Superstar, The Phantom of the Opera* and *Sunset Boulevard*.

When *Sunset Boulevard* joined *School of Rock—The Musical, Cats,* and *Phantom* on Broadway in February 2017, he became the only person to equal the record set in 1953 by Rodgers and Hammerstein with four shows running concurrently.

As a composer and producer, Lloyd Webber is one of an elite group of artists to have achieved EGOT status by receiving an Emmy, four Grammys (including Best Contemporary Classical Composition for *Requiem*, his setting of the Latin Requiem mass), an Oscar, and eight Tony Awards, including the 2018 Special Tony for Lifetime Achievement in the Theatre. Additionally he has been honored with seven Oliviers, a Golden Globe, the Praemium Imperiale, the Richard Rodgers Award for Excellence in Musical Theatre, a BASCA Fellowship, and the Kennedy Center Honor. He was knighted in 1992 and created a life peer in 1997.

He lives in Britain and owns seven London theatres including the Theatre Royal, Drury Lane, and the London Palladium. He is passionate about the importance of music in education, and the Andrew Lloyd Webber Foundation has become one of Britain's leading charities supporting the arts and music.